D1682824

10

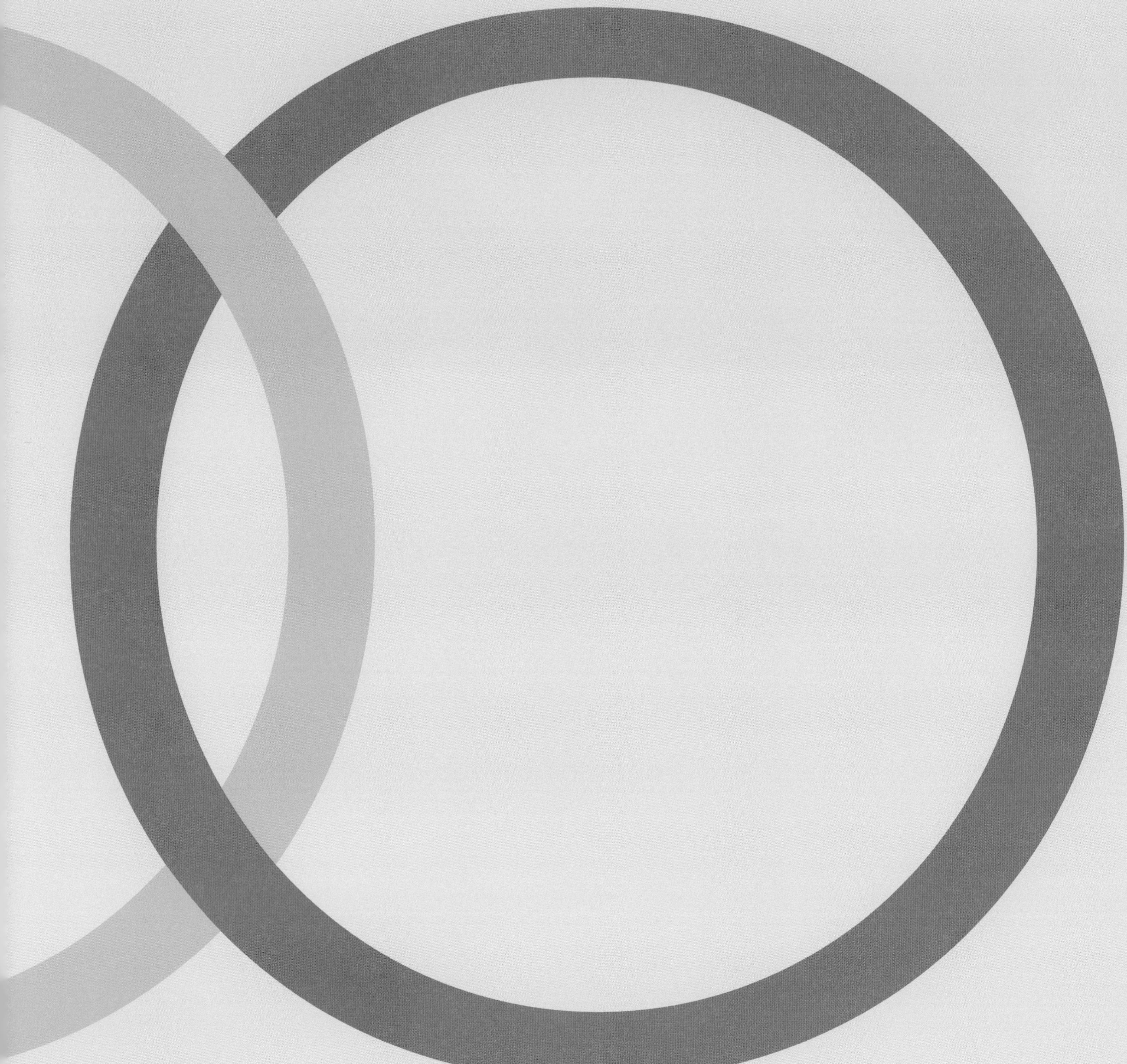

FAITH HUMANITY EDUCATION SERVICE

Preparing to celebrate the seventy-fifth anniversary of the 1893 founding of NCJW, Inc. Section members Judy Stahl, Pat Peiser, and President Edna Flaxman model dresses of various eras, 1967. (Richardson, *Dallas Times Herald*.)

repairing our world

the first 100 years of
the national council
of jewish women
greater dallas section

1913 to 2013

Compiled by
National Council of Jewish Women
Greater Dallas Section

TCU Press
Fort Worth, Texas

Copyright ©2018 by the National Council of Jewish Women,
Greater Dallas Section, Inc.

Library of Congress Cataloging-in-Publication Data

Names: National Council of Jewish Women. Greater Dallas Section, compiler.
Title: Repairing our world : the first 100 years of the National Council of
  Jewish Women, Greater Dallas Section, 1913-2013 / compiled by National
  Council of Jewish Women Greater Dallas Section, Inc.
Description: First edition. | Dallas, Texas : TCU Press, [2018] | Includes
  index.
Identifiers: LCCN 2018035617 | ISBN 9780875657028 (alk. paper)
Subjects: LCSH: National Council of Jewish Women. Greater Dallas
  Section--History. | National Council of Jewish Women. Greater Dallas
  Section--Biography. | Women--Texas--Dallas--Societies and clubs--History.
  | Jewish women--Texas--Dallas--Societies and clubs--History. | Jewish
  women philanthropists--Texas--Dallas--Biography. | Women
  philanthropists--Texas--Dallas--Biography. |
  Philanthropists--Texas--Dallas--Biography.
Classification: LCC F394.D21 N38 2018 | DDC 305.48/892407642812--dc23
LC record available at https://urldefense.proofpoint.com/v2/url?u=https-
3A__lccn.loc.gov_2018035617&d=DwIFAg&c=7Q-FWLBTAxn3T_E3
HWrzGYJrC4RvUoWDrzTlitGRH_A&r=O2eiy819IcwTGuw-
vrBGiVdmhQxMh2yxeggw9qlTUDE&m=oW_hPTTvsfAdJA975baT2enUXb
FAxvjAXb84nip-Z-E&s=-FQjZZ5hPkisni3AZfBUtPNP4tyhRMgYgBb3Zw-
7Dpw&e=

Any mistakes in this volume are purely unintentional. There is the possibility that
something or someone may be identified or characterized in error. A good faith
effort has been made to identify and give credit for all information, graphics,
photographs, and content presented in this publication. We ask flexibility and
forgiveness of those who find an error.

TCU Press

TCU Box 298300
Fort Worth, Texas 76129
817.257.7822
www.prs.tcu.edu
To order books: 1.800.826.8911

Book and jacket design by
Alan Lidji, Lidji Design Office
Dallas, Texas

This book is dedicated to all the Jewish women and men of the Dallas area who have responded to the challenge to heal the world, *Tikkun Olam*, and have sought to answer unmet needs for over a century through commitment to the National Council of Jewish Women, Greater Dallas Section, Inc. and its branches.

Our Mission–National and Local

The National Council of Jewish Women, Inc. (NCJW) is a grassroots organization of volunteers and advocates who turn progressive ideals into action. Inspired by Jewish values, NCJW strives for social justice by improving the quality of life for women, children, and families, and by safeguarding individual rights and freedoms. NCJW's programs and projects reflect the spirit of the organization itself—a faith in the future, a belief in action. Through education, community service, advocacy, and collaboration, we work to address the needs of all peoples and faiths within our community. Our advocacy efforts aim to correct the root causes of the social problems we encounter. We dare to have a vision of what is possible.

The Greater Dallas Section (the Section) is devoted to making a positive difference in the lives of women, children, and families in the community, responding to public needs with innovation and dedication. More than one thousand members devote thousands of hours annually to community service projects as well as to research, education, and advocacy to advance NCJW's mission.

Contents

Foreword — x
~*Vivian Castleberry, of Blessed Memory*

Preface — xii
~*Harriet P. Gross*

Introduction: Roots of the National Council of Jewish Women, Greater Dallas Section — 1

The First Decade: 1913-1922 — 7

The Second Decade: 1923-1932 — 15
Stitching Together for Thirty Years

The Third Decade: 1933-1942 — 21
Finding Homes for German Children

Recognizing Women of Purpose and Action
~*Katherine Krause*

Cooking Up *Cocktails to Coffee*

Being Welcomed to Dallas
~*Renate Fulda Kahn, of Blessed memory*

The Fourth Decade: 1943-1952 — 31
Supporting Israel Strategically
~*Sue Tilis*

Making a Difference at City Park School
~*Phyllis Somer*

The Fifth Decade: 1953-1962 — 37
Encouraging Young Women to Serve Dallas
~*Kathy Freeman*

Presenting a Study about Dallas Children as a Drama ~*Pat Peiser*

Lifting North Texans' Literacy
~*Pat Peiser*

The Sixth Decade: 1963-1972 — 47
Helping Children of West Dallas Study and Grow
~*Ann Folz*

Offering Consumer Advice with Operation READY ~*Rose Marie Stromberg*

Breaking Volunteer Barriers in Dallas Schools
~*Jeanne Fagadau, of Blessed Memory*

The Seventh Decade: 1973-1982 — 59
Winning at City Hall
~*Katherine Bauer*

Screening for the Tay-Sachs Gene
~*Judy Utay*

Safeguarding Dallas Area Seniors
~*Pat Peiser and Shirley Tobolowsky*

Advocating for Vulnerable Consumers
~*Sylvia Lynn "Syl" Benenson*

Educating Nonprofit Leadership
~*Betty Dreyfus*

Celebrating Shabbat
~*Janice Sweet Weinberg*

Advocating for Children in Foster Care
~*Brenda Brand*

Establishing the First Endowment Fund
~*Joy Mankoff*

Creating a Library Docent Program
~*Sharan Goldstein*

The Eighth Decade: 1983-1992 — 77
Serving the Refugees of Cambodia
~*Darrel Strelitz*

Working to Prevent Teen Pregnancies
~*Phyllis Bernstein*

Mediating Juvenile Issues
~*Kathy Freeman*

Lending a Hand with Housing for Women in Crisis ~*Claire Lee Epstein, of Blessed Memory*

Taking Israel into the Classroom
~*Denise Bookatz*

Strengthening Families with the Power of Education ~*Sylvia Lynn "Syl" Benenson*

Identifying Impaired Hearing in Infants
~*Frances "Sister" Steinberg*

Founding the Meyerson Docent Program
~*Sharan Goldstein*

Creating a Piece of History
~*Judy Utay*

The Ninth Decade: 1993-2002 — 93
Creating Guardians for the Most Vulnerable
~*Joni Cohan*

Building Bridges in Dallas
~*Jody Platt*

Soothing Fears of Kids in Court
~Judy Hoffman

Celebrating Children at Vickery Meadow
~Madeline "Maddy" Unterberg

Teaching English to Brave New Immigrants
~Myrna Ries

Living with "Gala" Memories
~Rita Doyne

Being Serenaded by Paul Anka

The Tenth Decade: 2003-2012   **105**

Celebrating with Coretta Scott King
~Jody Platt

Recovering from an Office Fire
~Marlene A. Cohen

Focusing on Food and Fitness
~Kyra Effren

Helping Youth Have Healthier Relationships
~Myra Fischel

Welcoming the Stranger
~Julie Lowenberg

Partnering with Other Faith Groups
in Vickery Meadow ~Cheryl Pollman

Celebrating "Let's Move" with First
Lady Michelle Obama ~Barbara Lee

11: Marking a Century of Achievement 117

Celebrating One Hundred Years of Service
~Robin Zweig

Piecing Together a Symbol of Our Strength
~Cynthia Schneidler

12: Creating Alternative Structures 125

Answering a Need for Working Women
~Joyce Rosenfield

Remembering Evening Branch
~Nita Mae Tannebaum

Branching Out with the Richardson-Plano Section
~Carol Wigder

Including Men for the First Time
~Carol Rieter Tobias

Ending a Good Thing
~Janine Pullman

Listing of Branch Presidents

13: Giving with a Purpose 141

Saving Pennies to Golden Galas
~Bette W. Miller

14: Women Power: Inspiring Agents of Change 157

A Century of Advocacy

15: 2014 and Beyond 177

Anticipating the Next One Hundred Years
~Caren Edelstein

16: Historic Leadership 185

Greater Dallas Section Presidents

Charter Members of the Section in 1913

Charter Life Members

Greater Dallas Section Members Who
Served on the Board of NCJW, Inc.

Greater Dallas Section Awardees through 2015

    Hannah G. Solomon

    Janis Levine Music Make-A-Difference

    Emerging Leader

    Pioneering Partner

    Lifetime Achievement

Awards Received by the Greater
Dallas Section

Community Partners

17: Acknowledgments 203

    Image Credits 207

    Selected Bibliography 210

    Index 212

Foreword

by Vivian Castleberry,
of Blessed Memory
*Journalist and Editor
of the "Living Section,"*
Dallas Times Herald,
1955–1984

Vivian Castleberry (center, seated) reviews awards with her *Dallas Times Herald* staff. The Section was named the newspaper's "Club of the Year" in 1961. Photo by Andy Hanson. ("Six Staffers Salute Six Clubs," *Dallas Times Herald*.)

What a gift!

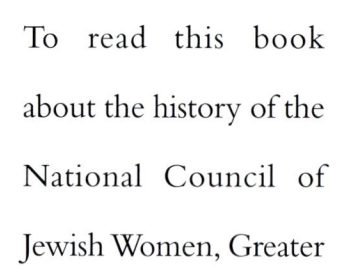

To read this book about the history of the National Council of Jewish Women, Greater Dallas Section's first one hundred years is to have a better understanding of the social, cultural, and psychological changes that have moved Dallas forward in the last century.

When I became an editor at the *Dallas Times Herald* in 1955, I had no training for leading its "Women's News" section (which we soon changed to "LIVING") and only scant knowledge of the unique history of my beloved city. Bert Holmes, managing editor, who hired me, told me, "Watch what the Jewish women are doing; they are always ahead of the curve."

He was right. Not only were the Jewish women and their NCJW organization first to recognize a need, but they were also first to respond to that need. They did their homework, enlisted those involved in the issue, and presented a plan of action.

By the time members introduced a project, the Dallas Section had the support of most community leaders—the City Council, Dallas County Commissioners Court, both local newspapers, radio, television stations, and places of worship. Volunteers trained themselves—and the community—to provide professional services in countless areas of human need: from youth to aging, from the foreign-born to the homeless, from education to health, from culture to justice, and more.

By the end of a half century of service, the Section had established many unique programs in Dallas public schools, helped develop services for seniors and the homebound via the Visiting Nurse Association, taught citizenship and literacy classes for new Americans, and created several charitable funds to support the Section's projects and involvement with other agencies. Here is a sampling of some firmly established groups in the community that the Dallas Section started in its second half century:

The year: 1961. The problem: approximately seventy-five thousand adults in North Central Texas were illiterate. NCJW's response: LIFT (Literacy Instruction for Texas), which provides volunteer instructors who have taught thousands of adults to read and write. LIFT has been an independent agency for more than fifty-five years.

The year: 1979. The problem: abused and neglected children had no advocates in the legal and foster care systems. NCJW's response: the creation of CASA (Court Appointed Special Advocates) to provide trained volunteers as advocates for these young people. CASA, after thirty-three years as an independent organization, now utilizes more than 770 volunteers to help find safe, permanent homes for over two thousand children each year.

The year: 1989. The problem: the need for tour guides at the new state-of-the-art Meyerson Symphony Center. NCJW's response: the Meyerson Docents Program, whose volunteers have been hosts, guides, and teachers for the past quarter of a century. Meyerson staff members now coordinate the scheduling of tours led by Section and community volunteers for visitors from around the world.

The year: 1990. The problem: some babies born at Parkland Hospital, without access to hearing tests, were sent home with unknown hearing problems. NCJW's response: expansion of Parkland's Infant Hearing Screening Program to diagnose hearing impairments in newborns early enough to provide medical intervention.

Breaking into the twenty-first century and opening the Greater Dallas Section's next one hundred years of service, the organization has continued to analyze unmet needs, to form alliances, and to solve community issues with the collaboration of nonprofits on similar missions. A recent educational effort, the "S.A.Y. What?" (Sound Advice for Youngsters) Coalition, has now developed into a new agency, the North Texas Alliance to Reduce Unintended Pregnancy in Teens.

Section members have been steadfast at one more thing: they innovate, create, cooperate, integrate, and sponsor programs and projects—and then they labor to find solutions and to work themselves out of a job. As soon as the infant they have birthed can stand alone, they, like good parents, cut the apron strings and allow it to become a separate entity or to attach itself to another community program. They love—and let go—and then pick up the next challenge.

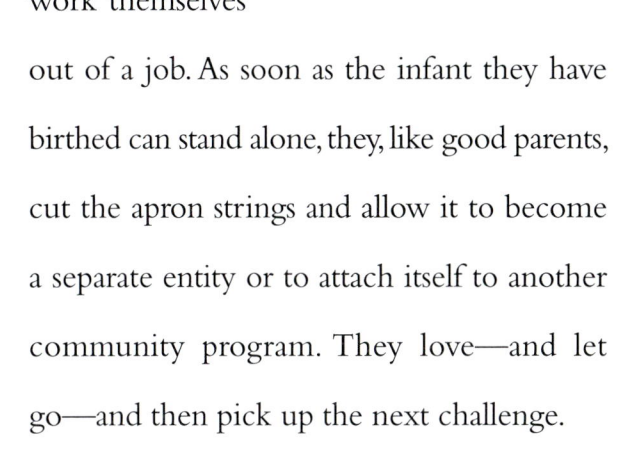

Read on! and discover the many other gifts that NCJW has contributed to Dallas.

Vivian Castleberry (far right) celebrates Women's Equality Day at Dallas City Hall with Section members Adlene Harrison and Pat Peiser (left and center), 2015. Photo by Caren Edelstein.

Preface

by Harriet P. Gross
Writer, Greater Dallas Section Member

Over twenty-five years ago, Miriam Jaffe led a team of fifteen National Council of Jewish Women, Greater Dallas Section★ members who researched and codified the Section's accomplishments over its first three-quarters of a century. Ms. Jaffe's overview at the time remains just as valid today and deserves repeating from the Section's book, *National Council of Jewish Women, Greater Dallas Section: Celebrating 75 Years of Service to the Community*, as we mark our Centennial:

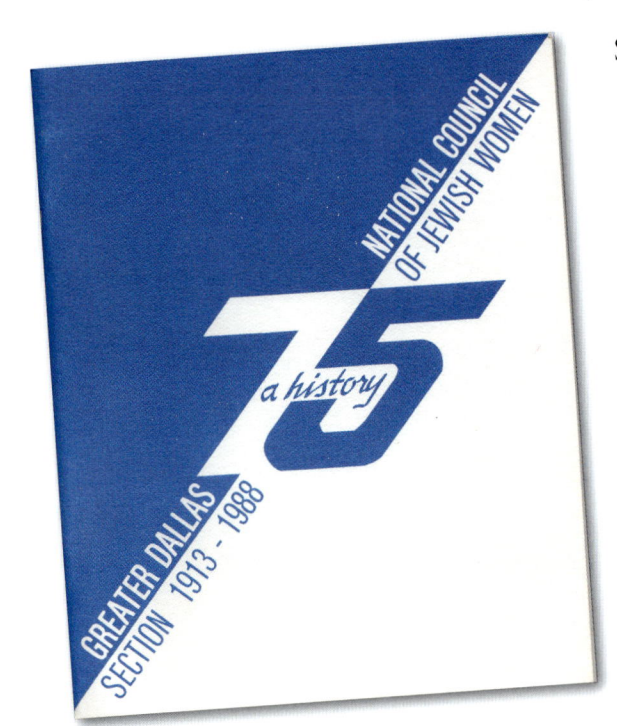

As Hannah G. Solomon, founder of the National Council of Jewish Women, titled her autobiography Fabric of My Life, *so we may think of Dallas Section's experience as fabric, where strands spun at its very inception are woven through the years as colorful threads. Some are continuous, some disappear completely, others reenter the design, and new ones are incorporated so that the finished tapestry symbolizes respect for tradition and continuity as well as openness to innovation and change.*

We hope you are as fascinated as we are to observe the Dallas Section in the context of world events, of the evolution of women's roles, of the growth of Dallas, of American Judaism, of the impact of technology and education, and of our National organization. We hope you appreciate the Section's response to challenges and its part in discovering and defining those challenges. Our history has been a labor of love.

At this milestone time, we look back for inspiration and forward to a future of similar accomplishments. We remember and salute those early women, our founding mothers, who somehow bravely dared to set their feet on a new path that no one had walked before. Today, members keep moving on that path, accepting future challenges with spirit and determination.

★ For purposes of brevity, the following designations are used throughout the book:

"National" or "NCJW" refers to the National Council of Jewish Women, Inc. whose main offices have been or are in New York City, New York, and Washington, DC.

"The Dallas Section," in early years called "the Council" and still later "the Greater Dallas Section," refers to the organization located in Dallas, Texas. "The Section" refers to all the former names of the Greater Dallas Section of the National Council of Jewish Women.

Three generations of Jewish women: Hannah G. Solomon (right), her daughter Helen S. Levy, and granddaughter Frances Levy Angel. Photographic postcard. Colorado Springs, Colorado, 1918. Hannah G. Solomon Papers. Manuscript Division, Library of Congress (204B).

Hundreds of attendees enter the World's Columbian Exposition grounds for the 1893 Chicago World's Fair. Photo by Frances Benjamin Johnston. (Library of Congress, LC-USZ62-104794.)

"Who is this new woman? She is the woman who dares to go into the world and do what her convictions demand."

Hannah G. Solomon (1858–1942), founder of the National Council of Jewish Women.

Introduction: Roots of the National Council of Jewish Women, Greater Dallas Section

Every organization has a primary "soul"—a reason to exist. In 1893, Hannah Greenebaum Solomon (Hannah G.) brought together ninety Jewish women from across the United States to take part in the Parliament of Religions, held during the Chicago World's Fair.

Responding to the world issues of those times, this gathering led to the development of the world's first large-scale Jewish women's organization, the Council of Jewish Women (National), and its mission. In 1928, the name formally was changed to National Council of Jewish Women (NCJW).

Hannah G. Solomon, 1893, founder of the National Council of Jewish Women. Courtesy of The Jacob Rader Marcus Center of the American Jewish Archives, Cincinnati, Ohio, at americanjewisharchives.org.

National's growth was so swift that by 1896 there were already fifty active sections across the country. All came together in New York City that year for its first convention, where the organization's constitution was adopted. From its beginning, National was involved in philanthropic endeavors and social reform, emphasizing services that provided education, health care, and employment for women and children. The federal government noticed and, in 1903, asked National of early involvements includes assisting immigrant families financially and through the work of settlement houses, providing vocational training for young girls, establishing free health clinics and day nurseries, and forming study circles for members to address these concerns.

During National's second decade, sections across the country established programs to deal with employment, incarceration, and health issues, and were the first to provide necessary services for

(Right) Women, from adults to infants, joined in a suffragist march to show support for women's right to vote, c. 1913. (Library of Congress, LC-USZC4-5585.)

for help in preventing young female newcomers to the country from being swept into prostitution or exploited by sweatshop owners.

In response, the New York Section organized a "Port-and-Dock Department." Members met all incoming ships to help arrivals pass through the immigration process and to assist them in locating relatives. The next year, National opened a permanent Immigrant Aid Station on Ellis Island.

As the nineteenth century closed and the twentieth began, there was a growth in social movements. The need for social reform in many areas, including the status of women, was evident to National's founders as they swung into action. A list

the Jewish blind and to make sure that affordable lunches were available to all school children.

In 1906, a probation officer whose salary was underwritten by National was accepted in a New York municipal court to work with delinquent Jewish children. Other sections provided this service in additional cities within the next five years. In even broader areas of service, National aided victims of Russian massacres and did the same for survivors of San Francisco's 1906 earthquake and fire. A national "Committee on Peace and Arbitration" debuted in 1908; four years later, during a meeting of the International Council of Women in Rome, the International

Council of Jewish Women was organized.

The White House Conference on Child Welfare in 1909 naturally drew National's participation, and the need for federal action was brought home to local members. During the 1911 National Convention, the women called for governmental programs to regulate food, drugs, and child labor, to legislate uniform marriage and divorce laws in all states, to provide low-income housing, and to enact anti-lynching legislation.

call for organization and action. They were in a different place from the women who had formed National and the original Dallas group, but they still coalesced around the same set of goals. Members were ready to support democratic values, to lead the way in providing local services, to train volunteers, and to cooperate with many other community groups. American Jewish women had already learned through experience that together they could do far more than any single one of them might accomplish alone, and that faith and devotion to a better society would be the driving forces to move them forward.

(Left) NCJW responds to the Statue of Liberty's call to "Give me your tired…" and helps settle the newest Americans, c. 1913. Courtesy of NCJW, Inc.

In Dallas, according to Hollace Ava Weiner in her book, Jewish "Junior League" (2008, Texas A&M University Press, pp.137–138), attempts to start an organization of Jewish women had met with limited success. In 1898, under the leadership of Rabbi George Alexander Kohut of Temple Emanu-El, Mrs. L. M. Guggenheim, Miss Gloria Wormser, and Miss L. Nora Wormser, a section of the Council of Jewish Women was formed. This section was represented at National's 1902 Baltimore triennial convention and was disbanded in 1905. By 1913, Dallas women were eager to form the Dallas Section when Sadie American, Hannah G.'s "deputy," arrived here with her

The women were quick to organize for a number of reasons. In the Jewish culture of the early twentieth century, women did not have many opportunities for either religious or higher secular education. They lacked the right to vote; therefore, they had little experience with public policy and few outlets for any exercise of meaningful advocacy.

Women's groups like NCJW began to spring up to enlarge the scope of their members' lives through mind-broadening study groups. These programs provided opportunities for members

(Center) Early coverage, 1894. ("A Dallas Lady Honored," the *Dallas Morning News*.)

Over a century, graphic styles have changed and so have NCJW's logos. Courtesy of NCJW, Inc.

to assess community needs and find meaningful volunteer ways to meet them, even as they enjoyed the very real comfort of socializing with others much like themselves. In coming together, these women found they could leave the imposed security of their own kitchens to interact with women who had similar goals. In doing so, they grew. They learned to listen. And in listening, they found their own voices and began to speak.

The Dallas Section's study groups were first led by men, primarily local rabbis revered for their religious education. But in studying with them, Dallas women learned that they, too, could lead and teach.

Section women took their skills outside the home to help those less fortunate, those with greater needs. When they saw hungry children in a local school, including Jewish children from families who had come to America much later and were much poorer than they, these Dallas women began making soup in their kitchens and taking it to the school. This homegrown effort was the start of the Dallas Public School's lunch program. When they found that babies were ailing, even dying from lack of milk, they began providing milk through a special fund that continues to make milk available to the needy in our area to this very day. These Dallas women started worshiping together on designated Section Sabbaths. Through all these early efforts they continued to gain the knowledge and experience that would serve to make them full citizens of their city, the country, and the world.

National's mission, principles, priorities, and resolutions always have served as a basic structure within which all sections operate. They reflect NCJW's faith in the future and belief in action by pursuing justice and respect for all. National also bases its efforts on a list of Jewish values taken from Biblical sources and the inspiring words of religious leaders. They include: Kavod Ha'broit, respect and dignity for all human beings; Talmud Torah, education and awareness; and Tzedek Tirdof, the pursuit of justice.

The Section, through changing times and differing communal needs, has embraced the National directives and has adapted great ideas from other sections in the country to initiate new programs. Volunteers have expanded the Section's vision as unique local needs arose, with all of their efforts under the umbrella of the broad National mission.

That same spirit lives on in Section members today. This nonprofit organization and its generations of strong women (and men) have proven themselves to be leaders of social change and advocates for women, children, and families. The members of today's Greater Dallas Section are still rooted in the ideals, Jewish values, and concerns of the pioneering heroes who gathered in Chicago in 1893.

A DALLAS LADY HONORED.

Appointed Texas Vice President of the National Council of Jewish Women.

Mrs. E. M. Chapman of Dallas, wife of Rev. Dr. E. M. Chapman, has been appointed vice president for Texas of the National council of Jewish women, whose headquarters is at Chicago. It is understood that this honor has been conferred on Mrs. Chapman as the result of the favorable impression created by her address at the Jewish women's religious congress, it having evoked not only great praise for its beauty but also because of the fact that although speaking for one-half an hour she did not have a scrap of paper in front of her. As vice president of the national organization Mrs. Chapman is ex-officio president of the state organization and she expects to organize sections all over Texas. The following is the letter announcing her appointment:

National Council of Jewish Women, Chicago, Jan. 19—Mrs E. M. Chapman, Dallas, Tex.—Dear madam: It is with pleasure that I beg to inform you that you have been appointed vice president for Texas of the National council of Jewish women, the association formed at the last meeting of the Jewish woman's religious congress.

We trust that the council will become a growing power for good, and are anxious for your co-operation. The duties of the office will consist in urging the organization for sections in the various cities. We earnestly hope for an early response signifying your acceptance of the position. Very cordially yours,

SADIE AMERICAN,
Corresponding secretary.

Colorful, dramatic image on the program for the "Woman Suffrage Procession" held on March 3, 1913. Illustration by Benjamin Moran Dale. (Library of Congress. LC-USZC4-2996.)

Nurses bound for Europe on the ship *Red Cross* typified the Section's spirit of national service, 1914. (Library of Congress, LC-DIG-ggbain-17121.)

1913	1914	1915	1916	1917
Current Dallas Section chartered	Dallas School volunteers; Penny lunches	Sewing classes at Neighborhood House	Immigrant Aid and Americanization courses	First health clinics in Dallas Schools

> "It is not your responsibility to finish the work of perfecting the world, but you are not free to desist from it either."
>
> *Rabbi Tarfon (c. 70–135 CE),*
> *Pirkei Avot 2:21*

The First Decade: 1913 to 1922

This was our world—a time of monumental change. World War I began in Europe in 1914. The following year, the British ocean liner, RMS *Lusitania*, on its way from New York City to Liverpool, England, was sunk by a German U-boat, killing almost 1,200, including many Americans. The United States declared war on Germany in 1917. Germany surrendered on November 11, 1918, Armistice Day. A worldwide influenza pandemic struck, killing nearly twenty million people. The Soviet States formed the Union of Soviet Socialist Republics (USSR). The tomb of King Tut was unearthed, and the Panama Canal opened traffic to join two oceans.

What did the United States face here? The start of the national income tax and the reestablishment of the Ku Klux Klan (KKK). But there were positives as well. Henry Ford

1918	1919	1920	1921	1922
WWI US Troops supported; Junior Council organized	Free school baths	US Nineteenth Amendment ratified; Council women voted	School Loan Fund started	Bible readings in public schools opposed

developed the first moving assembly line; the Nineteenth Amendment to the US Constitution ratified women's right to vote; the Lincoln Memorial was dedicated in Washington, DC; and the first woman was elected to the US Congress, representing Montana. Also, daylight saving time and dial telephones changed American patterns of commerce and communication.

As NCJW was forming in Dallas, the city was already a center of trade and manufacturing because of the presence of the railroad system. Troubles included a march by the KKK and stress from incursions as the Mexican Revolution crossed the Texas border. Grand openings were routine in this decade: a rebuilt Neiman Marcus store at Main and Ervay Streets, Parkland Hospital, the Woodlawn Tuberculosis Sanitarium, Southern Methodist University, WFAA radio, the Federal Reserve Bank of Dallas, and Union Station. The Texas/OU football game was moved permanently to Dallas in 1914. This decade also saw the first woman, Annie Webb Blanton, elected to statewide office in 1918.

The City of Dallas's population in 1920 was more than 159,000; approximately eight thousand of the residents were Jewish and lived in three distinct parts of the city. These areas were: Deep Ellum/East Dallas, "Goose Valley" (area bounded by Cedar Springs Road, Harry Hines Boulevard, and McKinney Avenue), and "The Cedars" (just south of Elm, Main, and Commerce Streets).

(Top) The Section's first president, 1913–1915, Grace A. Goldstein. Also president from 1923–1925, Goldstein became Grace Neuman after her marriage.

(Bottom) Minnie Hexter, the Section's second president, 1915–1919.

By 1920, the Jewish population became more concentrated in South Dallas, around Crowder, Corinth, South Akard, Beaumont, and Gould Streets. Temple Emanu-El and Congregation Shearith Israel, along with the Columbian Club and the Jewish Community Center, were located in this area.

BY 1913, JEWISH WOMEN IN DALLAS WERE AWARE OF COMMUNITY NEEDS AND READY TO ORGANIZE and to plan so they could tackle the problems of the city. Hannah G. Solomon's "deputy," Sadie American, was here for the official founding of the Dallas Section of the Council of Jewish Women in February of that year. The Section became the first independent Jewish women's group in Dallas. Seventy-five women made up the initial membership roster, paying dues of two dollars each at the start. It was not an inconsiderable sum when a loaf of bread could be bought for a nickel or less. By the time the first yearbook/directory was published in 1914, there were 219 members.

Margaret Sanger opened the first birth control clinic in 1916 in New York. Across the country, suffragettes demonstrated for women's right to vote, receiving it in 1920. The National organization backed these early feminists, but the Dallas Section, two decades younger, was not yet actively involved in these issues.

So, while the men transacted business, women were organizing. Middle-class women of the time founded numerous clubs and volunteer organizations in order to share experiences, seek self-improvement, and have an effect on home-front social issues.

How did Dallas Jewish women use this time? "Faith and Humanity" was the credo established nationally; our women added "Education and Service" to the Section's statement of purpose. Educational goals were focused initially on members' own personal improvement through exposure to art and literature, lectures on a variety of topics, and a number of discussion groups. Rabbis led two popular program series. Beginning

---

Hannah G. Solomon's "deputy," Sadie American, was here for the official founding of the Dallas Section of the Council of Jewish Women in February of 1913. The Section became the first independent Jewish women's group in Dallas.

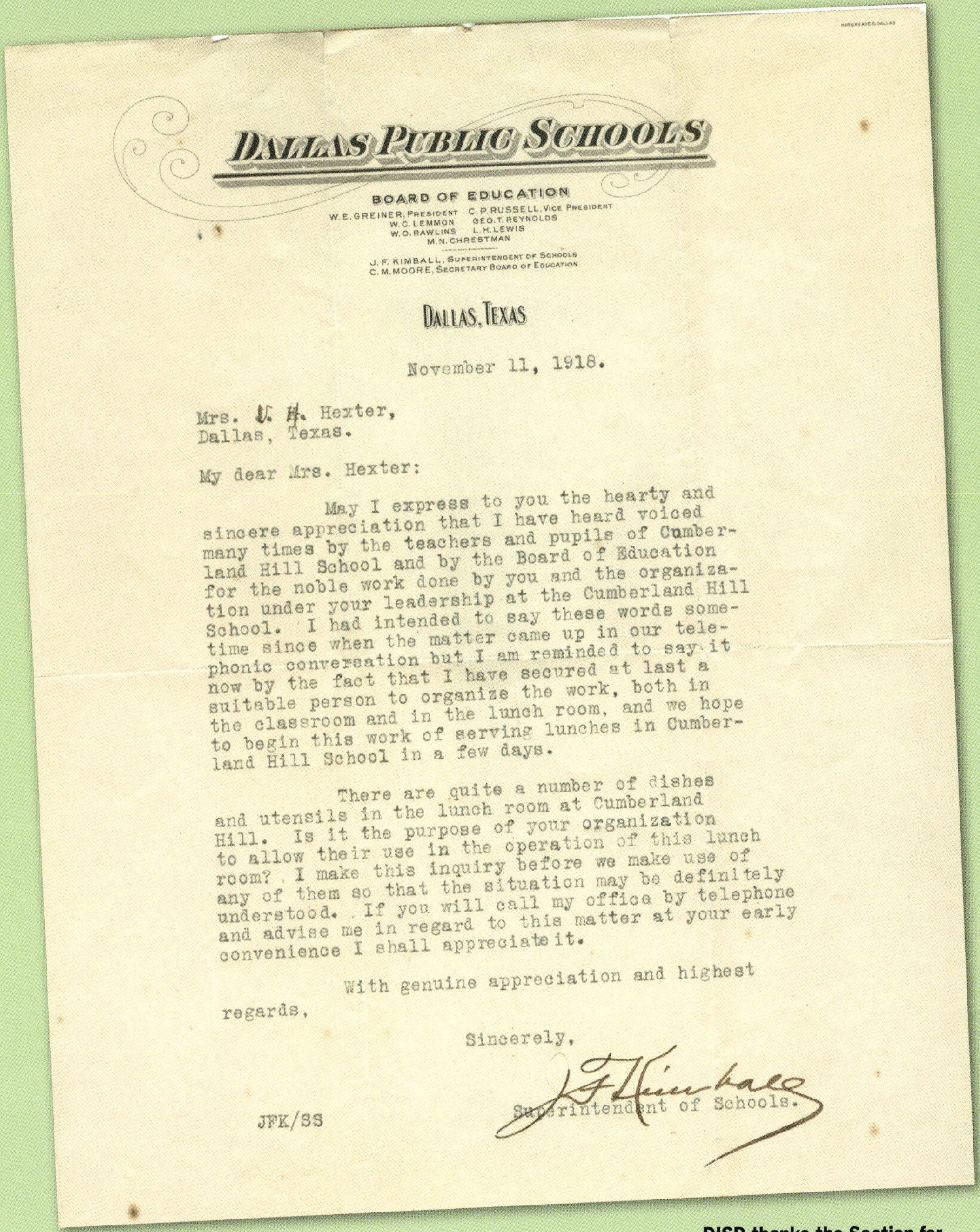

DISD thanks the Section for Cumberland Hill School's penny lunches.

E.M. Kahn employees march in a World War I preparedness parade in downtown Dallas, 1917. Photo by Marco's Studio. Courtesy of Dallas Jewish Historical Society.

Along with "Faith and Humanity," the credo established nationally, our women added "Education and Service" to the Dallas Section statement of purpose.

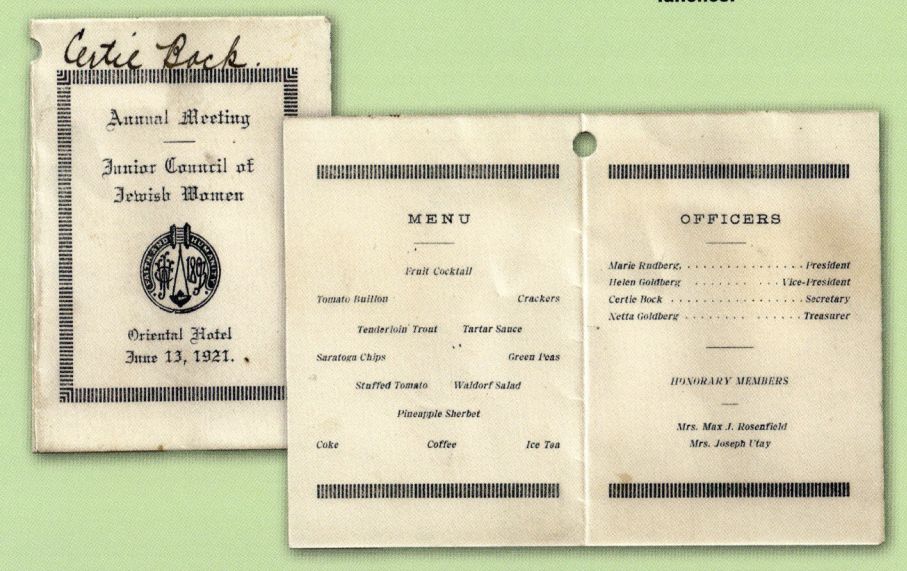

Program from the 1921 Annual Meeting of the Section's Junior Council, Marie Rudberg, president, and Certie Bock, secretary.

The "New" Temple Emanu-El, from 1899, located on South Ervay at St. Louis Streets, where the Section held many meetings from 1913–1916. Courtesy of Dallas Jewish Historical Society.

Sewing Class Conducted by Dallas Section Council Jewish Women

(Above) The Section's sewing class at the Neighborhood House, c. 1915. Photo by Frank Rogers.

COUNCIL OF JEWISH WOMEN.

New Organizations Have Been Recently Formed in Dallas, Galveston and Houston.

The National Council of Jewish Women has just completed its chain of sections and agents in the South, through the organization of Jewish women in Galveston, Houston and Dallas in Texas and Little Rock and Hot Springs, Ark., and providing of additional secretaries for social service in sections already formed in cities of the South and Middle West. The council's purpose, in so far as this new plan is concerned, is the care of Jewish girls coming to America and seeking work and homes in and near these cities. It is claimed that the most perfect system of immigrant protection for girls has been built up by the council.

A unique part of this Jewish immigration work extends also to foreign countries. Many girls coming to America are not allowed to land because of defective sight, possibly weak minds. Efforts are made at foreign ports to prevent the sailing of such girls, but many get through, only to be sent back again by our Government. The trouble is, however, that not a few who start on the return journey never reach their friends. Some commit suicide through disappointment, but more are robbed and led astray by men. The council has now what it claims is a perfect chain of sections and agents, both in the South and West here, and in Russia, Germany and Austria, from which largest numbers come, so that practically no deported girl need go wrong, and none remaining here may be for a moment without a capable chaperone.

The *Dallas Morning News* reports on the founding of the Section, 1913. ("Council of Jewish Women," the *Dallas Morning News*.)

in 1915, Temple Emanu-El's Rabbi William Henry Greenburg led the "Study Circle" that met every Monday evening at the Temple. A few years later, when Dr. David Lefkowitz became the rabbi at Temple Emanu-El, he led the "Jewish Fortnightly Current Events" program.

Few women of that day had opportunities for higher secular education, and most Jewish women were denied the religious education that was customary—almost mandatory—for males. Consequently, the Section provided these, and faith became an important element of the Section's purpose. During the first year, a monthly Section Sabbath was introduced. Like most early functions, they met at Temple Emanu-El. In March 1914, the first Section Sabbath was held at both the Temple and Congregation Shearith Israel, broadening the base of membership to include Conservative women along with the Reform-affiliated, who were the majority of the founding members.

Racial and ethnic exclusion were parts of the early Texas scene. Jews (and others) were not accepted for membership in many private clubs or as residents in some neighborhoods. As a result, the larger Jewish community founded the Columbian Club, which permitted Jews and others to join. This was the site of the Section's first birthday luncheon, an annual tradition that has been held in many different venues for more than a century.

Section members wasted no time in moving their efforts out into the larger community. Early on, a Section "Purity of the Press" Committee monitored local newspapers for signs of anti-Semitism and, in 1922, the Section took a stand in opposition to Bible reading in the city's public schools.

The Section's model process was born early and continues to this day: do research and identify a need, initiate and evaluate a pilot program, and then find appropriate people or organizations in the larger community who can help continue the work and eventually take it over altogether.

The City of Dallas began a unique partnership with the Dallas Section that has endured for more than one hundred years. When local children needed after-school care, when new immigrants needed acculturation, when its seniors needed meals, the women of the Dallas Section stepped forward to serve, eager to strengthen their community.

The Dallas Public Schools' first in-school volunteers were Section members. Initially, the women focused on helping school-aged children. They had a particular interest in the Cumberland Hill School, located in one of Dallas's poorest neighborhoods, where more than thirty nationalities, including many Jews and Hispanics, lived. This was Dallas's oldest public school, and its building still stands at 1901 North Akard Street. As early as 1914, the first volunteer project, the Penny Lunch for poor students attending this school, began. Section members cooked food in their homes. The food then was carried to the school. By 1918, the Dallas School District's Board of Education began supporting the lunch program and expanded it to include additional schools.

At the Neighborhood House, located at McKinney and Highland Streets and operated by the Dallas Free Kindergarten Association, the Section established a free health clinic and even free baths. Members furnished the clinic and provided medicines, bandages, soap, and towels. As many as 2,500 people were seen during that first year. At the House, the Section also taught sewing and cooking to those needing these skills and prepared young women of working age for jobs that would help support their families. Eventually, the Dallas School Board decided to place health professionals in all of the district's schools.

The Immigrant Aid Committee also was formed in 1914, and its first efforts were to organize Americanization classes in conjunction with the Dallas Public Schools. By 1925, the Section started Dallas's first English courses for adult foreigners.

A Junior Council of young, single Jewish women was organized by the Section in 1918 to engage those fourteen to twenty-one years old. Activities included drama, music, dancing, and religious circles. This group started with thirty-seven members and by the end of the decade had expanded to 123. As needs and interests shifted during the next fifty years, groups evolved, and various new age groups were included.

During World War I, Section volunteers sewed hospital gowns, made surgical dressings, sold more than $176,000 in war bonds, and gave a dance for Jewish soldiers stationed in this area. In 1919, as the Dallas population began to boom, Section President Mrs. Victor Hexter (Minnie) sent the following note of encouragement to the Section: "Now that the war is over, we should put forth our best efforts to do bigger work than ever before. Our membership ought to double because of the influx of newcomers into Dallas. Council not only opens up means of getting acquainted but (it) can be made the outlet for extensive and intensive work."

On the local scene, the Philanthropic Committee supported the "Free Ice Fund," started by the *Dallas Times Herald* newspaper, and provided business education scholarships for young men and women. Other beneficiaries of Section philanthropy included national and international organizations such as the Jewish Welfare Relief Fund, Hebrew Union College, the Zionist Organization of America, and the National Jewish Health Hospital in Denver.

A limited number of scholarships of $100 were given each year to Jewish

A new cooking class, ready to begin instruction from Section volunteers at the Neighborhood House, operated by the Dallas Free Kindergarten Association, 1917.

("To Organize Jewish Women," the *Dallas Morning News*.)

TO ORGANIZE JEWISH WOMEN.

Miss Sadie American of New York Will Speak Here Monday.

Miss Sadie American of New York City, the executive secretary of the National Council of Jewish Women, is in the city and is to deliver an address on Monday night before the congregation at Temple Emanu-El. Her work, which has taken her to pretty well every congregation of Jewish people in the United States, is of a benevolent and patriotic sort.

Dr. William H. Greenburg of Temple Emanu-El said last night: "Miss Sadie American is a remarkable woman. She is to be in Dallas Monday. Her purpose is to organize a section of the National Council of Jewish Women, an organization the most representative of Jewish womanhood of America. She will speak before the congregation of Temple Emanu-El Monday night, beginning at 8 o'clock. She has probably occupied every Jewish pulpit in the United States in the prosecution of her work. She is a very interesting speaker and she carries a message."

(Below) The Columbian Club, known as the "Jewish Country Club" of Dallas, was the site of the Section's first Birthday Luncheon.

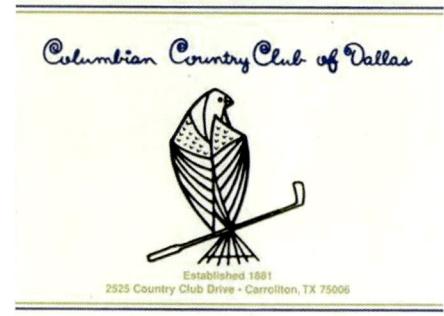

(Right) A Section hymn from the early years.

Early coverage of the Section's engagement in public education, 1918. ("Dallas Pupils Get Lunches at Cost," the *Dallas Morning News*.)

students attending universities in Texas that had a Menorah Society, the precursor of today's Hillel, a Jewish university campus organization. A student loan fund was started in 1921 to pay partially for the training of a future rabbi. More than $2,000 was raised through parties, teas, and—just once—a raffle for a car. A unique fundraiser was also employed: a penny a day was collected from each member to make sure the Section would be "of real service to Judaism."

In the earliest days of the Dallas Section, patriotism was a predominant theme. At meetings, members would sing "The Council Hymn" to the tune of "My Country 'Tis of Thee."

The hymn, which is reproduced here as it appeared in an undated program from a Dallas Section meeting, include the misspelling "dulfil." That most certainly should have been "fulfil." The single letter "l" at the end of both this word and "instil" suggests a British spelling preference still common in the early days of twentieth-century America; today, of course, the letter would be doubled. Lyrics to two full stanzas of "The Star-Spangled Banner" followed the Council Hymn.

According to the program, the meeting also included "Open Forum" and "Tea of All Nations," with Mrs. Ed Goodman (Gertrude) and Mrs. Charles L. Benson (Sybil) in charge. Note that these women's first names were not used; the custom of the time was to list married women by their husbands' names only. The women were given the joint masculine title of "Chairmen." According to instructions: "Everybody Must Sing–If You Can't Sing, Hum."

It was an expectation that Dallas Section women would take responsibility for repairing their world and training future generations to carry the torch. By the end of the first decade there could be no doubt that they would!

Open Forum.
Sing-Song .... Star Spangled Banner

Tea of All Nations .... { Mrs. Ed Goodman
                                                  Mrs. C. L. Benson
                                                  Chairmen

SONGS
Everybody Must Sing—If You Can't Sing, Hum

Council Hymn—to the air of "My Country 'Tis of Thee"

To Thee thy daughters sing,
Humbly our prayers we bring,
    To Thee above.
Into our hearts instil
Reverence for Thy will
Our duty to dulfil
    Through Faith and Love.
When we from Egypt's land
Marched forth a rescued band
    To Liberty,
Then, Freedom, noble word,
By mankind first was heard
And human hearts were stirred.
    To Thee we turn.
Since then throughout the world
Our flag has been unfurled
For Thee on high.
Justice, Love, Modesty,
    Duty, Fidelity,
Faith and Humanity!
    Oh, hear our Cry.

STAR SPANGLED BANNER

O say, can you see by the dawn's early light
What so proudly we hailed at the twilight's last gleaming,
Whose broad stripes and bright stars thro' the perilous fight
O'er the ramparts we watched were so gallantly streaming!
    And the rocket's red glare,
    The bombs bursting in air,
Gave proof through the night that our flag was still there!

O say, does that star-spangled banner still wave
O'er the land of the free and the home of the brave?
O thus be it ever, when freeman shall stand
Between their loved homes and foul war's desolation.
Blest with victory and peace, may the heaven-rescued land
Praise the Power that hath made and preserved us a nation.
    Then conquer we must
    For our cause it is just,
    And this be our motto, "In God We Trust."
And the star-spangled banner in triumph shall wave
O'er the land of the free and the home of the brave.

President Minnie Hexter notes in her president's report for 1918–1919 that February 22, 1919, President George Washington's birthday, was designated as Texas Arbor Day. On that day, the Section "planted pecan trees in City Park, in one of the most beautiful spots of that beautiful place, in memory of the three Jewish boys of Dallas who made the supreme sacrifice. Appropriate exercises were held. This tribute to our boys served a triple purpose, not only commemorating and honoring the dead, but by adding civic attractiveness, and, at the same time, perpetuating the nut trees indigenous to our soil." Mrs. Nathaniel Harris, NCJW National President, was in Dallas for several weeks beforehand, adding impetus to the tree planting event. Mrs. Harris "spoke most feelingly and impressively" at the event.

City Park, Dallas, c. 1920. Courtesy of Dallas Heritage Village.

Eleanor Roosevelt was an author, ambassador, social activist, and wife of the thirty-second president, Franklin D Roosevelt. (Keystone/Getty Images.)

1923	1924	1925	1926	1927
First Section fundraising rummage sale	Pioneer programs for seniors; City zoning ordinances advocated	First English courses for foreign adults	Initiated services for visually impaired	Dallas Juvenile Court supported; Council Comment published

"Whatsoever thy hand finds to do, do it with all thy might."
Ecclesiastes 9:10

The Second Decade : *1923 to 1932*

In 1923, John A. Macready and Oakley Kelly flew a single engine plane from New York to San Diego, the first ever nonstop transcontinental airplane flight. Four years later, Charles Lindbergh accomplished the first solo transatlantic flight. The attorney Clarence Darrow asked that mercy be granted to two young Jewish thrill-killers, Leopold and Loeb. The role of science and religion in public schools was put to the test during the famed Scopes "monkey trial," at which Darrow was victorious.

The stock market crashed in 1929, marking what would become the longest sustained economic depression in the Western world. Eleanor Roosevelt directed efforts toward feminism—although it wasn't called that yet!—when she

| *New name: National Council of Jewish Women* | *Celebrity authors visit; Junior Buds started* | *Sewing Circle ships to orphanages, immigrants* | *Magazine boxes for hospitals and jails* | *First classes for hearing-impaired* |

1928 — 1929 — 1930 — 1931 — 1932

wrote the essay "Women Must Learn to Play the Game as Men Do." Women were beginning to come into their own, including here in Dallas.

During the 1920s, Dallas established itself as a major center of finance and transportation. There were impassioned public calls for changes in governance and zoning and for improvements in schools, streets, and parks. In 1927, and again in 1930, voters approved Dallas charter amendments and bond proposals that promised better government coordination plus enhanced awareness and treatment of basic city needs.

THE DECADE WAS MARKED BY JUBILANT HIGHS AND DEMORALIZING LOWS ACROSS the country and the world. Members of the growing Dallas Section worked mightily to deal with some of the community's increasing burdens of the time, including poverty, illness, and disability.

The Section that had formed ten years earlier with seventy-five interested women now started its second decade with 618 members. Annual dues were now up to $4, and the organization's budget at the beginning of this decade was $2,700. Ten years later, it had increased to $4,000. The first decade had involved sixteen committees, but a Ways and Means Committee was not among them. That committee was finally created in 1923 to formalize fundraising, and a rummage sale was held as its first effort. This was the predecessor of the Section's Your Thrift Shop and later ENCORE resale shop and an early realization of how to use existing, easily available resources to help fund community service programs.

Both a free clinic and free bath programs, founded earlier at the Cumberland Hill School, were adopted by the Dallas School Board in 1924, further establishing the Section's pattern of identifying community needs and meeting them with new services that could later be handed over to other appropriate groups to continue.

During the early 1920s, tuberculosis was running rampant in Dallas. To broaden the Section's already existing efforts to improve infant and child health, members began to provide milk through the Tuberculosis Committee in 1928 and later through the Health Committee. A milk fund was established and remained a part of the Health Committee until 1945. Eventually, it became an independent tribute fund and was renamed The Minnie Hexter Milk Fund, honoring the woman who founded this program and headed it during its early years. This fund continues today as a source of free milk and infant formula for Dallas's needy families. Throughout this decade, the Section extended services to the visually challenged. Some members learned Braille to assist the blind; this early effort is recognized as the genesis of today's Dallas Lighthouse for the Blind. After that, the women convinced the Dallas Public Library to set up a collection of Braille books, and the Section paid for necessary surgery for a blind child. These accomplishments inspired Bishop Joseph Patrick Lynch—for whom a Dallas Catholic high school is named—to remind the city that not even one of the blind who had been helped by the Section was Jewish.

When these successes were reported at an NCJW National Convention, the Section was urged to add services for the hearing-impaired to its programs for the blind. The first step was hiring a teacher to offer a lip-reading class for deaf children; thirty-seven students, ages three to twenty, enrolled. Providing funds for speech therapy was the Section's natural follow-up.

Beginning in 1923, the Section provided services at the Hella Temple Crippled Children's Hospital (Scottish Rite Hospital for Children). Initially, the Section furnished a playroom at the hospital, and volunteers helped supervise play. This continued until the early 1930s. Beginning again in 1948, Section volunteers provided play therapy for ambulatory children in the Hospital's playroom until early 1954.

Additional activities in this decade included donating wheelchairs for hospitalized children, taking youngsters from low-income families to

---

The Section furnished library books, rockers, a Victrola, and a friendly, cultural environment at the Scottish Rite Crippled Children's Hospital, c. 1920s.

The Section hired Miss Louise Hillyear, a lip-reading teacher, during 1932–1933 to conduct summer classes for thirty-seven students at Dallas's Fannin Elementary School. ("Lip-Reading Will Be Taught in Schools; Teacher Elected," the *Dallas Morning News*.)

the Texas State Fair, and staging an ecumenical "coup" by organizing a citywide Easter egg hunt for children, which was held at Colonial Hill School Park. The Section sponsored a Girl Scout troop at Temple Emanu-El and provided for special Sunday School events there until 1928, when the Congregation's Sisterhood assumed those responsibilities.

The older generation was not neglected. Section volunteers made personal hospital visits to seniors and provided rides for elderly shut-ins so they could occasionally leave their homes. These were the first programs for older adults ever offered by any NCJW Section, and they became models for National's entry into this area of community service.

The Section helped with Red Cross and Community Chest fundraising drives. They campaigned to get all Jewish women registered to vote and to use the right finally granted to them in 1920. Section members also advocated for legislation directed toward improving treatment of those with mental health disorders and for restoring criminals to societal productivity. Mrs. Albert Mittenthal (Rae), Section president in 1928–1929, charged members, "We must be courageous enough to recognize which road we must travel, to move forward. . . . One for all, and all for the Council, in essential things. . . ."

Section life was far from all work and no play. There were a Drama Circle and a Literary Circle plus an annual Council Sabbath observed the Friday evening before Purim each year, alternating venues between Temple Emanu-El and Congregation Shearith Israel. At the 1924 Birthday Luncheon, Section members were treated to a talk by acclaimed Jewish novelist Edna Ferber, who was brought to Dallas just for the occasion. At the Birthday Luncheon the following year, every member brought a jar of jelly for the Council Jelly Closet, to be given as Purim gifts to the poor.

Members enjoyed the Section's Celebrity Course, a fundraising effort that offered a series of four lectures in 1928–1929. Presenters were: writer/dramatist Thornton Wilder on his book *The Bridge of San Luis Rey;* John Cowper Powys, a lecturer, critic, novelist, and philosopher; Sydney Thompson, a dramatic reader who performed plays, ballads, and folktales in costume; and Sir Douglas Mawson's moving pictures of the South Pole.

In the summer of 1929, the Philanthropy Committee awarded a scholarship to a promising young violinist, Zelman Brounoff, to continue his studies. He subsequently auditioned and was accepted into the Dallas Symphony Orchestra. In 1945, Brounoff became the assistant, and later the associate concertmaster, of the Dallas Symphony. He remained with the symphony until his retirement in 1983. This same committee also provided season tickets for forty blind individuals to enjoy the music of the concerts.

The Americanization Committee promoted English literacy while sharing information on business, hygiene, and citizenship with many immigrant women—a large number of whom later became Section members themselves. The Health Committee worked on improving sewage services in South Dallas, the screening of domestic workers for tuberculosis, and advocating for government inspection of meat.

Every Monday morning the Sewing Circle met to make necessary items for the continuing stream of newcomers who came through Ellis Island and for the Jewish Children's Home in New Orleans. To raise funds while they stitched away on donated materials, Sewing Circle participants paid ten cents for a cup of coffee—a heavy price

> In the summer of 1929, the Philanthropy Committee awarded a scholarship to a promising, young violinist, Zelman Brounoff, to continue his studies. He had been accepted into the Dallas Symphony Orchestra just three years prior at the age of seventeen. He retired as Concertmaster Emeritus in 1983.

Scholarship recipient Zelman Brounoff, violinist, entertained the Section at its 1927 program at Temple Emanu-El. Courtesy of the Brounoff Family Archive.

Children of students in the Section's Americanization class performed Russian dances for members of the Section, 1930. ("Little Americans Give Russian Folk Dances," the *Dallas Morning News*.)

President Thekla Brin (fifth from the right) and her Section board members are listed in the *Dallas Morning News* article, 1932. ("Newly Elected Officers of Council of Jewish Women," the *Dallas Morning News*.)

The Section's Sewing Circle was thanked by the Red Cross for its "beautifully made garments," 1930.

at a time when a full pound could be bought for as little as forty-seven cents!

Council Comment, the Section's earliest newsletter, made its debut in 1927. Following National's lead, the Section changed its official name to the National Council of Jewish Women, Dallas Section. The Section's bylaws were changed to end contributions to other philanthropic organizations, allowing the Section to have a broader local impact.

As its second decade drew to a close, Section President Mrs. Walter Brin (Thekla) reminded everyone to "replace, in our lives, depression with expression and activity," setting the stage for the next decade—years with plenty of opportunities for mighty efforts.

Stitching Together for Thirty Years

For three decades women from the Dallas Section stitched garments to clothe families in need. The Section's Sewing Circle began in 1920, and through the mid-1930s it turned out thousands of garments—first for local day nurseries and needy families and then for shipment to immigrants at Ellis Island. Demand continued to grow, and the women continued to sew for other beneficiaries including the Jewish Children's Home in New Orleans, Dallas Baby Camp (Children's Medical Center), the Tuberculosis Hospital, and Federated Charities.

This enormous endeavor cost the Section's treasury absolutely nothing. Sewing Circle volunteers persuaded local merchants to donate all the materials they needed.

During the mid- and late 1930s, the volunteers expanded their efforts further, creating handsome boxes of garments for the Shrine Hospital for Crippled Children, Hadassah, and the Bradford Memorial Home while continuing to meet the demands of the New Orleans Home and local Dallas needs. A Section report from 1937–1938 states, "It is our pride and pleasure to vote them (the Sewing Circle) a new electric sewing machine."

In the early 1940s, the Sewing Circle delivered 2,562 garments to the Red Cross for use in emergencies. The group continued cooperating with the Red Cross through 1946, working with the Temple Emanu-El Red Cross Sewing Unit in the Temple's South Dallas quarters—a special room that was open to the public on a non-sectarian basis. Throughout World War II, this cooperative effort resulted in the completion of some ten thousand garments: dresses, coats, pajamas, snowsuits, rompers, and trousers.

The Section's Sewing Circle resumed operations in its own sewing room in 1947 and continued until 1951, when it was discontinued.

The Section's Sewing Circle produced amazing numbers of garments and layettes for emergency use both locally and overseas, c. 1920s.

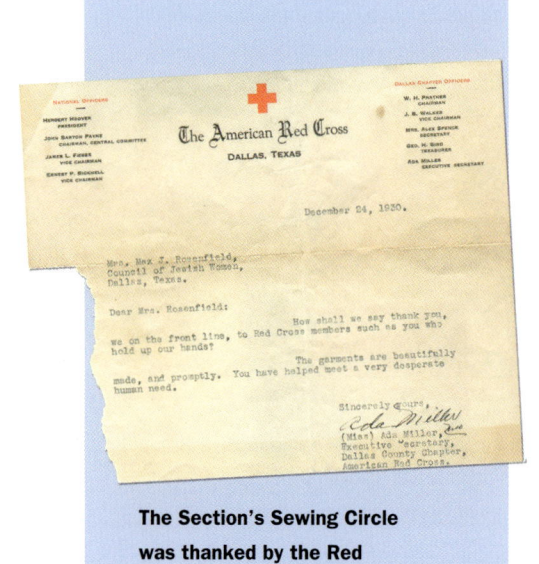

Dramas, musicals, and skits helped tell the Section's stories and engage many members. Here are representative samples of programs and events of the second decade.

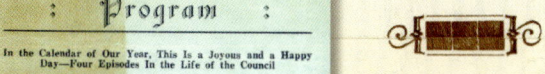

Unimaginable drought and dust storms, along with the Great Depression, robbed families of livelihoods and the basics for human survival, 1936. Photo by Dorothea Lange. (Library of Congress. LC-USZ62-131366.)

Section's Birth Control Committee formed — 1933

Milk Fund started; Section supports new Dallas VNA — 1934

Aid for German-Jewish children — 1935

Texas Centennial Exposition volunteers — 1936

Parkland Lending Library; Teacher for homebound students — 1937

"A little bit of light dispels a lot of darkness."

Rabbi Schneur Zalman of Liadi, Russia (1745–1812), founder of Chabad, a branch of Hasidic Judaism

The Third Decade : 1933 *to* 1942

The world desperately needed light during these tumultuous years. The Great Depression officially started in October 1929 and plagued the globe until the early 1940s. In Europe, Adolph Hitler was amassing unchecked power; war broke out there in 1939. Though the United States tried to stay out of the battles, when Japan attacked Pearl Harbor in 1941, we, too, were officially at war.

A monumental drought and dark clouds of life-choking dust scourged the central United States, stretching into the Panhandle of Texas, robbing farmers of their livelihoods, and destroying families. Dallas turned to manufacturing what was needed for the war effort, and the Ford plant on East Grand Avenue stopped making cars to grind out military trucks and Jeeps instead.

Some hope arrived for North Texas when the State's 1936

First German refugee child placed in Dallas	*Survey of Foreign Born, in cooperation with SMU*	*After-school programs for "latch-key" children*	*Dallas Council of Social Agencies' cases indexed*	*Day nurseries for military families*
1938	1939	1940	1941	1942

Centennial Exposition was awarded to Dallas. The attraction created about ten thousand jobs. Some fifty buildings were built in Fair Park where more than six million people attended the five-month celebration of Texas's one-hundred-year anniversary of independence from Mexico.

THE DALLAS SECTION SOMEHOW MANAGED TO MAINTAIN ALL ITS EXISTING SERVICE PROJECTS during the Depression, but barely. President Franklin D. Roosevelt's new programs, such as the National Labor Relations Board (NLRB) and Works Progress Administration (WPA), sparked new light with a redefinition of advocacy and a redoubling of social action.

A major Section effort continued to be service to the blind. Section volunteers staffed a Lighthouse for the Blind booth at the State Fair, ran a "Talking Book" program, and put together a history of blindness in the city for the Dallas School Board. Somehow, $75 was scraped together to purchase a car to transport the blind as needed.

Money, however, was the Section's main concern. The annual dues that had been raised to $4 during the past decade were rolled back to the earlier $3, yet membership did not grow. The Social Welfare Committee was formed in 1933. It started its work by providing three needy students at Forest Avenue High School (James Madison High School) with books, other supplies, and—as minutes of the day put it—"proper clothing." The Committee also sent volunteers to Baylor Hospital every day to assist with occupational therapy. Birth control clinics in Dallas were established in 1935, sixteen years after Margaret Sanger opened the first clinic in New York. By 1937, the Section's Civic and Communal Affairs Committee was supporting free legal aid and birth control clinics.

A major Section effort continued to be service to the blind. Section volunteers staffed a Lighthouse for the Blind booth at the State Fair, ran a "Talking Book" program, and put together a history of blindness in the city for the Dallas School Board. Somehow, $75 was scraped together to purchase a car to transport the blind as needed.

A hard-of-hearing project suggested earlier by National was started in Dallas in 1932, serving eight boys by its second year. The Dallas School Board took responsibility for this program in 1939, when it had grown to aid almost two hundred students in sixteen classes at eleven different city schools. At the end of the decade, three hundred were being helped.

Providing academic support to physically challenged children was the next agenda item. The Section's "Schoolchild Welfare Committee" conducted a survey of school-aged children who were unable to attend school because of their physical challenges, and appealed to the Dallas School Board to offer special classes for these children. With a slow Dallas School Board response, the Section went forward by itself in 1937, hiring a home teacher for these children. Later, a trained

(Right) Blanche Hirshfelder, chair of Committee on the Blind, teaches a child how to identify shapes, 1942.

Section member taught a class at the Scottish Rite Hospital for Children. These efforts inspired the local Women of Rotary to join in this program—with early financial support from the Section.

Tuberculosis was still a concern, and the Section supported the National Jewish Health Hospital in Denver, where patients received free treatment in a beneficial, sunny, dry climate. In Dallas, the Section gave oranges, cod liver oil, and four thousand quarts of milk every year to the city's needy children.

In 1931 the Section began distributing magazines to twenty locations, including all city hospitals and the city jail. This was the genesis of

Section member Bertha Goslin explains some of the complexities of the English language as part of the Section's Service to the Foreign Born project.

the Parkland Hospital Lending Library, which the Section established in 1937. Volunteers continued distributing magazines to patients for the next forty-five years.

The Section cooperated with Southern Methodist University in a 1939 major survey of Dallas's foreign-born population. Members were instrumental in helping Jewish newcomers from Germany connect with relatives, resettle locally, and find jobs. Two years later, following the lead of National, the name of the Americanization program was changed to "Service to the Foreign Born." To assist with the influx of new residents, the Section cooperated with an array of service providers, including the Jewish Welfare Federation, YWCA, Red Cross, Child Guidance Clinic, and the Dallas Public Evening School. Section members also found temporary foster homes for three refugee children.

In 1941, the largest volunteer social services project in Dallas, "Soundex," coordinated eighty-five Section volunteers who spent two thousand hours over eleven weeks codifying three hundred thousand case histories and updating the filing system of the Dallas Council of Social Agencies (Community Council of Greater Dallas). The new system eliminated more than four thousand duplicate listings and made enough room for a whole year's worth of new case files.

Continuing turmoil across the Atlantic created change in the Section's service agenda. In 1933, there had been thirty-five students in English language classes; by 1941, there were ninety students, as Jewish refugees began leaving Europe for America. To reach these immigrants, the Section hired two teachers to supplement a teacher provided by the city. Later, an additional English language teacher was hired by the federally funded WPA. Classes were held at Dallas Public Evening Schools all over Dallas and included coaching to help students of many generations attain citizenship.

To provide its sections with information to assist them in fighting anti-Semitic propaganda, National formed a "Committee of One Thousand" consisting of key NCJW women from all over the United States. A study of conditions in Nazi-controlled countries was proposed. The first of a series of pamphlets, "Anti-Semitism—A Study Outline," was published in 1934. Dr. David Lefkowitz, Temple Emanu-El's Rabbi, held monthly meetings using this study guide. However, National did not complete its outline of programs, and since the meetings were very popular with members, Rabbi Lefkowitz continued this series with his own study outline.

The Section continued to embrace sewing as a major project. Garments were sent to the Red Cross, British War Relief, and United China Relief.

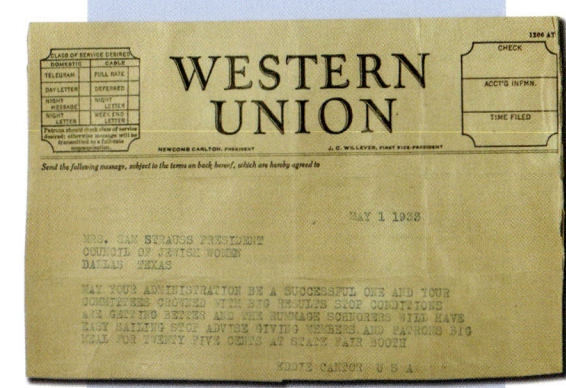

Entertainer Eddie Kantor sent a telegram to Sarah Strauss, incoming Section president, to wish her a successful administration and prosperous fundraising efforts, May 1, 1933.

Section members Rilla Beattle and Mrs. Abe Zimmerman (left to right) serve children of World War II armed forces at Silberstein Day Nursery, 1942.

(Left) Section members Dora Mayer and Doris Borley help a patient at Parkland Hospital select a magazine from the Section's free lending library, 1942.

(Right) Bernice Nussbaum, Section teacher, works with a student who requires homebound instruction; this was part of a joint effort with Scottish Rite Hospital, 1942.

Members sold war bonds and, through the United Service Organizations (USO), hosted dances and provided home hospitality for servicemen stationed in or near Dallas. One year the Section even prepared a Passover Seder for 184 Jewish soldiers.

With many women entering the workforce for the first time, the Section recognized the growing need for childcare. The Council of Social Agencies invited Section members to train to work at the Silberstein Day Nursery. By 1942, twenty-six volunteers were staffing the nursery year-round, five days a week.

Through it all, Section members continued to socialize and celebrate as well as serve. NCJW National President Mrs. Arthur Brin (Fanny) attended the Dallas Section's birthday luncheon in 1933. Members held a special meeting honoring the Texas Centennial in 1936. For the twenty-eighth Birthday Luncheon in 1941, the featured speaker was State Judge Sarah T. Hughes of the Fourteenth District Court, who spoke about the progress of women. Judge Hughes later became the federal judge who swore in Lyndon B. Johnson as president of the United States after the 1963 assassination of President John F. Kennedy in Dallas.

During these troubled years, there were constant efforts toward peace. The Section took part in a forum on the League of Nations in 1936 and the next year joined forces with Hadassah and the Sisterhoods of Temple Emanu-El and Shearith Israel to discuss the question of an organized peace movement. In 1940, the Section conducted a year-long study series called "The Future After the War—Is Isolation No Longer an Option?"

What were the findings of that series? There are no written records—perhaps because *Council Comment* had been replaced in 1939 by a simple monthly calendar, possibly in the interest of conserving paper. The newsletter was reinstated in 1941, but there was no yearbook for the decade's end. Instead, the $300 that would have gone toward its publication was sent to further National's program of aid to the foreign-born. As the Section moved into the mid-1940s, it did so with a new management approach in which two of its four vice presidents were assigned, for the first time, to take specific responsibilities for the committees addressing welfare and education.

Even the prospect of war did not deter the Section. Members endorsed the National Audubon

Society's 1941 stand against the use of wild bird plumage on hats.

In the middle of these challenging, dark days there were glimmers of light—heroes in the war effort, social change in Washington, economic improvement, and hard-working women who committed to services that helped stabilize and aid the community. The Section, which celebrated its twenty-fifth anniversary on March 1, 1938, continued to identify needs, seek light, and research solutions, and then provide healing hands.

Finding Homes for German Children

The Dallas Section began working with the New York City-based German-Jewish Children's Aid organization in 1934, when the need for child resettlement in the United States was first recognized. National prioritized this matter by resolution at the April 1935 Triennial Convention in New Orleans:

"Since the National Council of Jewish Women has always concerned itself with problems relating to women and children, the Board of Directors recommends that one of the major projects of the Sections during this ensuing Triennial period shall be continuation of the policy as applied to German Jewish refugees."

Less than two weeks later, Mrs. Arthur Brin (Fanny), National's president, sent all members an urgent appeal that she termed a "Special Emergency Matter which cannot wait until next fall," advising that "Action must be taken now...." That act was to locate American Jewish homes for German-Jewish children.

The Section was already engaged since a Dallas family had volunteered the winter before to take a child into their home. Section President Mrs. Asher Mintz (Amelia) received a letter in December 1934 from the German-Jewish Children's Aid organization: "The plan is going through. We ask that there be no publicity in the newspapers about it...."

Why no publicity? Mrs. Mintz received a letter from Cecilia Razovsky, executive director of German-Jewish Children's Aid, Inc., about a planned Dallas fundraiser for the cause:

We believe it is inadvisable to give newspaper publicity in connection with the German-Jewish children. If you wish to send copy to the newspapers, there is no objection to doing so, provided you do not mention that the children are here in the United States. You can mention that the purpose is to raise funds on behalf of German-Jewish refugee children, without mentioning that they are in the United States. We have not yet been given permission by the United States Government to publicize this work, and until we do receive this permission we must move with caution.

Financial arrangements were also carefully monitored. A transportation fund would pay the children's passage, but monies "must not be contributed by an organization or a Committee. Only individuals may pay...." Section women who wanted to participate had to write personal checks that would be mailed individually or pooled and sent by one individual to Paul Felix Warburg, treasurer of German-Jewish Children's Aid in New York.

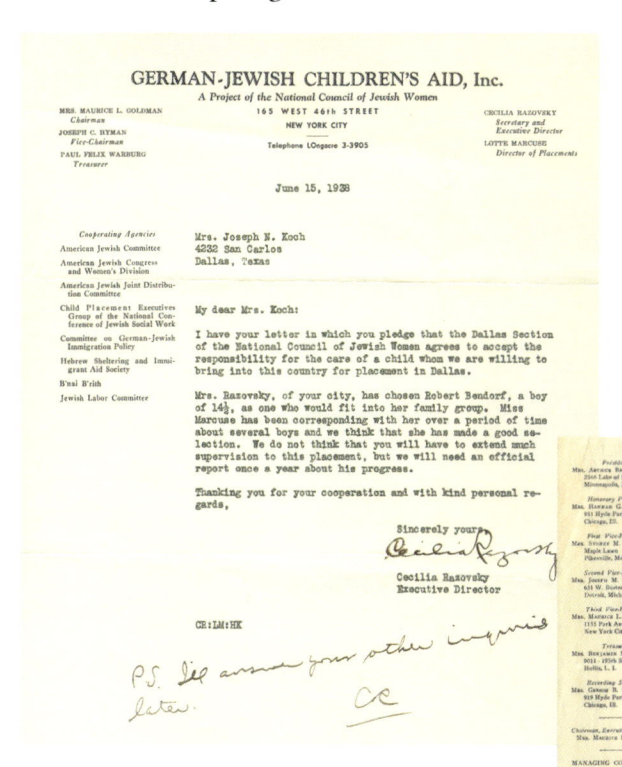

At that time, fifty-three children had already

(Left) Letter from German-Jewish Children's Aid, Inc., acknowledging placement of a refugee child in Dallas, 1938.

Emergency notice to the Section that action was required to bring refugee children to America, 1935.

25

VNA staff Victoria Hunter, Rose Bernice, and Florence Patterson (left to right) take a call and prepare to serve where needed, 1934. Courtesy of VNA Texas.

Even the prospect of war did not deter the Section. Members endorsed the National Audubon Society's 1941 stand against the use of wild bird plumage on hats.

arrived in the United States, with many of them immediately placed with private families. But the placement offer from the Dallas Section was originally excluded, showing how little was then known in New York about the vibrant Jewish life here.

A number of the Section's members combined their contributions so that Mrs. S. H. Marks (Rae), then Section treasurer, could write one single check for $100 in her own name as required. She received a warm letter of "thanks for the splendid cooperation toward the maintenance of a German-Jewish child in a private home in this country" directly from Warburg.

A similar letter almost two years later, again sent by Warburg to Mrs. Marks, expressed thanks for a much larger contribution of $1,166: "Will you kindly extend to the members of the Dallas Section my heartfelt gratitude for this evidence of their continued interest and cooperation in our work."

After another year, Mrs. Joseph N. Koch (Ruth) received notice from Mrs. Razovsky that a child was on his way to Dallas. "I have your letter in which you pledge that the Dallas Section of the National Council of Jewish Women agrees to accept the responsibility for the care of a child whom we are willing to bring into this country for placement in Dallas. Mrs. (Fannie) Razovsky of your city (no mention of any relationship with the letter writer who shares the same surname) has chosen Robert Bendorf, a boy of 14 1/2, as one who would fit into her family group. . . . We think that she has made a good selection."

It took until 1939 for Mrs. Koch to receive this brief note from Lotte Marcuse, Children's Aid's director of placement:

"I know you will be glad to hear that Robert Bendorf is on his way here (New York) and will arrive in Dallas within the next two weeks—finally!"

Recognizing Women of Purpose and Action
Essay by Katherine Krause
President & Chief Executive Officer, VNA Texas
Greater Dallas Section Member

The Visiting Nurse Association (VNA) began in Dallas in 1934 with encouragement and leadership from Sadie Lefkowitz, wife of Rabbi Dr. David Lefkowitz of Temple Emanu-El.

Mrs. Lefkowitz, seeing the need in the community, rallied prominent Dallas women, including Dallas Section members, to support the effort of Public Health Nurses of Dallas to provide healthcare in Dallas's poorest neighborhoods. This became the VNA, and Mrs. Lefkowitz became its first president.

The following year, VNA was endorsed by the Dallas County Medical Society and began receiving support from a variety of Dallas women's organizations. The Section contributed linens, and the Catholic Women's Guild donated a linen cabinet.

In 1957, the Women's Council of Dallas County started the Meals on Wheels program, delivering nutritious, freshly prepared meals to homebound individuals who had no access to resources like food banks and grocery stores. The VNA gave assistance to the program starting in 1966, later completely taking it over. From the program's beginning, Section members helped to deliver meals and continue to do so to this day. Today, Section members also volunteer with Jewish Family Service to deliver kosher meals.

In 2015, the VNA publicly thanked "the caring hearts of Sadie Lefkowitz, Temple Emanu-El, and the Dallas Council of Jewish Women of 1934" for founding this community institution that has been providing healthcare services to older adults in the Dallas area for the eighty-plus years since. The VNA, best known today for Meals on Wheels, but also for making hospice and private care available, said about Mrs. Lefkowitz and those who worked with her: "Helping seniors live with dignity and independence at home is a rich legacy and a tribute to these amazing women of purpose and action."

Cooking Up *Cocktails to Coffee*

In the mid-1930s, Dallas Section members began compiling recipes for their fundraiser cookbook, *Cocktails to Coffee*. The book sold for one dollar a copy. Fifty years after its publication, on the occasion of the Section's seventy-fifth birthday, an updated reproduction was given to attendees at the birthday gala.

Annette Florence McLemore, daughter of former Section president Mrs. M.E. Florence (Grace), wrote about her memories of the cookbook in a letter dated May 24, 1986:

Dear Ms. (Helen) Stern and Ms. (Barbara) Silberberg:

I saw your notice in the May Bulletin of the NCJW requesting information about the NCJW cookbook "Cocktails to Coffee." I also have a copy of that book—my mother—Grace L. Florence—(President of the Council 1929–31)—helped compile it. I also remember Thekla Brin (President 1931–33) and Myrtle Levy working on the book. I am not sure in whose administration the book was published, but if you will note on page 152 of the book, "the Texas Centennial–1936" was mentioned, so it must have been published previously.

The cookbook was an outcome of a project the aforementioned Council members and others conducted. The Council maintained a booth at the Texas State Fair for several years. They sold 'Jewish' food—restaurant style—and made considerable profit for Council. The women cooked the food at home and brought it to the booth in their cars—ruining many a family car. (I remember my father complaining that our car always smelled of matzo ball soup.) Many people requested their recipes. . . .

Sincerely,
~ Annette Florence McLemore

★★★

Mrs. McLemore doesn't mention Section President Mrs. Asher Mintz (Amelia), but she was obviously a force in this project. She had written to the law office of McCormick, Bromberg, Leftwich & Carrington with an important question about the cookbook, and received two answers in return:

October 13, 1934
Dear Mrs. Mintz:

I have investigated your inquiry as to the legality of mailing your Council Cook Book, including some recipes for mixing intoxicating drinks.

I am unable to find any statute of the United States bearing on the mailability of any such articles and, therefore, advise you that there is no limitation on your right to mail the book containing such recipes.

I trust that this sufficiently answers your inquiry.
With assurances of my pleasure at being of assistance,
Very truly yours,
~ H.L. Bromberg

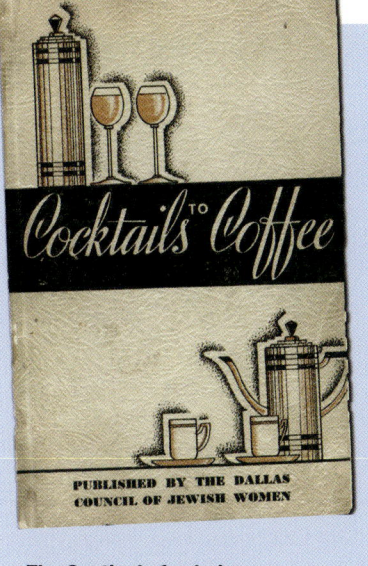

The Section's fundraiser cookbook sold for $1 in 1934.

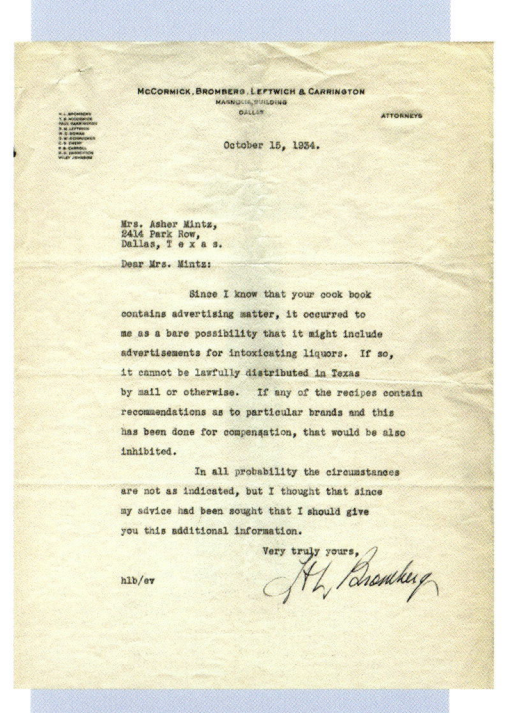

Correspondence between Section President Amelia Mintz and attorney H. L. Bromberg, concerning the Section's *Cocktails to Coffee* cookbooks, verified the legal aspects of selling a book with recipes containing alcohol. This was just after Prohibition in the US had ended, 1934.

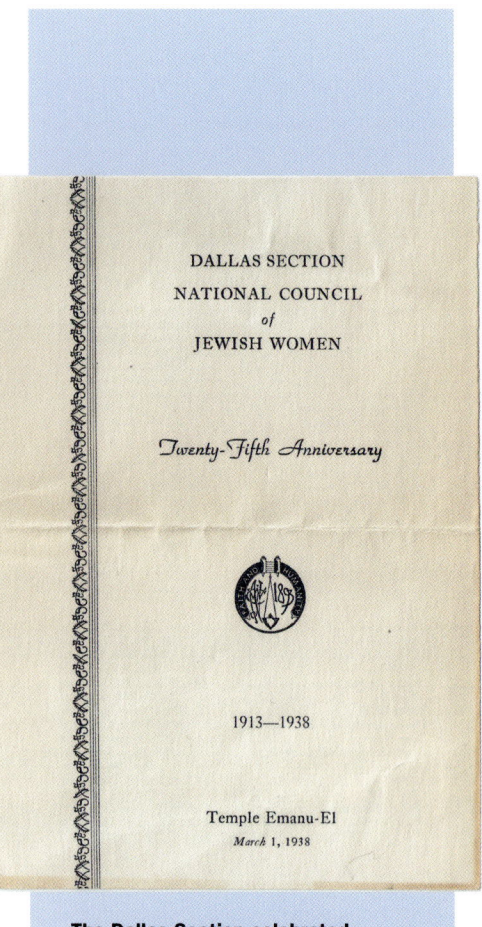

The Dallas Section celebrated its twenty-fifth anniversary with a Silver Tea on March 1, 1938, at Temple Emanu-El.

(Right) A grateful Renate Kahn retells how she entered into America with help from the Section and the Jewish community, 2013. Courtesy of the Dallas Jewish Historical Society.

October 15, 1934
Dear Mrs. Mintz:

Since I know that your cookbook contains advertising matter, it occurred to me as a bare possibility that it might include advertisements for intoxicating liquors. If so, it cannot be lawfully distributed in Texas by mail or otherwise. If any of the recipes contain recommendations as to particular brands and this has been done for compensation that would be also inhibited.

In all probability the circumstances are not as indicated, but I thought that since my advice had been sought that I should give you this additional information.

Very truly yours,
~H.L. Bromberg

Being Welcomed to Dallas
Essay by Renate Fulda Kahn, of Blessed Memory
Greater Dallas Section Member

My two grandmothers were so close; they shared an apartment in Germany. The family had apartments over my grandfather's coffee store. One of my grandmothers and I were eyewitnesses to the Kristallnacht (Night of Broken Glass) in November 1938. We hid behind heavy drapes as we watched people break store windows.

Times were changing rapidly, and my parents were forced to make new living arrangements. My grandmothers were unlikely to handle the chore of a big move to a new country, so they stayed behind.

My mother, father, brother Steven, and I arrived in New York, but with a big stumbling block—Mother had caught a severe case of tonsillitis during our crossing. She was hospitalized for almost two weeks. In the meantime, several NCJW ladies visited Mother frequently, and they visited us often as well.

The 1939 New York World's Fair was in full swing; what a treat for a kid like me! This was a great diversion for the family when Mother was recuperating. Mother left the hospital, feeling much better, and we stayed in New York for about another week.

Finally, my father, brother, and I caught a Greyhound bus to Dallas. Mother would join us after she felt strong enough to travel. We made the five-day journey with only seven dollars that had been given to us to use for meals. When we arrived in Dallas, I was almost thirteen, and Steven was six-and-a-half.

A contract was made for us two kids to live for one year with my parents' good friends, whom we had never met. My father knew Gretel Wolff from Darmstadt, Germany. Her husband, Dr. Paul Wolff, was a physician in Dallas. Steven and I would live for one year with the Wolffs, giving my parents time to get on their feet. The Section arranged all this and funded our financial support. My parents had a furnished room nearby and jobs that had been arranged by the Jewish Federation.

One of Steven's major problems was not knowing much English. Steven got off on the wrong foot with Mrs. Wolff from almost the first moment they met. Steven had seen photos of "Aunt" Gretel as a slender lady. Upon first meeting her, he saw a very robust woman. Without thinking, Steven blurted out in German, "You sure are fat." It took her many years to forgive Steven.

Steven was anxiously waiting to start school and meet other boys his age. Once he started kindergarten, he learned English rapidly. Our parents attended the English and Americanization classes offered them, and our family acclimated to our new home in Dallas. One of my grandmothers perished in the Holocaust; the other made it to Dallas and taught piano lessons for many years.

I graduated from Woodrow Wilson High School and Southern Methodist University, and much later, I became a CPA so I could give back to the community and do pro-bono work. I became a Life Member of the Dallas Section and took care of their financial books for many, many years.

RENATE KAHN

before my 13th birthday. I knew NO English.

Several Jewish agencies were a tremendous help - the Federation, NCJW, Temple Emanuel Sisterhood. One of these, probably NCJW, arranged for my brother and me to live with the Dr. Paul Wolff family, while our parents roomed and boarded 2 blocks away, so that we could see them every day, after work. These agencies also found jobs for both of our parents! Of course, with Jewish owned establishments - our Dad at the FINK Co.* (wholesale grocery) and Mom at Marcy Lee Mfg (owned by Ernest Wadel.)*
One year after our arrival, we moved together into a small apartment - much too small for all of our huge German furniture, which had arrived in large crates. Since we had NO money, (Hitler kept ALL except for the equivalent of $2.50 each = $10.00 TOTAL!)

I went to several schools here - Lipscomb, D.L. Long + Woodrow Wilson, and ultimately SMU where I majored in accounting, later be-

As Minister of Labour and Foreign Minister, Golda Meir poses with children of Kibbutz Shfayim at the opening of the Netanya-Tel Aviv highway, 1950. Photo by Teddy Brauner. (Government Press Office, National Photo Collection of Israel.)

War-time support; Civil Defense Aides	Volunteers at Office of Price Administration	Local Ship-A-Box collections	First NCJW Convention in Dallas; Golden Age Club	Dallas Society for Mental Hygiene; Foster children services
1943	1944	1945	1946	1947

30

"If I am not for myself, who will be for me? But if I am for myself only, what am I? And if not now, when?"

Hillel (c.110 BCE–10 CE), Jewish sage and scholar

The Fourth Decade : 1943 *to* 1952

In 1943, the world was in great turmoil. Germany's army suffered its first major defeat of World War II, yet the Warsaw Ghetto uprising failed, and surviving Jews were moved to concentration camps. The next year, Allied forces stormed Normandy, after which the Nazi Reich crumbled. Later, the world watched as Nazi criminals were tried in Nuremberg.

Peace, or the absence of war, didn't last long, though. Immediately after the creation of the State of Israel in 1948, the Arab-Israeli War began. And in 1950, North Korea invaded South Korea, and the United States joined the conflict as part of the United Nations' military force.

These years were also marked by big changes in Texas and Dallas. Lyndon B. Johnson was seated in the US Senate after a disputed Texas election. Movement toward racial equality

1948	1949	1950	1951	1952
"Your Thrift Shop" opens	*Student Education Fund renamed for Reba M. Wadel*	*Dallas School for the Blind sponsored*	*After-School Recreation at Dallas' City Park School*	*Evening Branch started*

CONTEMPORARY JEWISH AFFAIRS

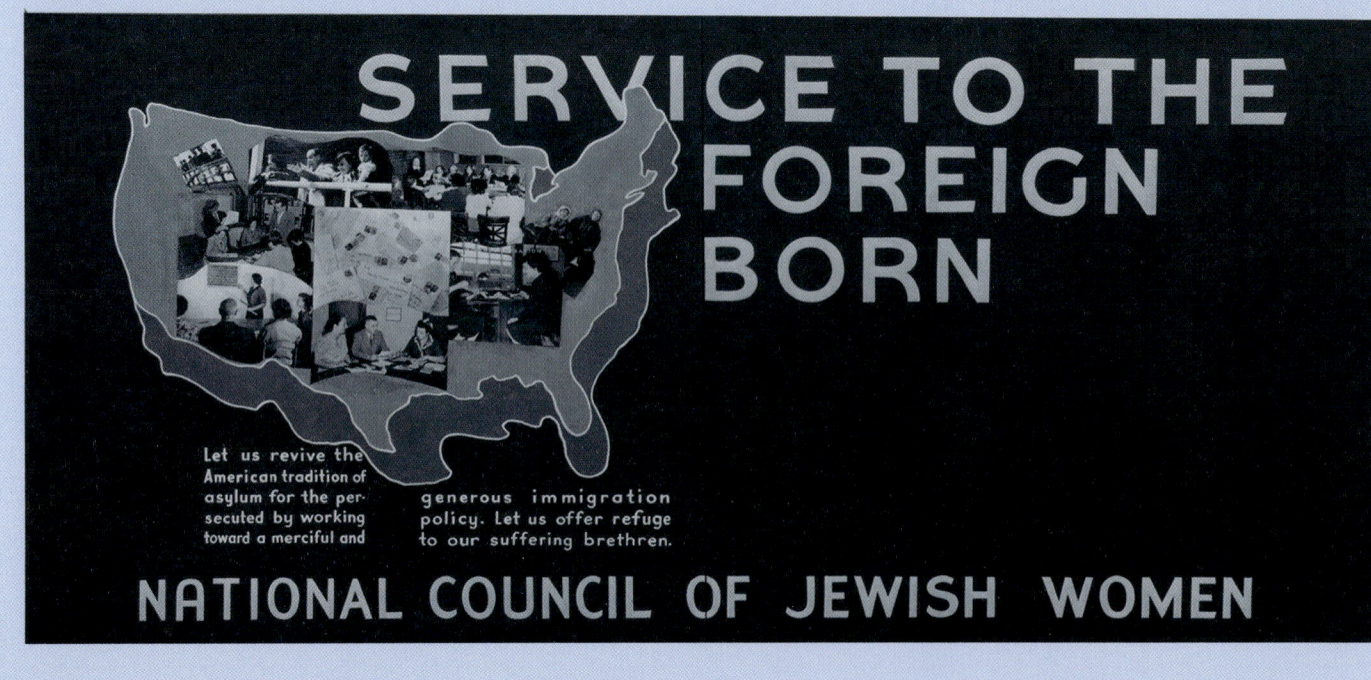

To serve democracy through understanding and unity. To serve the Jewish people through its traditions and faith. Our program is concerned with: Jewish education in religion and history. Interfaith and interracial understanding. Elimination of discrimination and anti-Semitism. Jews in postwar world.

NATIONAL COUNCIL OF JEWISH WOMEN

SOCIAL WELFARE AND WAR ACTIVITIES

Proper development of children makes for national welfare....

Protect them by Maternal health centers - nursery schools - adequate food - playgrounds and clubs - scholarships and vocational guidance. Your emergency jobs will hasten victory and peace.

NATIONAL COUNCIL OF JEWISH WOMEN

SERVICE TO THE FOREIGN BORN

Let us revive the American tradition of asylum for the persecuted by working toward a merciful and generous immigration policy. Let us offer refuge to our suffering brethren.

NATIONAL COUNCIL OF JEWISH WOMEN

After World War II, many local and national NCJW projects needed assistance and volunteer support. Large posters captured the attention of program attendees, encouraging them to get involved, c. 1946. Courtesy of NCJW, Inc.

was already in the air, especially throughout the University of Texas: The UT-Galveston Medical School admitted its first black student, and the Supreme Court ordered integration of the UT-Austin Law School. In Dallas, 1943 marked the opening of Southwestern Medical College, now known as the University of Texas Southwestern Medical Center.

THE DALLAS SECTION WAS NOW MORE THAN A GENERATION REMOVED FROM ITS FOUNDERS, but members continued to move forward with their bedrock belief in faith and humanity. These selfless, Jewish values continued to guide decisions on how to give services when and where they were needed. With each new decade, the Section proved its ability to identify problems and work toward solutions. The Section's fourth decade provided many challenges to test its resolve. However, members found a way to give both time and resources.

As part of the war effort, more than one hundred Section members sewed seven thousand garments and made surgical dressings for domestic and overseas use. They helped thousands of servicemen stationed in the Dallas area feel at home in their city. Volunteers continued to staff a day nursery for the children of defense workers, sell War Bonds, and coordinate and contribute to food and clothing drives. Emergency wartime activities also included work with the Committee on Home Defense, the American Red Cross, the Army and Navy Service Committee, the Office of Civil Defense, and the Aircraft Warning Center. Everything from donating a piano to "block organizing" and "fat drives" kept Section members busy.

Even during wartime, there were ongoing non-war needs to address. Section members taught immigrants at evening classes, emphasizing the English language and preparation for citizenship. Keeping children healthy and well-fed pushed the Milk Fund envelope, especially since tuberculosis was still a major problem in Dallas. The fund, renamed The Minnie Hexter Milk Fund in 1945, began distributing three thousand quarts of milk per year, a figure that grew to twenty-five thousand quarts by the end of the decade.

The aftermath of World War II created long-lasting challenges. Dallas members worked to help Holocaust survivors in Europe. They raised money to help support NCJW refugee homes located in Athens, Greece, and Paris, France, for women whose families had perished or could not be found. They also contributed to National's "Ship-A-Box" program that sent clothing and food to Jewish children's shelters in Austria, Hungary, and Palestine. When survivors and refugees began entering the United States, resettlement took on a new meaning for Section women, who helped the Jewish newcomers adjust to American culture and also arranged referrals for mental health professionals as needed.

The Section continued the established tradition of special programs and study groups. Members learned about topics such as local housing, international trade agreements, the Fair Employment Practices Act, and the special needs of schools, prisons, and parolees. A Mock United Nations session was held. Throughout 1948 and 1949, the Section's World Governments Group explored democracy, socialism, communism, and even fascism. Members also avidly followed the Nuremberg trials for Nazi war criminals and discussed both anti-Semitism and what they called "the Palestine problem." Members continued volunteer commitments, which had started before the war but accelerated during and after it, for the Red Cross and for the Veterans Administration, Parkland, and Scottish Rite hospitals.

At this time, through the work of its Health Committee, the Section officially affiliated with the Texas Society for Mental Hygiene (TSMH) to promote better mental health in Dallas. After the Section's intensive education program and

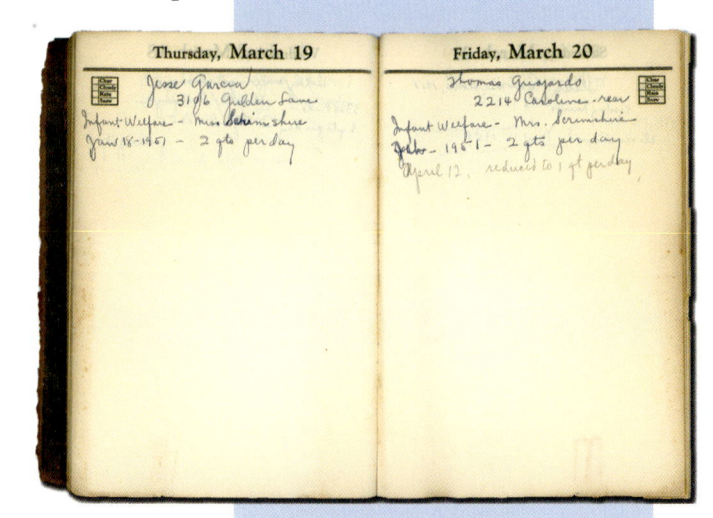

Detailed record keeping was required to monitor the distribution of thousands of quarts of milk via the Minnie Hexter Milk Fund, c. 1940s.

Thank-you notes from the Day Nurseries that were enriched by Section volunteers and donations, c. 1947.

(Above) Game days at the Golden Age Recreation Club, 1948.

(Right) As early as the mid-1940s, the Section was recognized for "outstanding hospital services" by the Dallas City-County Hospital System; the armband identified Section volunteers, c. 1946.

(Above) The Section's ongoing support of Israel since it became a nation in 1948 has been varied but focused. Forty-five years after Israel's founding, the NCJW, Inc. Centennial Summit brought Dallas leaders, among them past presidents Bette Miller and Brenda Brand (left to right), to Israel to visit the Research Institute for Innovation in Education (RIFIE), 1993. Courtesy of Bette Miller.

membership campaign, TSMH was successful in securing 154 members who, on June 17, 1947, became the Dallas County Society for Mental Hygiene. There were 350 TSMH members by year's end. This was the origin of the Dallas County Mental Health Society, which is now known as Mental Health America of Greater Dallas.

The Section launched other new programs. In 1946, members turned their attention to the elderly population. The Golden Age Recreation Club was organized to involve seniors in service-oriented activities and to provide them with social opportunities. The club drew seventy to its first Chanukah party. Seniors invested in the Ship-A-Box efforts, and their hand-crafted items later went on sale at Your Thrift Shop, Section's first local thrift shop, which opened in August 1948.

In 1946, the NCJW National Triennial Convention came to Dallas. The Dallas Section was the smallest ever to host a major national gathering, but two hundred volunteers made 450 delegates feel at home. This event wasn't to be repeated in Dallas for thirty-three years, but its organization and success became a model for major gatherings in other locales.

The Dallas Children's Bureau in 1947 asked for the Section's assistance. Members provided clothing for the foster children that the Bureau supervised. Over the years, volunteers also assisted with clerical work in the office, chauffeured the caseworkers, and gave holiday parties for the children and their mothers. Twenty years later the Bureau finally took over all these responsibilities.

As the workforce continued to change, so did the needs of families. Day nurseries provided care for preschool children, but many school-aged youths also needed supervision. In 1951, the Section launched a pioneering after-school program for children of working parents. The After-School Recreation Program was formed at Dallas's City Park Elementary School. Theology students at Southern Methodist University were hired to supervise the program, and fifteen Section volunteers served snacks, led games, and helped with homework. The effort proved so successful that parents of "latchkey kids" throughout the city requested transfers from their schools to City Park to take advantage of this program.

Employment conditions challenged how women could commit to volunteer service. The Section launched the Evening Branch to accommodate young working women who were not able to attend daytime meetings and activities. At its start in 1952, the Evening Branch's thirty-three members gathered to take part in a number of projects oriented toward service for children and youth with groups such as Hope Cottage and the Dallas Juvenile Detention Home. The Evening Branch also conducted a survey of mental health facilities for children.

Late in 1951, the *Dallas Times Herald* published a major article on the women in the Dallas Section, titled "Jewish Council's Time Consumed by Projects." Writer Pat Hendricks focused on three areas of service: Americanization and preparation of newcomers for citizenship, the elderly, and school-age children.

Here's a partial quotation from her article: "With a staggering list of projects, these clubwomen have set out to attain their goal, which in part is 'dedicated to the full achievement of the democratic way of life through education and service.'" Members highlighted in this story included Mrs. Albert Mittenthal (Rae), Mrs. S. Edward Sulkin (later Lorraine Schein), and Mrs. J. S. Fine (Dorothy), representing some one thousand Dallas Section women in a moment of public recognition.

The broad-based services to so many segments of society and the urgency of the times dictated the Section's Hillel-inspired response for selflessness and prompt action.

Supporting Israel Strategically
Essay by Sue Tilis
President, Greater Dallas Section 2006–2008

Since 1945, the Dallas Section has supported Israel through National's initiatives as well as its own programs.

For many years, the Section was involved with National's Ship-A-Box, a project that provided educational materials and supplies for those in need in Israel and Europe.

In 1968, National established the Research Institute for Innovation in Education (RIFIE) at the School of Education of The Hebrew University of Jerusalem, to develop and evaluate new educational methods, materials, and services for at-risk children in all segments of Israeli society. Major programs developed at RIFIE include HIPPY/Haetgar (Home Instruction for Parents of Preschool Youngsters); MANOF, residential, educational youth centers; and YACHAD, tutoring programs for school-aged children. The Section brought the HIPPY program to the Dallas area in 1988.

For three decades, enthusiastic Section volunteers have presented a curriculum called "Hello Israel," for sixth graders in public schools. This enrichment program introduces students to the history and people of Israel and the Middle East in an impartial, interactive way.

The Section in the 1990s, in conjunction with the Dallas Southwest Osteopathic Physicians, established the Rabin Peace Fund to provide travel scholarships for students in South Dallas high schools. The teens were invited to write essays about "Why I Want to Go to Israel," and three winners each year were awarded $10,000 scholarships for a supervised tour of the Jewish state. These trips continued until conditions in Israel posed a potential safety risk.

In 2007, the Section approved the establishment of Yad B' Yad (Hand in Hand), a tribute fund that, through National's Israel Granting Program, provides money for programs in Israel that mirror Section's volunteer work here in Dallas.

Making a Difference at City Park School
Essay by Phyllis Somer
Greater Dallas Section Member

The Dallas Section launched the After-School Recreation Program in 1951 as a way to help working mothers by providing supervised care for their children after school.

I chaired the program for two years, beginning in 1963. To acclimate our volunteers, I drove a new person every day to Dallas's City Park Elementary School, acquainting them with the school itself, its children, and the stark realities of South Dallas. At the time, this school was a sad, dilapidated, horribly rundown building in a depressed area.

On one of those outings, my new volunteer was a newlywed, new to Dallas and the Section. She loved the program and embraced it. A couple of weeks later, when I returned home, I found stacked to the ceiling in my laundry room boxes and boxes of Fruit of the Loom underwear for kids!

That new volunteer's husband worked for a department store, and she had told him about our project. These boxes came directly from the manufacturer, and we had enough for the entire school. One person can make a difference!

Another wonderful, previously anonymous friend of the program was Lee Pierce, father of Section member Pauline Gravier. Every year, during the week before Christmas, he bought shoes for every child at City Park Elementary School. It's unthinkable today, but back then we could take all the children in our cars to Phillip Segal's Shoe Store on Second Avenue where they were all fitted for the new shoes. They walked out with huge smiles!

Section members Jeanne Fagadau (left), Vivian Lowenthal (kneeling), and Aleyne Marks (far right), spend time at the After-School Recreation Program held at City Park Elementary School, 1962. Photo by Doris Jacoby. (McKee, "Golden Years Open Doors to Needs of the Community.")

Section members Phyllis Somer and Sharon Ross (standing, left to right) and City Park Elementary School teacher Mrs. J. E. Wilson (bottom left) enjoy some fresh air with children participating in the Section's After-School Recreation Program, 1964. Photo by Andy Hanson. (Castleberry, "Where the Need Is They Are There.")

Soviet Premier Nikita Khrushchev meets with US President John F. Kennedy at a summit in Vienna, 1961. (AFP/Getty Images.)

Volunteers at McKinney Veterans and Terrell State hospitals	First Encore Sale	Desegregation supported; Councilettes started	Jewish worship centers and Section members move north	Dallas Meals on Wheels begins
1953	1954	1955	1956	1957

"I ask not for a lighter burden, but broader shoulders."
Jewish proverb

The Fifth Decade : 1953 *to* 1962

The decade began with the Korean armistice and ended with the start of the Vietnam War. The Supreme Court ruled that public schools must be desegregated. Alaska and Hawaii became states, and "In God We Trust" was adopted as the United States' motto. President John F. Kennedy was confronted with the Cuban Missile Crisis. Disneyland opened in California. Elvis exploded onto the scene, and Marilyn Monroe made her final exit.

Life changed dramatically with Jonas Salk's polio vaccine, the invention of the integrated circuit by Jack Kilby at Texas Instruments in Dallas, and the first successful space explorations. Dallas continued to grow. Buses replaced streetcars when a new highway provided a direct link to Fort Worth. Notables visiting the city included Presidents Harry Truman, Richard Nixon, and Ronald Reagan, plus civil rights leader Reverend Dr. Martin

1958	1959	1960	1961	1962
Recruited social workers; UT Austin graduate social work scholarships	*Social services for Dallas youth researched*	*Survey of older adults' needs*	*Operation LIFT*	*Section's Preston Royal office opened*

Mrs. David Esquenaze (seated centered), a Cuban newcomer to America, studies English with Selma Ross (left), Nita Mae Tannebaum (standing), and Carol Wadel (right) 1962. Photo by Doris Jacoby. (McKee, "Golden Years Open Doors to Needs of the Community.")

Luther King Jr. In 1961, the Graduate Research Center of the Southwest was chartered and eventually became the University of Texas at Dallas.

During the Dallas Section's fifth decade, the members shouldered more responsibilities each year, advocating for emerging social issues in addition to fulfilling promises made by previous generations.

From the organization's start, the majority of the city's Jewish population lived in South Dallas. Section members were neighbors. During World War II, there had been no new residential construction, so when soldiers returned home and were ready to start families, they were faced with a serious housing shortage that lasted into the 1950s. Fewer homes became available in the central city areas, and new city ordinances allowed manufacturing facilities to be established next to residential buildings. This commercialization of neighborhoods and the availability of newer, affordable houses elsewhere motivated many first- and second-generation Jewish families to move away. The Jewish population of South Dallas relocated to the Park Cities, east to Lakewood, and to what is now called Old East Dallas.

The opening of North Central Expressway from downtown to Mockingbird Lane in 1952 enabled populations to move farther north. By the mid-1950s, most of the Jewish families of South Dallas had moved elsewhere. As a result of the government's acquisition of Congregation Shearith Israel's property for the development of the R.L. Thornton Freeway (Interstate 30) and the movement of its members' homes, the Congregation relocated from Park Avenue near City Park to Douglas Avenue near Walnut Hill Lane in 1956. To better serve its members, Temple Emanu-El acquired land at Northwest Highway and Hillcrest Road in the early 1950s and opened its new building in 1957.

The Dallas Section followed its members. Previously, the Section had stored supplies and records in members' closets and spare rooms. Temple Emanu-El also was used for storage. In the late 1950s, a donated space at Preston Road and Forest Lane was provided for the Section's mimeograph machine. The Section's first permanent office opened in 1962 in the Preston Royal Shopping Center.

During this decade, the Section's membership expanded to more than one thousand. Most members of this era were still full-time homemakers, given recognition merely with pins and certificates in acknowledgment of their volunteer activities. Yet they were not afraid to tackle important social issues and seek improvements. Programming emphasized speakers and subjects relating to the major signs of the times—events that captured the interest and imagination of the Section's members: aging, civil rights, mental health, desegregation, education, McCarthyism, the United Nations, and Israel in the Middle East.

As Dallas and the world changed, so too did the needs of its people. The knowledge gained from fact-finding enabled the Section as well as individual members to take decisive steps toward solving problems and effecting beneficial changes.

Section members continued to help immigrants become citizens (about forty individuals in 1954-1955)—and then celebrated by hosting parties for them. In the following two years, the arrival of Hungarian refugees claimed the attention of both the daytime Section and its Evening Branch.

Civil rights were a chief concern in Dallas as

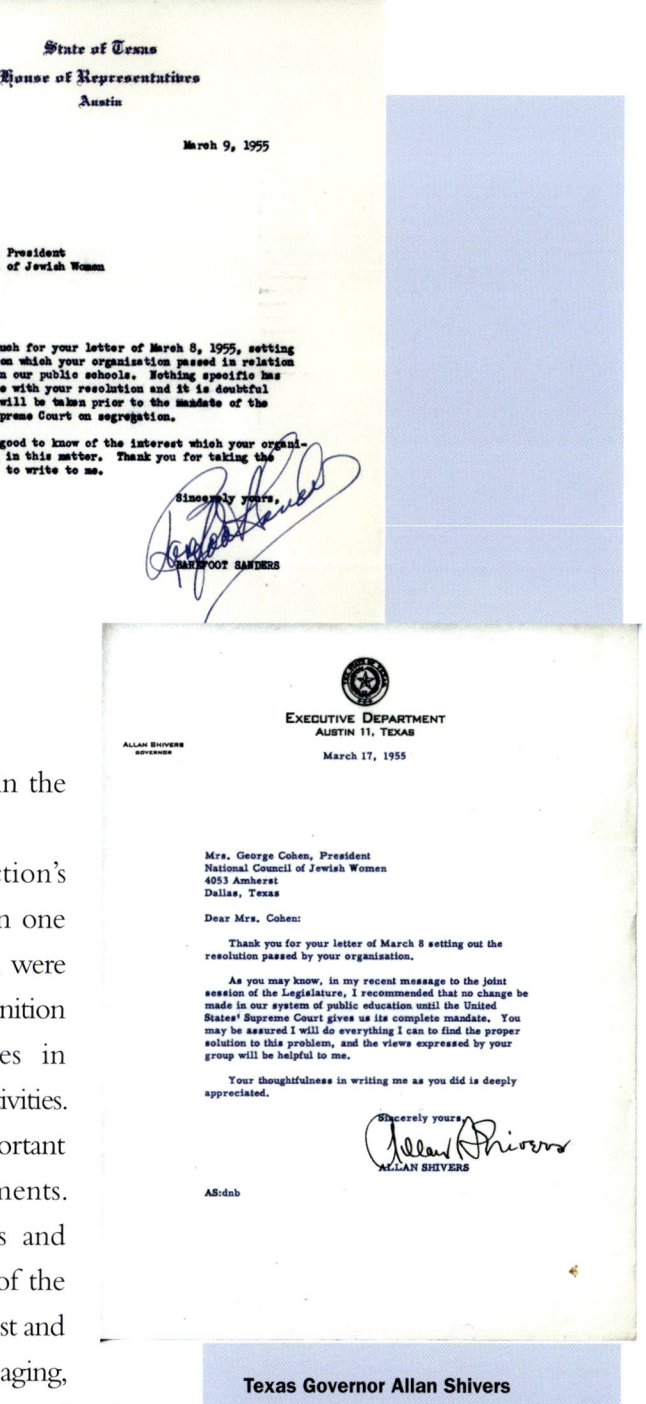

Texas Governor Allan Shivers and State Representative Barefoot Sanders individually thanked the Section for their February 1955 support of desegregation. Both thought the US Supreme Court should resolve the issue before the state took any action.

39

COMMUNITY SERVICES NEWS

SENIOR CITIZENS PROGRAM

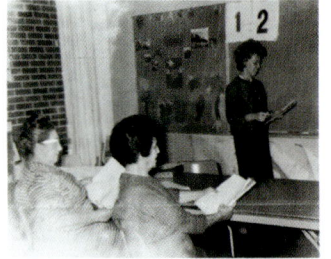

Mrs. Abe Hershman Instructing Senior Citizens in English Class.

Senior Citizens Displaying Some Items Made in Their Sewing Class.

(Above left) Section member Janet Hershman instructs senior citizens in English reading and writing to prepare for citizenship, 1964. ("Community Services News," *Council News*.)

(Above right), The Senior Citizens Recreation Club members exhibit some of their creative works from sewing class that were donated to Children's Medical Center, 1964. ("Community Services News," *Council News*.)

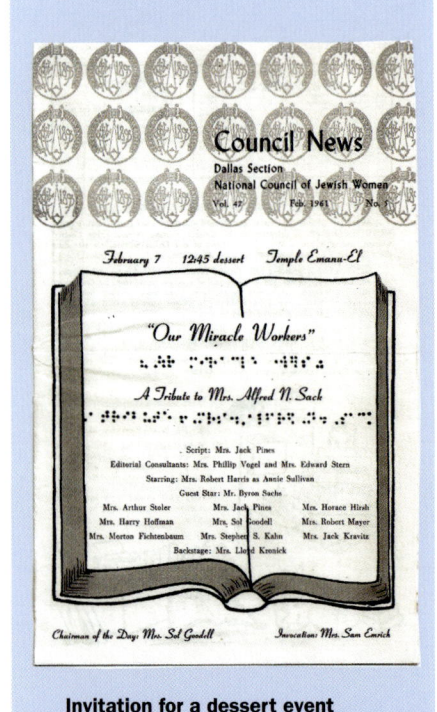

Invitation for a dessert event celebrating the Mildred R. Sack Tribute Fund for the Blind. (*Council News*, February 1961.)

well as across the country. In 1954, the Supreme Court ruled in *Brown v. the Board of Education*, declaring that racial segregation of children in public schools was unconstitutional. The Section had its own decision to make: would its members follow the request of National to pass a resolution in favor of desegregating the Dallas public schools and send the resolution to the Texas governor himself? With some trepidation, Section officers decided to put this matter to a vote of the entire membership. In March 1955, the resolution passed unanimously. Here is the text of that important document:

I. It is resolved that we of the Dallas Section of the National Council of Jewish Women contact other like-minded groups for the purpose of taking positive action in conjunction with them in favor of working out desegregation in an orderly fashion by contacting local and state officers when advisable.

II. It is resolved that the Dallas Section of the National Council of Jewish Women appoint representatives to go to Dr. Edwin L. Rippy, as spokesman for the Dallas School Board, to let him know that we have studied and understand the problems involved in desegregating the Dallas Public Schools, and that we express willingness to support measures which may be recommended by the Dallas School Board in order to implement desegregation.

Another top priority was services for the blind. Eight Section volunteers transcribed Braille textbooks for schoolchildren, and, in 1961, the Dallas School for the Blind Tribute Fund, which had started in 1950, was renamed the Mildred R. Sack Tribute Fund to honor Mildred and her family for all their support. This fund was used to provide services, specialized equipment, and scholarships for blind children. One scholarship recipient later taught in a Denton public school. His success paved the way for the hiring of other blind and physically challenged teachers.

An ongoing project, under the guidance of twenty-five volunteers, was the Golden Age Club. At the 1960 NCJW Southwestern Interstate Regional Conference in Fort Worth, the results of a survey of Golden Age Recreation Club members were presented. This was one of the first times that information was received directly from older adults. Also at this conference, Section past president Lorraine Sulkin (later Lorraine Schein) became a staff member for the NCJW, Inc., as National Field Service Representative. A daylong conference on the elderly, titled "Spanning the Generations," was held the same year.

Because of the Section's work with seniors, National's Texas State Legislative Chair, Mrs. C.A. Hurst (Barbara), a Section member, was appointed to Governor Price Daniel's Committee of the White House Conference on Aging. This committee was to prepare for the first White House Conference on Aging, to be held in Washington, DC, in January 1961. Barbara joined 2,800 representatives, including four other NCJW members from other states, at the DC conference.

Even though the members were involved in a growing number of complex community projects, needs were expanding beyond the Section's ability to address them. Furthermore, agencies needed more professionally trained staff to lead and supervise the volunteers. The Section decided in 1958 to conduct a study on the social worker's role in sharing responsibilities within a more complicated society. The two-year study concluded that it was crucial to secure more professionally trained personnel to enhance and expand social service programs and agencies in the Dallas area.

A campaign was mounted to interest high school students in future social work careers. The Section and the North Texas Association of Social Workers coproduced the film *Summer of Decision*, as part of this recruitment effort. The film won a special award from the Dallas Council of Social Agencies. This huge advocacy effort culminated in the ultimate realization of the Section's goal when, by an act of the Texas legislature, the Graduate School of Social Work was formally established in 1967 at the University of Texas at Arlington (UTA).

The Reba M. Wadel Scholarship Fund, established by the Section in 1948, previously was authorized to award an educational grant of $1,800 per year to a graduate-level social work student at the University of Texas at Austin if that recipient would pledge to return to Dallas for a minimum of one year of service after graduation. With the establishment of the UTA School of Social Work, this scholarship began to be awarded to UTA students.

To help meet the budget demands of the Section's many community service projects, Your Thrift Shop continued to produce revenue. In 1954, the Section began the Encore Sale, an offshoot of Your Thrift Shop, to sell designer and higher-cost merchandise.

Another Section study, begun in 1959, was a three-year effort to determine the needs of Dallas youth and the resources required to meet those needs. The study results were presented in a 1963 community forum, "Direction for Tomorrow," undertaken with the Junior League of Dallas in conjunction with the Juvenile Welfare Federation. The effort garnered major awards from the Council of Social Agencies and the Child Welfare League of America.

Section members continued with many other projects during this decade, including the Parkland Hospital Library, Meals on Wheels, and varied services to Terrell State and McKinney Veterans Administration hospitals. Members also volunteered at Dallas-area social service agencies on Christmas Day, allowing paid employees to spend some holiday time with their families.

The Section's longest-lasting effort undertaken during this complex decade may well have been Operation LIFT (Literacy Instruction for Texas), begun in 1961 with the cosponsorships of the *Dallas Morning News* and WFAA-TV. The program was created and still offers easily accessible classes to help functionally illiterate adults learn to read and write English. Section members managed this project until 1963, then continued in an advisory capacity when LIFT became an independent community effort. At one time, there were 250 volunteers working with six hundred students.

The Section won the *Dallas Times Herald*'s (DTH) 1961 "Club of the Year" Award for the LIFT project, the year the daily newspaper inaugurated this honor. This was part of the era in which Vivian Castleberry served as editor of the "Living" Section of the *Herald*.

During these eventful years, the nuts-and-bolts needs of the Section were well handled. The Section's first office served nearly 1,400 members, who paid annual dues of $5. The yearly budget was almost $30,000. A junior group, called Councilettes, attracted fifty-six girls, aged twelve to fourteen, in 1955. Thirty more young women joined by decade's end.

Those growing membership rolls and expanding budgets provided broader shoulders, ideal for taking on the increased needs of the community. The Section's extra resources would be crucial for blind residents, immigrants, school-age children, and older adults during the next, particularly tough, decade that would follow in Dallas.

Ongoing Section support for Parkland Hospital has included "Pink Ladies" volunteers. (Left to right): Ruth Brown, Jenny Bock, Margaret Nebenzahl, Mamie Commer, Gladys Asch, Eve Afray, and Sarah Goodman, c. 1970.

The Section asks for donations for Your Thrift Shop, 1962. (*Council News*, May 1962.)

A patient at Children's Medical Center plays with a hand puppet made and presented by Laurie Tycher, Councilette president (seated on right). Eileen Ray, Section's Councilette adviser, and Zelene Lovitt, Evening Branch president (standing, left to right), display a handmade wall hanging for the hospital, 1971. Photo by Andy Hanson. (*Dallas Times Herald*, September 26, 1971.)

Councilettes play games with young children as part of their "Let-Me-Entertain-You" birthday party service that helped raise funds for Councilettes' activities. (Left to right): Bridgett Kornblatt, Marianne Albert, Donna Daniels, and Marilyn Matthew, 1969.

Encouraging Young Women to Serve Dallas
Essay by Kathy Roth Freeman
President, Greater Dallas Section 1998–2000

As early as 1917, the Dallas Section created a program for girls aged fourteen to twenty-one. Originally called the Junior Council, it later became the Junior Auxiliary of the Dallas Section of Council of Jewish Women, then the Junior Buds in 1929, when the focus changed to engaging only teenagers. By 1945, that program had disbanded.

At mid-century, National fostered a new junior movement of young teenagers called "Councilettes." The Section organized its equivalent group in March 1955, allocating a budget of $300. Local girls aged twelve to fourteen met under the chairmanship of Shayna Schepps (later Shayna Selby); during this first year, membership reached eighty.

From the beginning, the girls were involved in community service. They hosted a theater party that raised $85 and earmarked those proceeds for the Section's tribute funds. The Councilettes worked with Your Thrift Shop, packed boxes for the Ship-A-Box project, created stuffed animals for the Dallas Society for Crippled Children, made Easter baskets for the Section's after-school recreation program at City Park Elementary School, and assembled scrapbooks for Children's Medical Center.

Through the years, the group took on additional projects, including stuffing five thousand envelopes with Easter Seals for the Crippled Children's Society drive, collecting magazines for the Section-sponsored library at Parkland Hospital, and producing a talent show at Golden Acres, Dallas's Home for the Jewish Aged.

I became chair of the Councilettes in 1956. On my watch, Councilettes was divided into two separate groups according to grade level, both doing the same things at the same time but meeting in different places—always in the homes of members. Group officers were installed at a Mother-Daughter Luncheon, which became an annual event for the duration of the Councilettes.

Membership started declining in the late 1950s and was further hampered in the mid-1960s, when National's age requirements changed, and seventh-grade girls were no longer eligible to join. Still, the teens continued to raise funds with great success with their "Let-Me-Entertain-You" birthday party service. For $10, the girls would entertain any size party, serve refreshments, and stage a puppet show. They used the proceeds to buy educational equipment for nursery schools in Israel as part of the ongoing Ship-A-Box project and were able to send fourteen boxes to Israel in 1968. That same year, a successful Father-Daughter Party was held in addition to the annual Mother-Daughter Luncheon.

Councilettes continued serving Dallas with visits to the Buckner Children's Home, the Children's Emergency Shelter, and Children's Medical Center. Within two decades, the girls posted an enviable record of service, combining fundraising for their favorite projects with support for the community at large. Finally, low membership resulted in disbanding the group in 1976.

Presenting a Study about Dallas Children as a Drama
Essay by Pat Peiser
President, Greater Dallas Section 1960–1962

In 1960, 190 women, including Dallas Section members, in cooperation with the Dallas Council of Social Agencies, began investigating the conditions of children living in Dallas County and the social services available to them. Over the next three years, these volunteers compiled a massive report consisting of twelve volumes that addressed every element of service for children and their families and then presented 282 recommendations. The publication was titled *Child Welfare Study of Dallas County*.

The Section determined that the findings and recommendations of this study needed to be promoted so that all Dallas-area residents would become aware of and participate in solving the problems of local child welfare. With the Junior League of Dallas as the Section's partner, *Direction for Tomorrow: The Challenge of the Dallas County Youth Study,* a dramatization, was born.

The partners designed this program as a drama in four acts, with narrative depictions of conditions found in the study, for presentation to city and county officials. A large booklet, *190 Took A Long Hard Look,* describing the findings was published and distributed to accompany the program. The drama *Direction for Tomorrow* was presented on June 13, 1963, at Dallas Memorial Auditorium Theatre, a part of Dallas's original Convention Center, in front of an audience of seven hundred that included city and county officials. It was later presented to many organizations throughout Dallas County.

The two volunteer organizations, with Emily Goyer representing the Junior League of Dallas and myself as the Section's cochair, were soon honored as recipients of the Child Welfare League of America's Edith L. Lauer Award, which was presented at the League's 1964 convention in Kansas City, Missouri.

The *Dallas Morning News* covered the youth study and its dramatization.

Direction for Tomorrow drama was presented to city and county officials after a two-year study. Dr. Floyd Norman, chairman of Health Services for the Citizens' Committee for the Dallas County Youth Study, and Gloria Hoffman, Section member, watch Ziona Balaban (left) rehearse, 1963. Photo by Doris Jacoby. (Brinkerhoff, "A Community's Call to Action.")

Lifting North Texans' Literacy
Essay by Pat Peiser
President, Greater Dallas Section 1960–1962

In the early 1960s, an estimated 75,000 adults in North Central Texas could not read or write beyond a fourth-grade level. They were classified as functionally illiterate.

The Memphis Section of NCJW proposed that the Dallas Section undertake a program to combat

> Operation LIFT was a major example of a community-wide program and the continuation of the Section's oft-repeated plan of action: research, begin a program, evaluate, seek collaboration, then turn it over to the community to be adopted.

illiteracy similar to the one they had begun in 1955. I, as Section president, called an emergency board meeting in February 1961, and the board voted to accept this challenge in a big way.

The Section collaborated with the *Dallas Morning News* and local television stations WFAA and KERA to form Operation LIFT (Literacy Instruction for Texas). The community-wide effort started with thirty-one classes in Dallas schools, public housing facilities, and churches. During the program's first year, one hundred volunteers taught 450 students, using a series of televised lessons produced by Dr. Frank Laubach, known as the "apostle of literacy" for his work in teaching English. By the end of that first year, 250 volunteers (150 of them were Section members) and eighty organizations aided in recruiting, interviewing, and enrolling more than 850 students.

Operation LIFT was a major example of a community-wide program and the continuation of the Section's oft-repeated plan of action: research, begin a program, then turn it over to the community to be adopted.

Maurice Carlson, who had provided rent-free office space for the project in his insurance company's offices, agreed to assume the chairmanship in the program's second year. Section member Margaret Hirsh served as LIFT's volunteer director and first teacher.

Eventually, LIFT moved its office to the Communities Foundation of Texas building on Live Oak in Dallas and engaged professional executive directors. In 1992, LIFT's Executive Director, Evelyn Patton, proposed that the Meadows Foundation erect a special building in the Wilson Historic District, a neighborhood of nonprofit organizations in East Dallas funded by the Foundation, to centralize all classes. LIFT relocated to this building in 1993. Unfortunately, this location decreased the number of people who could take advantage of LIFT's classes.

Because the Meadows Foundation allows occupancy in the Wilson District for only ten years, LIFT had to move in 2002. This turned out to be a blessing in disguise. The new location at 2121 Main Street in downtown Dallas offered space for only a few classes, so Jerry Mosman, executive director at that time, began establishing classes all over Dallas County, which followed the organization's original concept: take the classes to where the people are. Sixteen partners provided "hubs," with each space accommodating three to seven classes. Students met three times each week, with a combined total of ninety-four weekly classes taught by 248 regular volunteers.

In the first year of this new arrangement, LIFT served 3,649 students—almost double the number of the previous year. Since LIFT began, more than 45,000 adults have learned to read through this program. The agency currently serves about five thousand learners annually.

I rejoined LIFT's board in recent years, served as a vice president, and now continue to serve on its advisory board.

ORD-CHRONICLE
AY MORNING, APRIL 30, 1961

Group To Aid Problem Of 2,335 Illiterates

You hear a lot about why Johnny can't read but little about illiteracy among adults.

And there are many adults who can't read and write in Denton County. According to the Texas Literacy Council, 2,335 people in Denton County are "functional illiterates" which means they either can't read or write or barely can.

To these people, a newspaper is just a paper covered with meaningless symbols. When they sign their names to something, if they can, they have little knowledge about what they are signing.

To help correct this situation, Robert C. Likins, associate director of the Baylor Literacy Center, is coming to Denton this week for a literacy workshop. The purpose of the workshop is to train people to teach others to read and write. Sponsored by the Denton Unitarian Fellowship, the workshop is open to all who are interested. The workshop will be held at the Unitarian Fellowship Building on Cordell Street near Fulton Monday and Wednesday, from 6:30 to 9 p.m. On Tuesday, Likins will speak before the Business and Professional Women's Club. His speech will be entitled "Around the World in 30 Days with the Laubach Program."

Likins received his B. A. in English at San Diego State College in California. He then studied at San Diego State College in California. He then studied at the Koinonia Foundation in Baltimore, Md. In 1959, he became associate director of the Baylor Literacy Center, to which he went from November and December, 1960, Likins accompanied Dr. Frank Laubach, noted literacy expert, as a member of the literacy team of four specialists on a world tour. They did literacy work in 30 nations. In Viet Nam, Dutch West Guinea and Taiwan they helped make adult literacy primers in 30 tribal languages.

Using the simplified system devised by Dr. Laubach any literate adult can teach others to read and write. All that is necessary is to attend a workshop, provided free of cost, and to obtain inexpensive teaching materials provided by the Texas Literacy Council at cost. After studying with a volunteer teacher, an illiterate will be able to read about 1,793 of the most useful English words, and he should be able to pronounce almost any other word in the English language.

To emphasize the drive for literacy training, Mayor Frank Barrow has proclaimed May 1-6 as "Community Literacy Week" in Denton.

citizens to read. This is where the Texas Literacy Council comes in. It is its function to supplement the work of the schools by providing a teaching service to the adult members of the community where other services are inaccessible.

"Illiteracy is a community problem, and it must be met head-on by community action if we are to improve the literacy of Denton. It was with this in mind that the Denton Unitarian Fellowship decided to bring this workshop to Denton."

14—Section 1   The Dallas Morning News   Sunday, May 28, 1961

ORIENTATION
Workshop Planned For LIFT Teachers

Two crash teacher workshops have been set up to help orientate latecomers who plan to teach classes in the upcoming Literacy Instruction For Texas (LIFT) program starting June 5.

The initial workshop has been scheduled for Monday, the second for Thursday. Both will be staged at Newman Catholic Center—behind Fincher Hall at Southern Methodist University — at 3160 Daniels.

Time of both sessions will be from 7:30 p.m. until 9 p.m.

Mrs. Jerome Frank, recruitment coordinator of LIFT, said both these workshops are "vitally important" to all prospective teachers. At these sessions will be explained the best manner of helping the illiterate and, also, workbooks and materials will be distributed.

LIFT is the program organized by the Dallas Section of the National Council of Jewish Women and sponsored by The Dallas Morning News that will attempt to put an end to functional illiteracy in this area.

More than 600 students have already signed up for the free "learn to read and write" course. Only a small workbook and materials fee of approximately $2.50 is charged for the entire 26-weeks session.

The adult students, called functional illiterates because they cannot read and write the equivalent of fourth graders, congregate at viewing centers throughout the area and are instructed via television programs a half hour a day. Another half hour of study and practice follows each TV lesson.

The course begins at 7 a.m. on WFAA-TV (Channel 8). It will be repeated at 6 p.m. each day on KERA-TV (Channel 13). It will be at these times each Monday through Friday.

LIFT officials said Saturday students are still urged to contact the organization and that some teachers, viewing stations, TV sets and other voluntary things are still needed.

Anyone interested in any phase of the program can telephone LIFT officials at RI 7-9192 or write Box 8453, Dallas 5.

—Dallas News Staff Photo.

Mrs. Marvin Rubenstein (left), Mrs. James S. Wedeles and Mrs. Charles Marcus package information on Operation LIFT.

Several publications covered the Section's LIFT efforts: here, the *Dallas Morning News* and the *Denton Record-Chronicle* (above left and right) identify the training for teachers and volunteers and the large number of recipients who will improve literacy with the help of the program. (Above, left to right): Rita Rubenstein, Bette Wedeles (later Bette Schuttler), and Anita Marcus, 1961. ("Workshop Planned For LIFT Teachers," the *Dallas Morning News*.) ("Group To Aid Problem of 2,335 Illiterates," *Denton Record-Chronicle*.)

You CAN Learn to READ AND WRITE

(Please Read This Advertisement to Anyone You Know Who Cannot Read and Write)

An estimated ten million Americans cannot read and write well enough to understand safety signs, follow a cook book recipe, or serve in the armed forces. 800,000 adult Texans are functional illiterates. Over 70,000 persons, who live within a 100-mile radius of Dallas, cannot read and write English as well as a fourth grader.

If you cannot read and write, here is your opportunity. Lessons will be presented over WFAA-TV and KERA-TV. There will be five lessons each week, one each day, Mondays through Fridays, for 26 weeks.

Classes will be held in conveniently located TV viewing centers: in homes, public schools, housing projects, churches, industrial companies, etc. A qualified teacher will attend each class to explain the lesson as it is presented on television.

These lessons will be given to you FREE of charge.

The only cost will be for your textbook at a very low price . . . and that is all.

A whole new world can be opened for you. You will be able to fill a better job . . . . read a newspaper . . . . read your Bible . . . . pass a driver's test . . . . look up telephone numbers . . . . read recipes, medicine directions, street signs and a million other things. You will be able to read as well as your children in school.

Better still, you will be able to learn many other subjects after you have learned to read and write. Today, many adults are taking different kinds of courses after completing this program.

If you are an adult (20 years old or over) and cannot read and write, now is the time for you to help yourself, your family, your community and nation. Learn to READ and WRITE. Send in the coupon in this ad . . . do it now! Hurry for the time is short.

ACT NOW!
Enrollment Deadline — May 15
Lessons Start JUNE 5
WFAA-TV
7 to 7:30 A.M.
MONDAYS THROUGH FRIDAYS
Program will be repeated at 6 p.m. on KERA-TV.

NEEDED: STUDENTS—VOLUNTEER TEACHERS & INTERVIEWERS

COMMUNITIES OUTSIDE OF DALLAS ARE INVITED TO PARTICIPATE

If your town or city lies within the viewing area of WFAA-TV, why don't you participate with us in this important program? Many communities are doing so. For full particulars

WRITE TO:
LIFT
P.O. BOX 8453, DALLAS, TEXAS
Or Telephone RI 7-9192

FILL OUT AND MAIL TODAY

MAIL TO: LIFT—P.O. BOX 8453, DALLAS, TEXAS

PLEASE CHECK BOX APPLICABLE TO YOU
☐ STUDENT—I want to learn how to read and write. I understand the enrollment deadline is May 15.
☐ TEACHER—Please count on me. I want to help people learn how to read and write.
☐ INTERVIEWER—I want to help. I would like to do counseling and interviewing.

YOUR NAME _____
ADDRESS _____
CITY _____ PHONE _____
(Please Print)

LIFT
LITERACY INSTRUCTION FOR TEXAS
PROGRAM OF THE DALLAS SECTION, NATIONAL COUNCIL OF JEWISH WOMEN
SPONSORED BY THE DALLAS MORNING NEWS — WFAA RADIO AND TELEVISION

Advertisement to recruit LIFT students and volunteers, 1961.

You CAN Learn to READ AND WRITE

SIGN UP NOW!
Lessons Start June 5
WFAA-TV Channel 8 | KERA Channel 13

CONTACT **OPERATION LIFT**
P.O. BOX 8453 — TELEPHONE RI 7-9192

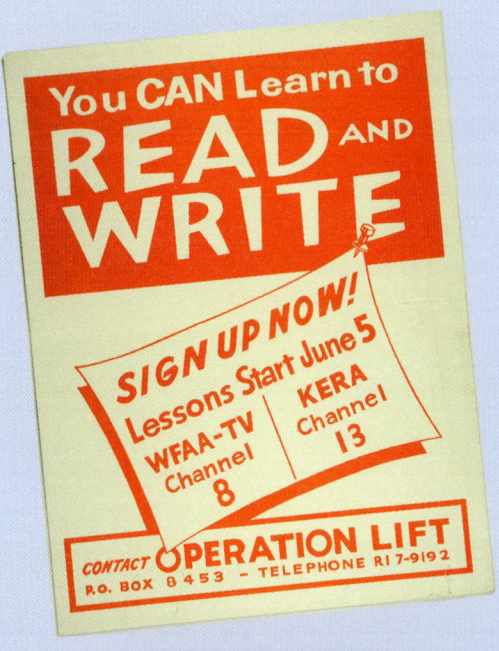

The Section's Operation LIFT sign promoting the free literacy classes cosponsored by WFAA-TV and KERA, 1960.

Marchers Reverend Dr. Martin Luther King Jr. (second from left) and Rabbi Abraham Joshua Heschel (far right) cross the Edmund Pettus Bridge, Selma to Montgomery, Alabama, in religious solidarity with the civil rights movement, March 21, 1965. © 1978 Matt Herron/Take Stock

1963	1964	1965	1966	1967
Community forum "Direction for Tomorrow"	West Dallas After-School Study Center	Volunteers for Dallas County War on Poverty	Operation READY; Goals for Dallas participants	Renamed NCJW, Greater Dallas Section; UT Arlington School of Social Work established

"Faith is taking the first step even when you don't see the whole staircase."

Martin Luther King Jr. (1929–1968), Baptist minister and American civil rights activist

The Sixth Decade : 1963 *to* 1972

Events in 1963 shook America and the world. It seemed as if civil rights would be the defining issue of that year, punctuated by the March on Washington and the emotional "I Have a Dream" speech from Dr. Martin Luther King Jr. It was the same year in which the US Supreme Court ruled against mandatory prayer and Bible reading in public school classrooms. But the globe seemed to stop turning when word spread of the assassination of President John F. Kennedy in Dallas.

Lyndon B. Johnson was formally elected president in 1964, and the following year the Voting Rights Act was signed into law. Medicare went into effect. Change was accompanied by social unrest as draft cards were burned in protest of the Vietnam War. The baby boom was ending, and the Beatles were beginning their musical reign.

DISD Frederick Douglass School Volunteer Program	People to People Panel; Sesame Street promoted	Dallas Police Department Social Worker; PACE Committee	Golden Acres's LIFE program; Richardson-Plano Section formed	Encore warehouse opened; "Windows on Day Care"
1968	1969	1970	1971	1972

This memorial cover of the Section's January 1964 *Council News* expressed the sorrows of Dallas and the world over the loss of President Kennedy. ("In Memoriam," *Council News*.)

(Center) Section member Hermine Tobolowsky greets President Lyndon Johnson, late 1960s. Courtesy of Dallas Jewish Historical Society.

Coordinating the Section's fiftieth anniversary activities are Section members (left to right) Fannie Kahn, Marie Bitterman, and Bette Wedeles (later Bette Schuttler), 1964. Photo by Doris Jacoby. (McKee, "Golden Years Open Doors to Needs of the Community.")

As the 1960s neared their end, all good news was eclipsed when both Martin Luther King Jr. and Robert F. Kennedy, brother of President Kennedy and a Democratic candidate for president, were assassinated. War protesters were killed at Kent State University. The voting age was lowered to eighteen. Cigarette ads were banned on television, and the first rumblings of Watergate emerged, even as Nixon was reelected to a second term.

STARTING ITS SIXTH DECADE, SECTION MEMBERS CONTINUED FORWARD WITH FAITH, CREATING groundbreaking research, seminars, and service projects, but history altered "best-laid plans."

The Section celebrated its golden fiftieth anniversary with a giant birthday party lunch in October 1962. More than five hundred members and community leaders attended, anticipating hearing the featured speaker, David Schoenbrun, chief correspondent of the CBS News Bureau in Washington, DC. Much to the audience's surprise, Schoenbrun was unable to attend as planned because of a crisis in Mississippi. The previous day the first black student to register at the University of Mississippi, James Meredith, was escorted into classes by Federal Marshals. Schoenbrun was needed elsewhere, but he spoke to the Section via closed circuit television.

The fifty-year celebration continued the following spring with a dinner gala that featured a speech by University of Texas Chancellor Harry Ransom, who challenged guests to serve as both "citizens and philanthropists." Tickets for cocktails and dinner were $6.50 each.

The timing of Mrs. Charles Marcus (Anita)'s term as president of the Section in 1963 placed her in a dramatic moment in history. She and her husband were invited to attend a November 22 luncheon at the Dallas Trade Mart that was to honor President John F. Kennedy, Vice President Lyndon B. Johnson, Texas Governor John Connally, and their wives. The events on that fateful day precluded any luncheon. Anita's telegram to the newly installed President Johnson was answered by him and was addressed to Anita as the president of the Section. It said, "Your thoughtful message was received with deep appreciation. I shall cherish your prayers and support in the days ahead." By February 1964, Anita and 164 other community leaders were summoned to appear in Judge Joe B. Brown's Dallas County Criminal District Court as defense witnesses in the dramatic murder of Lee Harvey Oswald by Jack Ruby.

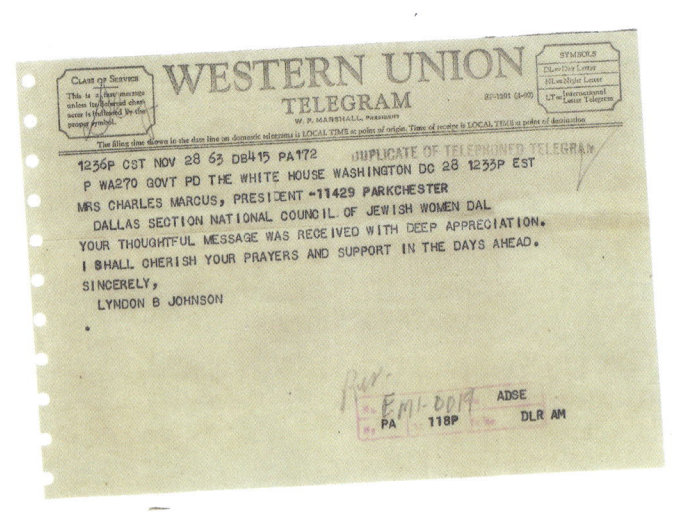

This telegram from President Lyndon B. Johnson to Section president Anita Marcus expressed gratitude for the Section's response to the tragic events in Dallas on November 23, 1963. Courtesy of Anita Marcus.

48

Schools for Community Action

Programming for this decade evolved from National's "Schools for Community Action," which identified specific issues to tackle with forums, community meetings, study groups, and more. The Section adapted National's program guides to reflect local issues.

School One

"Equal Opportunity for Youth" in 1964, the first of these "Schools," focused on dropout prevention. Dr. Willis Tate, then president of Southern Methodist University, opened the event with his speech, "We Are Living in Tomorrow's World." This forum helped publicize the findings of the three-year effort, *Child Welfare Study of Dallas County*, in which Section members participated. Guided by the study and the forum, the Section began an after-school study program in a disadvantaged neighborhood in West Dallas.

School Two

During his State of the Union address in January 1964, President Lyndon B. Johnson proposed legislation to reduce the national poverty rate. The Economic Opportunity Act was the first in a series of initiatives in the War on Poverty; others included the Health Insurance for the Aged Act (Medicare), the Food Stamp Act, Head Start, and the establishment of the Job Corps. That same year, the Section's second School for Community Action was "The Immovable Middle Class," a study of poverty in Dallas. As a result of this program, the Section provided volunteer aides for the Dallas County Department of Public Welfare.

The Dallas County Community Action Committee (DCCAC), a War on Poverty program established by the Economic Opportunity Act, asked the Section in 1965 to become the first volunteer group in Dallas to help with a study of Dallas poverty. Members, working with the Community Council of Greater Dallas (CCGD), assisted in the investigation of the prevalence of poverty and its characteristics in Dallas County, using information extracted from US census tracks, welfare rolls, and various Dallas area welfare agencies. Section volunteers were able to complete this task in five days instead of the two to three weeks allocated for this work. The Section subsequently worked with the DCCAC to promote Head Start for young children and to urge older adults to sign up for medical benefits under Operation Medicare Alert.

School Three

Then came the "Women on the Move" forum in 1966, which focused on women trapped in poverty and what could be done to free them from the cycle that passed from one generation to the next. Ruth Harvey, a consumer specialist on President Lyndon B. Johnson's Executive Committee, gave the keynote address. Projects originating from this program included Operation READY (Read, Educate, And Do-it-Yourself), the Consumer Alliance, and Consumer Education. Following National's involvement with Women in Community Service (WICS), the Section united with the local National Council of Negro Women, the National Council of Catholic Women, Church Women United, and the American GI Forum to recruit young women for the Women's Training Centers of the Federal Job Corps. Section members also provided supplementary services for the residents of the McKinney, Texas, Job Corps facility.

The Section's Schools were admired by many in the Dallas community. Midway through the series of six Schools, Roy Dulak, executive director of the Community Council of Greater Dallas, commented in the *Dallas Times Herald*, "[the Dallas Section is] one of the most effective, outstanding, and knowledgeable groups in Dallas on civic, health, welfare, and recreational problems." Barbara Richardson adds,

(Left) Roy Dulak, executive director of the Community Council of Greater Dallas, and Allan Maley, director of the Dallas War on Poverty, join with Section president Edna Flaxman and co-coordinators Anita Marcus and Bette Miller (left to right) in planning the Section's third School for Community Action, 1966. Photo by Jo Ball. (McKee, "Jewish Women Do Homework Before Forum.")

(Left) The Section's School for Community Action, held at SMU in 1964, covered issues affecting children and youth of low-income families.

Katherine Bauer, Pat Peiser, and Josephine Goldman (left to right) view food items provided to families in need at the Federal Foods Department of the Dallas County Welfare Department, 1966. Photo by Jo Ball. ("Jewish Women Do Homework Before Forum," the *Dallas Morning News*.)

The Section described the community's responses and goals for the Dallas County's War on Poverty from 1964–1969 in this brochure.

(Far right) Section member Janice Sweet (later Janice Weinberg) chaired the sixth School for Community Action, which discussed the survival of Judaism, 1971. (*Bulletin*, November 1971.)

Section members Thelma Vogel, Elaine Kimmelman, Phyllis Somer, and Betty Dreyfus (left to right) discuss plans for the Homemakers Arts Class for disadvantaged young women, 1968. Photo by Jo Ball. (McKee, "Jewish Women Plan Year of Helping Disadvantaged.")

"Their greatest contribution over the years, Dulak believes, has been their institutes and forums to inform the community of problems and possible solutions."

School Four

"Spotlight on the Family," held in November 1967, was the first public forum ever held in Dallas to deal with the issue of child abuse. Members studied the Texas Family Code and how it related to both middle class and disadvantaged families. The Section also continued its study of the War on Poverty and realized that the government initiative needed to be better understood. This led to the development of the People to People Panel in 1969, featuring persons knowledgeable about poverty. The National Council of Catholic Women, Church Women United, and National Council of Negro Women cosponsored this panel with the Section. Each time the diverse panelists spoke in various communities, they opened doors of understanding and broke down barriers that had divided people of different backgrounds.

School Five

"Urban Problems," held in 1970, emphasized problems of crime and urban decay. The program was followed by projects on police/community relations and alternatives to the traditional juvenile justice system. This was a unique School because Section members went into the community and experienced first-hand the difficulties of dealing with the agencies that work with those in poverty. Systems included medical services, safety net programs, and law enforcement. Out of this came a two-year pilot program in which the Section funded a full-time social worker, Phil Lewis, for the Dallas Police Department. He served prisoners and their families and worked with a group of Section volunteers who helped with the initiative. This pioneering effort in crime prevention was not only a first in Dallas but also a first in the United States. The City of Dallas assumed financial responsibility for this successful project in 1972.

School Six

The Section cosponsored "The New Jews" seminar with the American Jewish Committee in 1971. Its trio of issues included Soviet Jewry, the Six-Day War, and women's rights under Jewish law.

In 1966, the Section was invited to participate in Goals for Dallas, an organization that worked to define long-range objectives for the City of Dallas. One of the needs defined by this organization was the expansion of the Information and Referral Service, an important part of the Community Council of Greater Dallas. This agency provided referrals for individuals who needed help. Section volunteers helped identify agencies and their services and assisted in compiling the information into a manual. The Section gave funds for promotional materials and additional telephone lines for the service that still exists today as part of the 2–1–1 Texas system.

During the late 1960s, the Dallas-area population was growing and spreading quickly—fast enough that women in the communities surrounding the city were joining the Section and becoming highly involved in its projects and activities. So the Section—all 1,400 members—took on a new name in 1967: The Greater Dallas Section.

The Greater Dallas Section continued its longtime emphasis on improving the quality of social work by distributing three thousand social work recruitment brochures, hosting a high school career clinic, and cosponsoring a two-day college career conference. This advocacy built sufficient demand so that the University of Texas at Arlington formally established its Graduate School of Social Work in

1967. The Section donated $2,000 of seed money for the library. The first class of twenty-six students began to study for their degrees in September 1968; the very first student accepted into the school received the Section's Reba M. Wadel Scholarship. Today, the UT Arlington School of Social Work's enrollment tops 1,300, all working toward bachelor's, master's, and doctoral degrees in the field.

For many years, Section members had tried to convince the superintendents of the Dallas Independent School District (DISD) that trained volunteers were capable of tutoring reading, math, and English as a second language (ESL). Superintendent Nolan Estes agreed to allow the Section to pilot a program at Frederick Douglass Elementary School in 1968. The project became a model of volunteerism for other Texas school districts.

In 1969, the Section was asked to help promote a new television show for children called *Sesame Street*. Volunteers spent many hours at shopping centers and staffing a booth at the State Fair of Texas to ensure that children in low-income neighborhoods would tune in to the show and be better prepared for school.

The Greater Dallas Section hosted NCJW's Southern District Convention in 1970, at which Dallas won the award for having the largest percentage of Life Members. Section members were responsible for all the convention's arrangements, including hospitality, meeting room set-ups, award presentations, and souvenirs. City of Dallas Mayor Erik Jonsson was the keynote speaker. Rabbi Levi A. Olan of Temple Emanu-El was also included in the conference's program.

The PACE Committee (Public Affairs, Community Service, and Evaluation) was established by the Section in 1970. PACE was designed to evaluate new and ongoing Section community service projects to ensure their relevancy and efficiency.

As part of an additional evaluation process, it was decided that Encore needed a permanent space big enough to hold periodic sales and to store merchandise year-round. In 1972, Encore relocated to much larger quarters on Harry Hines Boulevard. The space provided more than six thousand square feet, enough for the selling and storage of merchandise plus accommodations for the organization's administrative office.

The Section participated in National's four-year study of poverty and women's needs. The finding that the most desperate need was for childcare led to National's study "Windows on Day Care." National published the results in 1972. The Section, having participated in the research that went into the study, held a news conference to announce the publication and submitted the report conclusions to the Dallas City Council. Members followed up locally with Dallas's first community-wide forum on childcare, held in conjunction with the Dallas Urban League. To turn knowledge into action, the Section approved a $5,000 grant to the Jeanetta Foundation Day Care Center in Dallas and joined the Parkland Hospital Day Care Committee to plan a day care center for its employees.

Also in 1972, Section member Hermine Dalkowitz Tobolowsky, known as the mother of the Texas Equal Rights Amendment (ERA) spearheaded support for the Federal ERA, which was approved by the Texas Legislature in March 1972.

During these ten tumultuous years, outstanding programs and study groups, evaluation processes, and advocacy at all government levels deepened the Section's commitment to fulfilling its greatest potential. President Jeanne Fagadau stated, "In spite of the chaos in the world or perhaps because of it, Council women rededicated themselves and redoubled their efforts to work toward the improvement of conditions in our own community and abroad." Indeed, members took steps of faith

(Left photo): Student Russ Coyle, member Barbara Hurst, member Judy Dorfman (now Judy Lifson), and DISD Superintendent Dr. W.T. White (left to right) discuss elementary school guidance and counseling.

(Center photo): Members Bette Miller (left) and Valerie Aronoff (right) confer about the hardships of those seeking unemployment benefits.

(Right photo): SMU President Dr. Willis Tate talks with Section member Ann Folz about the upcoming seminar (left to right), 1964. Photos by Andy Hanson. (Young, "New Dimensions in Education.")

Section president Katherine Bauer with members Sharan Goldstein and Janice Sweet (later Janice Weinberg) (left to right) review NCJW, Inc.'s plans for the twenty-fifth anniversary of NCJW activities in Israel, which include support of the School of Education at Hebrew University, 1971. Photo by Johnny Flynn. (McKee, "LIFE Is Concern of Jewish Women.")

for women, for children and families, for the poor, for prisoners, and for the elderly. These activities continued the journeys of past generations and established pathways for the coming decade.

Helping Children of West Dallas Study and Grow
Essay by Ann Folz
Greater Dallas Section Member

In 1964, the Dallas Section hosted its first School for Community Action, "Equal Opportunity for Youth," in order to explore and understand the needs of Dallas youth and school dropouts. After an extensive investigation, members determined that an after-school study center would benefit children in impoverished neighborhoods.

Jeanne Fagadau and I helped launch the West Dallas After-School Study Center as a pilot project, designed to provide a pleasant, professionally supervised environment for children whose homes had no physical places to study. The Study Center was more than a quiet place. It provided individual help with academics, field trips for cultural enrichment, and, above all, encouragement for each child.

With cooperation and guidance from the DISD and Edgar Ward Place (part of the Dallas Housing Authority), the Study Center opened on October 8, 1964, to serve students from Sequoyah Junior High School. The center, housed at Edgar Ward Place, was open every Tuesday and Thursday evening. Barbara Banks, a Sequoyah teacher, helped plan the program and provided professional supervision. Section members, plus some of their husbands and teenage children, served as volunteers.

The Study Center moved to the library of Sequoyah Junior High in 1965. Center hours were after school, under the direction of the school librarian, with assistance from Pinkston High School students. The project was underwritten with Section funds.

The Study Center received the 1966 Award for Service to neighborhoods from the *Dallas Times Herald*.

Offering Consumer Advice with Operation READY
Essay by Rose Marie Stromberg
Greater Dallas Section Member

One of the main findings of the 1966 School for Community Action, "Women on the Move," was the need for consumer information written in both English and Spanish for low-income families in Dallas.

After several months of research and planning, Operation READY (Read, Educate, And Do-it-Yourself) was developed, and a helpful information booklet was published. An initial printing of seven thousand pamphlets explained how to understand contracts. They were sent to sixteen agencies and neighborhood organizations and were distributed primarily in West and South Dallas.

Seven additional publications covered topics such as medical services, borrowing money, resisting door-to-door sales, and shopping for various household items. "How to Buy a Car"—in English and Spanish—was in great demand. I was part of the Section committee that wrote this purse-sized booklet. Later, the publications were distributed through home economics classes at DISD "Title I" junior and senior high schools. These schools had high percentages of students from low-income families.

The project continued through 1974 when it expanded into a new joint effort called the Consumer Alliance.

Some of the many pamphlets produced for Operation READY, 1967

Study Groups

A sampling of the study groups the Section offered during 1968–1970.

GREATER DALLAS SECTION
NATIONAL COUNCIL OF JEWISH WOMEN

Study Group presents

MENTAL HEALTH AND DRUGS
Yes, YOUR Child!

Speaker
DR. W. ROBERT BEAVERS,
Clinical Associate Professor
Dept. of Psychiatry, U of Texas
Southwestern Medical School

Date: Wednesday, December 10, 1969
Time: 10:00 a.m.
Place: home of Mrs. Henry Jacobus, Jr.
9500 Inwood Road

Chairman of the Day
Mrs. Herbert Mines

You and your friends are cordially invited to attend

GREATER DALLAS SECTION
NATIONAL COUNCIL OF JEWISH WOMEN

Study Group presents

COMPULSARY MILITARY SERVICE FOR ALL CITIZENS

A debate by the
Jesuit High School Debating Team

Mr. Edwin Brower, Coach

And now our daughters?

Date: Wednesday, February 19, 1969
Time: 10:00 a.m.
Place: home of Mrs. Milton Greene
4635 Park Lane
PLEASE NOTE CHANGE OF LOCATION

Chairman of the Day
Mrs. Philip Sanders

GREATER DALLAS SECTION
NATIONAL COUNCIL OF JEWISH WOMEN

Study Group presents

THE U N IN ACTION TODAY
Are We Really Moving Forward

Speaker
DR. R. RICHARD RUBOTTOM, JR.
a vice president of SMU,
20 year veteran of foreign service,
former ambassador to Argentina

Date: Wednesday, December 18, 1968
Time: 10:00 a.m.
Place: home of Mrs. Edward Greene
4616 Dorset Road
(north of Walnut Hill,
west off Strait Lane)

Chairman of the Day
Mrs. Herman Philipson, Jr.

GREATER DALLAS SECTION
NATIONAL COUNCIL OF JEWISH WOMEN

Study Group presents

THE CHALLENGE AND THE CHANCE
The Governor's filmed report on education

You asked for it --
and Dr. Estes recommended it

Date: Wednesday, March 12, 1969
Time: 10:00 A.M.
Place: home of Mrs. Lewis MacAdams
5233 Lobello Drive
(1 block south of Royal, east of Inwood)

You and your friends are cordially invited to attend.

GREATER DALLAS SECTION
NATIONAL COUNCIL OF JEWISH WOMEN

Study Group presents

YOUTH, SEX AND MORALITY
After Spock, No Camelot

Speaker
JOHN E. DAVIS
Psychiatric Social Worker

DATE: Wednesday, January 21, 1970
TIME: 10:00 a.m.
PLACE: Home of Mrs. Bud Sanger
4503 Catina
(1 block south of Royal,
between Inwood and Midway)

Chairman of the Day
Mrs. Albert Kronick

You and your friends are cordially invited to attend

GREATER DALLAS SECTION
NATIONAL COUNCIL OF JEWISH WOMEN

Study Group presents

THE BATTERED CHILD
Something *can* be done

Speaker
MRS. HARRIET M. STAMBAUGH

Ass't. Professor, Pediatrics, Southwestern
Medical School;
Director, Dept. of Social Work, Children's
Medical Center;
Chairman NASW Standing Committee on the
Battered Child.

Date: Wednesday, March 19, 1969
Time: 10:00 A.M.
Place: home of Mrs. Ben Rosenthal, Jr.
5350 Springmeadow
(between Royal and Northaven, east of Inwood)

Chairman of the Day: Mrs. Lynn Goldstein

You and your friends are cordially invited to attend

Breaking Volunteer Barriers in Dallas Schools

Essay by Jeanne Fagadau, of Blessed Memory
President, Greater Dallas Section 1968–1970

For several years in the 1960s, members of the Section attempted to start a volunteer program in Dallas's public schools. We wanted to help students with academic subjects, but there was reluctance from the DISD's administration. Were volunteers really capable of tutoring students in math, reading, and English?

At last, in 1968, the new superintendent of the DISD understood the vision. Superintendent Nolan Estes was delighted that the Section was willing and ready to start a volunteer program, the first of its kind in the state.

As president of the Section, I appointed member Joan Kronick to be the first chair of this project. Soon after, a pilot program at the Frederick Douglass Elementary School in West Dallas began. The principal was pleased, and volunteers loved their work as aides to the teachers. Students received essential extra help from Section volunteers, under the direction of classroom teachers.

The following year, Dr. Estes asked Joan to work for the District as the volunteer coordinator. When the idea of volunteers in the classroom was presented at a meeting of the District's principals, Section members sat on the stage and watched some troubled faces among those principals. Let the public into the schools? The administrators had to be convinced that it was a good idea and that their schools would benefit from additional resources.

The project was well organized. Records were kept. Volunteers were trained and appreciated. In fact, volunteers are credited with helping to pass critical school bond issues. Additional principals were soon clamoring to have a volunteer program in their schools.

Joan and her husband returned to New York the following year, and Dr. Estes asked me to serve as the new coordinator, which I did for the next few years. As the program grew, Margaret Dunlap, a former community volunteer from the Junior League of Dallas, joined me as the co-coordinator.

The project expanded to include a speaker's program and book donations. Community members would come to schools and share their experiences and skills. Many of the students had never owned a book before, so children were given free books to start their own at-home libraries.

When a court order desegregated the DISD schools, the program quickly expanded. Businesses, churches, and civic groups "adopted" schools, providing resources and time. The DISD volunteer program now required five additional employees to coordinate all the volunteer help.

News of the success spread, and I was invited to other Texas towns to share how to begin school volunteer programs–a win for students, teachers, administrators, and community members alike.

Karen Somer (later Karen Naseck), four-year-old daughter of Section member Phyllis Somer, joins cochairs Jeneane Pearlman and Ann Sikora in modeling fashion hats to publicize an Encore Sale fundraiser, 1968. Photo by Bob Vasek. (Richardson, "Now, Encore.")

(Above) Section volunteers head into the pilot program's class at Frederick Douglass School, 1969. ("School Volunteer Program," *Council News*, May 1969)

(Above right) Nolan Estes, DISD superintendent, honored hundreds of people on "School Volunteer Recognition Day" with the support of Section members Jeanne Fagadau (left), new coordinator, and Joan Kronick, the original coordinator of the DISD Volunteer Program, 1970. Photo by Jim Work. (McKee, "Education, Not Devastation Aided.")

The Dallas City Council, represented by J. Erik Jonsson, expressed its appreciation for the Section's grant to fund a social worker for the Police Department, 1969.

May 12, 1969

WHEREAS, The National Council of Jewish Women, Greater Dallas Section, has offered to grant the City of Dallas $20,000 for a two-year pilot program in the Community Service Division of the Police Department, and

WHEREAS, the Dallas City Council on May 5, 1969, accepted the grant offer and authorized the City Manager to contract for the employment of a trained social worker with correction experience to offer casework to crime victims, offenders and the families of both, and to furnish consultative assistance to the Police Department; and,

WHEREAS, the cooperative pilot program between the Council of Jewish Women and the City of Dallas could lead toward identifying potential repeat violators and preventing recidivism among youth and adults; Now, Therefore,

BE IT RESOLVED BY THE CITY COUNCIL OF THE CITY OF DALLAS:

SECTION 1. That the Dallas City Council express its grateful appreciation to the National Council of Jewish Women, Greater Dallas Section, for its generosity and community concern in support of the Dallas Police Department, Community Services Division pilot program; and

SECTION 2. That the City Secretary furnish a copy of this resolution to the National Council of Jewish Women, Greater Dallas Section.

SECTION 3. That this resolution shall take effect from and after its passage as in the Charter in such cases is made and provided.

-- RESOLUTION UNANIMOUSLY ADOPTED --

Erik Jonsson
Mayor

It's official! The Section, with 1,400 members, changes its Articles of Incorporation to recognize its new name of "The Greater Dallas Section" in June 1967.

NON-PROFIT

In the name and by the authority of The State of Texas

OFFICE OF THE SECRETARY OF STATE

CERTIFICATE OF AMENDMENT OF

GREATER DALLAS (TEXAS) SECTION, INC., NATIONAL COUNCIL OF JEWISH WOMEN, INC.
Formerly DALLAS SECTION-NATIONAL COUNCIL OF JEWISH WOMEN
CHARTER NO. 97255

The undersigned, as Secretary of State of the State of Texas, hereby certifies that duplicate originals of Articles of Amendment to the Articles of Incorporation of the above corporation duly signed and verified pursuant to the provisions of the Texas Non-Profit Corporation Act, have been received in this office and are found to conform to law.

ACCORDINGLY the undersigned, as such Secretary of State, and by virtue of the authority vested in him by law, hereby issues this Certificate of Amendment to the Articles of Incorporation and attaches hereto a duplicate original of the Articles of Amendment.

Dated JUNE 1, 1967.

John L. Hill
Secretary of State

Section members "Boots" Brin and Bette Miller (center and right) meet with Glynn Coker (left), executive director of the Dallas County Department of Public Welfare, in conjunction with the second School for Community Action, 1964. Photo by Andy Hanson. (Castleberry, "Where the Need is They are There.")

Katherine Bauer (left) and Janet Newberger greeted Mayor Wes Wise, who spoke about "Your Role in the Spirit of Dallas" when he addressed Section members at the 1971 opening meeting. Photo by Andy Hanson. (Richardson, *Dallas Times Herald*, September 26, 1971.)

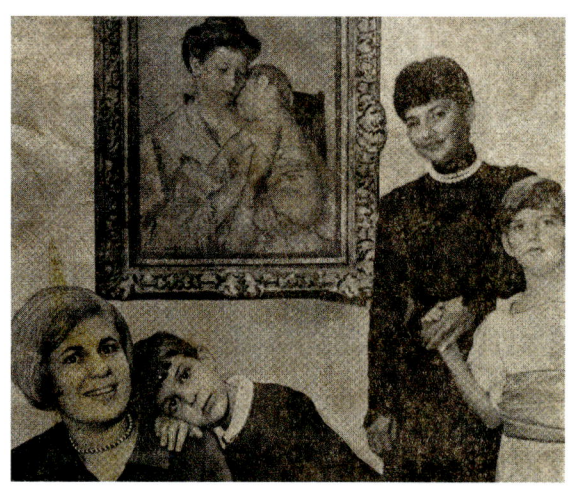

Section members Elissa Sommerfield, with her son Frankie, and Bette Miller, with her daughter Elka (left to right), recreate Mary Cassatt's "Mother and Child" at the Dallas Museum of Art to illustrate the importance of family, 1967. (Richardson, "Where There's a Woman, … There's a Way.")

Section members Janet Hershman, Sharlene Block, and Syl Benenson (left to right) display posters designating Dallas as "The All-America City." At that time—1971—over 1,450 Section members were serving the community. Photo by Johnny Flynn. (McKee, "LIFE is Concern of Jewish Women.")

The Section undertook a two-year study to determine if the City of Dallas Police Department needed a social worker. Social work consultant, Phillip A. Lewis (left), completes an interview, 1970. ("Revolving Door-Type Offender Helped," *Dallas Times Herald*.)

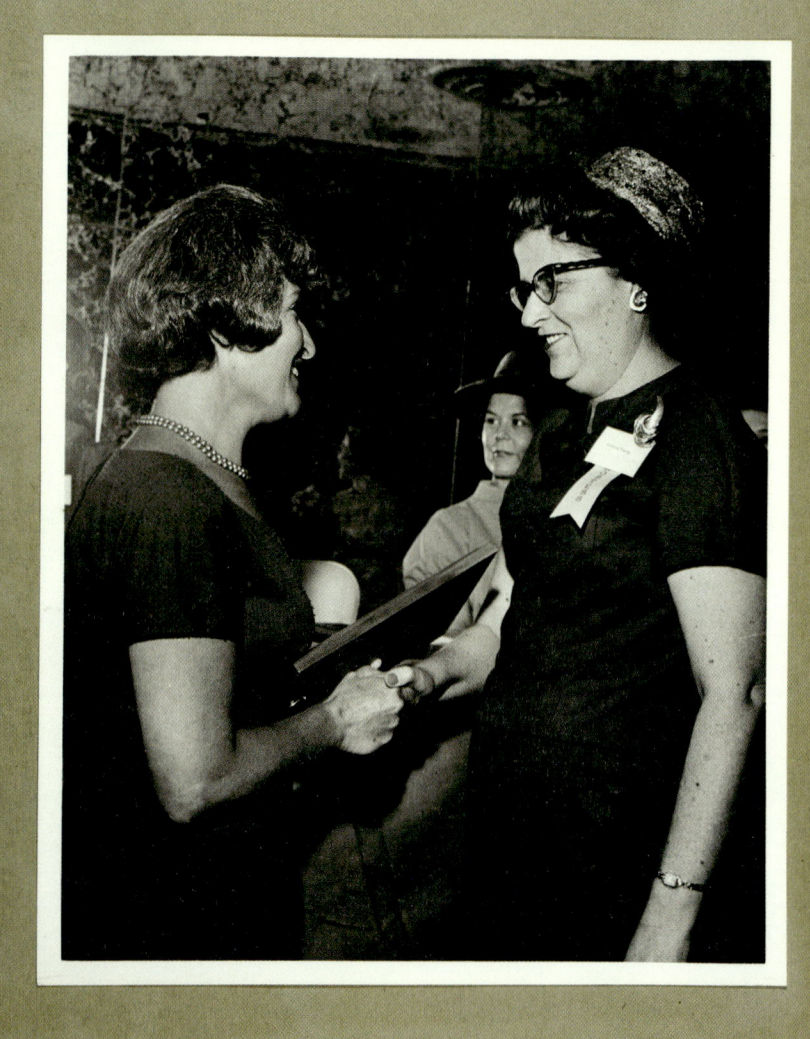

MRS Robert (Selma) I. Ross Receiving The times Herald AWARD FROM MILDRED YOUNG FOR THE WEST DALLAS STUDY Center!

Section member Selma Ross (left) accepting the service award for the Edgar West Dallas Study Center program from the *Dallas Times Herald* Club Editor Mildred Young, 1965.

(Below) Focusing on women in poverty, the Section's third School for Community Action featured Ruth Harvey, a member of President Lyndon B. Johnson's Executive Committee, 1966. (*Council News*, September 1966.)

The Section's fourth School for Community Action focused a spotlight on the family and its stresses and featured Pastor Dr. Thomas Shipp and Dr. Edward Rydman, 1967. (*Council News*, November 1967.)

The People to People Panel, an outgrowth of the Section's fourth School for Community Action, was featured at the Section's February 1969 meeting. (*Bulletin*, February 1969.)

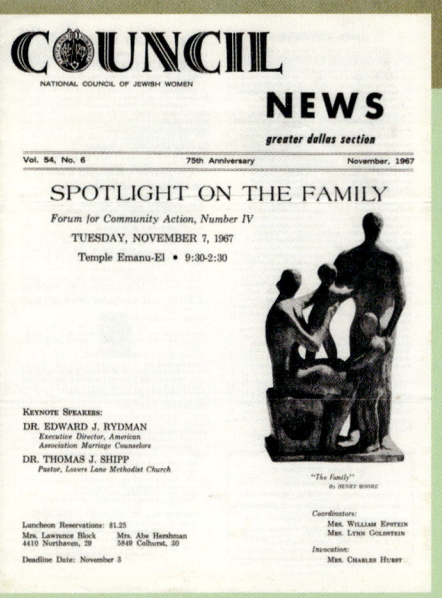

A successful champion of privacy and reproductive rights for women, Sarah Weddington served as an aide on women's issues in the administration of President Jimmy Carter, 1978. (National Archives and Records Administration, no. NLC-WHSP-C-07478-14).

1973	1974	1975	1976	1977
First Family Outreach program; Tay-Sachs screening program	*Elder Artisans Project; Day care staff training; Young Professional Branch organized*	*DISD consumer education; Outreach to New Americans*	*"Working Parents" forum; First Hannah G. Solomon Award*	*First Community Board Institute; Texas Coalition for Juvenile Justice*

"The future belongs to those who believe in the beauty of their dreams."

Eleanor Roosevelt (1884–1962), American activist, diplomat, and wife of President Franklin D. Roosevelt

The Seventh Decade: 1973 to 1982

The nation successfully launched its first space station, Skylab, in 1973. The United States' involvement in the Vietnam War came to an end. President Richard M. Nixon resigned and was pardoned the next year by President Gerald Ford. *Roe v. Wade* was argued before the Supreme Court in 1973 by Texas lawyer Sarah Weddington. Striking down Texas's criminal abortion laws, this case affirmed that a right to privacy under the Due Process Clause of the Fourteenth Amendment extended to a woman's decision to have an abortion. Though this confirmed women's reproductive rights, new challenges to these rights continue.

Bill Gates founded Microsoft in 1975. The first home computer hit the market just two years later, the same year Elvis Presley died. In 1980, Mount St. Helens erupted in Washington

1978	1979	1980	1981	1982
Domestic Violence Intervention Alliance	FOCAS begins	Morning Branch formed; Women's Issues Network organized	Dallas Central Library Docents; Professional Branch established	SHARE Endowment Fund

Thanks-Giving Square, Dallas, Texas. Photo by Leonid Furmansky. Courtesy of Thanks-Giving Square.

Mayor Pro Tem Adlene Harrison praises the Section for its humanitarian work, 1976. (Kennedy, "Harrison Salutes Council for Humanitarian Work.")

State. John Lennon was killed in Manhattan. The next year, Dallasite John Hinckley attempted to assassinate President Ronald Reagan. Sandra Day O'Connor became the first female Justice of the Supreme Court.

The Dallas/Fort Worth Regional Airport opened for commercial service in 1974, marking the beginning of one of the most integral drivers of the North Texas economy. Texas Congressman Jim Wright shepherded an amendment bearing his name through Congress in 1979, severely restricting service out of Love Field for the next thirty-five years.

A quiet achievement was the 1976 opening of Thanks-Giving Square, a haven of peace and prayer in the midst of downtown Dallas. Section member Adlene Harrison became Dallas's first female mayor and also the first Jewish mayor, filling the unexpired term of Mayor Wes Wise, who had resigned to run for Congress. This area became famous for *Dallas*, the prime-time television soap opera that debuted in 1978. It was filmed locally and kept the city's name on the national and international entertainment map for more than thirteen years.

THE WOMEN OF THE GREATER DALLAS SECTION NEVER STOP DREAMING ABOUT PROGRESS. No matter the challenges, the changes in society, the brokenness of the world, they plan for better—and they work toward making those hopeful outcomes a reality.

During the 1970s, the Section developed several programs based on National's priorities, leading to ten years of concentrated social action efforts. The major areas were children and youth, women's issues, aging, Israel, and Jewish concerns.

Children and Youth

The NCJW Richardson-Plano Section, which later became the Morning Branch of the Greater Dallas Section, proposed to the Texas Department of Human Services a volunteer program that would use trained volunteers to deliver supplemental casework services for at-risk families. In 1973, the Richardson-Plano Section helped open the Richardson Family Outreach Center, the first in the state. The Center was dedicated to strengthening families and preventing child abuse and neglect by providing support, encouragement, and parenting information.

Family Outreach assisted the Dallas County Child Welfare Unit in finding foster and adoptive homes for children in need. The program later expanded across the state. In 1976, the Section opened the Northwest Dallas County Family Outreach Center (Family Outreach Dallas). It was a joint venture with the Dallas County Child Welfare Unit. Volunteers worked with the families, did clerical tasks, and provided outreach to the community. The Richardson/Plano Center in 2014 merged with Family Compass (Child Abuse Prevention Center) to form an even stronger agency.

Also in 1976, the Section gave a $6,707 grant to National to support a forum on status offenders that was held in Washington, DC. This grant was matched by the federal Law Enforcement Assistance Agency (LEAA). Following the forum, the Section held its own program, "Trouble in Texas: Children and the Justice System," for professionals and volunteers. This directly led to the founding of the Texas Coalition for Juvenile Justice (TCJJ) in 1977. Anita Marcus, past Section president, was a cofounder and first president of the Coalition and subsequent executive director from 1978–1988. During Anita's tenure, TCJJ grew to be a statewide network of two hundred individuals and organizations, representing more than 500,000 citizens who were united in raising awareness of juvenile justice issues. Anita and TCJJ advocates were instrumental in establishing the Texas Juvenile Probation Commission and ending the practice of placing youths in city and county jails with adult offenders.

During this decade, a community-wide teen survey conducted by the Section concluded that young girls' pregnancies were both a cause and an effect of women's poverty. This study also concluded that both adolescent delinquency and so-called "status offenses" (legally defined as actions prohibited only to certain classes of people and most often applied to offenses committed by minors) were disproportionately linked to situations of child abuse and neglect.

With its lengthy history of family outreach efforts, the Section was chosen as one of three NCJW sections to participate in a pilot project that led to the creation of Foster Child Advocate Services (FOCAS). A grant from the Edna McConnell Clark Foundation, awarded through National, enabled the Section to partner with the Dallas County Mental Health Association to provide advocates for children in foster care. Section volunteers—almost fifty of them, responsible for one hundred cases—were trained by FOCAS and formed the first-ever corps of volunteers to serve in the Texas court system in 1980. Thanks in part to the Section, FOCAS later became an independent program called Dallas CASA (Court-Appointed Child Advocates), which currently engages more than seven hundred volunteers from throughout the county.

Women's Issues

The Section chose to focus on these topics: discrimination, childcare, economic and emotional needs of working women, how women could acquire new skills in order to become equal members of society, plus a little-discussed topic of the day: partner/spousal abuse.

As Bette Miller began her presidency in 1974, the Section changed the way it listed women's names in printed materials. Bette recalls, "We initiated the use of the member's 'given name' in minutes, *Bulletins*, etc., a display of our rights as women by using our own name, and not our spouse's. This was a groundbreaking move for many of our members, though years later they would not give it a second thought." It was not until 1980–1981 that the Section's yearbook/directory followed suit.

While formulating programs to meet necessary civic goals, the Section joined a coalition that petitioned the City of Dallas's

Past president Anita Marcus receives the 2006 Trailblazer of Youth Award from representatives of the Texas Network of Youth Services for her long-standing advocacy for children and youth, 2006.

Arrangements cochairs Janet Newberger, Betty Dreyfus, and Bette Miller (center, left to right, in cowboy hats) give a Texas welcome to NCJW conventioneers in Dallas, 1979.

In September 1974, a group of thirty-two young professional women met to form a new organization within the Section. Wendy Goldman, Susan Herz, Section adviser Ellen Lasser, and Raeann Lerman (left to right) celebrate the establishment of the Young Professionals at The Magic Pan Restaurant in NorthPark Mall, 1974. (*Bulletin*, September 1974.)

(Center, top) Section past president Anita Marcus (center) helps plan the Working Parents Forum with Lu McClellen (left), a professor at Eastfield College, and Madeline Mandell of the Day Care Association of Metropolitan Dallas, 1976. Photo by Johnny Flynn. (Cobler, "Parents Can Work It Out.")

(Center, below) Liz Carpenter, former press secretary to First Lady Mrs. Lyndon B. Johnson, was keynote speaker at the "Working Parents Forum," cosponsored by the Greater Dallas Section and Child Care '76, in cooperation with the Texas Department of Public Welfare, 1976. (Kennedy, "Working Parents Need Someone on Their Side.")

mayor and the city council to create an official commission to eliminate discrimination on the basis of gender. In 1975, designated the International Year of the Woman, the Dallas Commission on the Status of Women was established, and the Section was represented on the Commission.

Early in this decade, the Section researched how best to reach out to the growing number of younger working women in the community. The Young Professional Group was formed in 1974 for women in their twenties and thirties. Several years later, some Evening Branch members who were single parents decided that they needed a group that better reflected their interests and availability to serve. Thus, the Professional Branch was established in 1981 for both women and men. They met in the evening or on Sundays to pursue their interests in community service and public affairs.

Another identified critical community need was affordable, high quality day care for children, staffed by certified employees. Section members developed and funded a day care staff training course taught by professors at Eastfield College, one of the seven member schools in the Dallas County Community College District.

The Section worked with the Department of Public Welfare and the "Child Care '76" to present a daylong program, the "Working Parents Forum," attended by more than 525 people. The forum highlighted the need for affordable, high quality childcare. Liz Carpenter, the Texas feminist powerhouse of Washington journalism and Lady Bird Johnson's press secretary, was the keynote speaker and delivered the message "Balancing Babies and Bosses." This forum was duplicated in nine more cities throughout Texas during 1976. A Children's Advocacy Coalition was formed to work on the problems that were brought to light through the forum. Two years later, the Section spearheaded another city-wide childcare forum.

The Section sent delegates to the 1977 National Women's Conference in Houston. This conference was the first meeting of its type in the United States since the 1848 Women's Rights Convention held in Seneca Falls, New York. The twentieth-century event drew more than twenty thousand attendees.

In 1978, with Section leadership, the Domestic Violence Intervention Alliance was established. The Alliance published a directory of services available to women in crisis. The Section provided funds and volunteers for a shelter for battered women. Under the leadership of Section member Gerry Beer, this led to the establishment of The Family Place, which continues working to curb family violence and empower its victims.

The Section cosponsored the 1980 "Dallas Women: Progress into the 80s" symposium with the late Maureen Reagan, a strong supporter of the Equal Rights Amendment, as

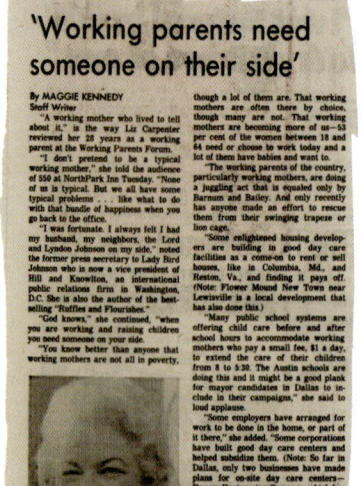

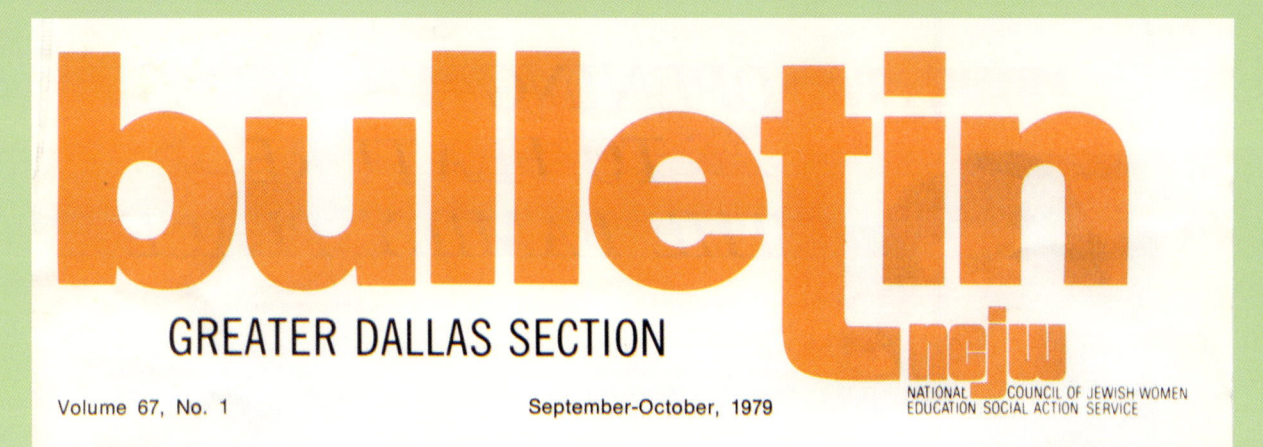

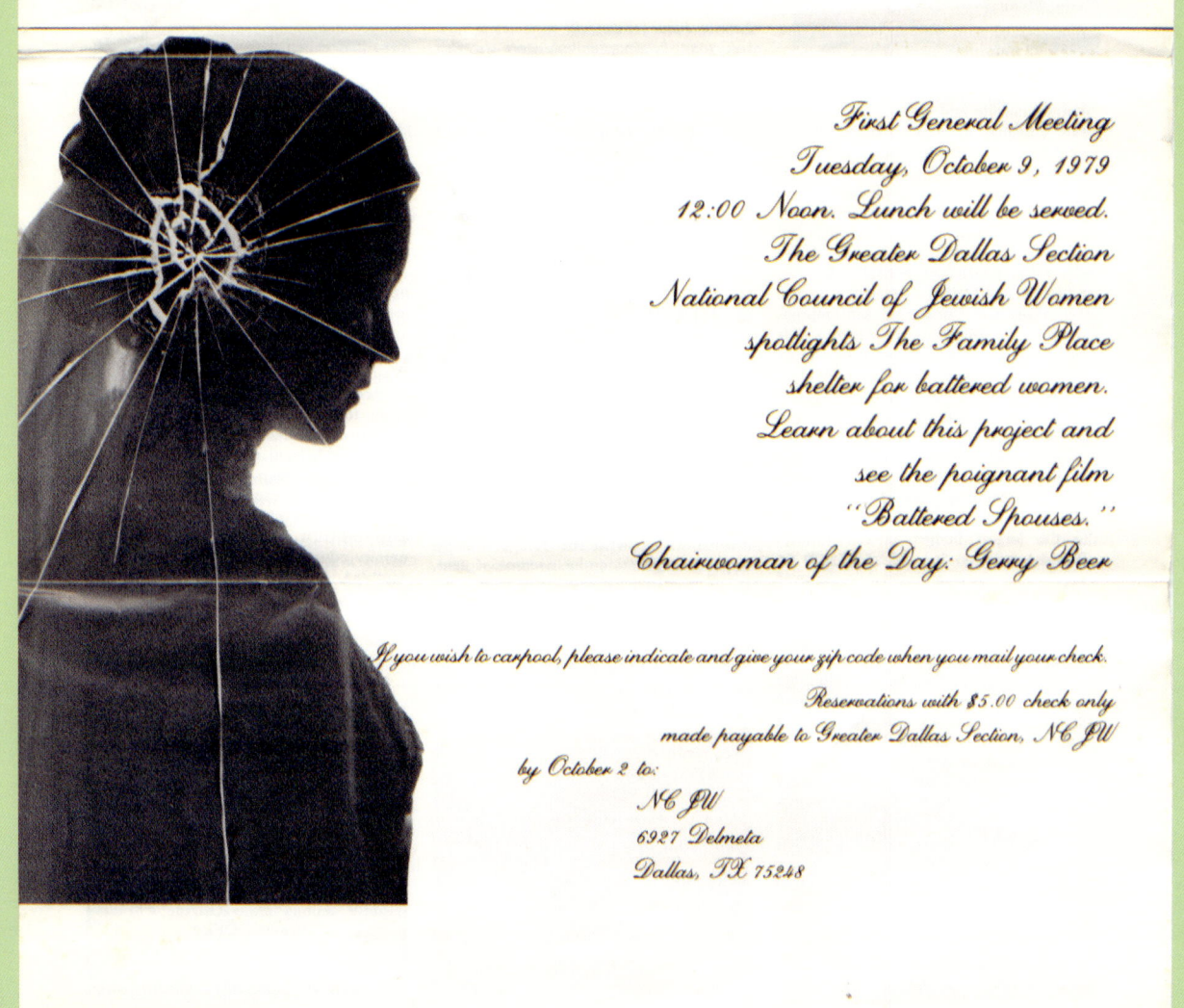

(Left) The Family Place program is introduced to the Section at its October 1979 general meeting. (*Bulletin*, September-October 1979.)

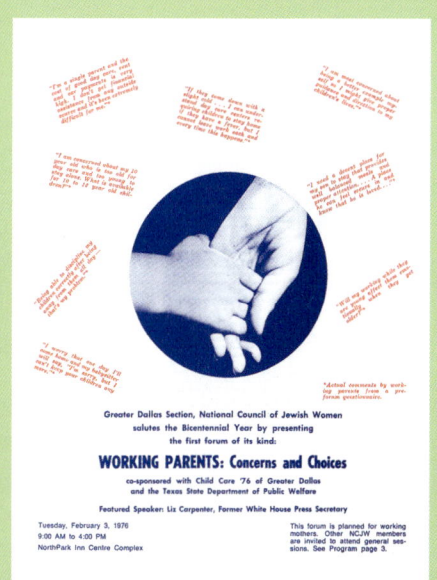

The Section saluted the 1976 Bicentennial by presenting the "Working Parents: Concerns and Choices" forum, cosponsored with Child Care '76 of Greater Dallas and the Texas State Department of Public Welfare, 1976.

the featured speaker. Afterward, Section members helped to organize the Dallas Women's Issues Network, whose purpose was to advocate for legislation promoting women's interests and rights.

Aging

Supporting research and projects for seniors has been an ongoing commitment of the Section for decades. In the early 1970s, a new effort was launched with the LIFE program, undertaken in cooperation with Golden Acres. The program (Love, Interest, Fulfillment, Enrichment) involved volunteers and funding for essential services plus education and enrichment.

Also, the Section—along with the Senior Citizens of Greater Dallas (The Senior Source)—spearheaded the Elder Artisans Project. It initially served residents of the Dallas Housing Authority's Brooks Manor, a high-rise for seniors, by helping to design and market their "Texas Collectibles" products. Later, eleven other area senior centers joined the project. From 1974 to 1979, the sale of these handcrafted items helped supplement the incomes of older Dallas-area artisans.

Evening and Professional Branch volunteers concentrated their efforts on the residents of Golden Acres and sponsored an art project and provided other entertainment for residents.

To encourage members to learn more about aging, the Section offered a study group called "How Does It Feel to Grow Old?" from a Dallas Geriatric Research Institute study on sensory deprivation in the elderly, begun in 1977. The Section's Grace L. Florence Fund underwrote the research, and Section volunteers helped North Texas State University (University of North Texas) student Jean Brophy conduct the study at Golden Acres. Her work won the annual Hammerman Memorial Award from the National Association of Jewish Homes for the Aged and was presented at their national convention. Ms. Brophy's master's thesis served as the nucleus for a major manual that was distributed nationally.

The Section also tackled complex issues related to aging with characteristic enthusiasm and thoroughness. In recognition of increasing victimization of the elderly, Section members hosted "In Search of Safer Senior Years: A Workshop Against Crime" in 1977. About three hundred people, representing the Departments of Human Resources, Visiting Nurse Associations, Area Agencies on Aging, law enforcement, and educational institutions from Texas and surrounding states attended the program.

Israel and Jewish Concerns

During this decade, the Section combined National's priorities of Israel and Jewish concerns. Ongoing study groups and an important annual meeting focused on anti-Semitism, the history of Jews in America, and the perpetuation of Jewish ethics. During the fall of 1979, the Section presented a course, "Defining Judaism," that was created by National. This was followed by a course developed by the Section in cooperation with the Minneapolis Section. "The Pot that Didn't Melt" used literature to examine the Jewish immigrant experience. Both of these programs were well attended. Volunteers also updated the annual Friday night service for Council Shabbat and later published its own prayer book.

The ethics of fair consumerism was also a Section concern. The Consumer Alliance, an outgrowth of Operation READY, began in 1974. In cooperation with Dallas Legal Services and other participating neighborhood groups, Section members researched consumer needs of low-income families and helped counsel Legal Services' clients who had consumer problems. As part of the Section's consumer education program, the Alliance created a "Survival Course" for high school students. The course, with help from the City of Dallas Department of Consumer Affairs and Dallas Legal Services, provided practical information to help students leave home as self-supporting young adults. It covered topics such as employment, tenants' rights, nutrition, health care and services, credit ratings, and buying a car. The course was piloted at six DISD high schools and later expanded to all DISD high schools.

In 1976, at its sixty-third birthday luncheon, the Section presented a new award, the Hannah G. Solomon Award, given in recognition of a member who "has a strong NCJW identity, has changed the lives of others through her

Seniors stitching up "Texas Collectible" items, 1975. Photos by Lee Langum. (Cobler, "Stitching loose ends.")

leadership efforts and service, has helped change and expand the role of women in vital areas of community life, and whose leadership in areas of NCJW concern—improving the quality of life for people of all ages and backgrounds—has motivated others to work for change and has resulted in progress and enlightenment in the community."

The first award was given to Fannie Kahn, a past Section president, who said in her acceptance: "This is my birthday wish: in an imperfect, troubled, and rapidly changing world, nothing is more important than for us to continue to work for the understanding and interdependence of groups, peoples, and nations."

Interdependence was a key word, as the Section joined forces in a long-range cooperative venture with the Women's Council of Dallas County, the Volunteer Center of Dallas, and the Junior League of Dallas. The goal of the five-year Volunteer Management Education Coalition (1979–1984) was the training of nonprofit leaders to direct project development and volunteer workshops, and evaluation processes. Various Section members took key leadership roles during this seminar series. These women included, among others, Norma Schlinger, the initial chair; Jeanne Fagadau; Ann Folz; Emma Sue Frank; Hanne Klein; Helen Stuhl; and Janice Sweet (later Janice Weinberg). Volunteer advocate, Marjorie Stitch, a New Orleans NCJW member, was the keynote speaker during an all-day workshop.

In the midst of these volunteer training efforts, the City of Dallas asked for help in introducing area residents to the new state-of-the-art Central Public Library, which opened in 1982. Section members were asked to organize and staff the library's volunteer program. Section member Sharan Goldstein took the lead in writing instructional material for the docent program, and the Section provided training and orientation for more than 175 community volunteers who served as docents, computer instructors, and library store clerks.

At the end of this seventh decade, the Section realized the need for a permanent endowment fund to support Dallas-area social service and public affairs projects not covered in its annual budget. The leadership established the SHARE (Service, Help, Advocacy, Research, and Education) Endowment Fund in 1982. Today, SHARE has more than $1 million invested to support new or expanding Section projects.

The decade closed with some dreams fulfilled and other plans reaching well into the future. The women of the Section continued to reflect the spirit of NCJW—a faith in the future; a belief in action.

Winning at City Hall
Essay by Katherine Bauer
President, Greater Dallas Section 1970–1972

During the presidencies of Edna Flaxman and Jeanne Fagadau, after researching the impact of incarceration on entire families, the Section launched a two-year pilot in 1970 that paid for a social worker in the Dallas City Jail to work with inmates and their families. Section volunteers Hortense Sanger and Carolyn Tobian (later Carolyn Clark) served as project cochairs. This effort was successful, and the Dallas Police Department, along with the City of Dallas, adopted the plan. This became the foundation for the police department's Social Services Section during the last year of my presidency in 1972.

Phil Lewis was hired as the social worker. Under police leadership, the Social Services Section expanded and began to work with people who police officers encountered on the street—people in need of social, economic, and emotional help. No other agency dealt with those types of situations or offered police officers that kind of professional assistance when an emergency occurred.

However, when the city's 1975-1976 proposed budget was presented, the Social Services Section

"Sometimes in this world, there are people who seem to be where the action is . . . where the great and exciting things are happening. And then, there are those few, exceptional people who are always there making things happen." —Ann Sikora, honoring past president Fannie Kahn with the Greater Dallas Section's first-ever Hannah G. Solomon Award. (Left to right) Ann Sikora, Fannie Kahn, and Section president Bette Miller, 1976.

Section president Janet Newberger (second from right) confers with the staff of the Dallas Police Department's Community Services Division, including social worker Phil Lewis (right), 1973. Photo by Andy Hanson. (Richardson, "Phil Lewis: Jail Social Worker.")

Section president Bette Miller (left) and vice president Joy Mankoff, armed with $10,000, convinced the Dallas City Council to reinstate a social worker in the Dallas Police Department, 1975. Photo by John Mazziotta. (Richardson, "$10,000 to the Rescue.")

had been eliminated. Knowing the research, the time, and the money invested in this valuable project, we decided to take action to reinstate it. Section members contacted City Council members and urged them to reconsider the program. We also informed other organizations of the budget cuts, and with the help of the Community Council of Greater Dallas, spread the word across the city.

A presentation by Section members was made at a City Council budget hearing. That was followed by more personal phone calls and letters to City Council members and Mayor Wes Wise. To further support the plea, we pledged $10,000 to emphasize our concern and belief in the Social Services Section.

Before the final budget vote was taken, funding for the Social Services Section was restored, along with financial support for the entire Community Services Division, which included storefront police operations. After the vote, an assistant city manager said that the pledge of money was key. Many groups come to the City Council wanting programs saved or work done, but none were as willing to participate as the Section had been.

Human services should be an essential part of any city's governance, and the Section was able to convince the Dallas City Council to share that belief and act on it.

> "I certainly have known and supported for years all that Section has done. Before my time on the City Council, the Dallas Police Department had no one to train them on domestic violence issues. Because NCJW never gave up, their $10,000 commitment made the difference. Without their support, I don't know when police training would have been instituted. I have always advocated for this training effort and the work of the City's Health and Human Services staff."
>
> **Adlene Harrison**
> *Former City of Dallas Mayor (1976) and City Council member (1973-1977)*

Screening for the Tay-Sachs Gene
Essay by Judy Utay
President, Evening Branch 1970–1971

The Greater Dallas Section and the Evening Branch brought together medical staff and volunteers in 1973 to discuss Tay-Sachs disease, an inherited disorder that causes the destruction of the nervous system. It was decided that the Evening Branch would lead an effort to screen the Dallas Jewish community for this disease.

According to medical research at that time, one in thirty Ashkenazi Jews was a carrier of the gene for Tay-Sachs, compared to one in three hundred for non-Jews. An infant with Tay-Sachs suffers a progressive deterioration of nerve cells along with mental and physical disabilities, usually culminating in death by age four. Because Tay-Sachs is a recessive gene disorder, both parents must be carriers for their child to be at risk for the disease.

The Evening Branch, hoping to serve families by offering a test that identifies the recessive gene, conducted three screening opportunities, including an all-day event at the Jewish Community Center. We also offered valuable information to families. These were the first mass Tay-Sachs screenings for the Dallas Jewish community. Working in conjunction with Children's Medical Center and University of Texas Southwestern Medical School, 1,447 people were tested for the Tay-Sachs gene. This screening was also the most successful of this type held in the United States.

The success of these screenings led to the establishment of the Dallas Chapter of the National Tay-Sachs and Allied Diseases Association. After the initial screenings, the Evening Branch continued to partially fund tests for individuals who were referred to the Branch by the local Tay-Sachs group.

Safeguarding Dallas Area Seniors

Essay by Pat Peiser
President, Greater Dallas Section 1960–1962
Shirley Tobolowsky
Greater Dallas Section Member

The Greater Dallas Section has long placed a priority on issues related to the community's senior citizens. Research during the early 1970s showed that seniors were particularly vulnerable to crime.

In 1974, the Section organized a Senior Safety Committee to coordinate a workshop to combat crimes against older adults. Three years later, the committee, representing eighteen agencies and organizations, convened "In Search of Safer Senior Years," a seminar on the physical and fraudulent victimization of the elderly. Section leaders in this effort also included Pauline Kress and Syl Benenson with Pat serving as director.

After the seminar, the steering committee became the Senior Safety Task Force, a component of the Community Council of Greater Dallas (CCGD). This task force identified banking, education, the police, and the media as areas of concern. The task force produced, with Section funding, a well-received listing of emergency numbers in the form of 150,000 paper "yardsticks," which were distributed to the community.

In the May 1976 Section *Bulletin*, it was reported that the Information and Referral Office (2–1–1 Texas) Dallas Region helpline at the CCGD, whose number was listed on the yardstick, received a phone call. It was from a woman who said the Section's colorful handout was the reason her sister is alive today. Mrs. X was having a heart attack. The person who was present panicked and became immobilized. Mrs. X somehow communicated to that person that there was an emergency number by the phone. This helped summon an ambulance; the woman was saved, and her grateful sister shared her appreciation.

Volunteers and professionals continued to work to implement the goals of the seminar on the abuse of the elderly. Plans were made to coordinate a new forum on the legal rights of the aged and to educate the community about senior issues through conferences on education, isolation, and more. The Section partnered with these social service agencies: Senior Citizens of Greater Dallas (The Senior Source), Visiting Nurse Association, the Volunteer Center (VolunteerNow), and Golden Acres.

Safeguards for Seniors, launched decades later in 1992, was the final effort of this task force with Pat as its director. It encompassed two major issues related to the well-being of older adults: proper use of medications and safety in the home.

To address medication use, screenings of high-risk individuals were provided in senior centers, churches, and other venues where seniors congregated. Volunteer pharmacists from Eckerd Pharmacy (later bought by CVS Pharmacy) conducted medication reviews with those who were at risk of dosage and medical problems, examining the bags of pills and prescriptions that participants brought to the free events. Seniors were then informed about the dangers of improper dosage, drug interactions, and use of outdated medications.

Community-wide conferences to bring attention to the problem of medication misuse were also presented. One daylong conference, "Helping Older Adults: Take It with Care," brought together physicians, pharmacists, geriatric specialists, and senior advocates who discussed the problem. The Section introduced the Safeguards program as one possible solution.

A joint effort between the Section, medical personnel, and the Evening Branch produced a program and three screenings for Tay-Sachs disease; Dr. Jorge Howard, Ron Mankoff, Dr. Robert Kramer, and Evening Branch member Noreen Goodman (left to right) met to review the results, 1974. (*Bulletin*, February 1974.)

The Section presented a five-state, two-day conference on the legal rights of the aged in Dallas. Paul Nathanson of the Senior Citizens Law Center was the keynote speaker, and Section member Joy Mankoff chaired the event, 1977. (*Bulletin*, December 1977.)

Section members Pat Peiser and Syl Benenson (left to right) flank Norman Moorhead (center), director of the Area Agency on Aging, as they prepare a program at Fair Park, 2002.

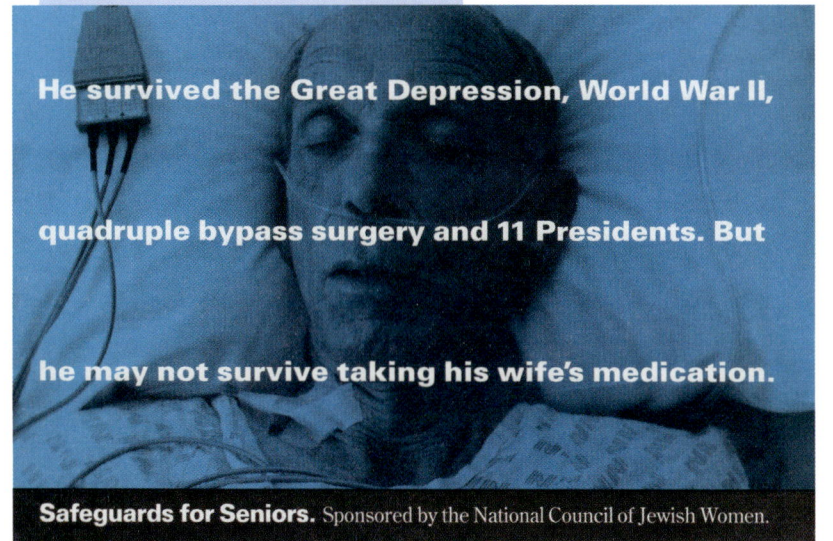

Safeguards for Seniors brochure, 1993.

The second phase of Safeguards was "Safety in the Home," a comprehensive education and intervention program. At the behest of Dr. Ron Anderson, CEO and President of Parkland Hospital, the Section, in collaboration with the Injury Prevention Center of Greater Dallas, launched this program in 1998. In 2000, a daylong conference, "Seniors-at-Risk: Pathways to Personal Safety and Independence," was held. The program offered presentations to senior groups throughout Dallas County, addressing these major factors: fire, falling, medications, burglary (at home and in the car), telephone and mail fraud, physical and mental abuse, and exploitation. Volunteers also made home visits to provide assistance with necessary minor repairs that added safety to the homes.

Section volunteers visited many community centers as well as individuals. One last conference, "Who Cares for the Caregiver," was held in November 2002 to bring awareness of the special problems and needs of caregivers to the professional community. After ten years, the Section turned over the program to Jewish Family Service for its continued operation.

Advocating for Vulnerable Consumers

Essay by Sylvia Lynn "Syl" Benenson
President, Greater Dallas Section 1978–1980

The Greater Dallas Section proved its ability to educate and advocate for Dallas's vulnerable consumers with its project Operation READY (Read, Educate, And Do-it-Yourself), which began in 1966. The success of Operation READY led to an invitation in the mid-1970s to expand further into the community through the new Consumer Alliance.

This Alliance was created as a cooperative effort of the Section along with Dallas Legal Services, the Consumer Affairs Department of the City of Dallas, and ten participating neighborhood groups of varying backgrounds. Section members Myra Fischel and Sharon Leviton chaired this project. They attended a class conducted by Dallas Legal Services for most of summer 1974 and began work in 1975.

The project was designed to research the greatest consumer needs of low-income families and to participate in an ongoing consumer education program.

The Section assumed a financial obligation of $7,000 and supplied volunteers to update and print new Operation READY pamphlets and to work with clients of Dallas Legal Services who had consumer problems.

Riki Rothschild (now Riki Zide) and Bill Stoner, paraprofessionals from Dallas Legal Services, were responsible for the education of all Alliance volunteers. Their mission: "We want to teach the consumer how not to be ripped off, and we want to teach them what recourse they have if they are."

More than thirty-five volunteers were trained to counsel on consumer rights, such as how to sue in small claims court and how properly to complete a contract. Part of the training included client screening. Volunteers would first ascertain the extent of help required. If a problem did not require professional legal help, trained volunteers could assist and lighten the load of the attorneys.

A survey of residents in the West Dallas target area was conducted. From these results, Section volunteers studied shopping patterns of the community and developed educational programs.

Volunteers stayed busy—speaking publicly about consumers' rights and publishing the booklet "How to Buy a Car" in both English and Spanish.

Members distributed "No Solicitors" signs

(Left) Eckerd's pharmacist (right) reviews medications for a client at the Martin Luther King Jr. Senior Center for the Safeguards for Seniors project, 1992.

(Right) A volunteer pharmacist from Eckerd Pharmacy (left) reviews medication of a resident of Golden Acres as part of the Section's Safeguard for Seniors, c. 2000.

(Left) Norma Schlinger (right) visits with a senior from the Lively Center in Irving as part of the Section's Safeguards for Seniors project, 1995.

(Right) Section members Gail Gilbert and Anita Marcus (left to right) explain the Safeguards for Seniors program to an interested health fair attendee, c. mid-1990s.

(Left) Section member Janet Newberger (right) visits with a senior resident at Cedar Crest Senior Center, 2000.

(Right) Engaging Section volunteers Jill Stone (front right) and Barbara Rabin (back right) check medications of older adults as part of the Safeguards for Seniors project, 1993.

(Left) Peggy Trubitt (right), Section volunteer, works with an older adult at Garland's Caruth Center as part of the Safeguards for Seniors project, c. mid-1990s.

(Right) Section member Nita Mae Tannebaum (right) presents information to an older adult attending a Senior Fair at Southfork as part of the Safeguards for Seniors program, c. mid-1990s.

Section members Syl Benenson (left) and Joy Mankoff (right) confer with Bill Stoner of Dallas Legal Services about materials for the Consumer Alliance, 1974. Photo by John Young. (Cobler, "Consumer Alliance Guards Right To Get What's Paid For.")

Staff Photos by John Young

Mrs. Murray Benenson and Mrs. Ronald Mancoff, NCJW vice-presidents, consult with Legal Services representative Bill Stoner. NCJW will be supplying printed materials such as the No Solicitors signs.

Consumer Alliance comparison shoppers check out prices in West Dallas. (Left to right) Yolanda Guerra, East Dallas Design Committee; Sharon Leviton, Section member; and Riki Rothschild (now Riki Zide), Dallas Legal Services, 1974. Photo by John Young. (Cobler, "Consumer Alliance Guards Right to Get What's Paid For.")

to residents who wanted to avoid falling victim to door-to-door salespeople and scams. The project also offered education on supplemental nutrition benefits (previously known as Food Stamps), tenants' rights, budgeting, and buying insurance. Soon, the Bethlehem Center and the Dallas County Community College District joined the education program.

A second phase of the West Dallas project involved comparison shopping in adjacent shopping centers to see if price and quality were consistent with those in other areas of town. West Dallas residents volunteered to do the shopping in their centers. Section volunteers shopped in a North Dallas center. A concluding step was to prepare a list of stores where consumers could find good items reasonably priced.

Residents of East Dallas also asked for a similar consumer program, with an added emphasis on buying used cars (there were many used car dealers in this area). Sharlene Block and I dressed very casually and visited a Ross Avenue car lot, armed with research. The dealership quoted a price for a specific car on the lot. Two weeks later, we dressed more formally and returned to the same site and were quoted a considerably lower price for the same car. We gave the documented results of our comparison shopping to the City of Dallas's Department of Consumer Affairs. This provided enough information to help close the lot, which already had a shady reputation.

The second year of this multi-faceted consumer education project widened the reach of the successful work with Consumer Alliance. This included working with the public schools. In 1975, the Section, in conjunction with the City of Dallas's Department of Consumer Affairs and Dallas Legal Services, piloted a consumer education information program for secondary schools in the DISD. The curriculum was designed as a full unit to be taught through civics or economics classes in six pilot high schools: South Oak Cliff, Skyline, Lincoln, W.T. White, W.W. Samuel, and Metropolitan.

The curriculum, called "Survival Course," provided practical information and projects for high school seniors so that they could better cope in society once they left the shelter of their school and/or home. Subjects included employment, housing, nutrition, advertising falsehoods, misuse of credit, health care and services, how to buy a new or used car, and understanding societal structures.

The Consumer Alliance and Education Project continued until 1981, empowering citizens all over Dallas to make informed decisions in a dynamic marketplace.

Educating Nonprofit Leadership
Essay by Betty Dreyfus
President, Greater Dallas Section 1976–1978

The Community Board Institute (CBI) provided affordable, high-quality training for the nonprofit sector of the Dallas area for over three decades.

This educational program, inspired by the NCJW section in Atlanta, Georgia, was designed to engage volunteers and build their capacity for board service and leadership within the extensive nonprofit community. CBI was initiated in 1976 during my term as president of the Greater Dallas Section. United Way of Metropolitan Dallas and the Community Council of Greater Dallas (CCGD) were cosponsors of the first program, which was held in April 1977. The forum quickly became an annual event for the Section. Over the years, Junior League of Dallas, the Volunteer Center of Dallas, United Way, Communities Foundation of Texas, CCGD, the Center for Nonprofit Management, and JCPenney Co. joined in as cosponsors for at least one year.

CBI featured prominent keynote speakers and highly qualified workshop presenters who donated their time and skills to lead workshops for nonprofit community organizations. Registration fees were kept at an affordable price. Many of Dallas's leaders were featured speakers, including Louis J. Weber Jr., Chairman, Goals for Dallas (1977); City of Dallas Mayor Jack Evans (1982); Nancy Brinker, founder of the Susan G. Komen organization (1995); Nina Vaca, founder and CEO of Pinnacle Technical Resources, Inc. and chair of the Greater Dallas Hispanic Chamber of Commerce (2004); and Gloria Campos, WFAA/Channel 8 news anchor (2007). In honor of the twentieth anniversary of CBI in 1996, City of Dallas Mayor Ron Kirk delivered the keynote address, and longtime WFAA/Channel 8 news anchor Tracy Rowlett was the closing speaker. At CBI 2008, Craig Watkins, Dallas County District Attorney, plus

2004

2008

Examples of the invitations for CBI.

1978

1977

English version of the Section's consumer book on buying an auto, 1975.

71

Oscar Joyner and Thomas Joyner Jr. of the Tom Joyner Foundation were the highlighted speakers. Panels and discussions covered current issues and were designed for new and experienced board members, volunteers, and agency personnel.

In light of economic challenges in 2009, a decision was made to postpone the next CBI program. It was felt that agencies were unable to employ as many people as they previously had and therefore couldn't spare personnel to miss a day of work for training. At the time, it was thought the program would be offered again in 2010, but the economic crisis continued. The program in 2008 turned out to be the final CBI event. During its thirty-two-year life, CBI offered valuable training and networking for thousands of community leaders and their nonprofit organizations.

As cochair of the 2003 event, Section member Sheryl Fields Bogen recalls, "I have such positive memories of working on CBI. It was a great opportunity for the bright and talented women of the Section to team with our counterparts in Junior League. We learned from one another as we organized the day and planned the breakout workshops. . . . This was truly a community-wide event, attracting people not only from the Section and Junior League but also from many nonprofit agencies and foundations. I always learned something new from attending."

Celebrating Shabbat
Essay by Janice Sweet Weinberg
President, Greater Dallas Section 1982–1984

In 1976, at the request of President Bette Miller, Section members compiled a creative Shabbat service booklet that was filled with art, poetry, and prayer. The Section used this publication to lead Shabbat services at Congregation Shearith Israel, Temple Shalom, and Golden Acres.

Section members and their children participated in these services with fervor and joy. My daughters played flute and guitar as they marched down the aisle, singing and ushering in the Kabbalat Shabbat. And, as we lit the candles and blessed the wine and the challah, all of us felt enveloped by the blessings of the Shabbat Queen.

Advocating for Children in Foster Care
Essay by Brenda Brand
President, Greater Dallas Section 1986–1988

Today's essential and well-respected CASA (Court Appointed Special Advocates) program began in 1979 as FOCAS (Foster Child Advocate Services), when the Section received one of three significant grants from National to pilot a program in which trained volunteers would become advocates for children in foster care. While the other Sections called their programs CASA, we initially chose FOCAS to avoid confusion with the name of a local YMCA program, Casa de Los Amigos, for runaway teens.

FOCAS started under the volunteer leadership of Section members Rose Marion Berg and Syl Benenson, with Marjorie MacAdams serving as staff. About thirty Section volunteers were trained by professionals from Dallas County Child Welfare, family court judges, and Guardians Ad Litem (attorneys appointed by the court to represent the child).

In just a year and a half, volunteers were handling more than one hundred cases. The Section had gained the confidence and respect of the courts, social services, clients, and the community. Testimony from "volunteers" at routine court hearings was deemed vital to the best interests and placement of children who were victims of abuse and neglect.

During the fiscal year 1982–1983, with more than fifty trained volunteers, FOCAS

Section members participated in Council Sabbath services, c. 1970s.

Section members Barbara Rose, Robin Zweig, and Celia Schoenbrun (left to right) at CBI 2004.

began generating its own financial support and recruiting volunteers from the broad community. A successful fundraising event, "April in Paris," brought attention and dollars from many donors. An advisory group of community leaders and professionals was formed, a board of directors was established, and bylaws were written. At the end of the first three years of service, more than 270 cases had been assigned and successfully completed, 530 children's lives had received a positive impact, and 1,200 court hearings had taken place.

In its fourth year, FOCAS became an independent, not-for-profit organization. Marjorie, who continued as executive director, was elected president of the National Court Appointed Special Advocates. At the same time, the National Council of Juvenile and Family Court Judges received a $3.3 million federal grant, which enabled state teams of professional advisers to establish CASA programs in all fifty states. FOCAS, as a beneficiary of this grant, hired a full-time supervisor to assist with the increasing number of cases assigned by the courts.

With a well-established program that had become an integral part of the protection of foster children who were victims of abuse and neglect, the Section turned FOCAS and its assets over to the newly named CASA in 1987.

As the Section's president and liaison to the FOCAS project, I took great pride in having initiated and demonstrated the need for this critical program that now has more than nine hundred volunteers and serves over 1,200 children each year. CASA is recognized as a huge success in Dallas and in other cities that have these services.

Establishing the First Endowment Fund
Essay by Joy Mankoff
President, Greater Dallas Section 1984–1986

Early in 1982, leadership began to explore the possibility of creating a fund to benefit the Section, the Jewish community, and Dallas at large. The result was SHARE (Service, Help, Advocacy, Research, and Education), the Section's first endowment fund. It was to be managed by a committee.

A December 3, 1982, letter from Section president Janice Sweet (later Janice Weinberg) formally announced the endowment:

Dear Member,

The Greater Dallas Section is pleased to announce the creation of a new general fund to be called SHARE: Service, Help, Advocacy, Research, and Education. Unlike our other funds which are directed toward specific concerns such as milk, scholarships, research, etc., the new fund will serve the dual broad categories of social service and public affairs, which represent the essence of NCJW. This fund will enable us to dream a little more and to complete services or projects not covered in our annual budget.

SHARE will be a permanent fund, an endowment fund. We shall expend only the income from the fund and keep the principal intact. Our gifts to SHARE, therefore, will be gifts of permanence. We shall, of course, seek large gifts and bequests to build on, but we shall also encourage, welcome, and acknowledge all contributions, with a minimum of ten dollars. Our gifts will remain here in Dallas, working for us and for our community.

Founding contributors, whose generosity has been evidenced by a gift of five thousand dollars or more, will be recognized. If desired, arrangements may be made to fulfill the obligation over a period of five years.

Carol Wadel, Barbara Rose, and Brenda Brand have agreed to put SHARE on a sound footing.

My personal gratitude goes to those loyal members who made their commitments to the Section's future.

The *Dallas Downtown News* characterized Marjorie MacAdams as a "tough cookie who has learned not to crumble," 1984. Photo by Bill Canada. (Tucker, "FOCAS Executive Director is a Tough Cookie Who's Learned Not to Crumble: Marjorie MacAdams.")

Founding and Sustaining Contributors of SHARE

Founding Contributors
(before December 31, 1984)

Phyllis and Richard Bernstein
Brenda and Stuart★ Brand
Jeanne★ and Sanford★ Fagadau
Dorace★ and Morton★ Fichtenbaum
Ann and Lorch★ Folz
Emme Sue★ and Jerome★ Frank
Belle C. Greene, in memoriam
Elsa Hirsh★
Dorothy★ and Henry★ Jacobus
Ann★ and Edwin★ Jolesch
Fannie★ and Stephen★ Kahn
Joy and Ron Mankoff
Betty Marcus, in memoriam
Bette and Bennett★ Miller
Janet★ and Morris★ Newberger
Lorraine★ and Sidney★ Schein
Carol★ and Louis Wadel
Marie Wolens★
A devoted member and husband
A Friend

Sustaining Contributors
(after January 1, 1985)
Friends and Family of Brenda Brand
Marjorie Kahn★
Doris★ and Joseph Metz
Marlene Meyerson★
Miriam Sternberg★

★Deceased

(Above right) Section members Sylvia Epstein (left) and Sharan Goldstein review training for docents at the Dallas Central Library as it transitions from cards to computers, 1982.

Creating a Library Docent Program
Essay by Sharan Goldstein
Greater Dallas Section Member

As the City of Dallas planned its state-of-the-art downtown public library in April 1982, library staff members anticipated its grand opening and the number of people who would need help navigating the new system. The staff recognized the need for a docent program. The Section was asked to take on this task.

Because the library's mission is to serve the entire community, there was a great effort to reach out to groups all over Dallas for the new Library Volunteer Corps. Under my leadership, instructional materials were written to help explain the collections in the eight-story library on Young Street. More than four hundred volunteers were trained to be docents.

For three years, Section and community volunteers led hundreds of groups of school children and adults through the entire building, familiarizing them with the library's collected treasures and special exhibits.

Computers were new to almost everyone then. Because there would be no more card catalogs, library technical staff members taught us how to use the computers. As docents, we, in turn, taught the public how to find books and materials instead of using that beloved old system.

Safeguards for Seniors

"SAFETY IN THE HOME"

This handy booklet was the product of the Section's collaborative work with more than two dozen agencies as part of the second phase of the Safeguards for Seniors project, 2000.

Cochair Sara Waldman and volunteer Elaine Marks (left to right) enjoy time with clients as part of the Aids in Medical Screening project for vision and hearing difficulties (AIMS), a collaboration with the Texas Department of

Safeguards for Seniors logo, 1992.

Long-term care was one of many issues addressed by the Section and various social agencies, 1980. (*Bulletin*, October 1980.)

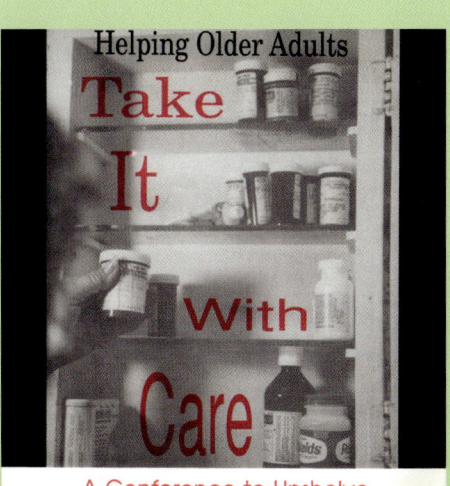

"Helping Older Adults Take It With Care," presented by the Section's Safeguards for Seniors program and nineteen other area agencies that served seniors, featured Walter M. Bortz II MD, geriatrician and host of the WFAA-TV series "Dare to Be 100," 1992.

Sally Ride, America's first woman astronaut, communicates with ground controllers during the six-day mission of the Challenger, 1983. (National Archives and Records Administration, loc. 541940.)

Khmer Outreach; DISD Teen Pregnancy Program volunteers	Alzheimer conference; Juvenile Court Mediation	"L'Chaim" program on teen substance abuse	DISD "Hello Israel" Project	First Section gala; Vogel Alcove Coalition; "Children As Witnesses"
1983	1984	1985	1986	1987

"Let your neighbor's dignity be
precious to you as your own."
Rabbi Eliezer (c. 40–120 CE)
Pirkei Avot 2:10

The Eighth Decade : 1983 *to* 1992

In 1984, scientists made a scientific breakthrough and discovered that the human immunodeficiency virus (HIV) caused AIDS. The first Martin Luther King Jr. Day was observed in 1986. Later that year, the country watched as the space shuttle Challenger exploded, killing the seven astronauts aboard. President Ronald Reagan, who asked Mikhail Gorbachev, leader of the Soviet Union, to "tear down this wall!" won a second presidential term. The Berlin Wall actually fell in 1989. Two years later, the Soviet Union dissolved, and the Cold War seemed to be over.

George H. W. Bush moved into the White House in 1989. Douglas Wilder, the nation's first black governor, took office in Virginia in 1990, and the Americans with Disabilities Act became a law later that year. Hurricane Andrew decimated the Gulf Coast in 1992.

1988	1989	1990	1991	1992
HIPPY in DISD launched	Coalition for Reproductive Freedom; Meyerson Docents	Parkland Infant Hearing Screening	Last Southern District Convention; "Preventing Teen Pregnancy" pilot	Safeguards for Seniors began

TREND SETTER

Woman is honored for NCJW work

The Greater Dallas section of the National Council of Jewish Women celebrated its 67th birthday with a luncheon at Brookhaven Country Club this week. Section President Syl Benenson presented the council's Hannah G. Solomon Award to Edna Cohen, past president of the organization and longtime financial administrator of its fund-raising event, the semi-annual Encore Sale.

The award, which is named after the founder of the National Council of Jewish Women, was given to Mrs. Cohen for her work as treasurer and bookkeeper of the Encore Sale and for her role in operating the council's now-defunct Thrift Shop. One of her friends recalled that the first sale in 1959 earned $650. Last year, the two sales brought in $90,000.

Mrs. Cohen, who has lived in Dallas since 1943, has been a member of the greater Dallas section for 37 years. Mrs. Benenson referred to her as "the spinal column that has kept us erect."

Sidney Stahl, a new member of the Dallas City Council, was the guest speaker at the luncheon. He began his remarks by saying that "there is no group in the city of Dallas, male or female, that I hold in higher esteem than the council."

Stahl cited transportation and the development of the central city as the major problems facing Dallas in the 1980s. "Once we were concerned about getting a man on the moon," he said. "Soon we will be concerned with getting a man downtown." He also expressed hope that development would be redirected to the southern half of the city rather than to the Oklahoma border.

— ERIKA SANCHEZ

Dallas City Council member Sidney Stahl, the keynote speaker at the Section's sixty-seventh birthday luncheon, said, "There is no group in the city of Dallas, male or female, that I hold in greater esteem than the Council." (Left to right): Edna Cohen received the Hannah G. Solomon award from President Syl Benenson at that luncheon, 1980. (Sanchez, "Woman is Honored for NCJW Work.")

(Right) The Section's *Bulletin* announced an upcoming program, The Innocent Victims: Sexual Child Abuse, 1987. (*Bulletin*, November/December 1987.)

The national spotlight was on Dallas in 1984, when the city hosted the Republican National Convention. It was the same year that the Dallas Museum of Art moved out of Fair Park, the site of the annual Texas State Fair, and into what became the Dallas Arts District. In 1986, Fair Park was declared a National Historic Landmark. Five years later, in Fair Park's Art Deco Hall of State, Queen Elizabeth and Prince Phillip came to dinner. In 1987, Section member Annette Strauss became Dallas's first elected female and Jewish mayor. The City of Dallas celebrated the 150th Jubilee year of its founding in 1991.

YEAR AFTER YEAR, AS THE WORLD AND CITY CHANGED, SO DID THE PRIORITIES OF the Greater Dallas Section. What has never varied, though, is the commitment from Section members to treat neighbors with dignity.

The Section continued to focus on immigrants, children and youth, women's issues, aging, Jewish concerns, and Israel—priorities highlighted by National a decade before. And often, the local community sought out assistance from the Section, because the organization had long ago established a reputation for offering solutions with dignity and compassion.

Immigrants

Acknowledging their immigrant roots, members hosted a fundraiser featuring the screen premiere of the 1983 film *West of Hester Street*, a Texas-produced film by Section member Cynthia Salzman Mondell and her husband, Allen Mondell. The film documented the arrival of a wave of Jewish refugees, who immigrated to the United States in the late 1800s through the port of Galveston, Texas. Actor Sam Jaffe, who narrated the film, was in attendance at the premiere.

During the 1980s, multiple generations of Cambodians, Laotians, and Vietnamese resettled in the East Dallas area. With renewed awareness of immigrant needs, the Section established the Khmer refugee project. This nearly full-service effort included hiring a Khmer-speaking caseworker/translator to help with Americanization, producing a newsletter in that language, tutoring both children and adults, working through legal issues, forming a job bank, and starting a community garden to grow fresh produce for the newcomers. From 1990 through 1996, Section volunteers tutored and mentored Amerasian and Vietnamese children, in coordination with the Vietnamese Mutual Assistance Association, and supported the Vietnamese Activity Center.

The Minnie Hexter Milk Fund now provided milk for the newest Americans as well as for others. Requests from the downtown Family Shelter for the Homeless helped about three hundred families and 547 children. These efforts earned the Section the ARCO Volunteer Center Award.

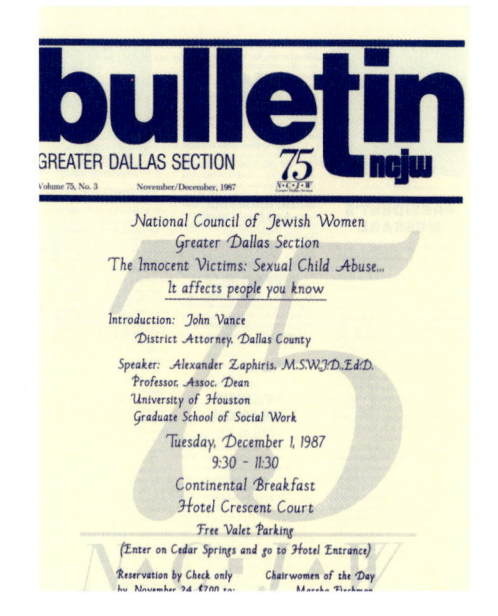

Children and Youth

In 1983, the Section, along with the Dallas Association of Young Lawyers and the Dallas County Juvenile Department, began addressing the needs of a specific group of children and youth through the Juvenile Court Mediation Project. The program allowed some young people to make constructive restitution for their misdeeds rather than having to enter the criminal justice system. Later in this decade, the program joined forces with the Section's Communities in Schools project, allowing mediation to be scheduled during and after school hours.

In 1985, the Section invited Tipper Gore, who

founded the Parents' Music Resource Center, to keynote a program. She spoke about the influence on children of sex, violence, and drugs portrayed in music videos and on album covers, offering perspective to the ongoing question of morality versus freedom of speech.

Later that year, the Section convened a community-wide program, *L'Chaim,* to address substance abuse among the young in the Jewish community. *L'Chaim* became a coalition of concerned parents and youth-serving professionals that formed a support group for parents and provided training for professionals in the Jewish community. A surprising six hundred young people and their families came together the next year for a second program on substance and alcohol abuse in this community. The large attendance showed the strong need for information on a subject barely discussed in prior years but now publicly identified as a growing concern.

The Section also worked with the Health Special High School, a DISD school for pregnant teens. Volunteers provided tutoring and mentoring to keep the girls in school and to encourage prevention of repeat pregnancies. In 1987, the volunteer services expanded by offering an infant care nursery for the students' children.

Through National's NCJW Center for the Child, Dallas became one of eleven research cities in a national project, Children as Witnesses in Child Sexual Abuse Cases, to help youths who had to appear as trial witnesses. The Section trained fifty volunteers in courtroom observation and monitoring. This program later became the Section's Kids in Court program.

The Section, as a member of the Dallas Jewish Coalition for the Homeless, helped found and supported the Vogel Alcove, which provides day care for homeless children. Members volunteered at the site, and scholarships were provided for children to attend summer camp. The Minnie Hexter Milk Fund provided milk and infant formula.

In 1988, past president Syl Benenson, after years of perseverance, successfully convinced the DISD to adopt the Home Instruction for Parents of Preschool Youngsters (HIPPY) program. This project prepares children ages three to five for school entry by fostering parental involvement in their sons' and daughters' early, at-home education. By 1998, the program was being offered not only in the DISD but also in the Richardson ISD. The Irving ISD adopted the program in 1999. More than a quarter-century later, this program still makes a vital academic difference for families in a variety of low-income communities.

Section members began volunteering with the Infant Hearing Screening Program at Parkland Hospital in 1990, and equipment necessary for early screening was provided. Tests were performed on three hundred premature babies during the first year of the project. More than 17,000 babies were evaluated during the program, which was taken over by hospital staff when State regulations no longer allowed volunteers to perform the testing.

Women's Issues

In 1989, the Section convened a meeting of community groups concerned about women's eroding reproductive health care rights. The meeting led to the formation of the Greater Dallas Coalition for Reproductive Freedom, cochaired by past president Joy Mankoff, representing the Section, and future Section president Julie Lowenberg, who represented the League of Women Voters of Dallas. The Section and this coalition worked as advocates, speaking out against

(Left) An article in the *Dallas Morning News* highlighted Section members Marilyn Segal and Paula Eilbott (left to right) for their work with the Children as Witnesses in Child Sexual Abuse Cases project; the article covered many of the Section's community service projects, 1987. (Miller, "A Tradition of Caring.")

The Section's Minnie Hexter Milk Fund has provided milk to appreciative youngsters at the Vogel Alcove since 1987.

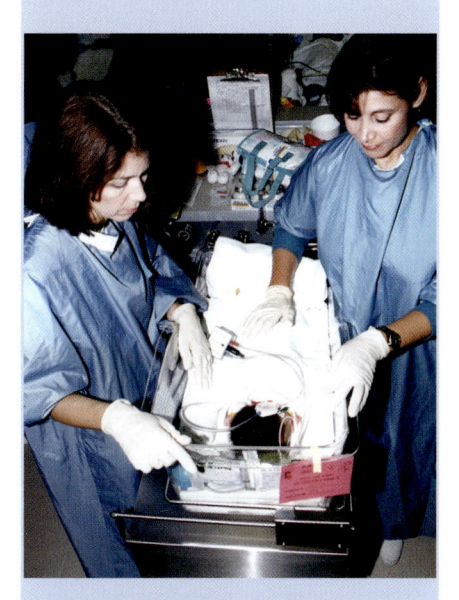

The caring volunteer hands of Section volunteers Zara Wettreich and Barbara DuBois (left to right) measure capabilities of newborn babies as part of the Section's Infant Hearing Screening Project at Parkland Hospital, 2003.

proposed state legislation that would restrict reproductive choice. Members attended marches held in both Austin and Washington, DC. In addition, with Jewish Family Service, the Section offered assistance to abused women, helping them find affordable housing and day care.

Aging

Turning its attention to the elderly, the Section convened the area's first conference on Alzheimer's Disease in late 1984. It led to the recruitment and training of a cadre of volunteers who helped families cope with this critical health issue. Section members also developed a speaker's bureau to educate the community on the increasing number and wide variety of dementia diseases. A second conference was held the following year to share community and caregiver concerns.

The Section's continuing interest in the elderly led the group to launch Safeguards for Seniors in 1992. It promoted the proper use of medication and safety in the home by providing helpful preventive information, education, and support. Presentations were conducted at senior centers throughout the city. Seniors were asked to bring their prescriptions and over-the-counter medications and supplements in brown paper bags, so registered pharmacists reviewed the contents. To facilitate the program's expansion, the Section funded a separate office and staff for this project. In 2002, Jewish Family Service brought this project under its umbrella of services.

Jewish Concerns and Israel

In 1986, Section members began taking the "Hello Israel" curriculum, an introduction to the land and its life, into sixth-grade classrooms at several Dallas public schools. The program helped fulfill National's mandate to concentrate on Jewish-Israel concerns.

The Section continued its Bible study group, and, in 1991, created a new course called "Our God and God of Our Mothers," facilitated by Rabbi Elisabeth (Liza) Stern, a rabbi at Temple Emanu-El, and Dr. Susannah Heschel, an assistant professor of religion at Southern Methodist University. Additional Israel-related projects, including Ship-A-Box, HIPPY, and NCJW's Research Institute for Innovation in Education (RIFIE) at Hebrew University, continued to have the Section's support.

The seventy-fifth year of the Section in 1988 was celebrated with a busy schedule of events and milestones. A special performance of *The Immigrant: A Hamilton County Album* on May 1, 1988, at the Plaza Theatre in Snider Plaza, included the distribution of an updated version of the fifty-year-old cookbook, *Cocktails to Coffee*. In addition, a special committee wrote and distributed a seventy-five-year history of the Section.

The Section stepped up to provide woman-power in 1988 as members took on what became a long-term, continuing project, serving as docents at the Meyerson Symphony Center. As a result of the success of the earlier Greater Dallas Section's Library Docent Program, the manager of the Symphony Center came to Section member Sharan Goldstein to implement its own symphony docent program. Volunteers from the Section and the community still conduct regularly scheduled public and special private tours of this beautiful downtown facility in the Dallas Arts District.

In addition to providing volunteers, the Section also financially supported the needs of other service organizations, including:

Pat Peiser, Section past president and director of Safeguards for Seniors, at the Harambee Fair at the Martin Luther King Jr. Senior Center, c. 1992.

Former Section president Joy Mankoff with members Gayle Johansen and Suzi Greenman (photo on left, left to right), president-elect Darrel Strelitz, along with past presidents Janet Newberger and Bette Miller (photo on right, left to right) are pictured at a seventy-fifth anniversary planning meeting, 1988. Photo by Randy Eli Grothe. (Goad, "Fete Set.")

The Section-designed docent training took place at the Meyerson Symphony Center while it was still under construction. The opening event highlighted the art world's positive reaction to the Dallas Symphony Center, 1989. Courtesy of the Morton H. Meyerson Symphony Center.

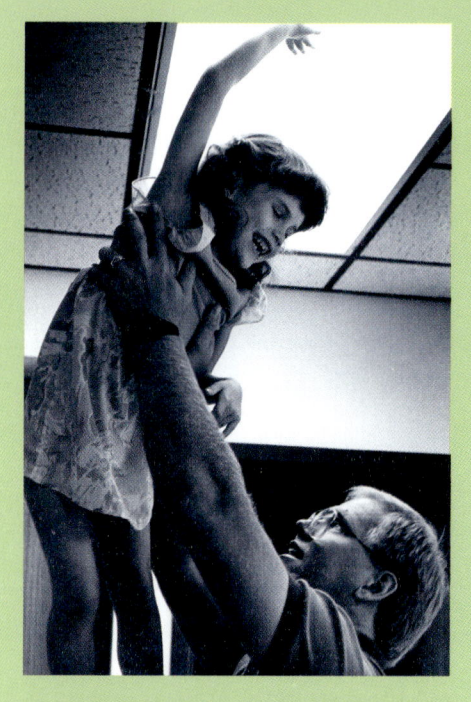

The Section provided summer camp scholarships to the Dallas Services for Visually Impaired Children, which gave "Sandra" hours of positive activities. Pictured: "Sandra" and her gymnastics teacher, 1987. Photo by Leon Unruh.

Section member and City of Dallas Mayor Annette Strauss was the Honorary Chair of the Section's Seventy-Fifth Anniversary Celebration performance of *The Immigrant*, 1988.

"Mr. Hamlisch requests the pleasure of your company" at the Section's Spring Benefit Concert, held at the Fairmont Hotel, 1987. (*Bulletin,* April 1987.)

A Section fundraising project, "Call Police" banners, provided many organizations with much-needed giveaways, among them the Dallas Board of Realtors, Diamond Shamrock, EDS, Interfirst Bank, Junior League of Dallas, Mary Kay Cosmetics, Presbyterian Hospital, Southwest Airlines, Zale Corporation, and the Dallas Cowboys, 1987.

The *Voice of Khmer* and the *Cambodian-Dallas Monthly* were two of the Section's efforts that engaged and acculturated Cambodian refugees to their new home in Dallas, c. 1980s. (*Voice of Khmer Dallas*, April 8, 1985. *Cambodian Dallas Monthly*, January 1987.)

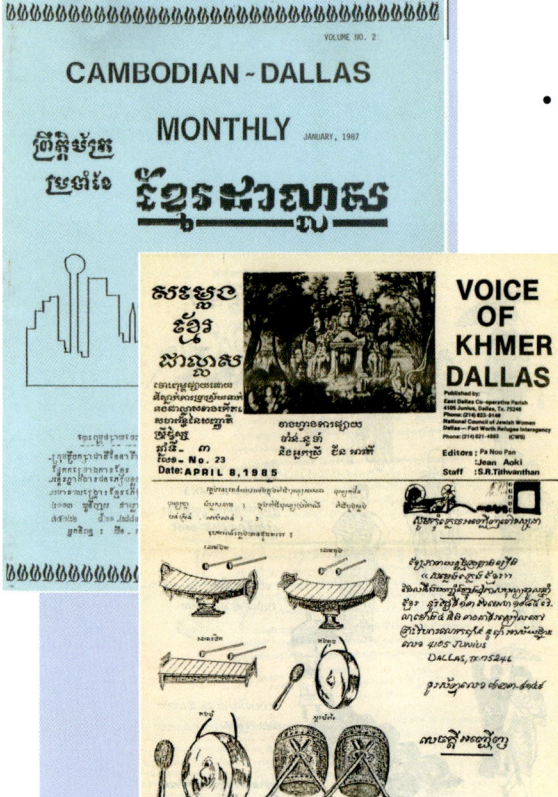

(Right) The Section sponsored the Khmer community garden for several years, c. 1988. ("E. Dallas Community Garden Grows Up," *Dallas Times Herald*.)

- **Children's Medical Center:** Apple computer and software to use as teaching aids
- **Dallas Jewish Historical Society:** audio recording equipment to use for oral histories of Dallas Jewish residents
- **Family Place:** support for a Hispanic Outreach Counselor
- **Dallas Independent School District:** volunteers and financial support for the Youth Leadership Program
- **Parkland Foundation:** medicine and lunch vouchers for the homeless
- **LIFT:** funding for classes at two Dallas Housing Authority sites
- **Dallas Services for Visually Impaired Children, Inc.:** special scholarship for a blind child to attend a summer camp.
- **Community Groups:** produced and distributed "Call Police" banners for drivers to put in their car windows when help was needed.

How was the money raised for all these contributions? The Section managed income from its Encore Sale, sought grants from various foundations, and launched large-scale fundraisers, which became the main sources of income. The Section brought Marvin Hamlisch to Dallas in 1987 for a musical show—a huge hit with members, their husbands, and the public. The tradition of stage performances continued through 2004.

By the end of its eighth decade, the Section began new research on how to meet additional community needs. Always keeping the dignity of others foremost in mind, the Section continued serving all age groups—from promoting Safeguards for Seniors to attempting to prevent teen pregnancy. Enthusiasm and more hard work helped lead members toward a more positive end of the twentieth century.

Serving the Refugees of Cambodia
Essay by Darrel Strelitz
President, Greater Dallas Section 1988–1990

Refugees started streaming into America in the late 1970s and early 1980s in the aftermath of inhumane excesses of the Khmer Rouge regime in Cambodia. They trekked long distances and escaped via boats or any way they could, with truly nothing but the clothes on their backs. The majority of the newcomers were illiterate because dictator Pol Pot had destroyed the intelligentsia on the "killing fields." Indeed, education in general in Cambodia was frowned upon.

The refugees had been forced to cope with extreme poverty and illiteracy at home. When they arrived in the United States they faced racism and hostility, as many of them were biracial, often Cambodian/African American, the result of the American presence there for many years. Many Americans were reluctant to get involved with the complicated challenges these families faced.

Catholic Charities settled large numbers of newcomers as they arrived from Southeast Asia, typically three generations in one tiny apartment, in very old sections of East Dallas. Only three months of their needs were covered.

In 1983, the Greater Dallas Section became

aware of these refugees and their harsh realities, a decision was made to help provide more promising futures for these families. The Section contacted the Dallas Police Department, as crime was an urgent issue, and supplied each family with a recommended door peephole so that the immigrants could have a means to ensure their security.

The Section asked a nursing school to provide basic health care, made sure that all newcomers were vaccinated, and started teaching the basics of illness prevention, though it was necessary to overcome the refugees' unease with American health practices. Limited communication was through the children, because the adults, both parents and grandparents, neither spoke nor understood English and were illiterate in Cambodian as well.

The Section worked with Parkland Hospital, but there were few translators, so we had health questionnaires translated into Khmer. The Section also managed to get a few Khmer typewriters and helped publish a small weekly newspaper in that language to disseminate important information and to help refugees develop a sense of community.

The longer the Section worked with this community, the more issues were identified. For instance, if a family had managed to find work and wanted to move into a slightly larger apartment, they would move without realizing that they were entitled to receive a refund of their initial rent deposits. Many Americans and others took advantage of the refugees' extreme poverty and inability to speak English. These newcomers had no understanding of what life was like in a sophisticated democracy; volunteer lawyers helped them work through the civic and legal systems, and gradually the immigrants started to cope with life here.

Section members noted that the new arrivals did not like American food and could not sustain a balanced diet. The solution: the Section worked with Kathy Dickey and James Falvo, who had some empty acreage on North Fitzhugh Avenue near Bryan Street in East Dallas. The two rented the property to us for a dollar a year. With guidance from the Texas A&M AgriLife Extension Program, we provided gardening implements, plants, seeds, and help with tilling the soil. Still, it became apparent that the refugees only wanted what they were used to eating, so the Section obtained special grasses and rice. The project took off, and many people busily gardened and harvested their native foods.

This entire project embodied the values of NCJW. The Section helped an isolated people become Americanized and helped them learn how to look after themselves. Knowing that we, too, were once strangers in a foreign land, we reached out to these people with their very complex needs as friends and helpers.

Working to Prevent Teen Pregnancies
Essay by Phyllis Bernstein
President, Greater Dallas Section 1992–1994

In the early 1980s, Texas and Dallas struggled with high teen pregnancy rates. Statistics showed that if a teenage girl had a baby at age fifteen or earlier, there was a fifty percent chance that she would become pregnant again before she was out of her teens. The Greater Dallas Section developed a volunteer component for the Teen Pregnancy Program at the DISD Health Special High School in 1983. The goals were to help reduce the number of second pregnancies among young teens and to try to motivate the girls to stay in school and complete their high school educations.

Section volunteers worked closely with the school's principal, counselor, life-skills teachers, and social workers, doing intake and exit interviews plus mentoring and tutoring. When necessary, volunteers consulted with the parents. During intake interviews, the girls were asked if they knew how they became pregnant. The younger ones, ages twelve and thirteen, and in some cases, even the fourteen-and fifteen-year-olds had no factual idea. They had believed and acted on many myths about their pregnancies.

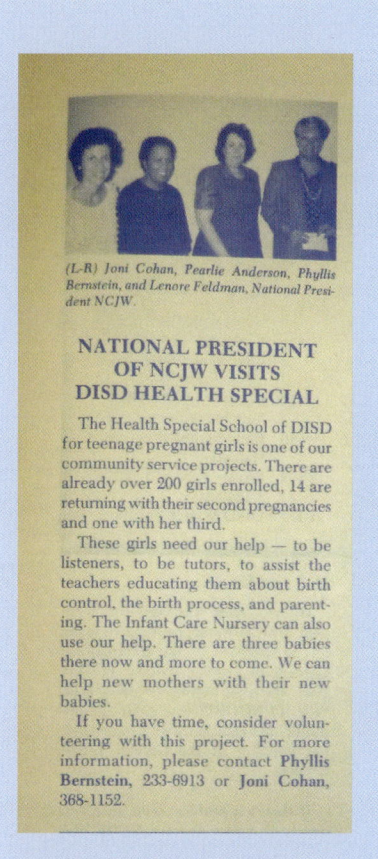

Section members Joni Cohan (left) and Phyllis Bernstein (third from left) join Health Special teacher Pearlie Anderson and National President Lenore Feldman (far right) on a visit to DISD's Health Special High School, 1985. ("National President of NCJW Visits DISD Health Special," *Bulletin.***)**

The Section's Khmer project aided Cambodian refugees in Dallas, 1984. Photo by Mark Graham. (Marshall, "Refugee Family Faces New Fears in a New World.")

(Left) Khmer Project Holiday Party, 1985.

(Right) Dallas County Assistant District Attorney Mark Thielman (center) addresses volunteers from the Section who will work with children who have to appear as trial witnesses, c. 1987.

(Left) Section members participate in a food collection in honor of the 150th anniversary of the City of Dallas. Phyllis Bernstein, Sharan Goldstein, unknown, employee of NTFB, Marcy Grossman, JoAnn Aronoff, Amy Goldstein (later Amy Roseman), Jacque Comroe, Beth Lasher, and Marjorie Cerf (left to right), 1991.

(Right) Section member Bette Miller (center) and Hannah Levin (right), director of National's Israel Programs, review some of the products received at the NCJW Ship-A-Box Mifal in Israel with site manager, 1988. Courtesy of Bette Miller.

(Left) Section member Sandy Nachman delivers "Meals on Wheels" to a homebound senior, 1991.

(Right) *SR Dallas Magazine* featured Section president-elect Darrel Strelitz and president Brenda Brand (left to right) as part of their coverage of community volunteers: "A Council of Caring," April 1988. Photo by Steve Krauss. (Bowles, *SR Dallas Magazine*.)

(Left) Section President Joni Cohan (left) and Section Executive Vice President Phyllis Bernstein (right) welcome City of Dallas Mayor Annette Strauss (center) prior to her receiving the Hannah G. Solomon Award, 1991.

(Right) The Section's volunteer historians Carol Sandfield and Helen Stern (left to right) worked diligently to organize the Section's records stored in the Dallas Jewish Historical Society's archives at the JCC, 1989.

(Left) Section members Marilyn Goldstein and Betty Lorch (left to right) assist HIPPY families with a creative experience at the Dallas Museum of Art, 1987.

(Right) HIPPY home instructors join Section members Syl Benenson (left) and Saralynn Busch (seated left) for a group photo after a training program, 1991.

(Left) HIPPY chair and past president Syl Benenson (second from right) along with HIPPY parents and children were honored at a DISD graduation celebration, 1997.

(Right) Section members Syl Benenson, Ellene Breinin, Sharlene Block, and Rita Sue Gold (left to right) pose for a picture with HIPPY children, c. 1990s.

(Left) Section members Bootsie Golden and Syl Benenson (left to right) join the fun on a HIPPY field trip to the Dallas Museum of Art, 2004.

(Right) Section President Sue Tilis congratulates a child and his family on completion of the Grand Prairie ISD HIPPY program, 2006.

(Left) Section volunteers Joanne Blum, Karen Stock, Connie Rudick, and Syl Benenson (standing, left to right), enjoying the lunch break at a HIPPY field trip to the Dallas Arboretum, 2014.

(Right) Section members Emme Sue Frank and Ruth Levi (left to right) prepare lunches for a HIPPY field trip during the program's early years, c. 1980s.

It was difficult to follow each girl through her time at the school. Many had not been in school at all for a year or two and came in order to be eligible for social service benefits. Often, they were absent for many days. The girls were allowed to stay only during the semesters of their pregnancies. After their babies had been born, the students were required to return to their home schools, so follow-up was difficult, if not impossible.

Many of the girls at the Health Special were not functioning at their academic grade level, and teachers were further challenged since there could be four different grade levels in one classroom at a time. The girls arrived and exited at different times during the semester, so the stability of the class was interrupted.

Section volunteers discussed how to hold a baby, change diapers, and choose whether to bottlefeed or breastfeed. Members also helped to find childcare when asked, but there were few affordable options available to these young girls.

As students shared their stories, volunteers learned of incest, rape, and abuse. The Section conducted a survey on the age of their babies' fathers. For the most part, men were at least three to six years older than the girls. These vulnerable youngsters did not want to press rape charges; they didn't even want to provide fathers' names to the Texas Attorney General's office, which would have helped them receive financial assistance.

Although the girls learned about birth control, many of the young students returned with a second pregnancy. We even saw one girl who, at age seventeen, was back with her fourth pregnancy. The teachers were dedicated and cared very much about their pupils. All school personnel tried very hard to help these challenged teens. The social workers attempted to start sex education classes for boys at various high schools, but these ideas were not well-received.

As a volunteer, I learned a great deal about a lifestyle to which I had never been exposed. I recall chaperoning a field trip to Parkland Hospital's labor and delivery rooms, which was an eye-opening experience for the girls—and for me as well! I realized that these girls would only rarely escape their cycle of poverty. Most came from impoverished single-parent homes, and their mothers had been teenage mothers themselves.

As DISD changed its policies on school-age pregnancies, the Section ended its involvement with this project in 1993. The lesson learned: to avoid teen pregnancy, preventive education has to be taught before teens become pregnant.

Mediating Juvenile Issues
Essay by Kathy Freeman
President, Greater Dallas Section 1988–1990

In the mid 1980s, the Dallas County Juvenile Department needed volunteers and funds to launch a Juvenile Mediation Project in an attempt to "divert certain juvenile cases from adjudication and incarceration." The Greater Dallas Section jumped in to provide the needed assistance.

In September 1984, Section member Claire Lee Epstein was named the chair of the newly created program. In the beginning, the Section provided eleven volunteers who received training from the Juvenile Department. This number would grow in coming years as needs increased within the county.

Juvenile mediation became my prime volunteer interest because I loved meeting with the offending, angry youth who were accepted into the program and with the victims who were sometimes angry as well. It was the job of the trained mediator to help both parties find common ground. Most often the accused juvenile wanted a quick way out of a bad situation. The victim typically wanted the youth to acknowledge how the perpetrator had wronged him or her. The goal was to give the offending youngster an appropriate assignment to right the wrong.

If anger was too strong between both parties and a dollar amount could be agreed upon, the

Section volunteer Ellene Breinin having fun with HIPPY families in the Children's Museum at the Perot Museum of Nature and Science during a HIPPY field trip, 2012.

Section volunteer Marilyn Boyd helps HIPPY children with an art project at the Dallas Museum of Art, 2012.

offender was sometimes asked to atone by doing chores for his family. The parent or guardian of the offender would then have to pay the proper sum to the victim. In this way, the youth learned to take responsibility for the wrongdoing, and the parent or guardian was included in the solution.

Over time, the Section's responsibilities grew, and we began scheduling the mediations. Later, we were invited into the Dallas public schools to conduct meetings on campus, during and after school hours.

Lending a Hand with Housing for Women in Crisis
Essay by Claire Lee Epstein, of Blessed Memory
Greater Dallas Section Member

Greater Dallas Section volunteers began working in 1986 with the Dallas Tenants' Association to help women in crisis find decent, affordable housing. I chaired the Section's project, Home Power for Women. To help break their cycle of poverty, volunteers planned and conducted seminars about finding employment, budgeting, and housing. We also provided assistance with counseling and record keeping.

Eventually, this nonprofit became the Housing Crisis Center (HCC), located in the Wilson Historic District, which was managed by the Meadows Foundation. When I arrived that first day after the name change, my volunteer duties had changed. I had no idea what I was to do, but was given a desk and a telephone and watched how others talked to those who called in. There was a lawyer on site who could guide us.

Dorothy Masterson was in charge. She was a volunteer who had launched the nonprofit HCC because she felt there was a need to help people with housing problems and evictions. Dorothy asked me to go to the Salvation Army twice a month to talk with the women there about the responsibilities of renting an apartment.

Dorothy has since retired, but the organization she started still goes on. I am glad to have been a part of this worthwhile project.

Taking Israel into the Classroom
Essay by Denise Bookatz
Greater Dallas Section Member

When Darrel Strelitz, as the Section's vice president of community services, attended an NCJW convention in 1985, she learned about a new project, "Hello Israel," that had been developed by an Ohio Section. The idea was simple: send a pair of volunteers into sixth-grade classrooms to present an enrichment program in conjunction with the regular school curriculum. The history, geography, culture, language, and politics of Israel and the Middle East would be taught in an entertaining, interactive manner. Most important, the program's content would be impartial, and presenters would not promote any political or religious positions.

Darrel Strelitz and Janice Sweet (later Janice Weinberg) attended NCJW training and then received permission from the DISD administration to institute the program in 1986. Volunteers contacted teachers in elementary schools to schedule "Hello Israel" in individual classrooms. Multiple schools participated.

The program continued with a succession of Section chairs through the years. Dorothy Roder led the program for almost fifteen years, bringing in new classroom volunteers and updating the presentation with new props, scripts, and videos. During Dorothy's leadership, the program expanded beyond the DISD to include some neighboring school districts.

The current program has evolved since its beginning more than twenty-five years ago. Volunteers present "Hello Israel" to almost one thousand students in twelve schools each year. New materials include products from the Dead Sea and books written in Hebrew. Presenters also show students the many technological advances and medical breakthroughs developed by Israel, a

The Section's "Hello Israel" cochairs Rosalind Black and Evelyn Bitterbaum (left to right) lead training for the "Hello Israel" program, 1987.

A student writes a letter of appreciation for a "Hello Israel" presentation, 2014.

(Left) Section member Evelyn Bitterbaum teaches the hora dance to DISD Preston Hollow Elementary School students during a "Hello Israel" presentation, 1990.

(Right) Section members Evelyn Bitterbaum and Evelyne Weinberg (left to right) present the "Hello Israel" program to students at DISD's Preston Hollow Elementary, 1990.

(Left) Cochairs Jo Reingold and Denise Bookatz with teacher Karlene Jolly (left to right) greet students before a "Hello Israel" class begins, 2011.

(Right) Section members Evelyn Bitterbaum and Liny Yollick present the "Hello Israel" program to a class at DISD's K. B. Polk Elementary School, 1987.

(Left) Section volunteer Ruth Stern (right) and a student demonstrate an item of interest in the "Hello Israel" class at Furneaux Elementary School in the Carrollton-Farmers Branch School District, c. 2000.

(Right) Section members Jeanine Chavenson (left) and Dorothy Roder (back) display items from the "Hello Israel" project with some eager sixth-grade students, c. 2000.

(Left) "Hello Israel" cochairs Greta Herskowitz and Denise Bookatz (left to right) point to the location of Israel on a wall map, 2009.

(Right) Section member Jo Reingold (right) with students during a "Hello Israel" presentation, 2011.

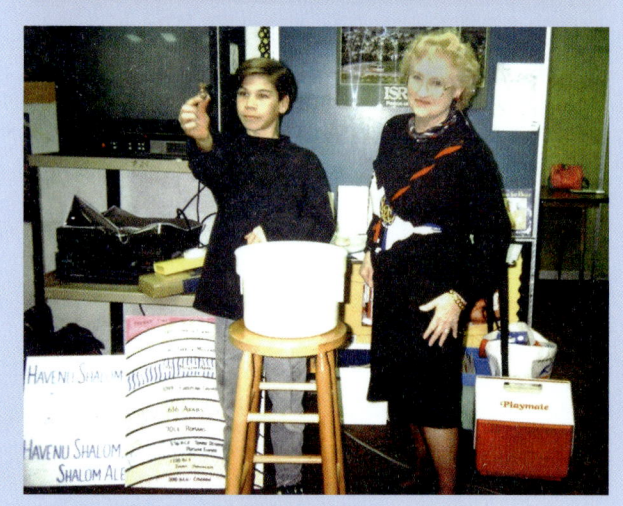

country whose land mass is only a third the size of the state of Texas.

Section members are truly goodwill ambassadors, giving young students a positive impression of both Israel and the Jewish people.

Strengthening Families with the Power of Education
Essay by Sylvia Lynn "Syl" Benenson
President, Greater Dallas Section 1978–1980

When you hear "HIPPY," you may think it refers to a radical free spirit from the 1960s, but the name has another meaning for the more than 20,000 families it has served in the greater Dallas area.

Home Instruction for Parents of Preschool Youngsters (HIPPY) is an evidence-based, international early childhood education program that teaches parents with limited income and minimal formal education (and in many instances limited English proficiency) to be the primary educators of their three- to five-year-old children. HIPPY was developed in 1969 at the NCJW Research Institute for Innovation in Education (RIFIE) at Hebrew University in Jerusalem. Today, HIPPY advances early childhood education worldwide. While the program instills the value of childhood education in the home, it also motivates parents to further their own education. This effort encourages adults to attain meaningful employment and improve their standard of living.

HIPPY is based on a community empowerment model. The program trains paid paraprofessionals (known as home instructors) to work with eligible families in their own communities, going into their homes weekly and teaching/role-playing learning activities with the parents. Then, parents spend twenty to thirty minutes a day teaching their children the curriculum, including school-readiness skills like recognizing shapes and colors, following directions, listening to and telling stories, and problem-solving. The opportunity to have a supervised job experience has enabled many of the home instructors to jump-start their careers. It is not unusual for children of home instructors to become instructors themselves; there are now examples of three generations working together in the HIPPY program.

I started this long journey with my friend, Section past president Bette Miller, to bring HIPPY to the Dallas area in 1979. After much perseverance, the DISD finally gave the green light for a Greater Dallas Section pilot program in 1988. Carla Weir (later Carla Mowell), who became the director of HIPPY Texas, was hired to implement this first effort. Since there was no training available in the United States, the Section funded Carla's expenses for training in Israel, where she not only learned about the operation but saw HIPPY in action with Israelis.

The initial HIPPY site in this area served seventeen immigrant families living in West Dallas. Based on the overwhelming success of this trial, HIPPY's acceptance grew quickly. By its sixth year, almost 1,200 families were enrolled, with the curriculum taught in English, Spanish, Vietnamese, and Khmer. There was also a Native American group. Building on the positive outcomes of the program in the DISD, the Section advocated expanding HIPPY to other school districts. Richardson ISD adopted the program in 1998; Irving ISD followed in 1999.

Each year, Texas HIPPY is evaluated by the University of North Texas Center for Parent Education. The results consistently indicate that more than 80 percent of the children who complete the HIPPY program are "ready for school," and more than 80 percent of the parents are more confident in their abilities to help their children learn.

The Section has played a significant role in HIPPY's growth and success by providing volunteers, funding, and advocacy. In the early years, the Section underwrote a large portion of staff salaries, training, and travel expenses to conferences. Currently, the Section funds bus transportation and provides chaperones for educational and cultural enrichment field trips. Area venues include the

Carla Mowell (previously Carla Weir) (standing on left), the original staff leader for HIPPY Dallas, conducted training sessions for project coordinators and local DISD personnel starting in 1988.

Past president and chair of the Section's HIPPY project, Syl Benenson, at a HIPPY graduation, c. 2000.

Section President Robin Zweig (right) having fun with HIPPY families in the Children's Museum at the Perot Museum of Nature and Science, 2012.

Dallas Museum of Art, the Perot Museum of Nature and Science, the Nasher Sculpture Center, and the Dallas Arboretum. The Section also underwrites incentives and refreshments for parent group meetings; backpacks for children who complete the program; funding for end-of-year celebrations; and college scholarships to deserving high school graduates who completed the HIPPY program when they were preschoolers.

The continuation of the Section's commitment to the local HIPPY programs follows clear evidence that this parent/child early educational program works. My name has become synonymous with the program (I am affectionately called Mother HIPPY) due to my ongoing passion for the parents, children, and communities who have grown and seen successes during their journeys with HIPPY and me.

Identifying Impaired Hearing in Infants
Essay by Frances "Sister" Steinberg
Greater Dallas Section Member

The relationship between the Greater Dallas Section and Parkland Hospital has been long and fruitful. The Infant Hearing Screening Project is one of the most successful examples.

In 1990, Section volunteers led by Phyllis Steinhart agreed to provide services and financial assistance for equipment and supplies to begin the initiative. The goal was to identify hearing difficulties in infants. The pilot program served babies in the continuing care nursery. As the program grew, government funding was added. Beginning in September 1999, Texas required hospitals to complete an audial screening on all babies before discharge, and Parkland, with the Section's assistance, expanded its program. These hearing tests became the standard of care for newborns in all of Parkland's nurseries.

Trained Section members were devoted to the project; most of them volunteered for at least fifteen years. They spent a minimum of three hours each week in Parkland nurseries. A bonus: we developed close relationships with one another as well as with Parkland nurse practitioners and audiologists.

The Section won the Volunteer Center of Dallas County's Twenty-Third Annual Outstanding Volunteer of the Year Award in 2003. During the project's duration, 17,121 babies were tested, and 473 newborns were identified with auditory impairment.

One day, when the chief of neonatology at Parkland was visiting with the volunteers, he told a story about a national meeting he had attended. He said that when asked how he was so successful with the screening project, he answered, "You get the Jewish women to do the job, and it gets done right!"

The project ended with the passage of new state licensing requirements for those doing the testing. At the conclusion of the program, Parkland staff members entertained volunteers with a beautiful tea at the Faculty Club of the University of Texas Southwestern Medical School. Also, the staff established a fund in honor of the Section to provide infant ear molds.

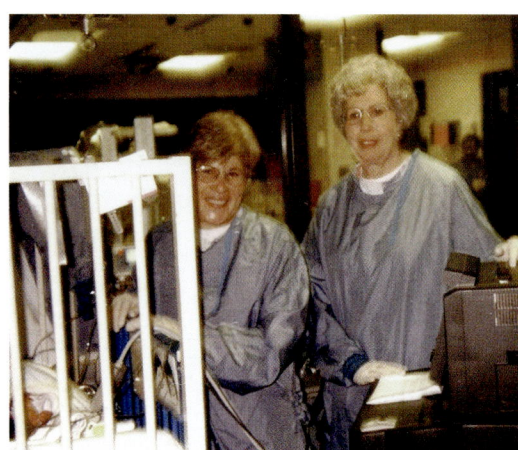

(Above) Section volunteer Bobbi Massman tests an infant's hearing at Parkland Hospital, c. 2000s.

(Above right) Section members Margaret Wilonsky and Betty Sue Sheinberg (left to right) prepare to test an infant's hearing, c. 2000s.

After twenty-two years, the Section's Infant Hearing Screening program was officially absorbed into the Parkland Hospital's routine process of testing newborns. Pictured at the concluding celebration are staff and Section volunteers. (Left to right): Parkland audiologist Kris Owen; a Parkland nurse; Rachel Emmet; Sister Steinberg; Phyllis Steinhart (first chair of the Screening program); Robert Smith, Parkland's interim president and chief executive officer; Bette Morchower; Karen Kurzman; Barbara DuBois (last chair); and Zara Wettreich, 2012.

Founding the Meyerson Docent Program
Essay by Sharan Goldstein
Greater Dallas Section Member

The Morton H. Meyerson Symphony Center, named for a Dallas arts patron and business partner of Ross Perot, opened in 1989. Perot provided $10 million for the construction of this early jewel in what has since become a major part of the City of Dallas Arts District. The concert hall was designed by renowned architect I.M. Pei and is home to the world-class Lay Family Concert Organ.

Anticipating a demand for tours of the new symphonic hall, the manager came to the Section to design and implement a volunteer docent program. Section member Miriam Jaffe created the training manual that is still in use. Barbara Rabin, Sondra Hollander, and I solicited not only the Section but also the entire community to send volunteers. In the year before the opening, we worked with symphony staff to set up a training program for guides who would lead both public and private tours. Of course, many Section members became docents. Sondra recalls her experience:

> What an honor it has been to showcase I. M. Pei's masterpiece building, the Meyerson Symphony Center, to the residents of Dallas and visitors from all over the world! It has been even more exciting to do this under the auspices of the NCJW Meyerson Docent Program. From the beginning of our training to the present time, the role of docent has been exhilarating and fulfilling, and the program has shown off the Section's ability in this field as well as the building itself.

During a special dinner celebrating the fifteenth year of the program, Melanie Armstrong, house manager and tour coordinator, said that Meyerson docents had given 3,043 tours to 162,000 people. In addition, Betty Switner, Director of the City of Dallas Cultural Affairs, said, "Volunteers such as NCJW members unlock the magic and wonder of this building every day, week, month, and year so people who would not know the story of the hall can appreciate the Meyerson and how it makes Dallas a richer place in which to live." (The *Turtle Creek News*, September 19, 2004.)

Since the Meyerson has been in the public eye for more than twenty-five years, there are fewer introductory visitors, but the Section is still involved, offering both public and private tours.

Creating a Piece of History
Essay by Judy Utay
President, Evening Branch 1970–1971

National celebrated its one hundredth birthday in 1993 with festivities in the United States and Israel. I was honored to have a small part in the celebration.

A commemorative quilt was created, with squares coming from sections and branches across the country. My square was chosen to represent Dallas and was included in the quilt. It depicts an image of a little boy with a syringe filled with blood to symbolize the testing for Tay-Sachs disease which began in 1973 by the Section and its Evening Branch.

I was unable to attend the one hundredth birthday convention held in Chicago to see the quilt. It eventually was placed on display at the Texas Capitol Building in Austin, where my husband and I finally were able to view it.

(Left) Section volunteers and Symphony staff gathered to celebrate the fifteenth anniversary of the Meyerson and the docent program. Front Row (left to right): Myra Fischel, Pat Peiser, Sharan Goldstein, Margaret Wilonsky, Dot Heller, and Syl Benenson. Middle Row: Sondra Hollander, Barbara Silberberg, Barbara Bubis, Shirley Christensen, Josephine (Jo) Herz, and Barbara Rabin. Back Row: Murray Benenson and Meyerson staff, 2004.

The *Turtle Creek News* recognized the fifteenth anniversary of the Section's docent program at the Meyerson Symphony Center, 2004. ("National Council of Jewish Women Honored," The *Turtle Creek News*.)

Judy Utay pointing to the square she created for the NCJW Centennial quilt, 1985. Courtesy of Judy Utay.

91

Mourning the loss of murdered Americans, expressed with flags at half-staff in the nation's Capital. Photo by Mark Wilson. (Getty Images.)

1993	1994	1995	1996	1997
Guardianship Program; "National Day of the Working Parent"	Kids in Court	After-school tutoring; First Women's Seder	Peace in the Middle East" essay contest; First male president of Professional Branch	"Literacy: Can Dallas Read the Future?" conference

"The only thing that is going to save mankind is if enough people live their lives for something or someone other than themselves."

Leon Uris (1924–2003), American author of Exodus

The Ninth Decade: 1993 *to* 2002

The United States was forced to address terrorism and mass murder when the first World Trade Center bombing in 1993 killed six and injured more than one thousand people. President Bill Clinton led the nation during a long period of peacetime economic expansion. The historic North American Free Trade Agreement passed. In 1993, the military adopted the "Don't Ask, Don't Tell" policy for gay and lesbian members of the military. In 1995, a domestic terrorist killed 168 people in the Oklahoma City bombing, and a year later Centennial Olympic Park in Atlanta was attacked. In 1999, two teens massacred students at Columbine High School in Colorado.

1998	1999	2000	2001	2002
Vickery Meadow Learning Center; Richardson HIPPY	*Anti private school voucher forum; Irving HIPPY*	*Last Encore Sale*	*Hannah's Advocacy Group*	*Operation Frontline minivan; Professional Branch ended*

The defining moment of this decade came early in President George W. Bush's first term when, on September 11, 2001, terrorists attacked the World Trade Center and the Pentagon and crashed another plane in Pennsylvania. Life all over the United States became marked by events before and after 9/11. Shortly after that, the United States invaded Afghanistan, starting Operation Enduring Freedom.

In Waco, the drama of the Branch Davidians Compound's fifty-one-day standoff with the US Bureau of Alcohol, Tobacco, and Firearms (ATF) ended with a fire that killed seventy-two men, women, and children. Dallas welcomed its first light rail system, DART (Dallas Area Rapid Transit), and the African American Museum opened in Fair Park. The Dallas Cowboys football team won the Super Bowl in 1993, 1994, and 1996, bringing a total of five wins to the team.

DURING THE NINTH DECADE OF THE GREATER DALLAS SECTION, AS THE TWENTIETH CENTURY was coming to an end, the Section continued to adapt to the needs of the time, and its members looked beyond themselves to study, plan, and work on behalf of their community.

Projects and Joint Ventures

In 1993, NCJW, Inc. and Marriott, Inc. cosponsored the "Day of the Working Parent." The model program called attention to critical issues facing families, which included the lack of high-quality child and elder care. More than two hundred people attended the Section's conference, "Juggling Jobs and Family: Making it Work at Work." The Dallas/Fort Worth Marriott Interdivisional Business Council was a major sponsor. The event, aimed at employers, discussed care issues and the Family and Medical Leave Act. Promotional "Food for Thought" cardboard lunch boxes, which included resource information, were delivered by Section members to area businesses and participants.

The Section also developed a guardianship program in 1993 to provide court-appointed guardians for older adults unable to make significant personal decisions. Jewish Family Service oversaw and adopted the program.

At the same time, the Dallas County District Attorney's Office and Section members spent months researching court familiarization programs. Kids in Court was created to help children who were victims of, or witnesses to, felony abuse so that they could become more comfortable with the courtroom process and be at ease when testifying. This program celebrated its twentieth anniversary in 2014.

During this decade, there was a broad expansion of the Section's community service projects, with some lasting only a year or two and others continuing for many years. Services started during this period and continuing for more than three years included:

- Image and clothing consultants for economically disadvantaged women at Attitudes & Attire
- Volunteers and vouchers for food and transportation for clients of Parkland Hospital's Homeless Outreach Program
- Volunteers and the Minnie Hexter Milk Fund supplied milk for Jonathan's Place, which provides a temporary home for drug-exposed infants and small children
- Tour guides at the Dallas Holocaust Museum
- Collaboration with Dallas Healthy Start to establish community health

---

Marriott, Inc. official Bob O'Brien (left) and Bette Miller (center), Section member and cochair of the "Day of the Working Parent," distribute a special "lunch box" of information to a Marriott employee, 1993.

(Right) Section member Barbara Lee (right) and her children Jonathan and Adrienne (left to right) prepare materials for the "Day of the Working Parent," 1993.

Section members Barbara Silberberg and Debbie Greene hand out "lunch boxes," 1993.

clinics with the goal of reducing infant mortality in Dallas

- Volunteers read and gave books to children in the Children's Medical Center's outpatient clinics via the Early Childhood Literacy Development program
- Field trips and enrichment activities for young women at Our Friends Place

The Section often partnered with other community groups to host vital community events. In 1997, the Section presented "Domestic Violence in the Jewish Community" with the Dallas Chapter of Hadassah, which focused on local cases. The program featured Rabbi David Stern of Temple Emanu-El and Ariella Goldstein of Jewish Family Service.

A conference, "Literacy: Can Dallas Read the Future?" in 1997, cosponsored with the Junior League of Dallas, featured Texas First Lady Laura Bush as the keynote speaker. The event "ADHD Across the Lifespan" partnered the Section with Jewish Family Service and the Teacher Learning Center of the Jewish Federation of Greater Dallas and attracted more than three hundred people.

The *Dallas Morning News* columnist and Section member Marilyn Schwartz was the keynote speaker at a 1999 conference titled "Coping with Breast Cancer: Body, Mind, and Spirit." The Section was a cosponsor of this event along with Jewish Family Service and the Galerstein Women's Center at the University of Texas at Dallas.

At the end of the decade, Safeguards for Seniors and the Dallas Area Agency on Aging copresented a conference for the professional community titled "Who Cares for the Caregiver?" Partnering with the Junior League of Dallas, the Section also cosponsored a free symposium, "Women on the Rise," presented by Jacob's Ladder, a program that transitioned women into the workplace.

Almost from its inception, the Section has created and supported nutrition programs, including "Penny Lunches" in 1914. The Section was the only Dallas-area volunteer organization involved in the Smart Shoppers program, a 1995 collaborative project led by the Special Supplemental Nutrition Program for Women, Infants, and Children (WIC). This effort, funded by the US Department of Agriculture, developed innovative ways to help low-income families learn how to use their food dollars effectively for a healthier diet. Members took small groups through grocery stores and talked about the importance of increasing fruits and vegetables in their meals, as well as how to read food labels and stretch their food dollars. The Section provided a food stylist and a professional food photographer to create a packet of easy, inexpensive recipes for the participants.

An outgrowth of the Smart Shoppers program was Operation Frontline, a project of the North Texas Food Bank. This effort used noted area chefs along with dieticians to teach proper nutrition and economical food choices to people with limited resources. In addition

Section volunteers join Dallas Holocaust Museum docents at the Memorial Stone as part of tours given for the community and school-age children. (Left to right) Unknown, Regina Roth, Sharan Goldstein, Freda Sobel, Marcy Grossman, unknown man, unknown woman, Felice Horwits, Arnold "Scotty" Darrow, and Gail Gilbert, 2000. Photo by A. Kaye.

(Left) Section member Jackie Waldman and Texas's First Lady Laura Bush (left to right) promote literacy.

Section member Kyra Effren demonstrates cooking techniques as part of the Section's partnership with the North Texas Food Bank's Operation Frontline, 2000.

(Right) Section volunteers Ynette and Ilyse Hogue (back row, left to right) gather up diverse English-as-a-Second-Language students at Vickery Meadow Elementary School for a group photo with teacher Heidi Thornton (back row, center), 2000.

Honorary National board member Bette Miller and Section member Lois Finkelman, a Dallas City Council member (left to right), take part in leadership and advocacy training as part of the Leadership Conference held in Dallas at the Fairmont Hotel, 2000.

(Right) A joint meeting of the Section and its branches focused on public education and featured Cecile Richards, founder of the Texas Freedom Network and president of Planned Parenthood Federation of America, 1998. (*Bulletin*, January/February 1998.)

to supplying volunteers, the Section in 2002 donated a minivan to the program so that the dieticians did not have to haul equipment and food in their own cars from one site to another.

Focusing on the local scene, the Section and other groups recognized the growing needs of new residents in Dallas's Vickery Meadow neighborhood, once an enclave of apartments filled with young professionals and empty-nesters. The 1988 Fair Housing Act required adult-only apartment complexes to accept children. Many residents left the area, and were replaced by many large, lower-income families, mainly minorities and newcomers from other countries who were being resettled by Catholic Charities.

In the mid-1990s, in response to the population surge, the Section launched much-appreciated programs at the Vickery Meadow Elementary School. These included tutoring and monthly birthday parties for children in the Vickery After-School program and assisting fast-track ESL classes, which provided accelerated basic language skills to students in grades one through six. Eventually, the language program expanded to include the parents.

Study Groups and Judaic Programming

The Section's interest in the state of world affairs fueled much programming during these ten years. Teaming with both Temple Emanu-El and Temple Shalom, the Section brought Dr. Deborah Lipstadt, Emory University professor of history and Holocaust studies, to Dallas for a special Section Sabbath in 1997. That evening, attendees learned about Dr. Lipstadt's personal fight against David Irving, a Holocaust denier. He had sued her for attacking the truth of his statements in her published writings. She was later vindicated, but only after a long and demanding trial.

Study groups on Jewish topics hit a high point during this time. The Section, Hadassah, Temple Emanu-El, and Temple Shalom joined in April 1995 to hold the first city-wide women's Passover Seder. The group wrote a special women's Haggadah for use during the Seder, which was led by Cantor Karen Webber Gilat from the Hebrew Union College-Jewish Institute of Religion.

Section member Rabbi Elisabeth "Liza" Stern, of Temple Emanu-El and Temple Shalom, was a favorite presenter. Packaged as a series of six sessions, her topics included Torah study, feminine spirituality and tradition, along with love relationships between Jewish men and women. Section member Rabbi Nancy Kasten, former head of Hillel and associate chaplain at Southern Methodist University, led programs on Jewish feminism and its impact on members' lives in the areas of ritual, community, and personal growth. Rabbi Kasten also conducted a book review series based on Abraham Joshua Heschel's *The Sabbath*. Member Rabbi Debra Robbins, also at Temple Emanu-El, joined Rabbi Kasten at a retreat at Greene Family Camp to connect participants more deeply with Judaism.

Other study topics included a diverse menu: the growing recognition of genes that increase the risk of breast cancer in Jewish women, cooking classes conducted by Section member Kyra Effren, and tours of the Dallas Museum of Art led by member Gail Sachson.

The Section and its branches usually presented their own programs, but once a year they worked together to sponsor a joint event. These were held in the evening so that Branch members could attend. Many of the programs addressed advocacy issues such as book censorship and the religious right's assault on public education with speaker Cecile Richards, founder of the Texas Freedom Network and president of the Planned Parenthood Federation of America. Abortion access/funding and National's areas of focus after the 2000 elections also were presented. Non-advocacy programs included author Nomi Eve, who reviewed her book, *The Family Orchard*, and Dr. Beck Weathers, a Dallas-area pathologist, who talked about changes in his life after his incredible survival from a 1996 disaster on Mount Everest.

In memory of the late Israeli leader Yitzak Rabin, Dallas Southwest Osteopathic Physicians funded the first of several Section-sponsored annual "Peace in the Middle East" essay contests in 1996. Entries were solicited from high school students in the DISD's southern sector. Three winners were chosen each year to spend three weeks as Youth Ambassadors in Israel; three semi-finalists received monetary awards. The essay contest and trips continued until 1999, when the Section felt that the political unrest in Israel posed a security risk for student winners. The physicians' group recognized the Section in 2000 with its Humanitarian of the Year Award, the first time it had been given to a group rather than to an individual.

Many other changes and accomplishments, large and small, were experienced as this decade drew toward its close. Area codes were added to the Section's yearly directories, a reflection of the growing North Texas area and the use of many pagers, cell phones, and fax machines. Credit cards now could be used to pay for annual dues renewals, a great help since membership had soared to more than 1,700 by the time the Section celebrated its eighty-fifth birthday in 1998. The Section entered the digital age with its first website, hosted by the Dallas Virtual Jewish Community.

National came to Dallas for the NCJW 2000 Leadership Conference. Outstanding scholars, survivors of violence, and women who achieved success in nontraditional professions led the event, which provided many opportunities for leadership and advocacy training. Dallas Section members provided the usual "Southern hospitality" and also conducted the Friday Shabbat candle-lighting service. Rabbi Debra Robbins led the Saturday morning service.

A first for the predominantly female organization: Tom Timmons, an active member of the Section's Professional Branch, became that Branch's first male president in 1996. The Branch's second male president, Jerry Raskin, was also its last president. The Branch discontinued its separate structure and programming in 2002 and joined forces with the Section. That same year, the Section began preparations for its ninetieth year of service to the community.

In 2001, the Encore Sale could no longer meet budget requirements, so the warehouse

Section members Rabbi Nancy Kasten, Jody Platt, and Debbie Massarano (left to right) lead Shabbat services at Temple Shalom during a Jerusalem 3000 Shabbat morning service, c. 1996.

Rita Doyne (right), Section Gala cochair, greets Dr. J.L. LaManna, chairman of Dallas Southwest Osteopathic Physicians, long-time Gala sponsors, 1999

(Left) DISD staffer Doris Freling (second from left) says farewell to students Kevin Wallace from South Oak Cliff High School; Maribel Ramirez from Sunset High School; and Maria Martinez from W. H. Adamson High School (left to right) as they prepare to leave for Israel as winners of the "Peace in the Middle East" essay contest sponsored by Dallas Southwest Osteopathic Physicians, c. 1997.

A gathering of presidents! Section past presidents Bette Miller, Phyllis Bernstein, Joni Cohan, and Jody Platt (standing, left to right) join Professional Branch president Tom Timmons (far right) and Section president Maddy Unterberg (seated, right) in welcoming National president Nan Rich (seated, left) to Dallas, 1997.

Section past president Joni Cohan (right), JFS Guardianship coordinator, reviews paperwork related to the program, 2000.

was closed, and the Sale was discontinued. The Section then depended on the galas that had begun in the 1990s to raise funds to support the organization and its many community service projects and programs.

Three past presidents from this decade reflect upon the Section's commitment to *Tikkun Olam*, "to heal the world," and to have a purpose beyond themselves.

Phyllis Bernstein said, "We have been serving our community in a variety of ways: helping women, children, the elderly, families, the environment, the homeless, the hungry, and youth in trouble. We make a difference!"

Kathy Freeman described the Section as "vibrant, involved, and wholly committed to helping make things better in the Jewish and general communities."

Jody Platt noted that her work with NCJW provided opportunities for solving difficult problems. Her involvement also had benefits like strategic and satisfying conversations with US Attorney General Janet Reno and First Lady Hillary Rodham Clinton. As Jody says, "The joys far outweigh the oys!"

Creating Guardians for the Most Vulnerable
Essay by Joni Cohan
President, Greater Dallas Section 1990–1992

The idea for an adult guardianship program originated with Dr. Carmen Miller Michael, who served as the first president of the Evening Branch of the Greater Dallas Section in 1952–1953.

Carmen saw a tremendous need in our community for such a program, recognizing that there are individuals who, because of mental, emotional, or cognitive inabilities, are unable to make decisions for themselves. These people needed guardians of their persons and their estates. Such individuals might be chronically ill, severely disturbed, and even homeless.

Guardianship is a legal procedure, only granted when a court determines that an individual's decision-making powers must be turned over to someone else. Most people have family members who can become guardians. If no one is available to be a guardian and there are some financial means, paid institutions such as banks may serve. But the most vulnerable, those who have neither family nor sufficient monetary resources, desperately need guardians.

A 1993 Guardianship Task Force of the Section went through a research and development process to explore bringing this service to our Jewish community. The group met for months, learning how other parts of the country provided guardianship, what was available in the Dallas area, and how to make the response to this need a local reality. Ultimately, the task force determined that Jewish Family Service (JFS) would be the appropriate agency to implement and oversee a guardianship program.

What I learned about guardianship as a member of the task force led to my becoming the first guardianship coordinator at JFS in January 1994. The program successfully served the most vulnerable in our community. Bunny Radman, head of the agency's gerontology department and a Section member, said that "if not for our guardianship program, these individuals would be living on the streets." With the program in place, clients were treated as one would care for a family member.

Building Bridges in Dallas
Essay by Jody Platt
President, Greater Dallas Section 1994–1996

Three months into my Section presidency, I was up to my elbows making gefilte fish for Rosh Hashanah. The telephone rang. Little did I know the ensuing conversation would result in building a bridge of understanding between the African American and Jewish communities in Dallas.

Gathered together in front of the *Dallas Post Tribune* banner at its offices are the paper's board members and Section member Harriet P. Gross (third from left), National president Nan Rich (fourth from left), and Section past presidents Phyllis Bernstein and Joni Cohan (second and third from the right), 1997.

Over the telephone, Dr. Theodore R. Lee Jr. introduced himself. He was president and publisher of the *Dallas Post Tribune*, a weekly African American newspaper founded in 1947. He had learned that I was president of the Greater Dallas Section and was told that our organization had a history of social action and justice in the Dallas community. One of the *Post Tribune*'s founders knew about our volunteerism in East Dallas schools and had told him, "If you want anything at all done, call NCJW." He had an idea, and he needed my help.

African American/Jewish tensions had surfaced at Dallas City Hall, and the media seemed to be blowing the situation out of proportion. Dr. Lee invited me to write an article about the Section's community activities as well as Jewish-related topics for his newspaper. He thought that if his 75,000 subscribers read a Jewish human-interest column, they would gain a better understanding of the Jewish community as a whole. If his readers became better educated about Judaism and understood more of that culture's traditions, perhaps together we would be able to help break down barriers. He also pledged to share my column with *La Vida News*, the African American paper in Fort Worth.

Dr. Lee was so convincing on the phone that I washed the gefilte fish off my hands and started writing—my deadline was two hours away! What followed during my two-year term as Section president (and continued for sixteen more years) was a weekly feature in the *Dallas Post Tribune* and *La Vida News*. My columns discussed Section community service projects, advocacy, workshops, study sessions, fundraising events, Jewish celebrations, guest-speaking engagements, friendships, and bridge-building opportunities between our communities.

Soothing Fears of Kids in Court
Essay by Judy Hoffman
Greater Dallas Section Member

Giving testimony in any trial can be a frightening, even overwhelming, experience for adults. Think about how much more it must be for children! Kids in Court is a partnership between the Greater Dallas Section and the Dallas County District Attorney's Office that gives youngsters the confidence, strength, and courage they will need to face this daunting experience in the courtroom.

Kids in Court is a unique project that is designed to help children ages two to eighteen who may have been victims of felony abuse. The program helps both the children and their families cope with the psychological challenges of an impending court appearance. Children can be more effective witnesses if they are made familiar, in advance of their scheduled hearings, with the courtroom environment, its processes, and the key personnel they will encounter.

More than twenty years ago, a team of Section members became involved in this effort. Paula Eilbott, Paula Jacobs, and Beverly Levy, with leadership and support from Section president Jody Platt, spent many months working together with Dori Reid, lead child advocate in Dallas County District Attorney's Office, researching court familiarization programs.

The result was a proposal that was approved by the Dallas County Commissioners Court

Dallas County District Attorney Craig Watkins joins Section members Robin Zweig, Marlene Cohen, Caren Edelstein, and Kathy Freeman (left to right) in celebrating twenty years of the Kids in Court program, 2014.

Section president Kyra Effren (far right) thanks Domino's Pizza of Dallas owners, Mr. and Mrs. Richard Hafner, and delivery person Tracy Gore (left to right) for providing eight years of pizza for the Kids in Court program, 2004.

Section member Paula Jacobs, first chair of Kids in Court, worked with the Dallas County District Attorney's Office to prepare children for courtroom procedures, 1995, Photo by Milton Hinnant. (Zethraus, "An Advocate for Children.")

99

Section volunteers Elaine Stillman (judge's bench at top) and Claudette Wolfe (bailiff's desk at far right), plus Children's Advocacy Center staff help children role-play the various jobs of courtroom personnel as part of the Kids in Court program, 2014. Photo by Laura Diamond.

(Right) Balloons and cheers are part of the Section's Birthday Bash at Vickery Meadow Elementary School, c. 2000.

Vickery Meadow Learning Center (VMLC) volunteer teacher Barbara Neill and Section member Hazel Byers (left to right) share a cheerful moment with ESL students at VMLC, c. 2000.

in March 1994. Shortly afterward, the Section and the District Attorney's Office sponsored the start of what would soon become a nationally recognized and acclaimed program.

The exemplary process, which is held on a Saturday morning every other month, includes a courtroom orientation session for the youngest victims. The children enact the roles of the various persons—judges, bailiffs, lawyers, and witnesses—who will be present in the court when the youngsters need to testify. Section volunteers along with members of the District Attorney's staff help guide the children through this process. Teenage victims and the parents/guardians have their own orientations, held at the same time, to help explain the courtroom procedures.

Printed materials, age- and situation-appropriate, some of which were written by Section members, are given to the children. At the end of the morning sessions, all join together to enjoy a pizza lunch provided by the Section.

Over the years, with the ongoing collaboration of the District Attorney's Office and the Dallas Children's Advocacy Center, more than 27,000 children and their families have benefited from a Kids in Court session. Even more have been helped by the materials specifically developed for this program.

Enthusiastic volunteers are present at every session, and the Section provides ongoing funding for all program expenses. We are proud to support Dallas County's commitment to its youngest residents.

Celebrating Children at Vickery Meadow
Essay by Madeline "Maddy" Unterberg
President, Greater Dallas Section 1996–1998

In fall 1996, Section member Jill Stone recommended that a monthly birthday celebration for the children in the Vickery Meadow After-School Care Program would be a positive experience. Jacqueline Eldridge, program director, loved the idea that came to be known as the "Birthday Bash."

Many of the children in this program had never experienced their own birthday party. The celebrations not only benefited the children in Vickery Meadow, but it also taught children of Section members the meaning of *mitzvot,* the Jewish obligation to do good deeds.

Once a month, volunteers and their sons and daughters planned a birthday party for all the Vickery Meadow children who had birthdays during that month. Activities included crafts, games with prizes, and a grand finale featuring a big birthday cake with candles.

Of course, everyone sang "Happy Birthday" and went home with favors. It was a fun, meaningful, and upbeat project for Section families and the children in Vickery Meadow until this project ended in 2002.

Teaching English to Brave New Immigrants
Essay by Myrna Ries
Greater Dallas Section Member

I love working with adults, teaching them English. I can't think of a more rewarding experience than I had in the late 1990s doing that at the Vickery Meadow Learning Center (VMLC), an organization that teaches English literacy skills.

No one coming to a new country can function, feed one's family, or move ahead in a new environment without help. The United States and Dallas must have been overwhelming to all those new immigrants, and it took great courage for them to come every day to learn about

American history and this strange new language.

I had enormous respect for my students. I enjoyed teaching them and felt so good helping these brave people try to make a better, safer life. They knew that they were not only learning for themselves, but also for their children. Many were on the road to becoming US citizens!

While teaching at VMLC with other Section volunteers, I felt that I was contributing to a project that was beneficial not only for these determined students but for our country as well.

Living with "Gala" Memories
Essay by Rita Doyne
Greater Dallas Section Member

I was a cochair of three Greater Dallas Section gala fundraisers, all of them with famous performers: Paul Anka in 1998 (see his lyrics here), Gladys Knight in 1999, and Mandy Patinkin in 2003.

It was a thrill to meet each of these stars personally, but my best memories aren't related to big-name personalities. Best of all were the Thursday meetings in advance of each gala. Working with wonderful Section cochairs and committee members cemented friendships that have long outlived these great events themselves.

Beyond the excitement of bringing such fabulous entertainment personalities here and getting to spend time with them was the goal and outcome that we found most important: raising money to support all of the Section projects and programs in our community!

Being Serenaded by Paul Anka

Tonight the "Lone Star" shines bright
What a delight to play this "Palace"
We praise the funds you raise, the many ways that you help Dallas
Indeed, with heart you lead, meeting each need in such a sure way
Dallas is wowed, yes downright proud
You reach out Your Way

Intent that this event be heaven sent
You gals were teamin'
You're blessed with Rita's zest, and
Council's best—That's Kathy Freeman
To get this evening set, Wendy and Bette,
How we applaud thee
Ticket sales flow, could you say "no"
To Lottye Brodsky?

NCJW you're well known
To be a chapter all your own
Jewish tradition thrives through you
You throw a "Kosher" Bar-B-Que
Forget the *traif,* you play it safe
And serve it Your Way.

Three cheers for volunteers who,
Through the years, found time for sharing.
Through art and "Healthy Start,"
Programs with heart
Show how you're caring.
It's true, because of you, Dallas shines
Through jewel of state here
Like Governor Bush, you bust your tush
You make life great here!

Dallas is home, proud of your land
You join together, hand in hand
To make your own community
The very best that it can be
Each life you touch, says thanks so much
For Caring Your Way.

The Greater Dallas Section's fundraising gala in 1998 featured singer and songwriter Paul Anka. He presented "Paul Anka: The Songs of Your Life," which included his performance of a song he wrote for the Section—sung to the tune of "My Way." The gala that year received rave reviews and raised more than $245,000.

Paul Anka is happily surrounded by the Gala's cochairs. (Left to right) Bette Morchower, Lotty Brodsky (now Lotty Lyle), Paul Anka, Rita Doyne, and Wendy Stanley, 1997.

The Section's *Bulletin* announces the 1998 Gala, "The Songs of Your Life," featuring Paul Anka.

(Left) Section Fundraising cochair Rita Doyne presents flowers to Mandy Patinkin after his encore performance for the Section's 2003 Gala. (*Bulletin,* November/December 1998.)

The brochure for the literacy conference cosponsored by the Section and the Junior League of Dallas, 1997.

(Below) The Honorable Mayor of Dallas, Section member Laura Miller, spoke at the opening meeting, acknowledging the many projects that are offered by caring volunteers, in anticipation of the ninetieth year of service, 2002. Photo by Deborah Silverthorn. (Silverthorn, "NCJW Begins Its 90th Year.")

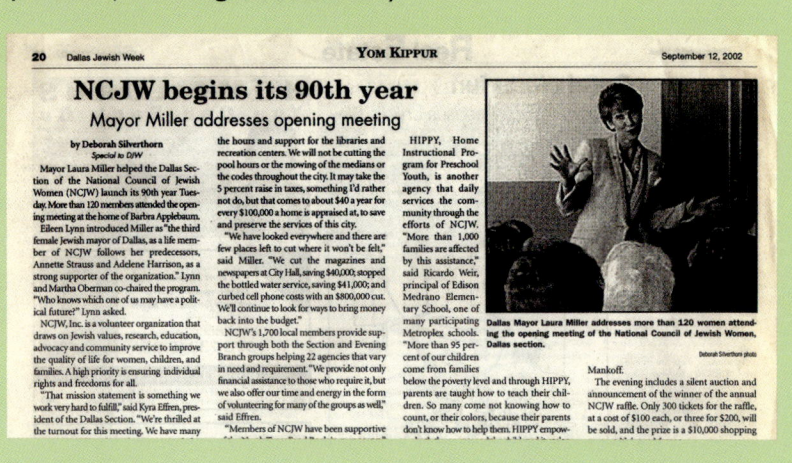

Teens in Court: Your Guide to Testifying, produced by the Section; artwork by Tam T. Ngyen.

The Section partnered with the Dallas Area Agency on Aging to present "Who Cares for the Caregiver" conference for professionals, 2002.

Advocacy and community services were highlighted at the 2000 National Leadership Conference in Dallas.

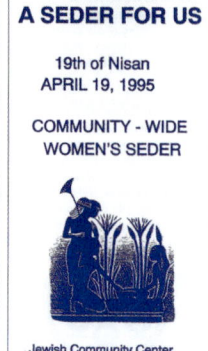

Women from many area congregations attended the Women's Seder that was cosponsored by the Section and several other groups, 1995.

Eager shoppers waiting for the opening of an Encore Sale, c. 1990.

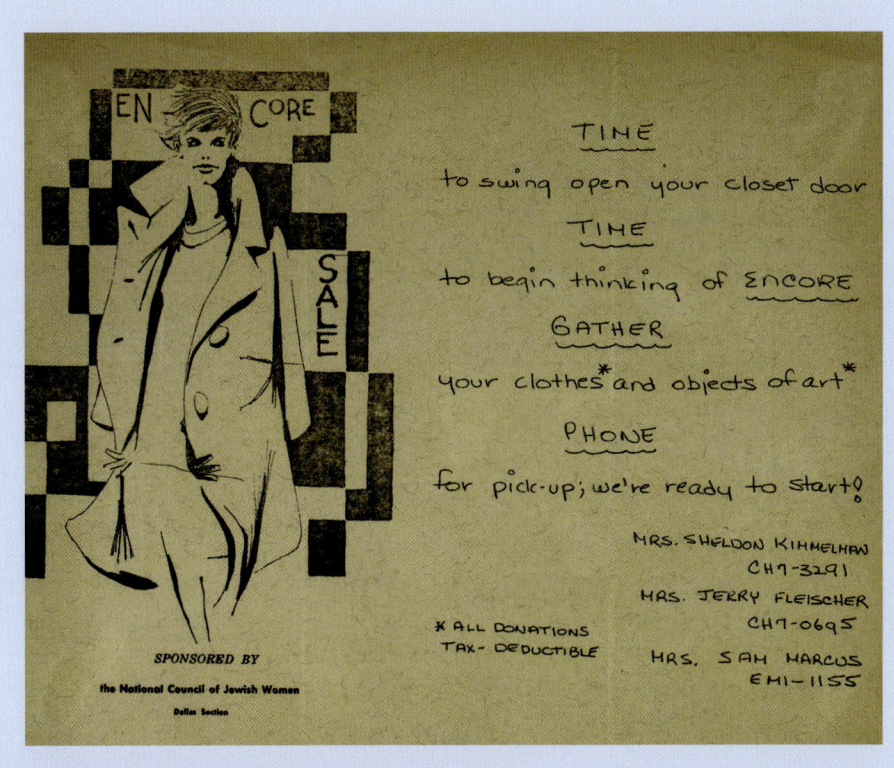

A stylish invitation to the Section's Encore Sale, 1966.

Presidents George W. Bush, Barack Obama, and Bill Clinton discuss aid for weather-disaster areas, 2010. (Official White House Photo by Pete Souza. P011610PS-0259.)

Coretta Scott King speaks at Section's ninetieth birthday; "Making the Connection"	Evening Branch disbanded	First Stay-at-Home fundraiser; Fire at NCJW office	VMLC civics classes	Women's Access to Comprehensive Health Services
2003	2004	2005	2006	2007

"We must not, in trying to think about how we can make a difference, ignore the small daily differences we can make, which over time add up to big differences we often cannot foresee."

Marian Wright Edelman (1939–), president and founder of the Children's Defense Fund

The Tenth Decade : 2003 *to* 2012

In 2003, United States troops, under President George W. Bush, entered Iraq. Anti-war protests followed. President Ronald Reagan died in 2004 at age ninety-three. Barack Obama was sworn in as the country's forty-fourth chief executive, the first African American to serve as president, in 2009.

The social network Facebook launched at Harvard University in 2004 and then expanded to include anyone thirteen and older in 2006. The next year, Nancy Pelosi (D-CA) became the first female speaker of the US House of Representatives. The Israeli–Palestinian conflict continued as rockets launched from Gaza racked the Jewish state.

Hurricanes Katrina, Rita, and Wilma in 2005 devastated New Orleans and the Gulf Coast. The Dallas area was not immune

2008	2009	2010	2011	2012
"Nation of Immigrants" conference; Voter Hotline	*Food + Fit = Fun* classes; "S.A.Y. What?" Coalition	*Vickery Meadow Neighborhood Alliance*	*Endow NCJW Dallas Fund; First Pioneering Partner Award*	*First Lady Michelle Obama recognizes Food + Fit = Fun*

The *Dallas Morning News* columnist Robert Miller acknowledged the ninety years that the Section has been active in Dallas. (Left to right) Section leaders Brenda Brand and Kyra Effren, plus Kit Prince, HIPPY Coordinator at RISD's Dobie Primary School, watch as a HIPPY mom and youngsters enjoy an art experience, 2003. Photo by Nan Coulter. (Miller, "Volunteers Still Helping Others After 90 Years.")

(Right) Michael and Amy Roseman (left to right) prepare books for distribution as part of the Section's "Making the Connection" project, 2005.

to tragedy. Tornadoes seasonally destroyed buildings and people. Gun violence took the lives of many local men, women, and children. Dallas became a human trafficking hub, facilitated by its proximity to several interstate highways.

THE LAST DECADE OF THE GREATER DALLAS SECTION'S FIRST ONE HUNDRED YEARS BEGAN WITH no signs of the Section slowing down. In fact, things were revving up, as old community service projects continued at the same time that new ones were introduced and implemented.

In honor of the Section's ninetieth year, Coretta Scott King, an influential, passionate, visionary woman and wife of the late Reverend Dr. Martin Luther King Jr., was invited to be the keynote speaker at its 2003 birthday luncheon. She spoke of her interest in educating our communities.

Section members researched, wrote, and published a colorful booklet, *Making the Connection,* to teach new mothers the importance of early brain development in their children. Health educators from Parkland Hospital were trained to present the material to the more than 4,400 pregnant women seen each year at two of Parkland's obstetrics and gynecology clinics. The Section also provided the patients with children's books, in both English and Spanish, which included informational bookplates that outlined the most important developmental issues for babies.

Continuing the Section's involvement in the Vickery Meadow area that began in the mid-1990s, volunteers taught adult literacy and ESL classes at Vickery Meadow Learning Center (VMLC). A citizenship class, its curriculum written and taught by Section past presidents Julie Lowenberg and Cheryl Pollman, was added in 2006. These services, along with volunteers and funds for the Vickery Meadow Food Pantry, continued throughout the decade and are still ongoing as the Section moves forward in its second century.

Other community service projects included: providing volunteers and funding for HIPPY and "Hello Israel," delivering Meals on Wheels for three agencies, and entertaining residents of Golden Acres (Dallas's Home for the Jewish Aged). Members participated in special events at Community Homes for Adults Inc. (CHAI), which provides ongoing services through group home living for the mentally challenged. Volunteers also mentored students from disadvantaged families by providing them with hands-on experiences based on science, math, and technology at the Science Place at Fair Park.

The Section continued leading tours at the Dallas Holocaust Museum. Working with Attitudes & Attire, members provided life-skills training and image consulting to economically disadvantaged women hoping to enter the workforce. Volunteers and financial support were provided for the forum "Families on the Rise," a daylong empowerment event for women presented by Jacob's Ladder.

At the January 2004 annual joint meeting with the Evening Branch, Dr. Nina Radford, a board-certified cardiologist and internist affiliated with the Cooper Clinic and UT Southwestern Medical Center, spoke about the facts and fiction of women's health issues. This meeting turned out to be the last event held jointly, as the Evening Branch dissolved that May.

In May 2005, in conjunction with the Dallas Jewish Historical Society, the Section presented a program, "Our World: Our Women. Big Doers in Big D." The event celebrated the 350th anniversary of the founding of North American Jewish communal settlements in 1654. A distinguished panel of Section members, Dolores Gomez Barzune, Syl Benenson, Adlene Harrison, and Jaynie Schultz, discussed the involvement of Dallas's Jewish women in cultural affairs, education, politics, and community service. A slide show highlighted photographs and a brief history of many of the Jewish women who had made significant contributions to the Dallas community.

The variety of volunteer projects that called for attention continued to broaden, and the Section met new needs as they arose. When Children's Medical Center added a Family Resource Center to its facilities, Section volunteers were there to help patient families access health information, prepare books for the shelves, and read to the children.

Eventually, the Section's leadership came to realize that there were many more needs than their funds or volunteers could handle. Knowing it takes a combination of research, education, advocacy, and direct service to make a difference, the Section discontinued their support of several programs in 2008 and refocused its resources on four specific issues: immigration, access to women's health, the well-being of children and families, and Israel.

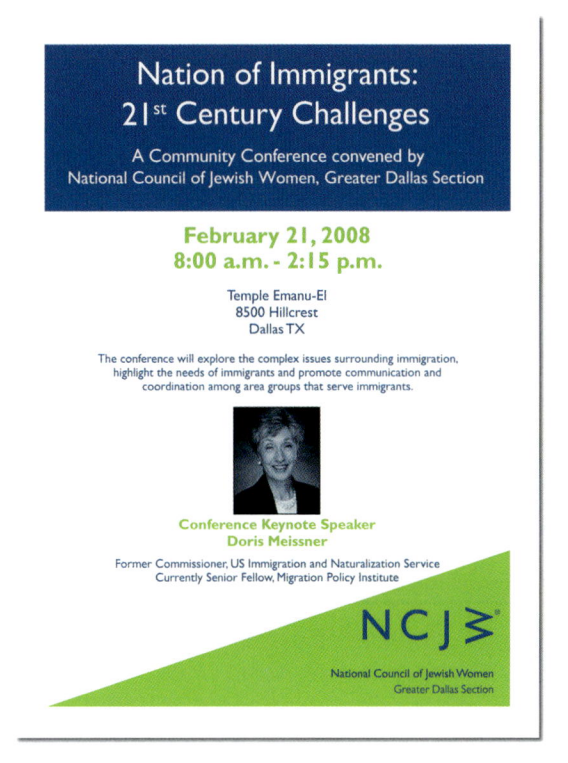

The Section's 2008 conference on immigration featured Doris Meissner, Senior Fellow at the Migration Policy Institute.

Immigration

The Section showed a renewed interest in comprehensive, humane immigration reform and convened a successful community conference, "Nation of Immigrants: 21st Century Challenges," in 2008. The conference addressed the needs of immigrants and facilitated communication and coordination among area groups that serve them. The keynote speaker was Doris Meissner, former director of US Immigration and Naturalization Services, who became a senior fellow at the Migration Policy Institute in Washington, DC. That conference led to the Section's continuing advocacy and services on behalf of immigrants.

Section volunteer Sondra Hollander (right) helps a client choose professional clothing at Attitudes & Attire, 2004.

Women's/Youth Health

WACHS (Women's Access to Comprehensive Health Services) began in 2007 and provided education and advocacy for comprehensive sex education and access to safe, effective contraceptive options. The project continues to use an age-appropriate sex education curriculum that Section volunteers created. In 2009, the Section, in conjunction with National's "Plan A: NCJW's Campaign for Contraceptive Access," received a

(Left) Section member Linnie Katz helps students in ESL and citizenship classes at VMLC, 2003.

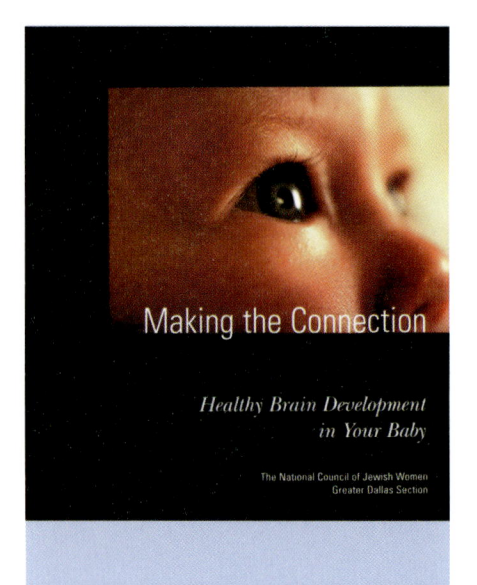

Ford Foundation grant and organized the "S.A.Y. What?" Coalition (Sound Advice for Youth).

Local faith-based organizations and agencies came together to determine the best approach to help implement a comprehensive sexuality education curriculum in the public schools. This coalition has become the North Texas Alliance to Reduce Unintended Pregnancy in Teens (NTARUPT), comprising more than thirty organizations and individuals that provide education along with health counseling and advocacy services for teens across North Texas.

Family Well-Being

Food + Fit = Fun, which began in 2008, teaches parents of young children the importance of healthy eating and staying active. Initial classes were offered in conjunction with the HIPPY program at Dobie Elementary School in the Richardson ISD and at Jill Stone Elementary School in the DISD. The project has now expanded to include all HIPPY families in Dallas and Irving public schools along with the Dobie program.

Israel Support

The focus on Israel involved holding programs that highlighted issues of concern. A newly designated tribute fund, *Yad B'Yad,* "hand-in-hand," was established to support National's Israel Granting Program (IGP).

Throughout the decade, general meetings and study groups that covered a wide range of topics enriched members' lives. The Section enjoyed being among the first to tour the new Nasher Sculpture Center. A Women's Seder, a joint project with Temple Emanu-El Sisterhood, was presented in 2008. Programs on health issues such as ovarian cancer, Alzheimer's disease, healthy eating, the HPV vaccine, and cancer prevention were presented. Members heard from local, Texas, and national speakers, experts, and elected officials on topics covering voting rights, redistricting in Texas, Israel, public education, sex education in Texas public schools, bullying, domestic violence, reproductive justice, and the intersection of politics and science.

A series of events held jointly with the Dallas Chapter of Hadassah began during this decade. Various medical topics were explored: the ethics of embryonic stem cell research with Nobel Prize Laureate Dr. Michael S. Brown and Rabbi Adam J. Raskin; "Genetic Disorders for People of Ashkenazi Descent" with Dr. Joel Weinthal, hematologist/oncologist; and Karen Heller, genetic counselor; and "Lifting the Veil of Sleep" with Dr. Philip Becker, clinical professor in the Department of Psychiatry at the University of Texas Southwestern Medical Center.

As the election season heated up in fall 2008, the Section continued its long history of promoting full voter participation. Members proclaimed, "Democracy is a verb!" Activities included sponsoring community voter education events, enabling voters who might not otherwise have been able to cast their ballots to do so, and providing "feet on the ground" on Election Day to ensure that every legitimate vote was cast and counted.

Section members worked with Oscar Joyner, president and chief operating officer of Reach Media Inc.; Bruce Sherbet, Dallas County elections administrator; and InfoVoter Technologies to develop a method to respond to a nationwide hotline's calls. Accessing the InfoVoter database of callers, the volunteers answered hundreds of inquiries about the voting process from throughout Texas. These voter protection efforts received local and national recognition and forged important long-term alliances within the community.

In 2010, the Section saw a renewal of programs led by area rabbis. Members Rabbi Nancy Kasten and Rabbi Ana Bonnheim led discussions on the lives of contemporary women in Israel who were studied through their poetry and other writings.

Endowment funds assured a vibrant future for the Section by providing permanent sources of revenue for current and future local needs. The Section's goal: to guarantee that its dedicated

---

The Section joined the Dallas Chapter of Hadassah to present a program on the medical and ethical use of stem cells. (Left to right) Section president Marlene Cohen, Congregation Beth Torah's Rabbi Adam Raskin, Nobel Laureate Dr. Michael S. Brown of UT Southwestern Medical Center, and Hadassah president June Penkar, 2006.

Claudia Fowler, a community leader of Joppa in South Dallas, and Casey Thomas, president of the Dallas Chapter of the NAACP, join Section members Cheryl Pollman and Terry Greenberg (left to right) to publicize voter protections, 2008.

volunteers could continue providing the high-quality community service, education, and advocacy that the community expects. Looking to the future, the Section felt the upcoming centennial year was a perfect time for members to be recognized as guarantors of the next one hundred years. A new tribute fund, "Endow NCJW Dallas," was established in 2011 to support operations. Additionally, the Section renewed its planned giving campaign, "Tamid: An Everlasting Legacy," encouraging members to make a bequest to the Section.

National brought its forty-fifth National Convention to Dallas in March 2011. More than three hundred women from around the country joined about forty Section members at this three-day event. National awarded their "Woman Who Dared Award" to former Speaker of the House and House Minority Leader Nancy Pelosi and her daughter, documentary filmmaker Alexandra Pelosi. Other speakers at the Convention included Congresswoman Debbie Wasserman Schultz (Florida); Hannah Rosenthal, special envoy to combat anti-Semitism at the US Department of State; Ruth Messinger, president of the American Jewish World Service; and Kathy Miller, president of Texas Freedom Network. The Section's Food + Fit = Fun project won the "Vision for America Showcase" Award.

Even longer than the Section's list of programs, partners, and projects is the list of members who, every day, make them happen. At one hundred years old, the Section is grateful to have members whose children, and even grandchildren, are now its members and advocates as well. Over time, their small daily contributions of caring and "days of service" add up to a better life for generations to come.

Celebrating with Coretta Scott King
Essay by Jody Platt
President, Greater Dallas Section 1994–1996

On March 4, 2003, the Greater Dallas Section celebrated its ninetieth birthday with the unprecedented opportunity of hosting Coretta Scott King as our luncheon keynote speaker. Mrs. King, an icon of the civil rights movement after the death of her husband, Dr. Martin Luther King Jr., discussed her struggle in educating our nation and our world on human rights issues. She focused on hunger, unemployment, voting rights, racism, and seeking equality and justice for all citizens.

To be in the room with one of the most visible and influential African American leaders of our time was indeed a privilege. This woman of wisdom, compassion, elegance, and vision passed away less than three years after her visit here. The presence of Mrs. King, a world-renowned champion of human rights, at the Section's Ninetieth Birthday Luncheon was a milestone and a memory for all our members and me to cherish.

Recovering from an Office Fire
Essay by Marlene A. Cohen
President, Greater Dallas Section 2004–2006
President, Evening Branch 2000–2002

On the evening of December 21, 2005, I received a call that there had been a fire in the stores below our office in Preston Royal Village. After recovering from the initial news, I prayed that nobody was hurt and feared what I would find when I went to the shopping center.

When I arrived, I learned that an elderly gentleman driving in the parking lot had suffered a fatal heart attack. His car jumped the curb, crashed through the window of the Copper Lamp Store, and sparks from his car caused a two-alarm fire.

Fearing that the fire had spread to the upstairs offices, firefighters broke through the street-level

Dallas ISD Superintendent Mike Moses with Mrs. Coretta Scott King at the Section's Ninetieth Birthday Luncheon, 2003.

Mrs. Coretta Scott King (seated), keynote speaker at the Section's Ninetieth Birthday Luncheon, is flanked by past presidents and luncheon cochairs Kathy Freeman and Jody Platt plus President Kyra Effren (left to right), 2003.

Adlene Harrison, one of the speakers at the "Big Doers" event, greets Harold A. Pollman, sponsor of the program that featured Jewish women who had made significant contributions to the Dallas area, 2005.

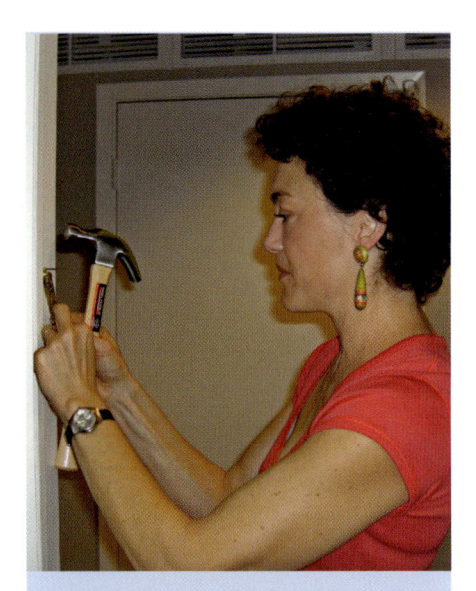

door and proceeded to break down every door upstairs, including the Section's office. Fortunately, no additional fires were found, but the offices were left in disarray. I discovered that everything in our office was covered in a fine layer of soot and reeked of smoke.

Working in semi-darkness, members and staff packed the office's contents and sent them to a restoration company. Because of the high cost of restoration and the invasive nature of smoke, we had an incredible stack of items to throw out. What a sad sight. Many boxes of records went to my garage with hopes that the smell would dissipate.

As news of the fire spread, offers of support poured in. Darrel Strelitz, area director of the Dallas Chapter of the American Jewish Committee and a former Section president, offered us temporary office space. We retrieved computers and other office machines from the restoration company, and we were up and running within a week. We were extremely fortunate that our lease required the management company to restore the interior of our office, and we had sufficient insurance to cover our losses. In seven weeks, we moved back into our newly cleaned space.

When I started my presidency, past presidents warned me that everyone has a crisis or disaster during her term of office. The fire definitely was mine, and I survived, as did the Section. A "little thing" like a fire couldn't stop us.

The Section returns to its office. Pictured is Rabbi Nancy Kasten as she prepares to install a mezuzah at the entry, 2006. Photo by Marlene Cohen.

Food + Fit = Fun Cofounder and Chair Sharan Goldstein (center, in black and white) enjoys a fun physical activity with VMLC participants, 2008.

Focusing on Food and Fitness
Essay by Kyra Effren
President, Greater Dallas Section 2002–2004

In 2007, Section member Sharan Goldstein and I recognized a need for a healthy living program for immigrants and people experiencing poverty.

Although there were many diet and exercise programs available, none offered a comprehensive course that included both nutritious meals and physical activities for a population that faces daunting challenges. With backing from the Section and a seed grant from General Mills, Food + Fit = Fun (FFF) was launched. Beginning in fall 2009, classes were offered to mothers of children enrolled in the HIPPY programs in the Richardson and Dallas ISDs.

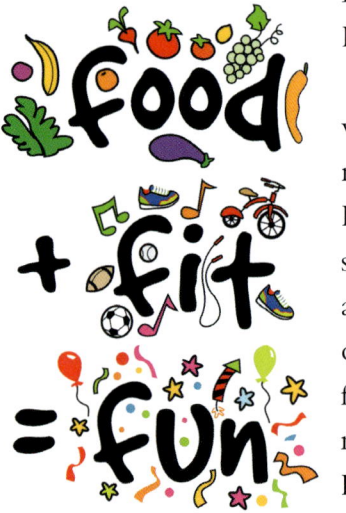

The target audience was consulted on their needs and challenges. From their feedback, a syllabus was created, and an advisory committee of participants was formed to continually monitor the program. FFF innovations include:

- A program designed to run for at least six months, allowing sufficient time for healthy habits to be adopted.
- Activities aimed at parents of preschool children in HIPPY, providing ongoing, in-home monitoring by home instructors.
- Family recipes from participants requested and tweaked to make them healthier, acknowledging that ethnically appropriate food might be more acceptable than recipes we might introduce.
- Equipment such as balls and pedometers provided, plus activity sessions for fun physical activity.

Outcomes are evaluated by:

- Asking participants to draw a picture of their previous night's dinner on a paper plate—first at the start of the program, then at its completion—thus providing before-and-after evidence of what they had learned.
- Holding a supermarket shopping spree, where the participants show their new skills in shopping for inexpensive, healthy foods.
- Hosting a "Look What We Learned!" potluck lunch at the conclusion of the course, where both participants and volunteers provide healthy dishes from many countries.
- Facilitating a final meeting with the advisory committee for a wrap-up critique.

We also learned that knowledge goes both ways. We gained insight into and respect for other cultures and were educated on the challenges faced by low-income populations. All of us realized that healthy living really could be fun.

In 2014, seeking a way to reach many more families, FFF leaders enhanced the program. Volunteers now teach the course to the HIPPY coordinators in the Dallas and Irving school districts. These coordinators then take the FFF message to more than six hundred enthusiastic families each year.

Helping Youth Have Healthier Relationships
Essay by Myra Fischel
Greater Dallas Section Member

Sixty percent of young women in foster care become pregnant within two years of leaving the program's protection. This startling national statistic helped provide direction for the Greater Dallas Section's program, Women's Access to Comprehensive Health Services (WACHS).

After a year of study and interviews with multiple agencies, the Section in 2008 began development of a curriculum geared toward teaching high-school-age children responsible sexuality. The Section chose to pilot the project with the Transition Resource Action Center (TRAC), a program of Central Dallas Ministries (CitySquare), to provide services to teens transitioning out of foster care.

Members designed three workshops that are equivalent to five hours of instruction. These same volunteers served as instructors and facilitators after the curriculum was tested. The topics, for both young men and women, covered healthy relationships, communication, and safer sex. The program has now expanded to serve other local agencies.

Volunteers also developed and produced a wallet-sized resource card with phone numbers of health care organizations that help youth who have questions or need help. These cards are widely distributed in the

Section members (left to right) Kathy Freeman, Debra Levy-Fritts, Harriet Mellow, Syl Benenson, and Freda Gail Stern prepare to lead the way on a supermarket shopping spree for Food + Fit = Fun participants from RISD's HIPPY program at Dobie Elementary School, 2012. Photo by Marlene Cohen.

Suzi Greenman (left) and Myra Fischel (right), WACHS founding cochairs, flank Evy Kay Washburne, executive director of TRAC, 2008. Photo by Laura Diamond.

foster care system and through other agencies in our community.

The hard work, research, and commitment of WACHS volunteers have yielded positive results. Local youth are benefiting from important education. This program led to the Section being selected by National to participate in an advocacy initiative funded by the Ford Foundation. This initiative was the "S.A.Y. What?" Coalition, which brought together individuals and agencies with a common goal of providing youth with accurate sexual education.

Welcoming the Stranger
Essay by Julie Lowenberg
President, Greater Dallas Section 2000–2002

Since its inception, the Greater Dallas Section has provided service to immigrant families seeking refuge in the United States. Many early immigrants came seeking a better life. Jews escaping the Nazis followed them. Cambodians fleeing the Khmer Rouge, Russian Jews leaving Communist countries, and unaccompanied children avoiding gang violence in Central America came in later years. The Section has been there, providing English language literacy and life skills, access to medical services, and assistance navigating the complex web of the American judicial system. The Section historically has sponsored public forums and conferences, participated in marches, spearheaded advocacy efforts, and provided education, all focused on assuring the fair treatment of the "stranger in our midst," those who come seeking freedom and justice.

In addition to developing member leaders who have made a positive impact on the Section and the broader community, another of the Section's great strengths is its ability to bring people and organizations together to work on common goals. Fast-forwarding to the first decade of the twenty-first century, the Section took up the cause of comprehensive, humane immigration reform and, to that end, convened a very successful community conference titled "Nation of Immigrants: 21st Century Challenges" in 2008. Along with Marsha Fischman, Bonnie Grossfeld, and Maddy Unterberg, I cochaired the conference. We recruited partner-sponsoring organizations, planned workshops, engaged plenary speakers, and organized a wonderful group of Section volunteers to ensure that everything ran smoothly.

That conference led to the Section's continuing advocacy and services on behalf of immigrants. "With One Voice," a coalition of diverse organizations and agencies that serve and/or advocate for immigrants, was formed to educate the general public, especially the business community, on immigration issues and the need for comprehensive reform. The coalition was active for several years under Section leadership, and its successes included the 2009 community forum, "The Business of Immigration Reform," featuring nationally syndicated columnist Ruben Navarrette Jr.

The relationships formed with individuals and organizations via "With One Voice" were critical to our Section's launching of a court-watch project in 2014 to monitor the deportation hearings of unaccompanied children in Federal Immigration Court. The Section also partnered with Catholic Charities in a Pro Se Asylum initiative to help parents and children file applications for asylum. Both of these activities are aimed at ensuring that the continuing influx of child refugees from Central America receive full and fair court hearings.

Partnering with Other Faith Groups in Vickery Meadow
Essay by Cheryl Pollman
President, Greater Dallas Section 2008–2010

The Vickery Meadow neighborhood is among the poorest and most densely populated areas of Dallas. The residents are primarily immigrants and refugees who were recently resettled in the apartments, and many do not yet speak English.

Section members Lauren Allenberg and Staci Bloom (left to right) teach a WACHS class to high-school-aged children at TRAC, 2011.

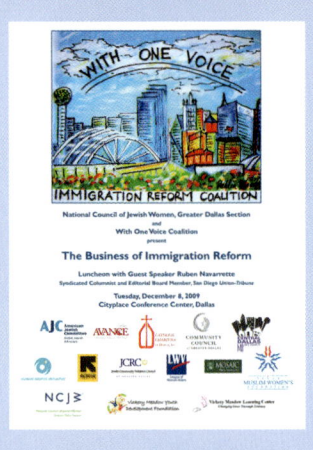

The Section brought together fourteen organizations to form the "With One Voice" Coalition, which jointly sponsored the "The Business of Immigration Reform" conference that featured columnist Ruben Navarrette, 2009. Original artwork by Dahlia Woods.

A plaque in memory of Section past president Janet Newberger's volunteer teaching at VMLC was given by the Section in her memory, 2008.

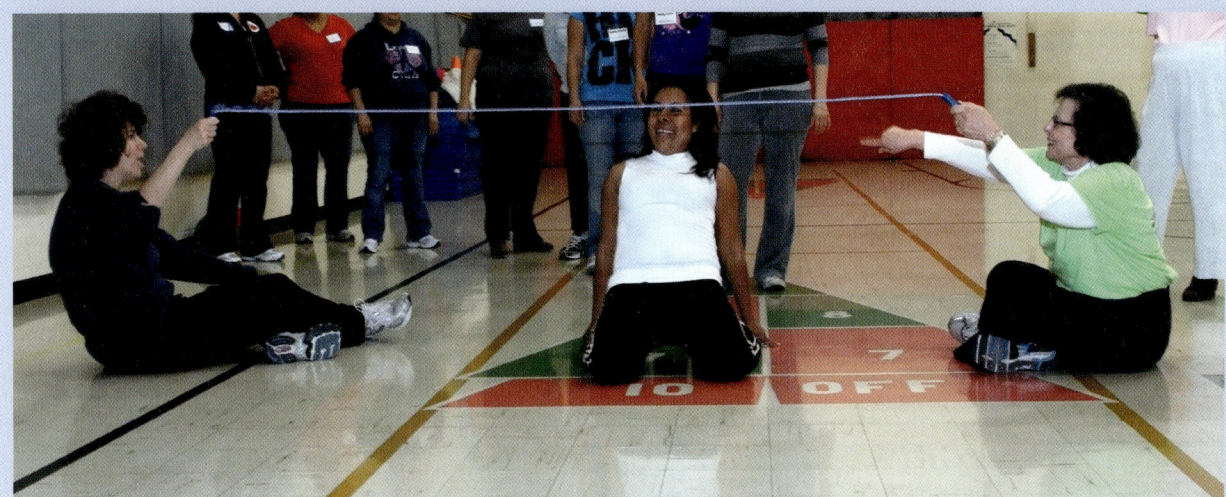

(Left) A HIPPY mom, Dobie Elementary School Principal Kay Reynolds, and Food + Fit = Fun cochair Kyra Effren (left to right) serve a healthy banana snack, 2009. Photo by Robin Sachs.

(Right) A big "Thank You" from the staff and parents of Dobie Elementary School shows appreciation for the Section's efforts to build a healthy lifestyle through Food + Fit = Fun. (Left to right) Kit Prince, director of RISD Family Literacy Program, and Maria Loera, Dobie staff member, 2010.

(Left) How low can you go? Project cochairs Debra Levy-Fritts and Sharan Goldstein (left and right) hold the rope as Food + Fit = Fun participants do the limbo, demonstrating that fun is possible while doing physical activity, 2011.

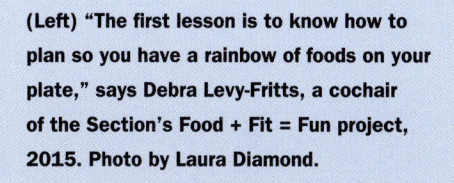

(Left) "The first lesson is to know how to plan so you have a rainbow of foods on your plate," says Debra Levy-Fritts, a cochair of the Section's Food + Fit = Fun project, 2015. Photo by Laura Diamond.

(Right) Section Food + Fit = Fun project leaders Marlene Cohen, Syl Benenson, Sharan Goldstein, Kyra Effren, and Debra Levy-Fritts (left to right) celebrate their "Vision for America Showcase" Award at the National Convention held in Dallas, 2011. Photo by Laura Diamond.

(Left) Up in the air: physical activity can be fun as Food + Fit = Fun participants show off their jumping skills, 2010. Photo by Robin Sachs.

(Right) Section volunteer Harriet Mellow (front) helps HIPPY moms from RISD's Dobie Elementary School pick out brightly colored produce at Fiesta Foods grocery store in Dallas, 2012.

Section President Kyra Effren (bottom center) with past presidents at the Ninetieth Birthday Luncheon. Front row (left to right): Syl Benenson, Pat Peiser, Betty Dreyfus, Joy Mankoff, Kyra Effren, Edna Flaxman, Darrel Strelitz, and Bette Miller. Back row: Julie Lowenberg, Janice Sweet (later Janice Weinberg), Maddy Unterberg, Anita Marcus, Marsha Fischman, Janet Newberger, Jeanne Fagadau, Kathy Freeman, Joni Cohan, Phyllis Bernstein, Jody Platt, and Brenda Brand, 2003.

(Left) Section member DJ Kassanoff assists new Americans as they improve their language skills at VMLC in West Dallas, 2015. Photo by Julie Lowenberg.

(Right) Regina Montoya, then senior vice president and general counsel for Children's Medical Center, with Cheryl Pollman, Section president, at the "Business of Immigration Reform" conference, 2009.

Section members and community partners celebrate the opening of the Vickery Meadow Food Pantry. Front row (left to right): Madlyn Rosenbaum, Myra Fischel, and Saralynn Busch. Back row (left to right): Jane Manaster, Deidre Cizon, Temple Emanu-El's Rabbi Asher Knight, Carol Weinstein, Cheryl Pollman, Lynn Goldstein, Debby Stein, and Rose Watel, 2012. Photo by Laura Diamond.

(Left) Section members Marlene Cohen, Bette Miller, and Janet Eickmeyer (left to right) examine the many historical items being gathered in preparation for the one hundredth birthday celebration of the Section, 2012. Photo by Laura Diamond.

(Right) Several generations of Section volunteers finish up their tasks during the Martin Luther King Jr. Day of Service at the North Texas Food Bank. (Left to right) Robin Zweig, Syl Benenson, Ellen Jackofsky, Mimi Platt Zimmerman, Pat Peiser, Beth Brand Stromberg, Benjamin Stromberg, Molly Zimmerman, Jackie Fleschman, Lauren Zweig, and David Zweig, 2012.

In fact, an estimated thirty-three languages are represented in this diverse community. The families are often in need of food, clothing, jobs, and other social services.

The Section's involvement in the Vickery Meadow area began in the mid-1990s when volunteers from the Section helped with after school tutoring. Later, they taught ESL classes and an enrichment program for children in kindergarten through sixth grades at Vickery Meadow Elementary School. When Vickery Meadow Learning Center (VMLC) opened in 1998, Section members taught adult literacy and ESL classes there. A year later, the Section became a member of VMLC's Board of Directors.

In 2010, the Section joined Catholic Charities, Ladies of Charity, Park Cities Baptist Church, Society of St. Vincent de Paul Diocesan Council, Jewish Family Service, and Temple Emanu-El to create the Vickery Meadow Neighborhood Alliance. The organizations work together to provide supplemental food through the Vickery Meadow Food Pantry along with clothing, social services, and employment counseling.

Section members serve the residents with respect and dignity, making them feel welcome in their new surroundings. The Section is represented on the management team of the Alliance, and our volunteers are integral to the success of the project. The truly positive aspect of this undertaking is the close working partnership with the other groups.

Celebrating "Let's Move" with First Lady Michelle Obama
Essay by Barbara Lee
President, Greater Dallas Section 2010–2012

In February 2012, First Lady Michelle Obama came to Dallas as part of a three-day tour to celebrate the second anniversary of her "Let's Move" initiative that was designed to solve the problem of childhood obesity in the United States within a generation. I was among about forty North Texans invited by the White House to meet Mrs. Obama at the City of Dallas's Kleberg-Riley Recreation Center.

The White House staff had learned about the Section's Food + Fit = Fun (FFF) program from Nancy K. Kaufman, CEO of NCJW, Inc. Working with families who have preschool-age children, FFF strives to reduce the impact of poor eating habits and obesity through interactive nutrition education and physical activity.

Each invited guest had a photograph taken with the First Lady. We joined a few hundred children from DISD's Nancy Moseley Elementary School who were in the gym. After a cooking competition, Mrs. Obama chatted with all the student groups. She stressed the importance of eating as healthy as possible and being active.

It was an honor to represent the Section and a privilege to meet the First Lady. I thanked her for all that she was doing to raise awareness and to promote local action on this critical issue. Her recognition of the Section was another shining moment in the one hundred years of our history and our service to the Dallas community.

Three generations of Section members enjoy their volunteer time together. (Left to right) Sarah Yarrin, Jackie Waldman, and Melissa Plaskoff, 2011. Photo by Norm Diamond.

(Above) Section president Barbara Lee, representing the Section's Food + Fit = Fun program, met First Lady Michelle Obama at a "Let's Move" program held at the DISD's Nancy Moseley Elementary School, 2012. Courtesy of Barbara Lee.

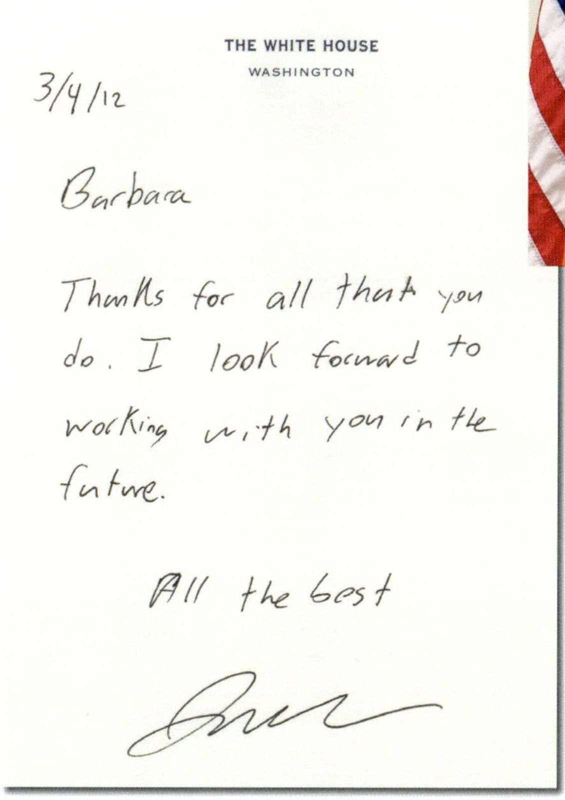

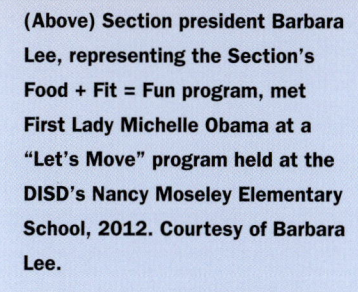

(Left) First Lady Michelle Obama expressed her gratitude to Barbara Lee for her assistance with the "Let's Move" program, 2012. Courtesy of Barbara Lee.

Happy Birthday! Joyous members release balloons in celebration of one hundred years of service, 2013. Photo by Lara Bierner.

"One question is always relevant: how can I use this to move forward?"

Rebbetzin Tziporah Heller, Jewish scholar

11 : Marking a Century of Achievement

Early in 2013, following the resignation of Pope Benedict, Cardinal Jorge Mario Bergoglio of Argentina became Pope Francis, the first Jesuit and first non-European Pope since 741 CE. Prince George Alexander Louis of Cambridge, the third in line to the British throne, was born to Prince William and Catherine, Duchess of Cambridge. Late in the year, Nelson Mandela, the first president of South Africa elected in a fully representative democratic election and a Nobel Prize winner, died at the age of ninety-five.

The year was the fiftieth anniversary of many events in the civil rights movement, including the Ku Klux Klan bombing of the Sixteenth Street Baptist Church in Birmingham, Alabama, where four young girls died, and Dr. Martin Luther King Jr. wrote the famous letter from the Birmingham jail that defended nonviolent resistance to racism. Also, 2013 marked the one-hundredth anniversary of the birth of Rosa Parks,

Section member Renee Karp enjoys the Day of Service activities with her grandchildren at the Jewish Community Center. (Left to right) Shira Karp, Renee Karp, Macy Golman, and Grey Golman; back: Rachel Chaput and son, 2013. Photo by Laura Diamond.

Section "buddies" Beth Brand Stromberg and Karen Stock (left to right) take a break from packing food for the Day of Service at the North Texas Food Bank, 2013.

(Right) The Centennial logo reflects the Section's pride in its home city, Dallas, 2013.

a civil rights activist who refused to give up her seat on a segregated bus.

The Eighty-Second Session of the Texas Legislature passed many contentious laws, including a requirement for a government-issued photo ID in order to vote in an election. Another law required a detailed explanation of the fetus in the womb before an abortion. Lawmakers issued new redistricting maps and appropriated $5 billion less in funds for public education.

In Dallas, all living former US Presidents and President Barack Obama were present for the dedication of the George W. Bush Presidential Center on the grounds of Southern Methodist University. Later that year, thousands of people gathered at Dealey Plaza to solemnly honor the memory of President John F. Kennedy, who was assassinated in Dallas on November 23, 1963.

ANY NONPROFIT GROUP THAT ORGANIZES AND SURVIVES FOR ONE HUNDRED YEARS IS A CAUSE for rejoicing. But to spend a century growing, serving, and being productive—these are real reasons to celebrate and to move forward!

As the Greater Dallas Section reached its century birthday, the kick-off began on January 21 with—what else?—a community day of service! About 160 members participated by working at such sites as the North Texas Food Bank and Our Friends Place, a transitional living center for young women whose histories reflected abuse, neglect, abandonment, homelessness, or poverty.

The Section had been asked to decorate one bedroom. Volunteers instead refreshed an entire apartment—painting walls, washing windows, scrubbing cabinets, providing new bedding and window treatments, installing a tile backsplash in the kitchen, and completing the look with custom-made pillows and artwork.

Meanwhile, another group of volunteers met at the Aaron Family Jewish Community Center to make small decorative items that they took to Our Friends Place. Parents, grandparents, and children created magnets, message boards, and paper flowers to brighten individual apartments and the common living area.

On February 14, the *Texas Jewish Post* (*TJP*) highlighted the Section's century of service with a cover story. The article emphasized the Section's commitment to community service from its early beginning—starting with help for immigrants in 1914. *TJP* selected the following pioneering initiatives to feature in its story: after-school programming, a recreational club for seniors, Family Outreach, HIPPY, and the Greater Dallas Coalition for Reproductive Freedom. According to the *TJP*, "NCJW Dallas was one of the first women's organizations in the area. Committed volunteers and passionate women in the community have made the organization what it is today."

The Centennial Celebration was preceded by a sponsor's reception, followed by a luncheon on February 26, 2013, almost one hundred years to the day of the Section's founding. There were tributes galore, among them a City of Dallas proclamation presented by Mayor Mike Rawlings. Also, Dr. Ron Anderson, former CEO of Parkland Health & Hospital System, presented an award from the Parkland Foundation honoring decades of Section volunteerism at Parkland Hospital. At the end of the meal, the audience was surprised when balloons popped out of a giant birthday cake!

The main event was the keynote speech by journalist Laura Ling, who told her story of bravery while working for human rights.

Celebrating 100 Years of Leadership, Advocacy and Community Service in Dallas

NCJW
National Council of Jewish Women
Greater Dallas Section
1913 - 2013

(Left) Section member Ellen Marks and her grandson work on a craft project at the Jewish Community Center during the Section's Day of Service, 2013. Photo by Laura Diamond.

Section member Susan Swartz and her grandson Max Weinstein (on ladder) tidy up the windows at Our Friends Place during the Section's Day of Service, 2013. Photo by Laura Diamond.

(Left to right) Max Weinstein along with Section past president Jody Platt and her grandchildren Molly and Saul Zimmerman help move books at Our Friends Place, 2013. Photo by Laura Diamond.

The Centennial Luncheon was preceded by a sponsors' reception. Key leaders (left to right): President Robin Zweig, Maddy Unterberg, Janice Sweet (later Janice Weinberg), Speaker Laura Ling, Adrienne Rosen, Marsha Fischman, Jody Platt, Rhona Streit (also known as Rhona Frankfurt), and Patty Traub, 2013. Photo by Lara Bierner.

Part of the Section's decorating team on the Day of Service at Our Friends Place. (Left to right) Sue Hesseltine, executive director of Our Friends Place; Joyce Bruce-Starling, resident manager; Section members Joyce Rosenfield and Carol Tobias; and Donna Fadal, interior decorator who donated her services, 2013. Photo by Laura Diamond.

The Parkland Foundation presented a special award to the Section. Section past president Jody Platt accepted the award from Dr. Ron Anderson, CEO of Parkland Hospital, at the Centennial Luncheon, 2013. Photo by Lara Bierner.

One hundred Chanukah menorahs light up the century of Section's service to the community at a celebration at the home of Section member Jody Platt, 2013. Photo by Laura Diamond.

121

Laura Ling, keynote speaker at the Section's Centennial Luncheon, joins past president Katherine Bauer at the sponsor's reception, 2013. Photo by Lara Bierner.

(Right) Cynthia Schneidler, Section member, displays the Centennial Quilt that she created in honor of the Centennial. The quilt symbolizes acts of service, advocacy, and Jewish values, 2013. Photo by Lara Bierner.

Ms. Ling had been arrested in early 2009 and imprisoned for 140 grueling days in North Korea. Her "crime"?—reporting on the sex trafficking of that country's women across the border into China. Her personal account of captivity, hope, and, finally, freedom inspired the attendees.

The Centennial Committee found an ideal way to acknowledge one hundred years of accomplishments and to say goodbye to the last twelve months of celebration. December 4 was the last night of Chanukah in 2013. That evening, a crowd of members entered the home of Jody and Mel Platt, each bearing a dinner dish and a personal menorah. Then, together, participants chanted the holiday blessings, lit one hundred Menorahs for one hundred years, and stepped forward into the Section's new century.

Celebrating One Hundred Years of Service
Essay by Robin Zweig
President, Greater Dallas Section 2012–2014
President, Evening Branch 2002–2004

Serving as the Greater Dallas Section president during the time of our Centennial will always be among my most treasured memories. Committees planned an array of events that gave us a unique opportunity to tell our story of service to the entire community. This incredible year also reminded all our members and stakeholders about the Section's mission as we recognized our progress and success in all aspects of our long organizational life.

Our biggest event of the year was the one hundredth Birthday Luncheon. The guest speaker was author and journalist Laura Ling. A centennial video, narrated by local television news anchor Gloria Campos, premiered at the celebration. It showed, in both words and pictures, a century of Section volunteer work for the Dallas area, the United States, and Israel.

Temple Emanu-El hosted an exhibit that represented our one hundred years of service, and special Section Shabbats were observed at several area congregations. These milestone twelve months came to a close with a Chanukah party at the home of Jody and Mel Platt.

Piecing Together a Symbol of Our Strength
Essay by Cynthia Schneidler, MD
Greater Dallas Section Member

To commemorate a century of commitment and strength, I created a quilt to honor the women of the Greater Dallas Section.

The pioneering leadership that characterizes our initiatives is reflected in my original design, which I made without a formal pattern. The pieces fit together as a portrait of the Section, invoking both the solidarity and power of our organization and the essential and unique contributions of each individual. The design is asymmetric, but at the same time, it resonates harmony in the pattern of shapes and colors, reflecting the nature of our work.

In the rhythm of the quilt's angles and spaces, in the interplay of the bright and the dark, and in the symbols of our core values, we hear and see our call to action and our response.

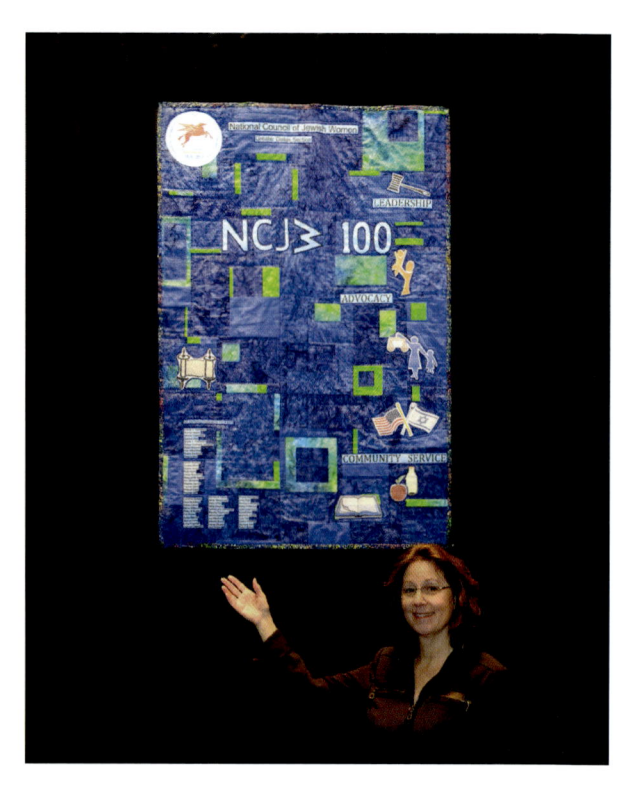

The Section's presidents, serving from 1960 to the present day, gathered to celebrate the upcoming Centennial. Seated (left to right): Bette Miller, Sue Tilis, Julie Lowenberg, Joni Cohan, Pat Peiser, Katherine Bauer, and Syl Benenson. Standing (left to right): Barbara Lee, Cheryl Pollman, Kyra Effren, Anita Marcus, Marlene Cohen, Jody Platt, Robin Zweig, Betty Dreyfus, Joy Mankoff, Phyllis Bernstein, Marsha Fischman, Brenda Brand, Janice Sweet (later Janice Weinberg), and Kathy Freeman. Not pictured: Jeanne Fagadau, Darrel Strelitz, and Maddy Unterberg, 2013. Photo by Lara Bierner.

The February 14, 2013, edition of the *Texas Jewish Post* honors the Section's commitment to the community. Photo by Lara Bierner. (Weinstein, "Happy Hundred.")

Section members (left to right) Jody Platt, Robin Zweig, and Rhona Streit (also known as Rhona Frankfurt) celebrate the conclusion of the Centennial year, 2013.

CITY OF DALLAS
Special Recognition

WHEREAS, in 1913, National Council of Jewish Women, Greater Dallas Section (NCJW) was granted a charter by the national organization and became the first Jewish women's organization in Dallas; and

WHEREAS, NCJW has launched, maintained and funded numerous community service projects to meet needs within the Dallas community during 100 years of volunteerism; and

WHEREAS, NCJW has worked in coalition, collaboration and partnership with numerous community organizations over these 100 years, striving for social justice by improving the quality of life for women, children and families and by safeguarding individual rights and freedoms; and

WHEREAS, NCJW initiated the first penny lunch program and first volunteer program in Dallas Public Schools, and established the Family Outreach program to counsel at risk families and to prevent child abuse and neglect; and

WHEREAS, NCJW was instrumental in the founding of the Texas Juvenile Justice Coalition and the Dallas Mental Health Association (now Mental Health America); and

WHEREAS, NCJW established and continues to maintain the Minnie Hexter Milk Fund, providing free milk and baby formula to families in Dallas; and

WHEREAS, NCJW founded LIFT (Literacy Instruction for Texas) in 1961 and CASA (Court Appointed Special Advocates) in 1979; and

WHEREAS, NCJW conceived and implemented Kids in Court preparing children to testify in Dallas County, and Safeguards for Seniors providing education for seniors regarding proper use of medications; and

WHEREAS, NCJW initiated HIPPY (Home Instruction for Parents of Preschool Youngsters) which empowers parents to be their children's first teachers and is presented in collaboration with the Dallas, Irving and Richardson Independent School Districts; and

WHEREAS, NCJW created and continues its involvement with the Meyerson Symphony Center Docent Program; and also created and ran docent programs at the Dallas Central Library and The Women's Museum; and

WHEREAS, NCJW established Food + Fit = Fun, a bilingual program run by NCJW volunteers that promotes a healthy lifestyle; and

WHEREAS, NCJW (as an extension of its Women's Access to Comprehensive Health Services initiative) designed and presents a healthy relationships curriculum for teens.

NOW, THEREFORE I, MIKE RAWLINGS, mayor of the city of Dallas, and on behalf of the Dallas City Council, on this 26th day of February 2013, do hereby extend special recognition to the

NATIONAL COUNCIL OF JEWISH WOMEN

on celebrating their 100th anniversary, and thank and congratulate NCJW for its pioneering programs and services that have improved lives and made a significant, positive difference in Dallas during its first hundred years; and wish this outstanding organization continued success as it enters a 2nd century of striving for social justice and a better quality of life for all.

MAYOR

Twelve "Whereases" from the City of Dallas honor the Section's one hundred years of service.

Louis and Robin Zweig join the Honorable Mike Rawlings, City of Dallas mayor (right), at the Centennial Celebration Luncheon, 2013. Photo by Lara Bierner.

April 1966

Evening Branch President Elaine Kimmelman passes the gavel to the newly installed president, Phyllis Putter (left to right), 1966.

"To everything there is a season, and a time to every purpose under the heaven."

Ecclesiastes 3:1

12 : Creating Alternative Structures

Resilience is the mark of a viable organization that survives over complex times and many generations. For some members of the Section, temporary or permanent situations required adjusting their volunteer commitments and schedules. Members' abilities to serve could be compromised by growing families, full-time employment for husbands and/or wives, responsibilities for aging family members, or longer distances between homes and service sites.

As activities of the Section increased and more volunteer time was required, members' availability was also challenged. Wise leaders then suggested creating alternative ways to organize, meet, and answer the dilemmas that members faced. The new groups that developed during those years were called "Branches." As long as the goals, personally and organizationally, were being met, the Branches continued. When new options were needed or presented, members chose what was better for their situations.

ALL SECTION BRANCHES OPERATED UNDER THE SAME MISSION AND VISION THAT WERE ALIGNED WITH National and the Greater Dallas Section values and principles. Branches have come and gone, but the participation and leadership that they developed remain. Here is an overview of the various branches.

Teens and Youth

From its earliest years, the Section engaged young women and teenage girls in organized, meaningful activities. From 1917–1946, several different efforts (Junior Auxiliary, Juniors, Junior Buds, Junior Council) drew young women into service. From 1955–1976, the Section's Councilette teenagers volunteered in the community.

Evening Branch

Establishment of this group began in 1951. The expectation was to serve young mothers, many newcomers from various parts of the United States as well as from overseas, and working women who were not able to attend daytime functions. After a reorganization in 1957, the Branch continued to provide community service, education, and social opportunities until it disbanded and merged its activities with the Section in 2004. The Branch's last president, Robin Zweig, said in an April 2004 *Constant Comment* article, "I believe that the legacy and history of Evening Branch will be characterized by outstanding leadership, outstanding service to the community, and, most importantly, a great group of people."

Richardson/Plano Branch

As Jewish women moved into Dallas's rapidly expanding suburbs, the travel times to Section activities grew prohibitively longer. In 1971 a Section was formed to serve these women more conveniently. The Richardson-Plano Section was an independent section, responsible for its own fundraising and projects. When this section could no longer sustain itself financially, it merged with the Greater Dallas Section in 1980 and became the Morning Branch. Later, in 1984, this group joined the Evening Branch.

Young Professionals and Professional Branch

A substantial number of young working women with an interest in serving the community decided to organize in the mid-1970s. As professionals between the ages of twenty to thirty, these women had volunteer needs which differed from those of Evening branch members. With this in mind, a new Branch, the Young Professionals, was started. Many of its members were former Councilettes. This branch completed its first year in 1975 with twenty members, a full slate of officers, and plans already outlined for the next year's programs and projects. Unsuccessful efforts to recruit leadership saw the group take a hiatus in 1977.

During the following years, a group of single parents expressed an interest in studying via National's Self Development Series. In order to take this course, one had to be a member of NCJW. This led to the recruitment of members for the newly named Professional Branch, which included five men and two women. With these seven as part of the Branch's Charter membership, there seemed to be an interest in what else NCJW had to offer. The 1981 Professional Branch evolved into a group of eighty members who met in the evening or on Sundays to pursue their interests in public affairs and community service. This branch dissolved in 2002.

Answering a Need for Working Women
Essay by Joyce Rosenfield
President, Greater Dallas Section 2016–2018
President, Evening Branch 1975–1976

During the late 1940s and early 1950s, more women were working outside the home, and many young mothers had nobody to watch their children during the day so that they could volunteer. Dallas Section past presidents Fannie Kahn and Mildred Sack urged the Section to form a group for those women who

The Evening Branch lightheartedly made sure their husbands knew they were doing important work, 1963.

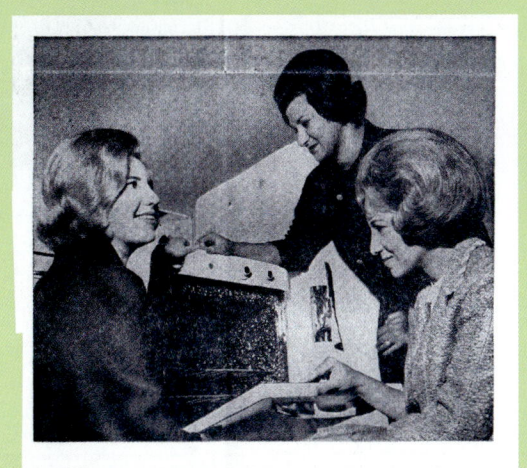

After she was president of the Evening Branch, Nita Mae Tannebaum (center) joined Section members Elissa Sommerfield and Sarah Yarrin (front, left to right) in helping to plan the Section's "Women on the Move" conference, 1966. Photo by Jo Ball. (McKee, "Jewish Women Do Homework Before Forum.")

Junior Buds to Stage Play at Temple Emanu-El

Fifteen young Junior Buds from the Section pose for a photo before presenting a College Day performance at Temple Emanu-El. Front Row (left to right): Marjorie Lichenstein, Lois Davis, Jeanette Ornish, Charlotte Donosky, Sara Lee Barshop, and Rae Engle. Back Row: Leah Leventhal, Louise Philipson, Annette Florence, Miriam Zesmer, Evelyn Rosenberg, Maxine Kay, Felice Novich, Sara Hart, and Rowena Kaplan, 1929. (The *Dallas Morning News*, September 17, 1929.)

THE EVENING BRANCH

Regular Meeting: January 8, 1952, 8 p.m.
Chairman: Miss Carmen Miller, Presiding.

The Evening Branch, Dallas Section, National Council of Jewish Women, is already in action. The group organized December 11, 1951, at 8 p.m. in the home of Mrs. John Franklin. Miss Carmen Miller was elected Chairman, Miss Marilyn Rachofsky Vice-Chairman, Mrs. Cecelia Crow Secretary. The girls are also going to have their own Study Group, and will also do work on a Community Service Project. Their regular meetings will be the first Tuesday of each month. Anyone in Council interested in attending the night meetings are welcome.

The Evening Branch was organized on December 11, 1951. ("The Evening Branch," *Bulletin*, January 1952.)

HELPING HANDS ncjw
Richardson - Plano Branch   Greater Dallas Section
October, 1980   Leslie Neumann — Editor

ELECTION 1980:
Are Our Basic Freedoms Being Tampered With?

The Richardson-Plano Branch focused on advocacy at this program about election issues, 1980. ("Election 1980," *Helping Hands*, October 1980.)

Evening Branch members created wall hangings for the Bradford Baby Clinic (which eventually became Children's Medical Center). (Left to right) Flo Marks, Rochelle Gartenlaub, and Judy Utay, 1966.

The Evening Branch's banner shows that the group won National's Fund Raising Award in 1988.

Section and Branch leadership posed for a group picture at National's Southern District Convention in Houston. Front row (left to right): Susan Combs, Elaine Scharf, Denise Mayoff, Susan Johnson, Myra Fischel, and Robyn Goldman. Middle row (left to right): Bette Miller, Lorraine Schein, Janet Newberger, Janice Sweet (later Janice Weinberg), and Syl Benenson. Top row (left to right): Susan Herzfeld, Kathy Freeman, Phyllis Bernstein, Sharon Cohany, Carol Rieter (later Carol Tobias), Anita Marcus, Pat Peiser, Joy Mankoff, Ruth Lurie, Maddy Unterberg, Jackie Goldman, and Sandy Kaman, 1982. Courtesy of Sharon Cohany.

(Right) It's time to honor the Professional Branch's membership with a French-themed dinner, 1982. ("Versailles Tonite," *Professional Branch Newsletter*, January 1982.)

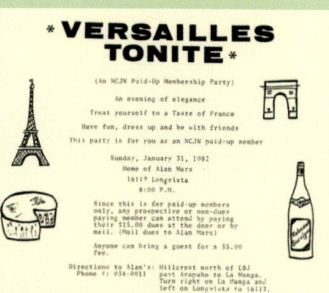

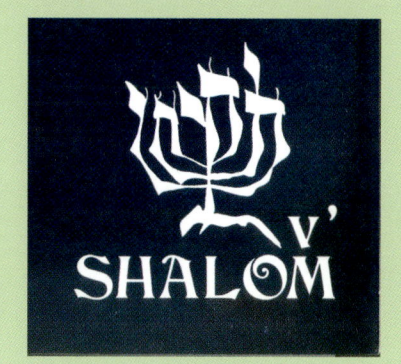

The Evening Branch, along with Jewish Family Service, developed this pamphlet, *V'Shalom*, in English and Russian to help new immigrants learn about important things to know and do in Dallas, 1975.

The Friendship Fone project, sponsored by the Evening Branch, reached out to elder shut-ins with friendly visits by phone. (Left to right) Section members Edna Flaxman, Katherine Bauer, Ann Folz, and Evening Branch President Gwen Benjamin, 1969. Photo by Bob W. Smith. (McKee, "NCJW Serves Fellowman.")

To many an older shut-in this season, the ring of the telephone will mean a member of the Greater Dallas Section is making a friendly "visit." The Friendship Phone program was started by the Evening Branch. With Mrs. Alfred Benjamin, right, Evening Branch chairman, are from left, Mmes Carl Flaxman, Herbert Bauer, executive vice-president, and Lorch Folz. Mrs. Flaxman, current parliamentarian, is past president of the Greater Dallas Section of the NCJW.

could not attend daytime meetings and events. As a result, thirty-three young women met and founded the Evening Branch on December 11, 1951. Most of the women were single and employed.

Dr. Carmen Miller (later Carmen Michael), who was a clinical psychologist at UT Southwestern Medical School in Dallas, was the Evening Branch's first chair. With her guidance, the Branch conducted an exhaustive study to determine the need for care facilities to serve emotionally disturbed children. The research revealed an inadequate number of available beds. Members advocated for state legislation to establish a hospital or group home for these children. Carmen published an article about the findings in the March 1953 *Texas Hospitals* journal.

Focusing on newcomers to the Dallas area, the Branch, in partnership with the Women's Division of the Dallas Jewish Federation, launched a significant newcomer's welcoming project, "Your Key to Big D." It contained a listing of cultural, educational, and welfare agencies in Dallas.

Other early community service projects included volunteering at Hope Cottage, the Juvenile Detention Home, Wadley Blood Center, or Parkland Hospital and making surgical dressings for the American Cancer Society. Members donated boxes of needed items to Israel via National's Ship-A-Box program. Branch members also volunteered at the Section's Your Thrift Shop.

In March 1957, a reorganizational membership coffee was held. Many of the new members were married and had small children. They found it easier to attend evening meetings. At the first regular meeting of the reorganized branch in October of that year, Judge Beth Wright of the Court of Domestic Relations spoke.

Bilingual Section volunteers, including branch members, befriended and advised a "Know Your Community" group of fifty-five Jewish New Americans who were chauffeured to monthly meetings that featured programs, refreshments, and congeniality. The work was so effective that the branch assumed full responsibility for this program in 1960.

Branch members were an active, talented, and social group. They presented puppet shows, had a bowling league, and enjoyed card parties and potluck dinners. The Travelling Troubadours, formed in 1962 and directed by Bernice E. Danhi, spread their good cheer with performances at Golden Acres, Senior Citizens Club, USO, and other nonprofit centers. Members served as hostesses for the 1963 Dallas Public Library's $1 million exhibition, "Words That Changed the World."

Beginning in the mid-1960s, branch volunteers provided weekly activities for clients of the Manning House, a social center for former mental patients, located at the Mental Health Association of Dallas. In cooperation with Jewish Family Service, Friendship Fone was launched in 1968. The Evening Branch paired members with older adults who needed social contact and access to someone for help in an emergency. They kept in touch by weekly telephone calls.

The Branch began a Tay-Sachs screening program in 1973. Tay-Sachs is an inherited disorder, one hundred times more common in Ashkenazi Jews than in other populations. The Branch devoted an entire program year to planning three screenings that were held in March 1974.

Many of the Branch's community service programs included "in projects." These events were often held in a member's home and involved creative activities. Members made Halloween masks, bags, and hats for Children's Medical Center patients and sometimes took the young patients trick or treating. Stuffed animals were made for the Thelma Boston Home for disabled foster children. Other

—Dallas News: John Rhodes.

With the aid of Scarecrow (Charlot Rosenburg), left, and the Good Witch (Nonie Schwartz), Council Player's Dorothy (Libby Svidlow) has found Toto, her dog.

Players following Yellow Brick Road

The Yellow Brick Road has been lengthened and extended into the community this fall by Council Players, the drama group of the National Council of Jewish Women, Evening Branch.

The young women have developed an amateur production of "The Wizard of Oz," which they are taking to underprivileged and handicapped children throughout the Dallas area.

Costumes and sets have been built by the group and are portable for setting up in such places as Scottish Rite Hospital, where it will perform Sunday afternoon at 2 p.m.

The production has been held once before, according to director-chairman Robyn Poss, at Crossroads Community Center. Other "bookings" are Parkland Hospital Pediatric Ward, Dec. 16; Mount St. Michael Home, Jan. 6; Juliet Fowler Home, Feb. 17 and Denton State School, March 24.

Performance at the Denton School will include a taping for closed circuit television.

This is the first year the council players have gone into the community with one show planned for several performances. It is free of charge.

The volunteers have been practicing three months and gave one dress rehearsal—for their own kids— before the first "curtain."

—SHARON COBLER

Members of the Evening Branch's Council Players, "Scarecrow" Charlot Rosenburg, "Dorothy" Libby Svidlow, and "Good Witch" Nonie Schwartz (left to right), performed in the *Wizard of Oz* at numerous area locations that served children, 1973. Photo by John Rhodes. (Cobler, "Players following Yellow Brick Road.")

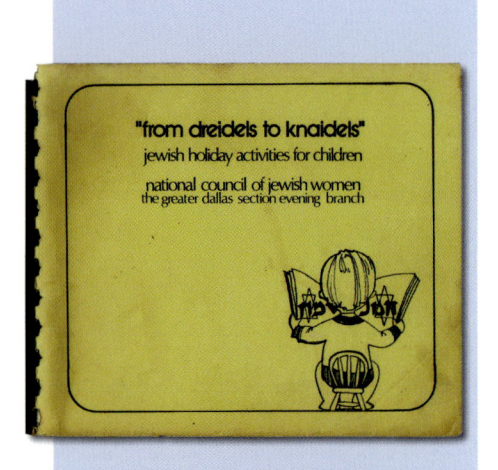

The Evening Branch compiled and sold this book of Jewish holiday activities and recipes to raise funds for community service projects, 1978. Courtesy of Caren Edelstein.

(Opposite, bottom left) The Evening Branch members and their families enjoyed activities with residents of area skilled nursing facilities. Here they are pictured at Heritage Park in Plano, TX, 1990.

(Opposite, bottom right) Lt. Maurice S. Kaprow, Jewish Chaplain of the USS *Saratoga* (CV60), sent this letter of thanks for the gift packages sent to servicemen during Operation Desert Shield, 1990. (*Constant Comment,* January 1991.)

works included teaching aids for the deaf students at DISD's Stonewall Jackson Elementary School, holiday decorations for Golden Acres, and favors and cakes for a birthday party for patients of Denton State School. A perennial favorite was making baby caps. Hundreds of head coverings were distributed to infants in the nurseries at Parkland Hospital.

In cooperation with Jewish Family Service, the program for New Americans was updated and focused on Russian immigrants. The Evening Branch wrote and distributed a handbook, *V'Shalom,* written in English and Russian. A map with pinpointed key locations, prepared by the Richardson-Plano Section, was also distributed. The handbook was later translated into Vietnamese for use in that community. The Branch prepared baskets with a Kiddish (wine) cup, candlestick holders, candles, and other items needed to celebrate the Sabbath. The gifts were given to each newly arrived Jewish family.

The Travelling Troubadours performed *The Wizard of Oz* early in 1974, and *Peter Pan* debuted at Terrell State Hospital later in the year. The group was renamed The Council Players and then became The Council Singers in 1977, led by Babette Davis. A video that showed highlights of the performances was produced and showcased at an NCJW Southern District Convention.

Branch members, despite being busy with family and jobs, continued with a multitude of community service projects during the 1980s. Volunteers participated in a Special Olympics Bowling Day and held parties for the children at the Dallas Ronald McDonald House. They collected maternity clothes for students at the DISD's Health Special School, provided services for New Americans, and Valentine sacks for Hope Cottage. Members held a special birthday party that featured Israeli dancing at a Community Homes for Adults, Inc. (CHAI) residence.

Volunteers corresponded with senior citizens in an Adopt-a-Grandparent program and organized a Senior Citizen/Children Talent Show at Golden Acres. Tay-Sachs screenings continued, and members delivered Meals on Wheels. Members addressed more than 14,000 customer postcards for each Encore Sale

and helped prepare and sell the merchandise.

In August 1990, the news was dominated by the first war in Iraq. Operation Desert Storm included an increase in US troops in the Persian Gulf. To support Jewish military personnel, the Branch sent care packages to several carrier ships stationed in the Gulf.

The Branch expanded its community service projects and continued its partnership, which began in the late 1980s, with the Samaritan Inn, a homeless shelter in Collin County. In 1991, members began volunteering at the Wonderland Express train exhibit, held at the Galleria Shopping Center, which benefited the Dallas Ronald McDonald House. Volunteers staffed the exhibit on December 24, so those celebrating Christmas could spend time with their families. This holiday attraction moved to NorthPark Mall in 1999 and became the Trains at NorthPark.

Members and their families celebrated many of the Jewish holidays, including Chanukah and Purim, with the residents of Golden Acres. Volunteers also served at the JCC's Senior Olympics.

Food donations for the North Texas Food Bank continued as did delivering Meals on Wheels in both Dallas and Plano. Branch members enjoyed presenting the Section's "Hello Israel" program to area schools and volunteering at Encore. The Branch also provided materials and toys for the therapy rooms at the Richardson Child Guidance Center. Twice-yearly meals were provided for Vogel Alcove employee meetings, and members were thrilled to step in and watch the sleeping infants for the staff.

As the twentieth century ended and the new century began, Branch members were trained to be volunteers at the New Beginning Center, a transitional, temporary emergency shelter for victims of domestic violence. Old cell phones were collected and sent to a company that refurbished them to provide a lifeline for victims. Residents of CHAI were treated to manicures, and volunteers helped the residents plant flowers to beautify their homes. A favorite community service activity for members and their children was preparing peanut butter-and-

Evening Branch past president Carol Robberson (right) provides a manicure for CHAI resident Barrie Burstyn during a community service project, 2003.

The Evening Branch's "Shopping Spree" chair Cindie Kurtz (right) has fun with a vendor, 1989.

```
LIEUTENANT MAURICE S. KAPROW
OFFICE OF THE CHAPLAIN
USS SARATOGA (CV 60)
FPO MIAMI, FL 34078-2740

                                            8 Dec 90

Resident
6511 Gretchen
Dallas, TX 75252

Dear Friend,

    On behalf of the Jewish community aboard the USS SARATOGA (CV60),
let me take this opportunity to thank you for the gift packages
you sent to us.  Unfortunately, you did not include your name so
I can not address you correctly.  I will be distributing them to
the Jewish personnel aboard over the next few days.  Believe me
when I tell you that they are really appreciated.

    It is always good to hear that members of the community support us
while we participate in Operation Desert Shield.  You certainly
know how important support is for us.

    Our morale is high and we are prepared to do whatever is necessary.
We have regular services and classes aboard the ship which are
attended by many of our Jewish sailors.  In addition, as the only
rabbi assigned to this battlegroup, I helicopter to all of the
smaller ships with us to provide for Jewish needs.  I can attest
to the dedication of our young men to the ideals we hold so dear.

    Again, thank you for your support.  If there is anything I can do
for you, please let me know.

                                            Sincerely,

                                            M S Kaprow

                                            M. S. KAPROW
                                            Lieutenant, Chaplain Corps
                                            United States Naval Reserve
                                            Jewish Chaplain
```

Good friends get together in the kitchen as part of the Evening Branch's "Cooking for a Cause" to benefit families served by the Vogel Alcove. Pictured: Jane Lofton, Julie Bank, Felicia Rubin, and Beth Brand Stromberg (left to right), 1998.

Joanna Byrne, Susan Levick, and Robin Benjamin Bock (left to right) paint decorative plates during a Paid-Up Membership Party (PUMP) that the Evening Branch held each year to celebrate its members, 2002.

jelly sandwich sack dinners for children whose foster parents were attending Child Protective Services' group meetings at Community Partners of Dallas's Rainbow Room.

Originally, the Section provided funds to the Branch to cover its administrative costs. Small fundraisers, such as raffles, bingo nights, and annual appeal letters, were held to supplement the Section's money. These funds usually were earmarked for the Branch's community service projects. A formal Ways and Means Department was established in 1973 when the Branch developed formal Bylaws and Policies and Procedures. These documents set a precedent for other NCJW branches since their parent Section traditionally governed them.

In 1986, the Branch began a "Shopping Spree" that featured vendors selling holiday and gift merchandise. The first year's effort raised $2,300. At the third event in 1989, over $8,000 was netted. That same year, the Branch used some of those funds to establish a special tribute fund to help support its community service projects. "Shopping Spree" had a very successful run of five years.

Passport Entertainment coupon books were very popular in the 1980s-1990s. These books provided discounts to many area restaurants, and the Branch earned a commission on each book sold. Members created and sold a booklet, "From Dreidels to Knaidels," about the Jewish holidays that had recipes and activities for families. "$CRIPT" certificates for grocery stores and restaurants were also sold. The Branch bought the certificates at a discount and then resold them at face value. Later, the sale of pins in the shapes of books and houses helped support literacy and homeless programs.

The Branch held a "Stay-At-Home" Ball in 1994. The invitation advised that there was "no shopping to do, no fancy attire, no speakers to sit through, no sitters to hire." Donations "excused" members from attending the event. Later, fundraising featured bingo extravaganzas, raffles, events with sponsorships, and large "garage" sales.

After serving the community for over fifty years, the Evening Branch disbanded in May 2004. At the last event, a dinner was held to celebrate the past successes and the lasting friendships that had been made. The Branch's funds were merged into the Section's treasury. Financial support and volunteers for the Collin County Committee on Aging's Meals on Wheels, Rainbow Room, Golden Acres, CHAI, and the Trains at NorthPark continued for several years under the auspices of the Section.

The legacy of the Evening Branch's service and leadership has been carried over into the Section. Marlene Cohen, Robin Zweig, and I, all previous Evening Branch presidents, have been presidents of the Section. Numerous other past Branch presidents and members who got their start in NCJW with the Branch also have served in leadership and community service roles since the Branch dissolved.

Remembering Evening Branch
Essay by Nita Mae Tannebaum
President, Evening Branch 1961–1963

We were young, some newly married or new parents, some new to Dallas, and others longtime Dallasites. The Evening Branch of the Greater Dallas Section was our answer: the social place to be. We could have fun while doing important things for the community.

As an old saying goes, "Some of my best friends are from the Evening Branch." We celebrated Jewish holidays together, many of our husbands became good friends, and we helped support one another. We had potluck suppers and created numerous cookbooks with members' recipes. I remember selling poll taxes to help get out the vote when John F. Kennedy and Richard M. Nixon were running for president. I met many of my closest friends while in the Evening Branch.

Established in December 1952, the Evening Branch was connected to the Dallas Section via a liaison from the Section's board. We were represented in the Section's *Yearbook* with a roster and details of our activities. We were honored that we were invited to be delegates to National's meetings, and it was a big deal when we were asked

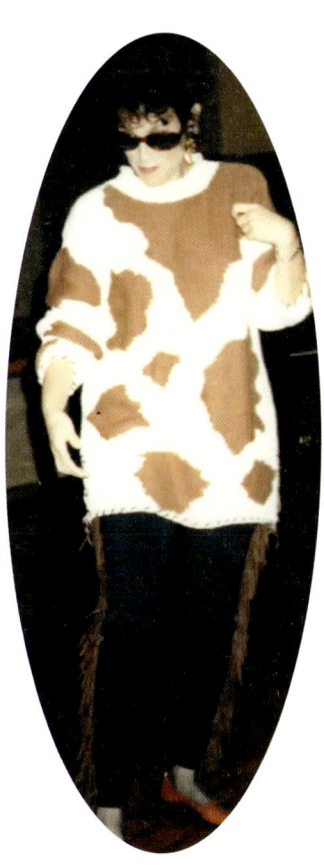

Evening Branch members Diane Garber and Kathy Higier (top to bottom) modeled chic outfits to kick off a new year of activities, 1992.

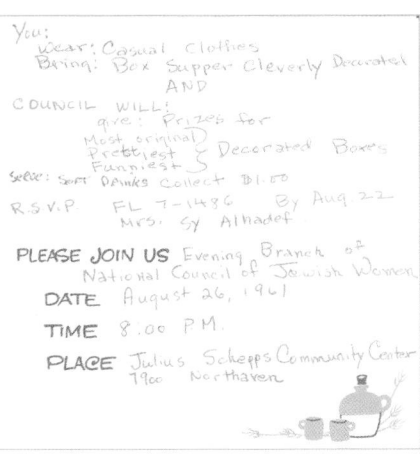

Handwritten notes, such as this engaging Evening Branch invitation, were used to notify members of upcoming events, 1961.

(Opposite page, top) The past presidents of the Evening Branch came together for a final dinner at the official closing of the Branch. Front row (left to right): Sandra Kaman, Sherri Shidlofsky, Felicia Rubin, Joyce Rosenfield, and Kathy Higier. Back row (left to right): Nonie Schwartz, Marlene Cohen, Robin Zweig, Elinore Brown, Judy Utay, Carol Tobias, Ellen Samuels, and Diane Lifshen, 2004.

(Opposite page, bottom) Evening Branch volunteers Judy and Robert Utay and Jerry and Ellen Samuels (left to right) take a break from assisting at the Trains at NorthPark on the day before Christmas, 2002.

to be ex officio members of the Section Board.

Just like in the Section, we all developed initiative, creativity, administrative skills, and compassion for others. Many of the best Section leaders of today received their start in the Evening Branch. It was a good time for all of us.

Branching Out with the Richardson-Plano Section
Essay by Carol Wigder
President, Richardson-Plano Section 1979–1980

The Dallas area once had more than one Section of the National Council of Jewish Women. In September 1971, fifteen women formed a daytime unit to provide needed services in the Richardson-Plano area. In spring 1973, the unit officially became a "section" of National, responsible for its own fundraising and projects. By June 1980, this Section could no longer sustain itself financially and was disbanded. It became the Morning Branch of the Greater Dallas Section.

In its early days, the Richardson-Plano Section (R-PS) compiled a "Directory of Social Services" and also conducted a survey of child abuse in the region. The results were presented to the Dallas County Child Welfare department (DCCW). Collaborating with DCCW for a pilot project, R-PS opened the Child Protection Center in 1973 to bring protective services for children closer to this suburban area. They hoped to reach those in need and to educate the public on issues of child abuse and neglect.

Members trained as paraprofessionals and worked under the guidance of the professional staff. Nine months later, the program's name changed to Family Outreach Center to reflect an expansion of services to general family problems, not only child abuse and neglect. By 1975, the Texas Department of Public Welfare offered its support and expanded the facilities. The success of this program prompted other cities to develop their own centers.

As R-PS became a Branch in June 1980, members were involved in several community service projects. In conjunction with Jewish Family Service, the group developed a news and information pamphlet, "Shalom Dallas," in English and Russian to mail bimonthly to Russian immigrants. The publication provided information about Jewish and United States holidays, local schools, and other topics relevant to their daily lives. The Hebrew Immigrant Aid Society (HIAS) awarded the Branch a certificate of appreciation for its outstanding contribution to resettlement of Soviet Jews in Dallas.

Members also volunteered with seniors at Golden Acres and with children at Scottish Rite Hospital. Toys were collected for the toy closet at The Family Place, a shelter for victims of abuse. And in 1981, at the request of Women in Community Services (WICS), Morning Branch members planned a Women's Day Seminar for residents at the McKinney Job Corps Center; the event was repeated the next year.

By 1983, the Branch members' lives had begun to change. Many returned to the workforce or were without available childcare. The Evening and Professional Branches, as well as the Greater Dallas Section, offered programs that were a better fit for the Morning Branch's members, so there was less need for this Branch. The Morning Branch, after four years, officially merged with the Evening Branch in 1984.

Including Men for the First Time
Essay by Carol Rieter Tobias
President, Evening Branch 1974–1975
President, Professional Branch 1981–1982

My interest in the Evening Branch waned when I became a single parent, but my interest in NCJW never wavered. I loved what the organization represented, and there were other women—including Sharon Cohany, Karen Stromberg, and Barbara Fried—who felt the same. I imagined there must be a group of men who shared our devotion to community service and who, like-minded, would want to join a group of women to work together. I was correct.

Lorraine Sulkin (later Lorraine Schein), a Greater Dallas Section past president and National's Southern

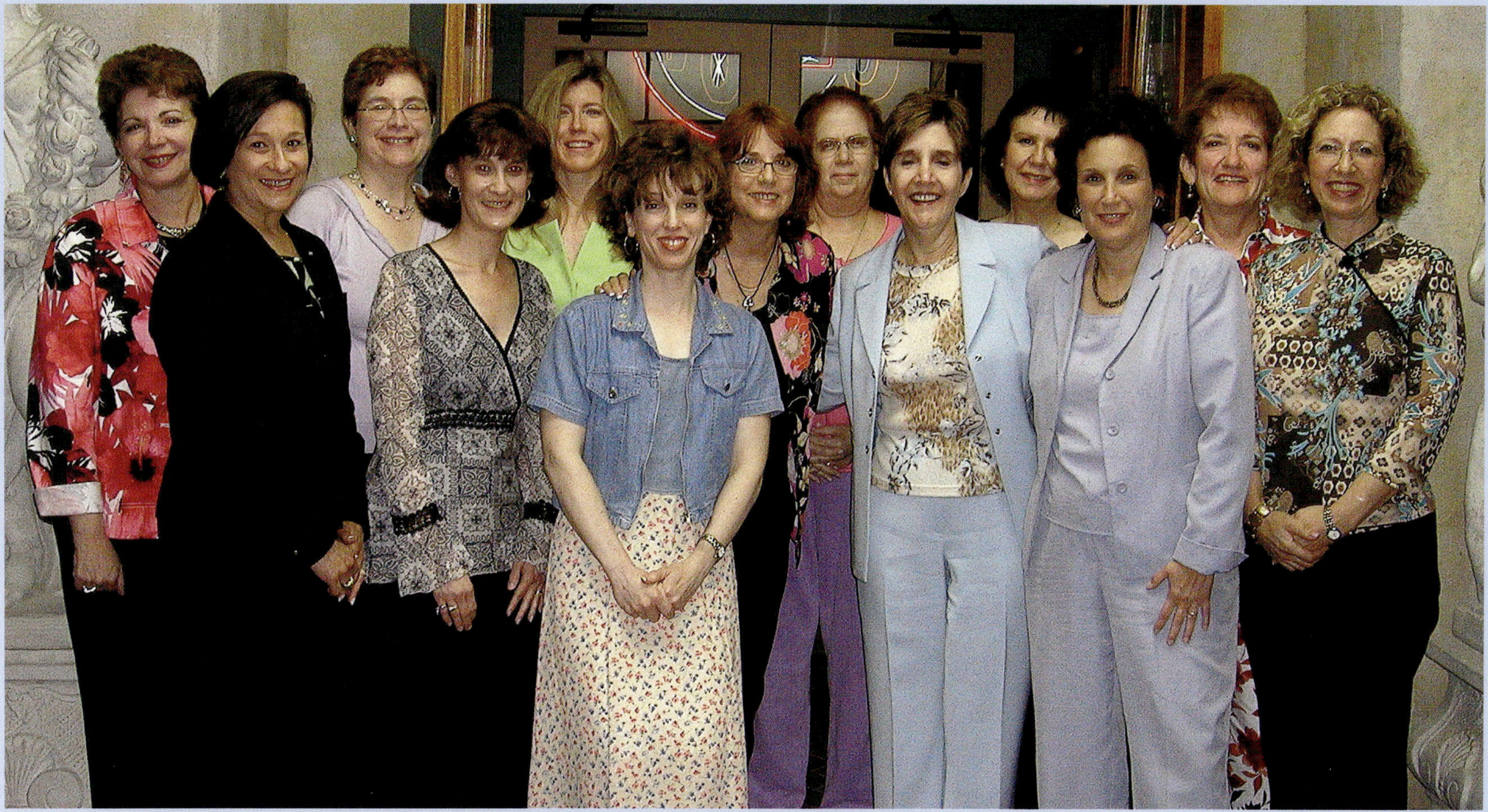

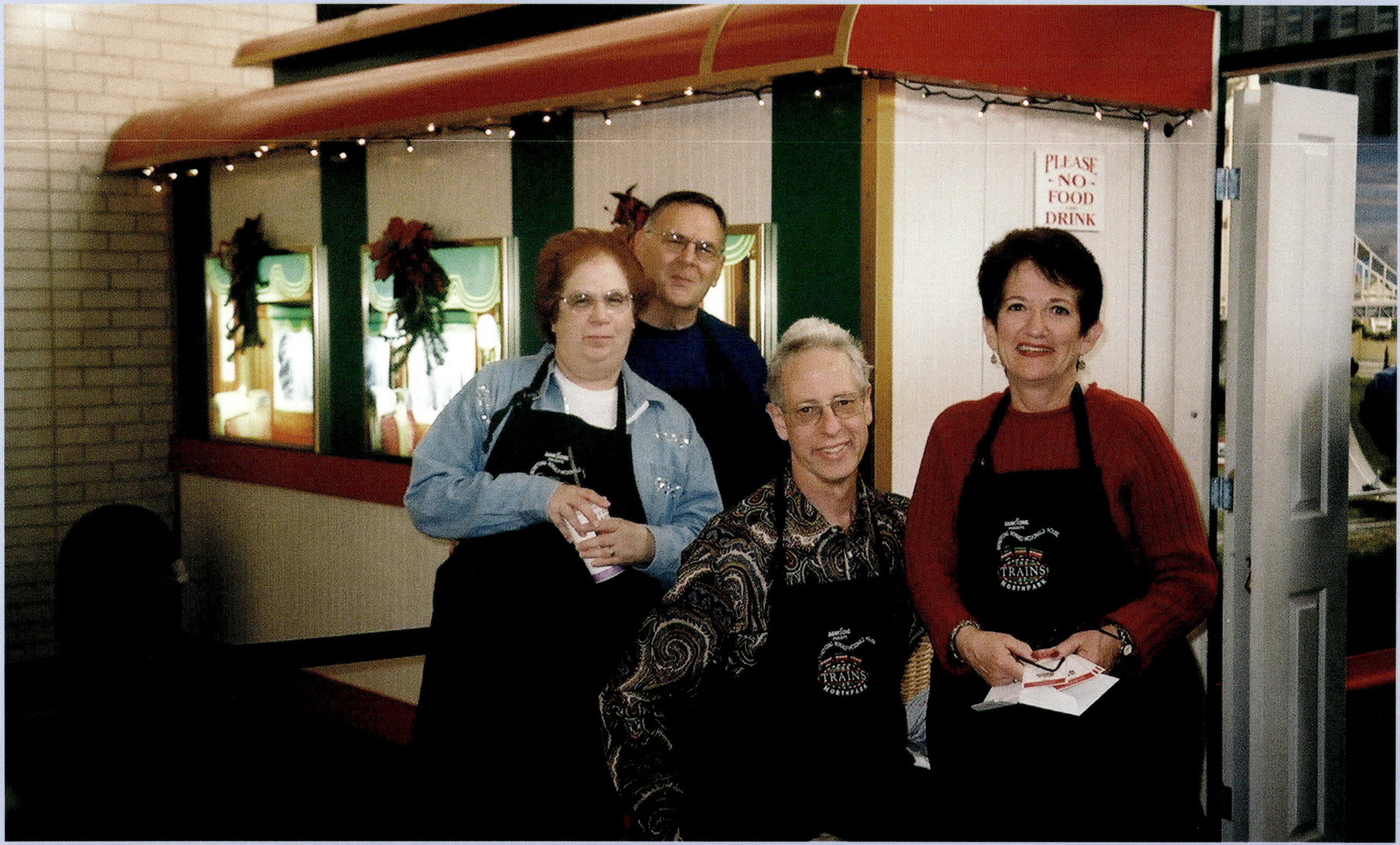
PLEASE
-NO-
FOOD
DRINK

(Left) Past Professional Branch president Carolyn Marcus (later Carolyn Abrams) conducts the Branch's installation, 1998.

(Right) Carol Rieter (later Carol Tobias), a past president of both the Evening Branch and the Professional Branch, prepares for the Self-Development Series presentation, c. 1980s. Photo by Sharon Cohany.

The Evening Branch provided funds for new cabinets in the remodeled kitchen at the Samaritan Inn, the Homeless Shelter for Collin County, located in McKinney. Front row (left to right): Debbie Wills, Debbie Jones, and Stacy Veeder, cochairs for the Samaritan Inn Project, presenting the check to George Chrisman, president of the board; Sandra Veeder; and Renee Stone holding infant daughter Jennifer. Back row (left to right): Roy Sherwood, a volunteer at Samaritan Inn; Col. Wes Geary, director; Harold Biggs, member of the Building Committee; and Phyllis Unell, 1991.

Carol Rieter (later Carol Tobias), the first Professional Branch president (center), celebrates the group's sixteenth birthday in 1997 with other founding members Marty Gross, Rich Morris, Bobbie Stein, and Jerry Raskin (left to right), 1997.

District Field Representative in the 1970s, was our guiding light. We knew that establishing a Branch for men and women was uncharted territory, but Lorraine presented the idea to National. I know she received some "grief" but only alluded to it in passing as we moved forward to welcome men into the Section's Professional Branch in 1981.

Our first program topic was about sex. What better way to pique the interest of singles! We approached the subject as a study group, and my friends still talk about that night in my living room with our lively guest speaker. The program worked, and we were off and running. Members volunteered at Golden Acres, the Ronald McDonald House, and The Family Place; held programs ranging from financial planning to women's issues; and offered an assertiveness training program.

I was president for only one year. My work life and family life took precedence over the leadership of this group. However, the Branch flourished for several years.

The Professional Branch was dissolved in 2002 after membership declined. I can say, without reservation, that while this Branch existed, it served an essential need for both the members and our community.

Ending a Good Thing
Essay by Janine Pulman
President, Morning Branch 1983–1984

When I joined the Greater Dallas Section's Morning Branch in the early 1980s, I wanted to meet other mothers who lived in the northern suburbs, to become more informed about public affairs, and to get involved in activities and projects that fit into my limited available time.

I took advantage of many of the opportunities that were presented, including attending National's Joint Program Institute in Washington (Washington Institute), state public affairs events in Austin, and, later, the Teach-to-Train Institute. I served as president of the Branch from 1983 to 1984.

Eventually, though, the Branch began to feel, in the words of the Morning Branch's first president, Elaine Scharf, "superfluous." Members weren't available during the day, and the other Branches had activities, presented at different times, that had greater appeal to members than our programs.

The Branch continued to enjoy occasional get-togethers, but we weren't participating in social action projects. We did produce an excellent monthly newsletter that included NCJW public affairs information from both the State and National organizations.

In my role as president, I believed it was time to end the declining group. There was disagreement from the Greater Dallas Section leadership, so we entered into in-house mediation.

As a result, the Morning Branch merged with the Evening Branch in 1984. Members were given a choice to work with the Evening Branch or the Professional Branch or to give their time to the Greater Dallas Section.

I always valued the experience, and, as president, accepted responsibility for what was best for both the Morning Branch and the Section.

Evening Branch members Susan Rosenbloom, Dolores Staffin, and Gwen Fine Roberts (left to right) making "pb&j" sandwiches for the Rainbow Room's foster children, 2003.

When the Evening Branch disbanded, President Robin Zweig (left) received the Branch's banner as a memento from member Susan Rosenbloom (right), 2004.

Professional Branch members show off their dessert creations at a membership party. Front row (left to right): Carolyn Marcus (later Carolyn Abrams), Barbie Wohlner (later Barbie Simpson), Sally Hein, and Linda Scrinopskie (later Linda Heath). Back row (left to right): Sharon Cohany and Susan Combs, 1985. Courtesy of Sharan Cohany.

(Left) Professional Branch members Jerry Raskin and Carol Rieter (later Carol Tobias) enjoy a moment together at a gathering after Rosh Hashanah, 1983. Photo by Sharon Cohany.

(Right) Tom Timmons, the first male president of Professional Branch, at a Branch dinner with his wife Jan, 2000.

Branch Presidents

Evening Branch

1952–1953	Carmen Miller (later Carmen Michael)★ #
1953–1955	Marilyn Rachofsky (later Marilyn Taubman)★ #
1955–1956	Elaine Shain #
1957–1959	Renee Stanley #
1959–1960	Ellen Salenger #
1960–1961	Anita Alhadef★
1961–1963	Nita Mae Tannebaum
1963–1964	Joan Weinberg★
1964–1966	Elaine Kimmelman★
1966–1968	Phyllis Putter★
1968–1970	Gwen Benjamin ★
1970–1971	Judy Utay
1971–1972	Zelene Lovitt
1972–1973	Harriet Silverman
1973–1974	Diana Gordon
1974–1975	Carol Rieter (later Carol Tobias)
1975–1976	Joyce Rosenfield
1976–1978	Eileen Muslin
1978–1980	Nonie Schwartz
1980–1982	Elinore Brown
1982–1984	Sandra Kaman
1984–1986	Susan Amster
1986–1988	Diane Lifshen
1988–1990	Ellen Samuels
1990–1992	Elise Gold★
1992–1994	Debra "Debbie" B. Greene EdD
1994–1996	Kathy Higier
1996–1998	Felicia Rubin
1998–2000	Sherri Shidlofsky
2000–2001	Marlene A. Cohen & Carole Robberson
2001–2002	Marlene A. Cohen
2002–2004	Robin Zweig

\# *Used the title Chair*
★ *Deceased*
★★ *Dates unknown*

Richardson-Plano Section

1971– ★★	Gayle Weinrobe
	Suzanne Sheinbein
	Jane Immerman
1980	Carol Wigder

Morning Branch

1980–1982	Elaine Scharf
1982–1983	Presidium: Leslie Neumann, executive vice president Denise Mayoff, administrative vice president Debra Ginchansky, community services vice president Janine Pulman, public affairs vice president Candy Brown, membership vice president
1983–1984	Janine Pulman

Young Professionals

1974–1976	Carol Newberger (later Carol Weinstein)
1976–1977	Leslie Greene (later Leslie Dworkin)

Professional Branch

1981–1982	Carol Rieter (later Carol Tobias)
1982–1983	Karen Stromberg
1983–1985	Sharon Cohany
1985–1987	Barby Wholner
1987–1989	Susan Combs
1989	Sally Hein
1989–1991	Carolyn Abrams
1991–1993	Ilene Goldsmith Sporkin
1993–1995	Amy Applebaum
1995–1996	Wende Yellin
1996	Anita Simon
1996–1998	Tom Timmons
1998–2000	Audrey Falk
2000–2002	Jerry Raskin

Mrs. Milton Loeb Sr. (Helen) and Mrs. Edmund Kahn (Louise) (left to right) give a preview of the costumes they would wear at the Section's "Gay Nineties" party where 1,500 attendees were expected, 1941. Photo by Meisel. ("Hostesses," the *Dallas Morning News*.)

"No one has ever become poor by giving."

Anne Frank (1929–1945), German-born Jewish diarist and a victim of the Holocaust

13 : Giving with a Purpose

There are many types of generosity. Some people volunteer time, and some lead with fresh, new ideas. There are others who may do all of the above and also give generously of funds to support the Section's goals.

The following essay covers the many types of fundraising activities that the Section developed over the years. A description of the Tribute Funds that bear the names of their major supporters and donors or the causes and purposes for which they were created is listed afterward.

Saving Pennies to Golden Galas
Essay by Bette W. Miller
President, Greater Dallas Section 1974–1976

Jewish women who volunteered in the community were often met with an assumption: they must be financially well-off and able to give money or assist because they had abundant resources and extra time. That myth, which is an extension of other Jewish stereotypes, was far from the truth or reality. Greater Dallas Section women, similar to National's members, represent a broad cross-section of economic capabilities and life situations.

Members are, for the most part, educated. Many are from middle-class backgrounds, and some are from single-earner families or are children of immigrants. Many have had to balance family time with volunteer activities, and others who worked outside the home could volunteer only during evening or weekend hours.

It was the Section's challenge not only to supply leadership, volunteer time, and skills to answer local needs but to acquire the money and other resources that would bring projects to fruition. Here is a quick look at some of the creative methods that the Section employed to raise funds.

In the early years, members were encouraged to save a penny a day to give to the Section. A "Salmagundi" Party, an evening of games and difficult skill tests, was created and held in 1916. Rummage sales were popular in the 1920s, and a celebrity lecture series was held in 1927. Sales of the *Cocktails to Coffee* cookbook, written by Section members, raised funds in 1935; the raffle of a diamond watch followed the next year. The early 1940s brought a Gay '90s party, selling chances for $50 war bonds, and holding an automobile raffle.

When additional funds were needed for a project, members often wrote personal checks to make up the difference.

In 1948, the Section raised $6,000 by holding another raffle. While that was a tremendous sum in those days, it was not adequate to support the Section's and National's goals. Leaders recognized the need to organize a permanent fundraising project to ensure a firm and continuous financial basis. The answer was Your Thrift Shop.

Planning for the original thrift store began when Mildred Sack was Section president. The idea became a reality under her successor, Rosine Olff. Past president Fannie Kahn, along with Laura Darver, were the driving forces that got the doors open.

The Shop debuted on August 15, 1948. Laura chaired the new project and set it up like a regular retail business. She established a system for merchandising, marking, and tracking inventory, and then trained Section members in all facets of the work. Except for a paid manager and a paid salesperson, volunteers maintained Your Thrift Shop. Over the years, the number of employees varied based on the health of the economy.

The store, located on Ross Avenue near Hall Street, expanded year by year, with the net profit increasing steadily. This retail effort was not the easiest of fundraisers because it required long hours and constant hard work. At the same time, the shop offered a service to people with limited income by offering low-cost merchandise. Even young people benefited: the Section participated in a federal employment program that provided for the hiring of a deserving Bishop College student to work fifteen hours per week. Members' tax-deductible donations of used merchandise plus items from merchants and manufacturers sustained the operation. The motto of Your Thrift Shop was "We can sell it if we have it to sell."

Hundreds of devoted volunteers, led by a series of determined vice presidents of Ways and Means, kept Your Thrift Shop profitable for almost thirty years. Leadership set the bar high for volunteer participation, providing the necessary woman-power needed to run the store. Inventive measures were used to increase the number of available volunteers. One chairwoman received a week of volunteer services from her children as a birthday gift. Others were encouraged to come to work by providing them with transportation to the shop—and then to

Section members Peachy Rudberg, Rusti Heilbron, and Myra Fischel (left to right) wear and display items that were available at the Fall Encore Sale, 1974. Photo by Jay Dickman (Richardson, "Encore Time.")

The Section's Encore Sale was also a place for member Carol Wadel and Cathy Saba, Section office assistant, to promote the sale of "Call Police" banners, c. 1970s.

Delta Airline flight attendants Annie Fairchild and Patricia Christenson (left to right) volunteered at Encore to have the first choice of high-fashion designer clothes, c. 1990s.

Section volunteers wore cheery smiles and bright aprons when they greeted Encore and Your Thrift Shop customers. Pictured: Judy Utay (above center), Syl Benenson (below center), and Joy Mankoff and Barbara Silberberg (above right, left to right), 1987.

the grocery store when the job was finished.

Seeking an upscale method of sales promotion in 1954, the Section encouraged members to donate their designer and better clothes to be sold at Encore, an extension of Your Thrift Shop. Selling name-brand merchandise to a select clientele at a different location yielded promising results and made the Encore sale a reliable fixture in the Section's fundraising program. Without a large enough location to store merchandise, clothing that was not sold during Encore was donated to Head Start of Greater Dallas, the Brookhaven College Theatre Department, and agencies that had clients in need.

Ten years after the first Encore Sale, the Section preceded its fundraiser with a style show and coffee at the downtown Neiman Marcus's Zodiac Room. This event became known as the "Encore Fete." Admission was the donation of a "better" used garment for the sale. The Fete became a social highlight of the Section's year.

In 1970, Encore added a spring sale in addition to the successful fall event. Until this time, Encore had been held in donated or rented spaces as varied as the ballroom at NorthPark Inn and an empty savings and loan building in Preston Center.

Encore offered men's, women's, and children's clothes, shoes, furniture, bric-a-brac, and giftware. About 10,000 customers were on the mailing list, and they eagerly anticipated and planned their schedules to shop the sales. More volunteers were needed, so the Section welcomed retired men to its volunteer ranks, and even attracted airline flight attendants who wanted to volunteer in order to get the first choice of the designer clothes and better items that were for sale.

Encore grew larger, and Your Thrift Shop on Ross Avenue became less profitable. As vice president of Ways and Means, I convened a men's advisory committee to review the financial situation. Their 1972 recommendation prompted the search for larger quarters. The Section leased a building on Harry Hines to house the Section's administrative office as well as to provide a space to store and sell Encore merchandise and sales. The Section had interesting neighbors and customers since the building was located between a taxidermy store and a bar-nightclub!

Your Thrift Shop remained open on Ross Avenue until 1978. Due to increases in rent and the downturn in the economy in the mid-1980s, the Section returned to its former office space at Preston Road and Royal Lane in 1985. The following year, Encore relocated in northwest Dallas. At an early sale in this new location, it was noted by one of the loyal customers, "This place is just like 'Last Call' at Neiman Marcus."

Both the Evening and Professional Branches partnered with the Section at Encore, running departments and providing volunteer staffing. The Evening Branch also held a "Kiddie Fete" with admission a donation of children's clothing.

Although Encore Sales were still raising substantial funds, the Section began exploring and experimenting with other types of fundraisers. In 1983, *West of Hester Street*, a film docudrama, was premiered at a Section event. The Section launched its first annual Gala, which featured artists and entertainers, with renowned musician Marvin Hamlisch in 1987. The next year, Section presented *The Immigrant,* a play based on the true-life experience of a Russian Jew who immigrated to a small Texas town in the early 1900s. Between 2005–2010, Section leaders decided to hold "nonevent" fundraisers to encourage donations without the effort of preparing a gala.

Over time, it became more difficult to maintain the leadership, volunteers, and paid staff required to run the Encore sales. Since overhead for the operation made the sales less profitable, the Section closed Encore's doors in 2000.

As history has shown, the Section's projects, programs, and fundraising efforts tried to answer the unmet needs and issues of the times. Current leaders and members are confident that contemporary methods of support will meet the new challenges of the Section's second century.

(Left) Encore's jewelry ladies Norma Levitan, Rosalie Wiman, and Margie Lipman (left to right), c. 1990s.

(Right) Three loyal Encore volunteers, Rhona Streit, Ellen Silverman, and Mollie Glazer (left to right), wear aprons made by the Section's "Texas Collectibles" project, c. 1990s.

(Left) Not wanting to miss out on any fun, Arthur Stern joined his wife, Helen, and Margie Cerf (left to right) as an additional Encore volunteer, c. 1990s.

(Right) Need a tie? Encore troopers, Al and Laura Darver (left to right), volunteers since the 1940s, will sell you one for $3.00, c. 1990s.

(Left) Myra Fischel posed with her "vintage" wedding dress that she donated to Encore, c. 1990s.

(Right) Section members Bess Kaplan and Jody Platt (left to right), volunteering at Encore, pack up a customer's purchase, c. 1990s.

Volunteering at Encore was a family affair. Nine-year-old Rachel Rubin, Aunt Adelaide Berman (left photo), and Rachel's mom, Felicia, assist young shoppers (right photo), c. 1991.

Guess Who Were Involved with Section's ENCORE Sale–This Forty-Six-Year-Old Beneficial Community Project?

Addressing invitations to the Sixth Encore Sale are Mrs. Theodore Strauss, chairman, seated left; Mrs. Julius Wolfram, seated right, and Mmes Robert Pollock, Melville Ros[e] and Phil Schepps, standing from left

—Dallas News Staff Photo by John Flynn

Invitations Announce Encore Sale By the Council of Jewish Women

(Above) Members Annette Strauss and Rhea Wolfram (seated, left to right) and Gwynne Pollock, Jeanette Rose, and Emilie Schepps (standing, left to right) address invitations for the Section's sixth Encore Sale, 1964. Photo by John Flynn. ("Invitations Announce Encore Sale by the Council of Jewish Women," the *Dallas Morning News*.)

Mrs. Herbert Lee, chairman, and her cochairmen get signs in readiness for the annual Encore Sale at NorthPark Inn Oct. 10-16. Nearly new clothing and art objects will be for sale. Standing at the sign are Mmes Irving Glazer, Gerald Weenick, Lee and J. B. Wolens, from left to right. The sale finances the section's many activities.

(Above) Section members Fonda Glazer, Raye Ann Weenick, Marilyn Lee, and Jackie Wolens (left to right) prepare for the fall Encore Sale, 1969. Photo by Bob. W. Smith. (McKee, "NCJW Serves Fellowman.")

The Jewish Ladies
3300 Ross Avenue
Dallas, Texas

Dear Friends,

I want to thank you for your help the past fifteen years or more in helping make it possible for me to clothe my children through your store, which made it possible for me to buy them clothes and other necessities on the price saving scale.

Rhonda Sue, my daughter who just graduated from Dallas Baptist College, is working now in Corporation Court and possibly will be the first woman teacher at the Dallas Police Academy.

George, my nineteen-year-old son, received three separate scholarships and is going into his second year at Dallas Baptist. He wore last year mostly khaki shirts bought in your little store. That saved us lots of money. Every time he came home he would say, "Mother, I need some shirts," and he would go by to see if you had the kind he had to wear.

Thanks again for the help you have given my children by having your little store. May you prosper in your church and your personal lives.

I remain,

Yours truly,
Mrs. Lucille B. Cooper

Letter to "The Jewish Ladies" as reported in the September 1972 Section *Bulletin*.

(Below) Section members Syl Benenson (upper left), Marilyn Schaffer, and Brenda Brand (left to right) model nostalgia clothes from the 1930s, 1940s, and 1950s that were available at the Spring Encore Sale, 1973. Photos by John Mazziotta. (Richardson, "It's Second Time Around.")

An article by Vivian Castleberry, Women's Editor at the *Dallas Times Herald*, announced the upcoming Encore Sale and featured Section members Selma Ross, Annette Strauss, Pearl Silverman, Gloria Jacobus (left to right), and Edna Flaxman (seated), 1964. Photo by Andy Hanson. (Castleberry, *Dallas Times Herald.*)

Your Thrift Shop ads put creative drawing and poetry together to gather items for the store, 1960. (*Council News*, November 1960.)

Section members Louise Eiseman (center) and Edna Flaxman (seated) admire Jan Beren (left) as she models a gown that was available at the Seventh Annual Encore Sale, 1965. Photo by Andy Hanson. (Young, "Encore.")

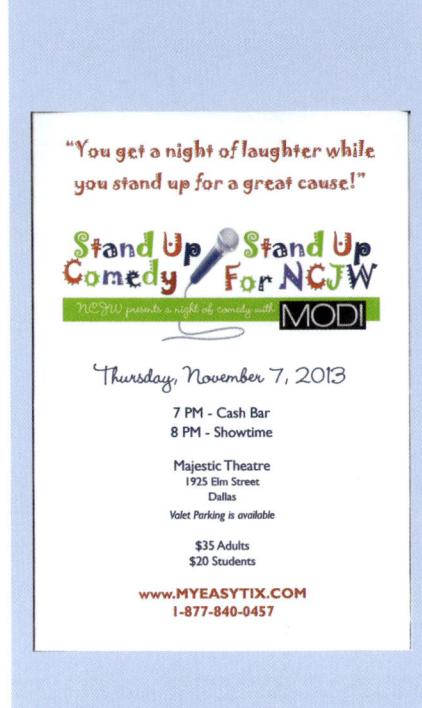

Galas

1987	Marvin Hamlisch
1988	*The Immigrant,* a play
1989	Marlo Thomas
1990	Polly Bergen (replaced Mariette Hartley)
1991	Dallas Brass
1992	The Capitol Steps
1993	Gregory Hines
1994	Bernadette Peters
1995	The Manhattan Transfer
1996	Mandy Patinkin
1997	Dionne Warwick and Burt Bacharach
1998	Paul Anka
1999	Gladys Knight
2000	Kenny Rogers
2001	Vanessa Williams
2002	Roberta Flack (replaced Natalie Cole)
2003	Mandy Patinkin in Concert with Paul Ford on piano
2004	Jim Brickman
2013	Laura Ling (journalist, replaced her sister Lisa Ling)
2013	MODI (comedian)

Stay-At-Home Events (Mail Campaigns)

2005	Cruise into the Future
2006	NCJW Dallas is Going Green
2007	Planting Seeds of Change
2008	Elect to Make a Difference
2009	Reaching New Heights
2010	Building Bridges/Changing Lives
2011	The Sky's The Limit
2014	Rededication

Support with Tribute Funds

Tribute funds are an outgrowth of early Section volunteer efforts to meet a need at a particular time. They were established to manage contributions in specific accounts that had restrictions on their use. As the Section's goals addressed community concerns, the startup and closure of various funds reflected new challenges and circumstances that required temporary or permanent support.

When an individual Section member's passion for a particular issue or a special group of people became her "torch," she provided ongoing leadership for that cause. The enthusiasm of individual members and their friends supported these efforts with funds, advocacy, and volunteer time as needed.

The following is a chronological list of the Section's Tribute Funds and significant dates.

Memorial and Happy Day Fund

1917: First general tribute fund.

1922: Endowed a hospital room in a new wing of Parkland Hospital in memory of Section member L. Nora Wormser.

1950: Last funds distributed and Fund discontinued.

Student Education Fund

1920: Fund established to send a young man to a Jewish theological school.

1921: Second fund, The Student Loan Fund, started to provide business training for boys or girls living in Dallas. Loans given to graduate students to continue their education. All loans were repaid by the students.

1921: Endowed yearly scholarship for students at Texas universities that had a Menorah Society (forerunner to today's Hillel).

1923: Name changed to the L. Nora Wormser Educational Fund in memory of Miss Wormser; used only for scholarships for local individuals.

1934: Early loans provided funds for several medical students.

1934: Provided non-interest-bearing loans and scholarships to qualified students in the community.

1946: First time loan was given to an African American student. The student attended Wiley College near Marshall, Texas.

1948: Provided scholarships for Dallas public school teachers to attend annual summer workshops of the National Conference of Christians and Jews.

Reba M. Wadel Scholarship Fund

1949: Student Education Funds transferred to this fund named in memory of Section member Reba Wadel.

1958: Provided scholarships for graduate study in social work at the University of Texas at Austin.

1967: Scholarships moved to the University of Texas at Arlington (UTA) to support graduate study in social work.

1975: Emphasis changed to graduate work in early childhood development at Texas Women's University (TWU).

1976: Scholarships given to three students studying child development at Eastfield Community College.

1991: Scholarships awarded for either social work or child development.

2013: Scholarships awarded to students studying child development.

Current: Fund continues to receive tributes and award scholarships at UTA and TWU.

Endowment Fund, (NJHC Denver)

1922: Fund initially established to endow a bed in the children's ward of the National Jewish Hospital for Consumptives in Denver, Colorado.

1937–1938: Endowed a bed and a room in the Texas Pavilion for Women at the hospital.

1948: Additional funds provided for hospital rooms and furnishings for a recreation room.

1950: Last funds distributed and Fund discontinued.

Milk Fund
Renamed Minnie Hexter Milk Fund

1934: Fund established to provide tubercular, undernourished, and indigent sick infants and children with the only source of free milk and baby formula in the city.

1945: Fund renamed in honor of Minnie Hexter, who was the second president of the Section.

1951: Fund provided more than 22,000 quarts of milk to needy sick children.

1974: Distributed free whole milk on an emergency basis to needy children in Dallas County.

1976: Provided four kinds of infant formula, including whole milk and non-dairy varieties.

1990: Supplied 427 high-risk pediatric patients in Children's Medical Center's Low Birth Weight and REACH (child abuse and neglect) clinics as well as children who required specialized formulas received free milk and formula.

1992: Provided $6,000 to Children's Medical Center for milk for needy patients.

1999–2004: The Vogel Alcove, a childcare provider for children of the homeless, became a recipient.

2001–2005: Jonathan's Place, a foster home for abused, abandoned, drug-exposed, or neglected children whose parents are seeking drug treatment, became a new recipient.

2007: Provided a year of special formula for a four-year-old child with phenylketonuria (PKU), which prevents the body from breaking down an amino acid called phenylalanine.

2011: Fund provided for and still purchases shelf-stable milk for Vickery Meadow Food Pantry and Jewish Family Service Food Pantry.

Section member Linnie Katz stands beside the shelf-stable milk contributed to the Vickery Meadow Food Pantry by the Section's Minnie Hexter Milk Fund, 2014. Photo by Laura Diamond.

Edward L. Protz (left), a former Wadel Scholarship recipient, discusses Dallas County Juvenile Department social work services with Section President Anita Marcus (right) and Rose Marion Berg (center), 1962. Photo by Doris Jacoby. (McKee, "Golden Years Open Doors to Needs of the Community.")

Audley Blackburn (left), a Section Wadel scholarship recipient, talks with Carol Wadel and Betty Dreyfus (center and right) regarding career options for the blind, 1970. (McKee, "Awareness Inspires NCJW.")

Current: Fund continues to receive tributes and distributes money for milk. The Section is grateful for an annual support gift from the Carrie Orleans Foundation.

Children's Sunshine Fund

1947: Fund established to provide volunteers and funds for the purchase of equipment, toys, clothes, and entertainment for the children at the Silberstein, Marder Street, and Margaret Bale Day Nurseries.

1955: Last funds distributed and Fund discontinued.

Dallas School for Blind Children Fund, renamed Mildred R. Sack Tribute Fund

1950: Fund established to support the Dallas School for the Blind and purchase special educational and play equipment for the preschool program.

1951: Provided college scholarships for blind individuals.

1961: Provided funds for Braille machines, records for sound scriber machines, and a psychiatric social worker.

1961: Fund renamed in honor of past president Mildred R. Sack.

1970: Scholarships for three blind students attending North Texas State University (University of North Texas), including Audley Blackburn Jr. In 1975, he became the first blind probation officer in the United States, serving Denton, Texas.

1980: First blind Jewish college student received a scholarship.

2000: The Reading & Radio Resource, which provided reading alternatives to the printed word, became the beneficiary of the fund.

2003: Last funds transferred to the Minnie Hexter and Wadel Scholarship Funds, and Sack Fund discontinued.

Terrell Hospital Adolescent Center Tribute Fund, renamed Bromberg Adolescent Center Tribute Fund

1972: Fund established to provide furnishings and equipment for the Adolescent Center at the Terrell State Hospital.

1973: Renamed in honor of Section member Billie Bromberg. The fund provided new tables for the recreation room.

1976: At the request of the Center, the Fund purchased thirty-three wall murals to add warmth and bright color to the residence.

1988: Provided sports equipment and bicycles.

2003: Last funds distributed to purchase personal computers, learning software, and décor for the new Learning Center at the hospital. Fund was discontinued.

Grace L. Florence Fund

1976: Fund established in memory of past president Grace L. Florence to fund geriatric research and programs for seniors.

1977: Funded Dallas Geriatric Research Institute's study of sensory losses.

1982: Funded a quality of life project at Golden Acres.

1984–1990: Provided underwriting for regional conferences on Alzheimer's Disease and gave funding for community education and support for families of Alzheimer's patients.

1992–2010: Provided initial funding and continued support of Safeguards for Seniors.

Current: Fund continues to accept tributes and supports programs for seniors.

SHARE Endowment Fund (Service, Help, Advocacy, Research, and Education)

1982: Permanent, general endowment fund established to support Dallas-area social service and public affairs projects and programs not covered in the annual budget.

1985: Funded the Section's *L'Chaim* drug education program.

1987: Funded the Section's 75th Anniversary history book.

2002: Provided funding for a Planned Parenthood of North Texas survey of regional hospitals that provide treatment to survivors of sexual assault.

2008 and 2009: Provided funding for keynote speakers at Section immigration conferences.

2013: Provided funds for the Section's Centennial Celebration, including significant underwriting of this Centennial History Book.

Current: Fund continues to receive tributes and supports Section projects and speakers for Section's events.

Rita O. Black Tribute Fund

1992: Fund established in memory of Section Charter Life Member Rita O. Black to support programs that strengthen families.

2002: Provided funds to the North Texas Food Bank to purchase a van for Operation Frontline to transport supplies and food.

Ongoing: Funds a HIPPY Dallas booth at "Get Kidz Fit," an annual Dallas Area Coalition for the Prevention of Childhood Obesity event, promoting healthy living for families.

Current: Fund continues to accept tributes and to provide funding for programs that strengthen families.

Yad B'Yad (Hand-in-Hand) Fund, renamed Israel Granting Fund

1998: Fund established to support National's Israel Granting Program (IGP) for targeted programs in Israel.

2008: Cosponsored a project in the Halfway House program at the Jerusalem Shelter for Battered Women, assisting women and their children as they escape family violence.

2009: Supported the Center for Women's Justice in Israel, a program that works to protect the rights of women in civil and rabbinic courts.

Current: Fund continues to receive tributes and supports National's programs in Israel.

Home Instruction for Parents of Preschool Youngsters (HIPPY) Fund

2011: Fund established to support the Section's HIPPY project.

Ongoing: Provides support for HIPPY field trips, backpacks, and school supplies to five-year-olds graduating from the program and college scholarships to graduating seniors in area school districts who participated in the HIPPY program.

Current: Fund continues to receive tributes and supports the HIPPY program.

Endow NCJW Dallas Fund

2011: Endowment Fund established to further the mission of the Section.

MILDRED R. SACK TRIBUTE FUND FOR THE BLIND

"Cast Your Bread Upon the Waters: "for thou shalt find it after many days." Mark Noble is 24 years old, Jewish, and blind since birth. He was graduated from Stephen F. Austin College and has been a senior counselor at the Greene Family Camp in Bruceville, Texas, this summer. Mildred Sack Tribute Fund is providing him a partial scholarship to begin work on his Master's Degree at the University of Texas at Arlington in social psychotherapy this September. Believing that he has deep insight into the needs of handicapped children and their families, he plans a career in counseling.

For many years our own NCJW member, **Sara Suwal**, has worked in the areas of teaching and rehabilitating the blind, understanding the special problems involved since she, also, is blind. **Sara** is trying to obtain additional help for Mark from the Texas Federation for the Blind.

We are so proud to be a part of Mark's future. You can help Mark by supporting the Mildred Sack Tribute Fund.

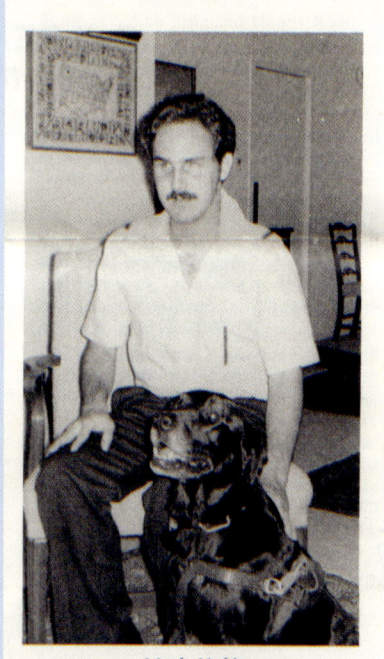

Mark Noble

Mark Noble and his assistance dog received coverage for his scholarship from the Mildred Sack Fund in order for him to attend graduate school at the University of Texas at Arlington, 1979. (*Bulletin*, September 1979.)

The Section's Fundraisers Featured Headline Performers

Jim Brinkman was the featured star at the Section's 2004 Gala at the Eisemann Center.

The 1996 Gala, dedicated to the memory of Elsie Pearle, featured Mandy Patinkin at the Morton H. Meyerson Symphony Center.

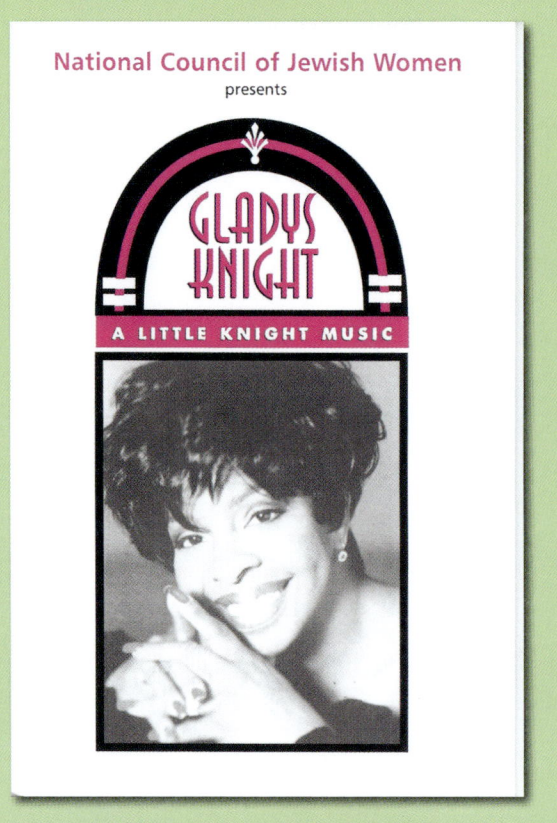

Gladys Knight presented "A Little Knight Music" at the Section's 1999 Gala at the Morton H. Meyerson Symphony Center.

Roberta Flack was the featured artist at the Section's 2002 Gala at the Meyerson Center.

Guest speaker Marlo Thomas attracted eight hundred women for the annual fundraising luncheon at the Fairmont Hotel, 1989. (*Bulletin*, October 1989.)

Dionne Warwick and Burt Bacharach were featured at the Section's 1997 Gala at the Meyerson Center. Photo by A. Kaye.

(Left) Roberta Flack, who replaced performer Natalie Cole at the Section's 2002 Gala, greets Executive Director Don Hicks of Dallas Southwest Osteopathic Physicians, the Gala's lead sponsor.

(Right) Bernadette Peters (third from left), guest star at the 1994 Gala, is surrounded by (left to right) Paula Jacobs and Julie Bleicher, cochairs, and Section members Marcy Grossman, Judy Schecter, and Jody Platt at the Morton H. Meyerson Symphony Center. Photo by A. Kaye.

Burt Bacharach and Dionne Warwick (center) lighten the mood for the Section's leaders (left to right) Sue Tilis, Lizzy Greif, Wendy Stanley, Barbara Stein, Janice Sweet (later Janice Weinberg), and Maddy Unterberg at the 1997 Gala at the Morton H. Meyerson Symphony Center. Photo by A. Kaye.

Paula Jacobs (second from left) and Julie Bleicher (fourth from left), chairs of the 1995 Gala, pose with the Manhattan Transfer performers at the Morton H. Meyerson Symphony Center.

(Left) Jim Brinkman, the featured star for the 2004 Gala, with President Marlene Cohen and her husband, Arnold Kaber (left to right), before an evening of music at the Charles W. Eisemann Center.

(Right) Event cochairs Staci Mankoff (far left) and Sheryl Lilly Pidgeon (far right) join President Robin Zweig and comedian Modi (center, left to right), the featured performer at the Section's November 2013 Centennial Celebration, before the start of the show at the Majestic Theater.

President Kyra Effren greeted Mandy Patinkin when he performed at an Encore performance for the Section, this time at the Charles W. Eisemann Center, for the Section's 2003 Gala.

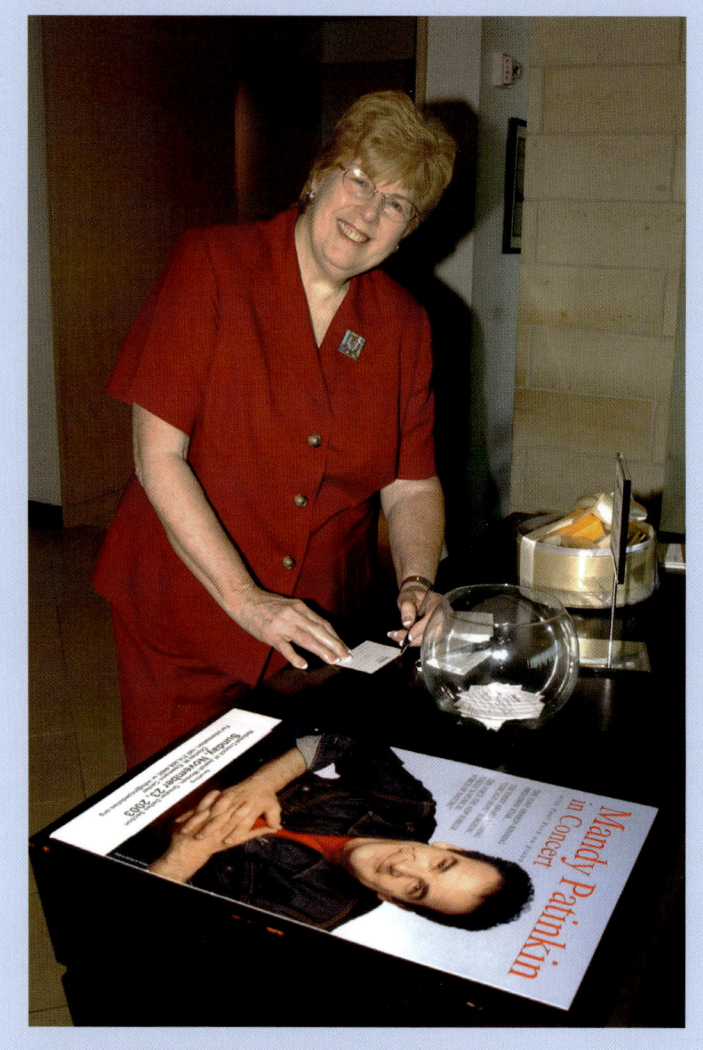

Member Lys Denenberg collected names for a door prize at the pre-Gala event sponsored by Neiman Marcus Dallas-Willow Bend, 2003.

Event chair Helen Frank joins Beth Brand Stromberg (left to right) in preparing the invitations for the Section's first "Stay-At-Home" fundraising event, 2005.

2006 Stay-At-Home Event

2011 Stay-At-Home Event

2010 Stay-At-Home Event

2008 Stay-At-Home Event

2007 Stay-At-Home Event

2009 Stay-At-Home Event

155

National's eleventh Triennial Convention in Washington, DC, attracted "change agents" from around the country, 1926. Courtesy of NCJW, Inc.

"Be the change that you wish to see in the world."

Mahatma Gandhi (1869–1948), leader of the nonviolent civil disobedience movement in India

14 : Women Power: Inspiring Agents of Change

Who are they? Who are the women who articulate societal issues that require change? Who analyze complex parts of human and civic systems and recommend actions that improve outcomes? They are the advocates, and they are the many generations of women in NCJW.

Why pursue change? Since its founding in 1913, the Section has been at the forefront of problem solving. The goal: to improve the well-being of women, children, and families that Section members saw around them. It became clear that to ensure, protect, and advance individual rights, they would have to stand up for those least likely or not able to speak for themselves.

During the formative years of the Section, women did not have the right to vote. They solved identified problems directly, without formal acknowledgment that what the members were doing was a part of advocacy. For example, volunteers established penny lunches after convincing the school board that lunches were necessary and that the volunteers could provide them.

Pat Peiser, Cheryl Pollman, and Julie Lowenberg (left to right) at a pro-immigration rally in Dallas, May 1, 2010.

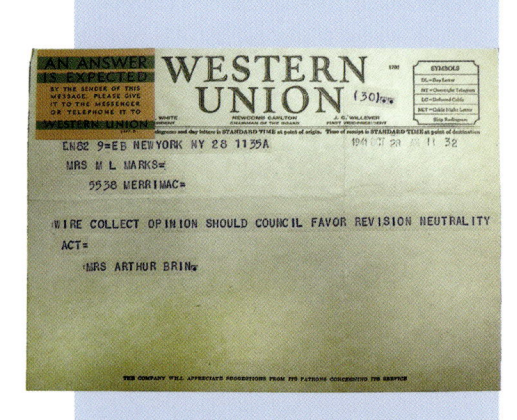

Before the internet existed, the quickest way to reach NCJW sections across the country was to send a telegram like this one from the National president, Fanny Brin, who sent it to the Section's president, Marguerite Marks, 1941.

When the program became too big, the Section convinced the Board to take it over—and to add health clinics as well.

Advancing Society through Advocacy

HOW DOES ADVOCACY WORK? THE FORMULA BEGINS WITH DOCUMENTATION OF A NEED. Once a situation is observed and particularized, research seeks out solutions that may already be in place. If a gap emerges, where no system or persons are present to address the problem, a proposal is carefully prepared and brought to Section decision makers for review. If approval is given for further action, an assessment is made to measure volunteer support and budget capacities. Often, a pilot project tests the progress and outcomes of the primary efforts, and adjustments are made if needed. Evaluation of the work is documented, and partners are sought to join the effort. Finally, when the project has matured enough to become institutionalized, the Section advocates for partners in the larger community to take responsibility for the matter. Members then can step back to participate along with other leaders and volunteers. Literacy Instruction for Texas (LIFT) is the perfect example of this Section's advocacy process.

When does the Section engage its members? From day one, whether they are giving community service volunteer hours or appearing at a board meeting to propose a new project, members are involved in advocacy. Education for being a spokesperson, an advocate, is an ongoing part of the Section's life. Through articles in the Section's *Bulletin*, programming at meetings and study groups, and Action Alerts that inform of upcoming issues, local members are kept abreast of pending matters of concern. Officers are briefed on must-know emerging issues, and they, in turn, notify project chairs of important information concerning their services. On a state and national level, training and informational (issue analysis) sessions are conducted at Texas Day on the Hill events in Austin, at NCJW's Washington Institute, and at conventions and retreats.

Using Tools of the Times

How has advocacy changed over the decades? Just think, from the Seneca Falls women's rights movement and fighting for the right to vote to today's struggle to assure access to voting booths, the Section's energy has never waned for everyone's full engagement in political decision making.

Early on, Section members were limited to addressing local leaders in person. In the mid-1930s, Rabbi David Lefkowitz of Temple Emanu-El helped members learn how to develop informed opinions on public issues. For decades, letters and telegrams that encouraged peace were sent to congressmen in Washington. By 1981, the Section fostered the Austin Committee, which was an important contact for state legislative action. That group grew under the Section's auspices until it achieved independent Section status in 1987.

Over the decades, the Section trained and organized its many voices: from quiet letter writers to noisy cheerers, whether presenting research data or individual case testimonies to governmental committees or parading printed signage, members prepared themselves to be effective. They created conferences and study groups that explored complex issues or focused on a single problem to address. They invited the community to step up; they called press conferences. They encouraged participation in the election process. Always, advocates and volunteers sought ways to demonstrate their serious commitment.

Courageous members remain willing to speak truth to power. Advocates have learned to bring in many voices through assorted devices: from mailed letters and telegrams to phone calls, faxes, emails, the internet, Facebook posts, texts, and tweets. However, whether the Section addressed issues alone or with coalitions, in person at city hall, in the state legislature, or in Washington, DC, members have made sure that their voices have been heard and could not be ignored.

"They Made a Difference"

The Section acknowledged many of the past presidents of the Section and its Branches who "Made a Difference" at its Ninetieth Birthday Luncheon, 2003.

Top row (left to right): Selma Ross 1964-1966; Elinore Brown/Evening Branch 1980-1982; Nita Mae Tannebaum/Evening Branch 1961-1963; Gussie Utay 1921-1923; Sara Waldman 1952-1954; Marsha Fischman 1980-1982; Kathy Freeman 1998-2000; Renee Stanley/Evening Branch 1957-1959; Marlene Cohen /Evening Branch 2000-2002/Section 2004-2006; Amelia Mintz 1934-1936.

Second row (left to right): Judy Utay /Evening Branch 1970-1971; Edna Cohen 1954-1956; Kyra Effren 2002-2004; Nonie Schwartz/Evening Branch 1978-1980; Susan Amster /Evening Branch 1984-1986; Mildred Sack 1946-1948; Anita Marcus 1962-1964; Joni Cohan 1990-1992; Ruth Koch 1937-1940; Julie Lowenberg 2000-2002.

Third row (left to right): Sherri Shidlofsky/Evening Branch 1998-2000; Grace Goldstein Neuman 1913-1915/1924-1925; Janet Newberger 1972-1974; Carol Robberson/Evening Branch copresident 2000-2001; Thekla Brin 1931-1933; Jody Platt 1994-1996; Marie Bitterman 1956-1958.

Fourth row (left to right): Joyce Rosenfield/Evening Branch 1975-1976/Section 2016-2018; Elaine Kimmelman/Evening Branch 1964-1966; Lorraine Sulkin (later Lorraine Schein) 1950-1952; Kathy Higier/Evening Branch 1994-1996; Sarah Strauss 1933-1934; Bette Miller 1974-1976; Sylvia L. Benenson, 1978-1980.

Fifth row (left to right): Felicia Rubin/Evening Branch 1996-1998; Minnie Hexter 1915-1919; Betty Dreyfus 1976-1978; Zelene Lovitt/Evening Branch 1971-1972; Katherine Bauer 1970-1972; Joy Mankoff 1984-1986; Phyllis Bernstein 1992-1994; Edna Flaxman 1966-1968; Janice Sweet (later Janice Weinberg) 1982-1984; Maddy Unterberg 1996-1998.

Sixth row (left to right): Darrel Strelitz 1988-1990; Fannie Kahn 1944-1946; Rosene Olff 1948-1950; Ellen Samuels/Evening Branch 1988-1990; Marguerite Marks 1941-1943; Brenda Brand 1986-1988; Grace L. Florence 1929-1931; Robin Zweig/Evening Branch 2002-2004/Section 2012-2014; Pat Peiser 1960-1962; Debbie B. Greene/Evening Branch 1992-1994.

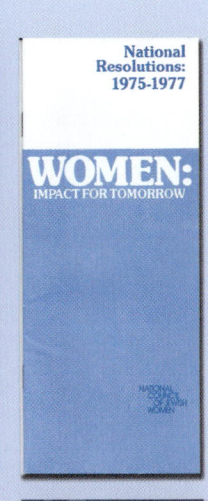

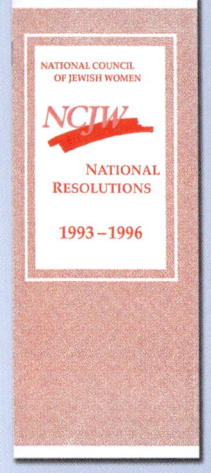

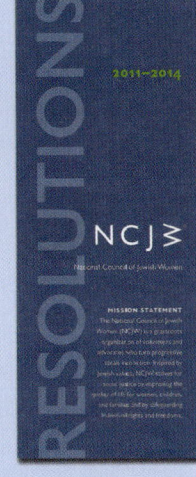

National's Resolutions, updated every two to three years, outline the major issues for which Sections can advocate.

Here and abroad, the Section's connection to Israel continued. (Below) Raymond Nasher (left) and Mayor Annette Strauss (right) visit with Professor Chaim Adler of the Hebrew University in Jerusalem to learn about pioneering educational research through the RIFIE program, 1989. (*Bulletin*, January 1990.)

Identifying the Work

What are some of the issues that the Section has addressed over the years? Some problems have been approached as community service efforts. Many solutions have resulted in the Section's project becoming part of the fabric of the community's life.

The listings below reflect highlights and starting points of many of the Section's historic engagements on urgent issues. Some concerns have reappeared over decades and have required continuous vigilance. The dates indicated do not reflect the ongoing duration of the Section's commitments and constant advocacy. The broad areas cover education, family/gender issues, health and human services, voting rights, the development and implementation of public policies, and immigration/international concerns–including Israel.

All efforts, however, support the following priorities of NCJW, which have evolved over the years. The recently stated goals are to:
- Advance the Well-being and Status of Women
- Advance the Well-being of Children and Families
- Enhance the Quality of Jewish Life
- Ensure and Advance Individual and Civil Rights
- Support a Secure Israel and the Well-being of All Its People

If you have been a Section agent of change, you will surely recognize the people and places where you or your friends have had a stake in *Tikkun Olam*, helping heal the world.

A Century of Advocacy

Education

1914: Provided first volunteers in Dallas Public Schools

1918: Encouraged Dallas School Board to adopt school lunch program

1922: Advocated for educating special needs children

1922: Opposed Bible reading in Dallas's public schools

1923: Proposed a peace program for Dallas school children

1927: Pioneered work on education for visually or hearing-impaired adults and children

1932: Advocated for in-home services for children not able to attend school because of disabilities

1935: Demonstrated need for lip reading classes in Dallas public schools

1940: Piloted after-school programs and study centers for "latch-key" children

1949: Conducted a survey of visually impaired preschool children that led to the formation of the Dallas School for Blind Children

1951: Developed After-School Recreation Program at City Park School

1951: Successfully advocated for a bill to allow visually impaired children to attend Texas public schools

1953: Supported first nonresidential public school classes for visually and hearing-impaired students

1955: Resolved to support public school desegregation

1961: Founded Literacy Instruction for Texas (LIFT)

1964: Piloted dropout prevention study center in West Dallas

1964: Published Operation READY as a part of consumer education

1968: Initiated and staffed DISD's formal school volunteer program

1974: Developed certification courses at Eastfield College for day care workers

1975: Wrote "Survival Course" of consumer education for DISD high school seniors

1976: Founded Community Board Institute to train nonprofit leadership

1979: Advocated for in-home early childhood education

1981: Created the docent training program for Dallas's new Central Library

1986: Enhanced Middle East cultural understanding with the "Hello Israel" program for sixth graders

1988: Launched Home Instruction for Parents of Preschool Youngsters (HIPPY) in Dallas area

1995: Advocated against private school vouchers

1998: Coconvened a literacy conference with Texas First Lady Laura Bush

1999: Cosponsored community-wide forum against private school vouchers

2001: Supported increased oversight of charter schools

2005: Advocated for state funding of pre-kindergarten public education

2007: Opposed academic study of the Bible in public schools

2009: Testified against the inclusion of creationism in Texas textbooks

2009: Supported expansion and increased state funding for day care and early childhood education

2010: Advocated for the separation of religion and government in Texas public schools

2014: Promoted accurate Jewish content in Texas public school textbooks

2015: Section Advocacy Continues
- Supporting early childhood education and accurate representation of Israel and Jews in Texas textbooks
- Opposing private school vouchers

Family/Gender Issues

1933: Established Section's Birth Control Committee; volunteered at Dallas County Birth Control Clinic

1942: Supported the war effort with day care services for working mothers and fathers in the military

1946: Initiated first geriatric recreation program

1960: Conducted groundbreaking survey to document seniors' needs

1961: Advocated against Texas laws that discriminated against women

Section members Joni Cohan, Janice Sweet (later Janice Weinberg), and Phyllis Bernstein (left to right) voting on changes to the National Resolutions, early 1990s.

Section volunteer Rita Sue Gold (center) helps HIPPY students with hands-on activities that increase early childhood learning, c. 2000.

Section member Rabbi Nancy Kasten at the healthcare rally with her poignant sign supporting children, 2012. Photo by Marlene Cohen.

Tuberculosis was a major concern in Dallas during the 1920s. The Section provided free milk at lunch to school children who had been referred by a supervising nurse of the Dallas Tuberculosis Association in an effort to improve children's health. At that time, lunchroom milk cost five cents per half-pint. The Section was concerned that some children needed to drink a pint of milk and could not afford the ten cents.

In 1927, members convinced the school board to lower the price to six cents a pint at Milam and Crockett Schools, where the Section had provided free milk. The Superintendent of Dallas Public Schools agreed to institute this change in any school where there might be a demand. After that, the Section recommended that Alamo and Cumberland Schools implement this price change and it was put into effect.

1964: Convened Dallas's first community-wide forum on childcare

1967: Advocated for Texas Marital Property Act

1972: Supported the federal ERA, approved in Texas in March 1972, and the Texas ERA, approved in November 1972

1972: Documented research on day care needs of women in poverty

1973: Established family outreach programs with Texas Department of Human Resources to prevent child abuse and neglect

1977: Identified major legislative issues on status of women at the International Year of the Woman Conference in Houston

1978: Cofounded the Domestic Violence Intervention Alliance

1978: Published a directory of services for female victims of family violence

1979: Founded FOCAS (CASA) for children in foster care

1980: Pursued women's rights by helping organize the Women's Issues Network (WIN)

1986: Assisted with NCJW's Center for the Child's study of "Women in the Workplace"

1987: Worked to help establish Vogel Alcove, which provides services to homeless children

1989: Cofounded the Greater Dallas Coalition for Reproductive Freedom to protect access to family planning services

1992: Held community forum, "Parenting in the '90s," with Dr. T. Berry Brazelton

1993: Convened "Juggling Jobs and Family" forum for employers and caregivers

1999: Advocated for increased federal funding for childcare services

2004: Participated in the March for Women's Lives, Washington, DC

2005: Supported reforms for Child Protective Services

2005: Opposed a Texas constitutional amendment that defined marriage solely as a union between a man and a woman

2006: Championed the rights of Jewish women unable to get religious divorces

2009: Advocated for male/female wage equality

2010: Worked to alter domestic violence by improving the economic status of women

2015: **Section Advocacy Continues**
- Supporting services for victims of domestic violence and trafficking
- Opposing discrimination based on sexual orientation/gender identity and additional restrictions on access to family planning

Health and Human Services

1914: Promoted child well-being by supporting neighborhood baths, penny lunches, day nurseries, and first aid services

1917: Advocated for free baths and the first medical clinics in Dallas Public Schools

1920: Proposed certificates of health for domestic employees

1922: Sought improved sewer services for South Dallas

1924: Encouraged purchase of only federally inspected meats

(Left) Ongoing Section support for public education is appreciated by former DISD Superintendent Linus Wright and Vivian Castleberry (seated, left to right); early DISD Volunteer Coordinator and Section past president Jeanne Fagadau celebrates with them at the Centennial Birthday Luncheon marking the Section's one hundredth anniversary, 2013. Photo by Lara Bierner.

(Right) Section members Barbara Lee and Sue Tilis (left to right) at Washington Institute, 2010. Photo by Laura Diamond.

(Left) Section members Joni Cohan, Jody Platt, and Mimi Johnson (left to right) pause for a moment outside the Texas State Capitol during Day on the Hill, 2001.

(Right) Section members Sharan Goldstein, Gail Johansen, and Phyllis Bernstein (left to right) attend a Dallas rally for women's health services, 2012. Photo by Marlene Cohen.

(Left) Section members Laura Diamond, Julie Lowenberg, Phyllis Bernstein, and Jayme Cohen (left to right) on their way to another round of briefings during Washington Institute, 2013.

(Right) Section member Rabbi Nancy Kasten (at podium) speaks about the issue of teaching fact-based evolution and climate change in Texas public school science classes during a press conference in Austin, 2008.

(Left) Section past president Kathy Freeman (left) "drops a card" in favor of home visitation programs such as HIPPY, at a Texas Senate hearing during Day on the Hill, 2013.

(Right) Former Texas Governor Ann Richards (center) marching with thousands of women, including Section members, in a Washington, DC, pro-choice demonstration that questions "Who Decides," 2004.

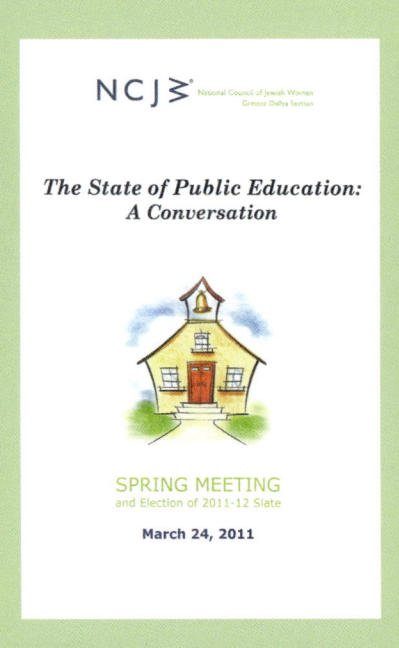

A panel of area educators from the Dallas and Richardson ISDs discussed public education at the Section's Spring Meeting, 2011.

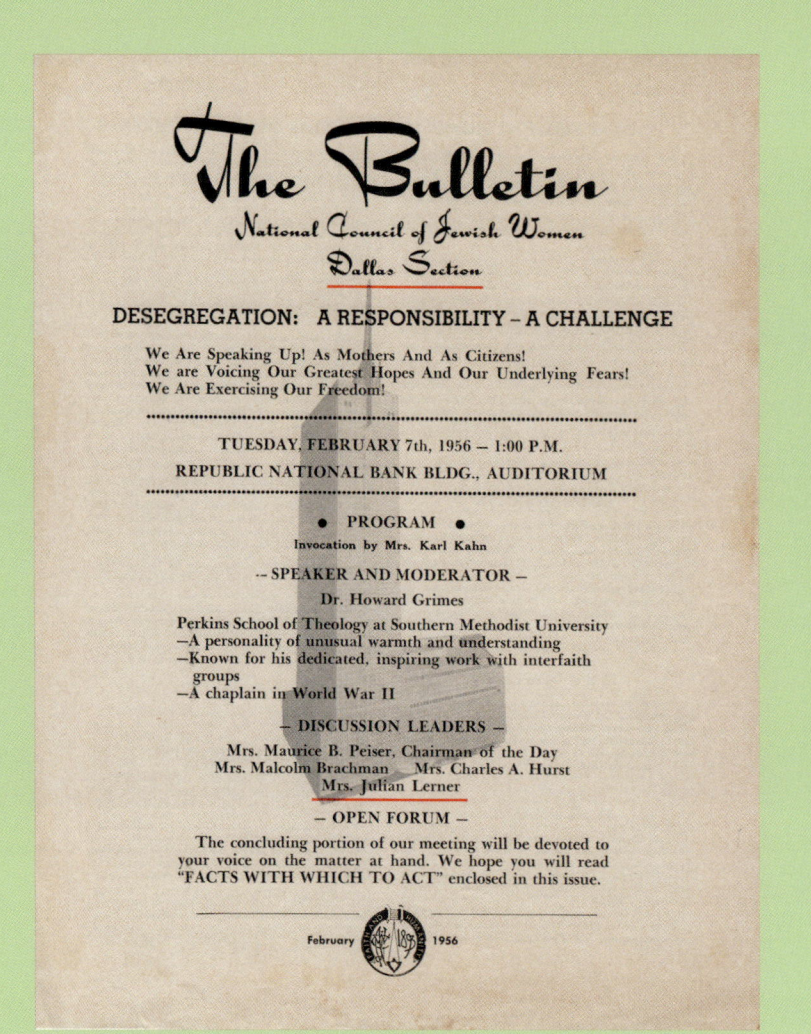

The Section's members were strong supporters of desegregating Dallas public schools, 1956. (*Bulletin*, February 1956.)

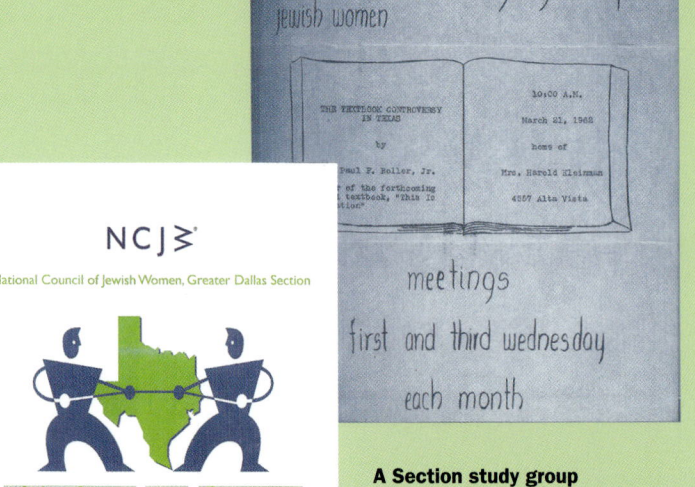

A Section study group concentrated on textbooks in Texas, 1962.

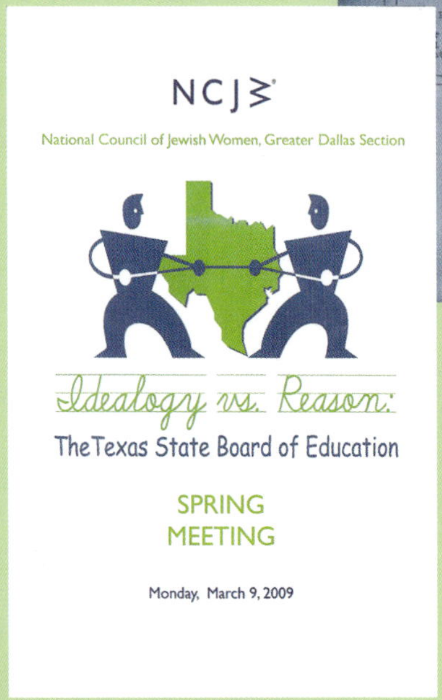

The Section's Spring Meeting focused on education decision-making at the state level and featured Texas State Board of Education member Geraldine "Tincy" Miller and SMU professor of anthropology Dr. Ron Wetherington, 2009.

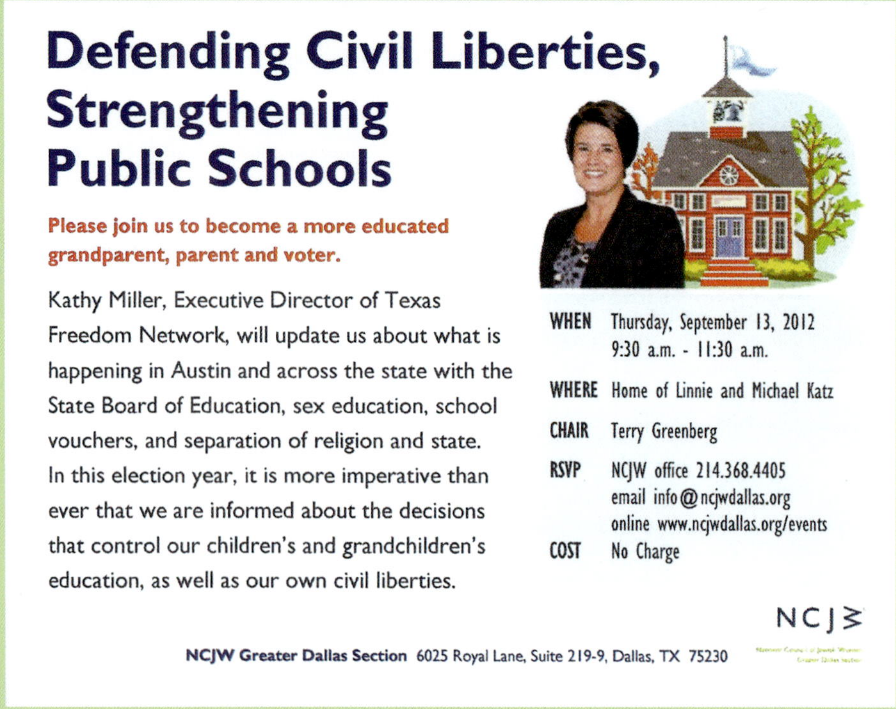

A Section study group featured Kathy Miller, executive director of the Texas Freedom Network, talking about the state of public schools in Texas, 2012.

1927: Persuaded the Dallas School Board to lower its price of milk in response to a Dallas Tuberculosis Association request

1934: Established the Milk Fund (Minnie Hexter Milk Fund)

1934: Assisted in founding the Visiting Nurses Association

1934: Supported the expansion of federal inspections of food, drugs, and cosmetics

1947: Helped establish the Dallas County Society for Mental Hygiene

1958: Advocated for expanded role of social workers in nonprofit service agencies

1963: Informed senior adults about and enrolled them in federal health program (Medicare)

1967: Promoted establishment of Graduate School of Social Work at UT Arlington

1970: Documented need and funded first social worker in the Dallas Police Department

1970: Advocated for more access to women's reproductive services

1976: Sought repeal of Hyde Amendment that bars federal funding of abortions, except in special cases

1979: Identified the urgent needs of disadvantaged girls through National's Adolescent Girls' Survey

1980: Provided public information about services for the terminally ill (the hospice program)

1983: Worked to reduce teen pregnancies as a factor in poverty

1984: Convened community conference to educate about dementia diseases and to recruit and train volunteers

1985: Formed a coalition to address substance abuse among Jewish youth

1991: Partnered with community groups to reduce unintended teen pregnancies

1992: Cosponsored "Paths to Prevention" conference on substance abuse among Dallas County youth

1992: Advocated for elder well-being via Section's Safeguards for Seniors

1994: Objected to cuts in the City of Dallas Health and Human Services budget

1995: Participated in nutrition programs for low-income families

1997: Opposed laws that required parental consent to supply contraception for minors

1999: Joined with the Texas Campaign for Women's Health to support increased state funding for women's health care

1999: Worked to prevent parental notification, informed consent, and further restrictions on abortion access

1999: Supported children's health insurance (CHIP), infant immunizations, and programs to reduce infant mortality

2001: Advocated for Texas government to request federal funds for women's health care programs

2002: Surveyed area hospital emergency rooms for availability of emergency contraception

Dr. Susan Wood (right), former director of the FDA Office of Women's Health, and the guest speaker at the Section's Opening Meeting, with Section member Dr. Cynthia Schneidler (left), 2008.

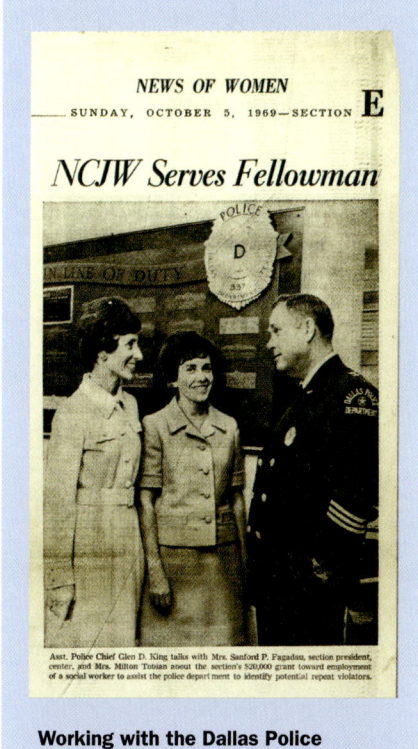

Working with the Dallas Police Department, the Section provided a grant to employ a social worker in the jail system to assist families of inmates. (Left to right) Carolyn Tobian (later Carolyn Clark), President Jeanne Fagadau, and Assistant Police Chief Glen D. King, 1969. Photo by Bob W. Smith. (McKee, "NCJW Serves Fellowman.")

Section members Yolanda Clark, Phyllis Bernstein, and Marlene Cohen (left to right) hold signs in English and Spanish to advocate for women's health services, 2012.

Section member Stacy Blank adds her name to NCJW's campaign that supported basic health care services for all, 2012. Photo by Laura Diamond.

2003: Designed "Making the Connection" to educate new parents about infant brain development

2004: Joined coalition to restore Texas CHIP benefits and change eligibility levels

2005: Endorsed expansion of Medicaid for pregnant women

2006: Identified pharmacists who would provide emergency contraception

2007: Opposed restrictions on stem cell research in Texas

2007: Supported "Plan A: NCJW's Campaign for Contraceptive Access" to secure availability of information and options

2008: Addressed childhood obesity and food insecurity through the Food + Fit = Fun project

2009: Advocated for women's health coverage as part of the Affordable Care Act

2009: Trained advocates to support comprehensive sexuality education in public schools

2010: Promoted Medicaid expansion in Texas

2011: Opposed mandatory sonograms before abortions

2011: Supported state-funded school nutrition and fitness programs to reduce obesity

2013: Advocated against new restrictive Texas abortion laws

2015: **Section Advocacy Continues**
- Supporting sexuality education, reproductive justice, the Affordable Care Act, and full funding of CHIP and Medicaid
- Opposing the Hyde Amendment and new barriers to reproductive choices

Immigration/International

1914: Established Immigrant Aid Committee to assist newcomers with documentation

1919: Conducted Americanization classes for new arrivals

1920: Promoted US's membership in the League of Nations

1922: Began first English classes for adult immigrants

1922: Monitored pending bills through the Legislation, Peace, and Arbitration Committee

1923: Encouraged foreign-born Jewish women to become citizens

1928: Supported international agreements to prevent another world war

1933: Petitioned foreign governments to send representatives to a Women's World Congress at the Chicago World's Fair

1934: Wrote to Congress to spread enlightened public opinion for peace

1934: Supported federal resolutions condemning Nazi oppression of Jews

1934: Advocated for increased size of the US Navy in response to actions by China and Germany

1935: Established the German Jewish Children's Aid Committee

1936: Cosponsored a community peace-seeking program with First Lady Eleanor Roosevelt

1939: Surveyed foreign-born residents for an SMU study

1939: Advocated to bring three German immigrant children to Dallas

1940: Supported aid to Great Britain and China and opposed aid to Japan

1940: Provided employment assistance for immigrants

1945: Promoted establishment of the United Nations and the World Court

1957: Assisted Hungarian refugees' resettlement in Dallas

1962: Supported National's effort to build Hebrew University High School in Jerusalem

1967: Participated in a Washington, DC, emergency meeting on the Israeli-Arab War

1977: Supported services for Jewish/Russian New Americans

1983: Established outreach programs for resettled Khmer communities in Dallas

1984: Opposed the Mexico City global gag rule on international family planning programs

1990: Supported a woman's full right to pray at the Jerusalem Western Wall

1995: Provided English and enrichment classes to children and adults in the Vickery Meadow area

1996: Administered the Dallas Southwest Osteopathic Physicians, Inc./DISD essay contest, "Peace in the Middle East"

1997: Opposed Israeli Chief Rabbinate's authority to limit conversions

2000: Promoted state and federal immigration reforms

2003: Developed new citizenship class for non-English speaking adults in the Vickery Meadow area

2008: Highlighted the needs of immigrants at "Nation of Immigrants: 21st Century Challenges" conference

2008: Formed the "With One Voice" coalition to educate the general public on immigration issues

2008: Supported efforts to allow immigrant youth to remain in the US

2014: Monitored and reported on Federal Immigration Court proceedings for unaccompanied minors

2015: Section Advocacy Continues
- Supporting comprehensive immigration reform, services for refugee children fleeing violence, and Israel's security
- Opposing anti-Semitic behavior in all its forms and locations

Public Policies

1920: Represented the Section at City of Dallas civic and community functions

1920: Supported universal suffrage and encouraged voter registration

1921: Monitored newspapers for anti-Semitic content via the Purity of the Press Committee

1924: Advocated for development of City of Dallas zoning ordinances

1924: Encouraged local Jewish women to vote in national elections

Section members Bette Miller, Betty Dreyfus, Sharlene Block, and another Texas Section delegate (left to right) with Senator Lloyd Bentsen during Washington Institute, 1972. Courtesy of Bette Miller.

During Washington Institute, Section members Bette Miller, Betty Dreyfus, and Sharlene Block (left to right) met with Congressman Jim Collins, 1972.

(Left) Section members Julie Lowenberg, Debbie B. Greene, Pat Peiser, Kyra Effren, Joni Cohan, Jody Platt, and Sandy Cohen (left to right) demonstrate that "All Kids Count, Quality Child Care Now" during a rally at Washington Institute, 2004.

(Right) Continuing support for reproductive freedom is illustrated here by Section members Beverly Tobian, Syl Benenson, and Betty "Bootsie" Golden carrying signs that question who decides at the Washington, DC, March for Women's Rights, 2004.

(Left) The Section rallied with Planned Parenthood to support women's health care at the Women's Health Express bus stop in Dallas, 2012. Photo by Marlene Cohen.

(Right) Section members Debbie B. Greene, Marlene Cohen, Sue Tilis, Julie Lowenberg, Pat Peiser, and Joni Cohan (left to right) at an NCJW rally against human trafficking at the United Nations, New York City, 2005.

(Left) Doris Meissner, former Commissioner of the US Immigration and Naturalization Service, pictured with Conference cochair Julie Lowenberg (left to right), was the keynote speaker at the Section's 2008 conference, "Nation of Immigrants: 21st Century Challenges."

(Right) Section members Pat Peiser and Barbara Lee (left to right) wear red noses at a Grandparents as Parents Coalition event that featured Hanoch McCarty, coauthor of *Chicken Soup for the Grandparent's Soul*, 2006. Photo by Marlene Cohen.

(Left) Temple Emanu-El was the site for the Section's Immigration Conference, where members Phyllis Bernstein and Sheryl Fields Bogen (left to right) were two of the speakers, 2008.

(Right) Section president Cheryl Pollman and State Representative Rafael Anchia, 2010. Photo by Laura Diamond.

For many years, the Section supported services for the visually impaired; here, Susan Weiss instructs a child at the piano, 1974.

(Below) A Braille calendar is one of many Section publications made available for visually impaired students. Pictured: calendars from 1964 and 1978.

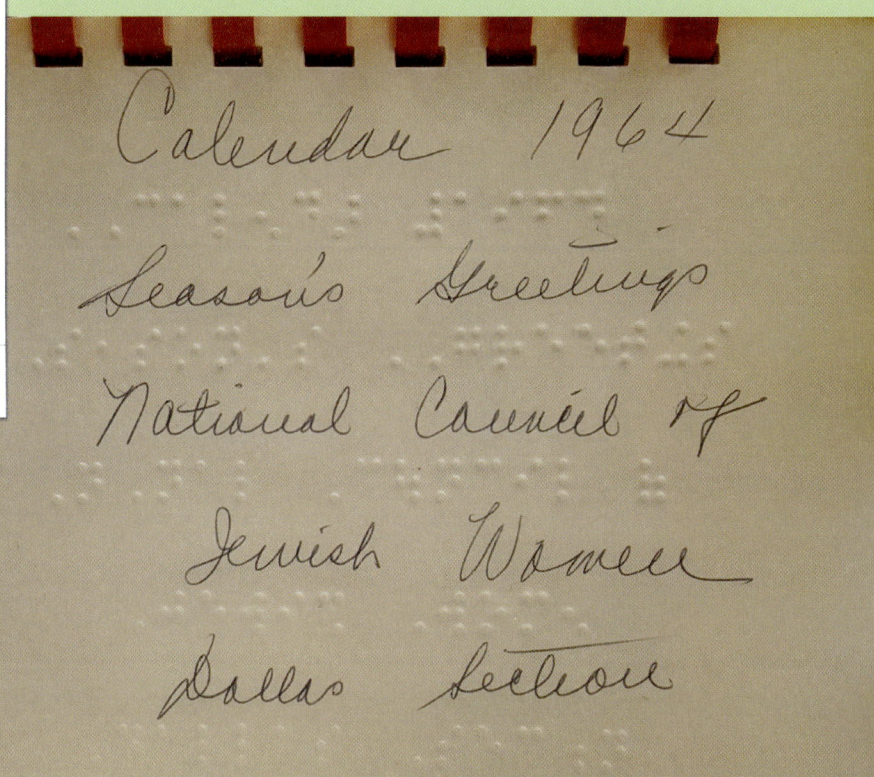

Aid to the blind is one of many projects of the Dallas Section. Examining a new Thermofax machine for the Dallas Services for Blind Children, a United Fund agency, are Mmes L. B. Wadel, Richard Eiseman and Seymour Bernstein, chairman of volunteer recruitment, from left to right.

Section members Carol Wadel, Louise Eiseman, and Margery Bernstein (left to right) show off the new Thermofax machine purchased for the Dallas Services for Blind Children, 1968. Photo by Jo Ball. (McKee, "Jewish Women Plan Year of Helping Disadvantaged.")

1978 CALENDAR

produced by

National Council of Jewish Women – Dallas Section

and

Dallas Services For Visually Impaired Children

Section member Debbie B. Greene's daughter Samantha (center) receives a warm welcome from President Bill Clinton at Washington Institute, 1998. Courtesy of Debbie Greene.

Governor George W. Bush greets Section members at Day on the Hill, 1999.

1924: Worked to improve the criminal justice system and supported treatment rather than imprisonment for the mentally ill

1927: Advocated for a juvenile court in Dallas County

1933: Worked with the Free Legal Aid Committee in Dallas

1941: Pressed for expansion of Texas social services for low-income residents

1947: Supported establishment of the Texas State Juvenile and the Dallas Family Courts

1955: Testified before the DISD School Board in support of desegregation of Dallas public schools

1959: Researched and advocated for social services for Dallas youth

1961: Participated in the policy-making White House Conference on Aging

1961: Worked for the repeal of the Texas poll tax

1963: Supported passage of the Civil Rights and the Voting Rights Acts

1964: Worked on voter education and peaceful implementation of the Civil Rights Act

1966: Encouraged establishment of the Dallas Human Relations Commission

1966: Worked with the Dallas War on Poverty office to assist access to social services

1967: Participated in National's first Washington Institute on advocacy

1974: Formed "Texas Collectibles" to enable older adults to supplement their incomes

1977: Founded the Texas Coalition for Juvenile Justice after in-depth research

1979: Monitored Dallas City Council, Dallas County Commissioners, and DISD School Board meetings

1981: Convened regional conference, "Patterns for Progress: Texas Models in Juvenile Justice"

1984: Helped establish the Juvenile Court Mediation Project in Dallas County

1988: Trained volunteer court monitors for the Children as Witnesses Project

1993: Developed Guardianship program to protect older adults and intellectually disabled persons

1993: Funded summer intern for Dallas County Park and Open Space Program

1994: Advocated for services for children who testify in abuse cases (Kids in Court)

1994: Appeared on public television's "McCuistion" program to oppose prayer in schools

1996: Implemented National's "Promote the Vote" campaign locally

1997: Cosponsored the "It's Time for Justice March" in Austin to support the Texas Hate Crime Bill

2000: Deputized entire Section Board to be voter registrars

2000: Joined Million Mom March to advance common-sense gun controls

2001: Educated Section members about federal court vacancies

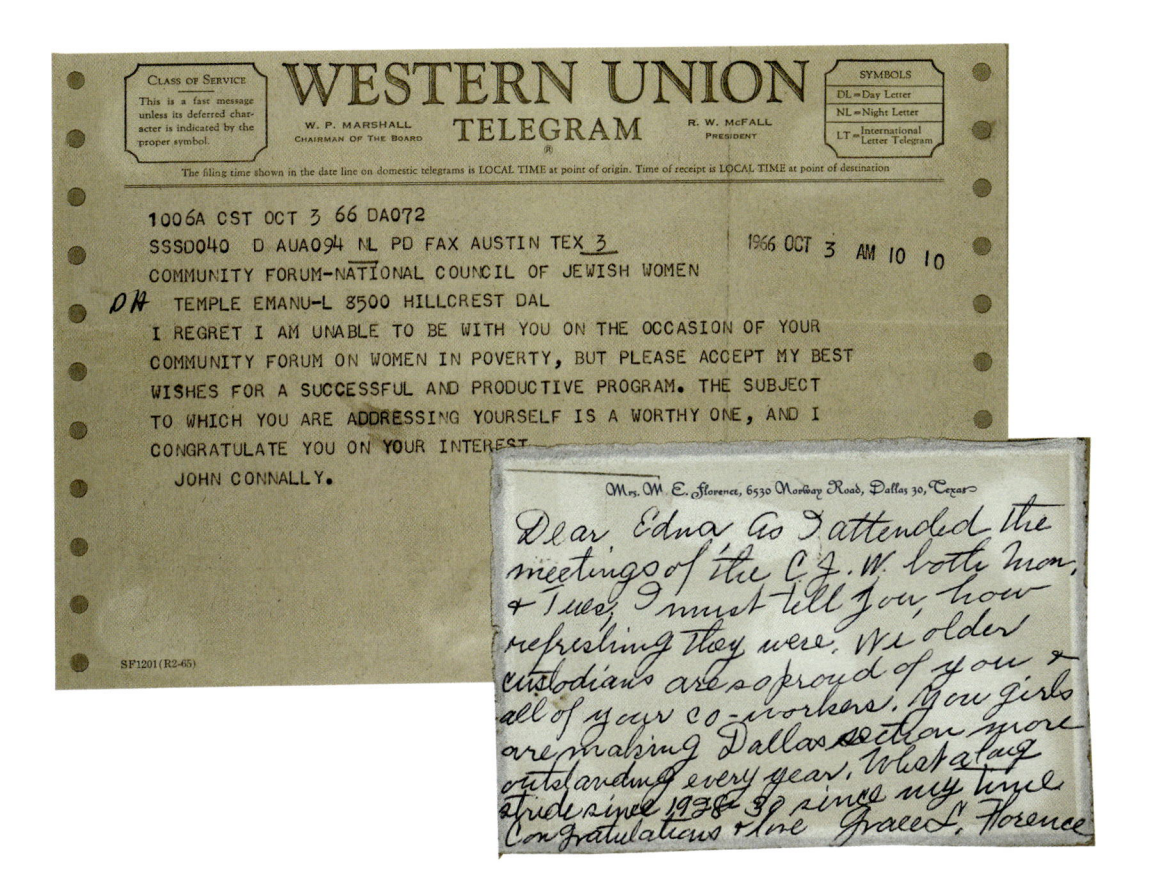

Telegram with best wishes from Texas Governor John Connally for the Section's "Women on the Move" forum along with compliments from Section past president Grace Florence, 1966.

2001: Opposed federal faith-based initiatives that would permit discrimination in hiring and services

2001: Established Hannah's Group to inspire Section advocacy efforts

2001: Advocated for the Texas James Byrd Jr. Hate Crimes Act

2003: Joined "Let the Sun Shine" campaign to require recorded votes in the Texas legislature

2005: Rallied at the United Nations to launch National's campaign to combat human trafficking

2008: Championed legislation to prevent gun violence

2008: Supported the abolition of the death penalty, both state and national

2008: Monitored voter information hotline

2009: Advocated for stronger protections for victims of trafficking

2010: Opposed predatory lending practices in Dallas and in Texas

2011: Objected to state voter identification requirements

2013: Promoted state legislation that addresses food insecurity

2015: Section Advocacy Continues
- Supporting gun violence prevention and rights of trafficking victims
- Opposing predatory lending, imposition of state limits on local ordinances, and laws that disenfranchise voters, including partisan redistricting

Note: Section's terms of office run twelve months (from May to the next May), so identified years may vary slightly from actual date of occurrence.

National's 2011 convention "Woman Who Dared" honoree, House Speaker Nancy Pelosi (left), with Section president Barbara Lee, 2011. Photo by Laura Diamond.

LETTERS

Perry should rethink prayer meet

As representatives of the National Council of Jewish Women in Dallas, we are seriously troubled about Gov. Rick Perry's endorsement of and participation in the prayer event called "The Response."

NCJW believes that the protection and preservation of the constitutional principle of religious liberty and the separation of religion and state are keystones of a free and pluralistic society, and that a democratic society is one that values diversity and fosters mutual understanding and respect for all.

Perry gives the appearance of endorsing one religion over another when he uses his office to promote a sectarian event. In addition to the constitutional concerns, his active promotion of this event is disturbing. As governor of a diverse state, he would have more sensitivity to minority religions, we had hoped.

NCJW is a national faith-based volunteer organization dedicated to improving the lives of women, children, and families. Since 1913, NCJW has been serving the Dallas area community, founding agencies such as LIFT and CASA. We respectfully implore Perry to reconsider his support of this event.

Barbara Lee, president, Greater Dallas section, and Marlene Cohen, state public affairs co-chair, National Council of Jewish Women, Dallas

(Left) Section president Barbara Lee and NCJW Texas State Public Affairs Cochair Marlene Cohen speak truth to power in a *Dallas Morning News* "Letter to the Editor" opposing Governor Rick Perry's participation in a prayer event, 2011. (Lee and Cohen, "Perry Should Rethink Prayer Meet.")

Senator Phil Gramm with the Section's delegation to Washington Institute: Janis Levine Music, Darrel Strelitz, Bette Miller, Carolyn Marcus Abrams, Brenda Brand, Senator Gramm, Sharon Sherman, Barbara Silberberg, Joy Mankoff, Rhona Streit, and Anita Marcus (standing, left to right), and Paula Eilbott, Syl Benenson, and Kathy Freeman (front row, left to right), 1989. Courtesy of Bette Miller.

Section president Katherine Bauer (right) and two other Texas Section delegates greet Senator John Tower at a Washington Institute in the early 1970s.

Section leaders Marie Bitterman, Pat Peiser, and Bette Wedeles (later Bette Schuttler) (left to right) meeting with Congressman Bruce Alger during Washington Institute, 1962.

Section leaders Syl Benenson, Myra Fischel, and Esther Jacobs (front, left to right) with Congressman Martin Frost during Washington Institute, c. 1970s.

(Left) Section members Caren Edelstein, Debra Levy-Fritts, and Pat Peiser (left to right) meet with Congressman Joe Barton during Washington Institute, 2010. Photo by Laura Diamond.

(Right) Section members Laura Diamond, Pat Peiser, State Representative Carol Kent, and Julie Lowenberg (left to right) at Day on the Hill, 2009.

(Left) Section members Sharan Goldstein, Linda Levine, Renee Karp, Samantha Greene, Randi Smerud, and Debbie B. Greene (left to right) at their Day on the Hill meeting with State Representative Jason Villalba, 2013.

(Right) Section members Laura Diamond and Joni Cohan (left to right) peruse the latest news about the healthcare bill while waiting in Senator John Cornyn's office before their visit with his staff, Washington Institute, 2010. Photo by Marlene Cohen.

(Left) Section members Caren Edelstein and Julie Lowenberg (left and right) with Sammie Moshenberg, National's director of Washington Operations (center), in front of the Texas State Capitol on their way to Day on the Hill, 2013. Photo by Laura Diamond.

(Right) Section members Caren Edelstein, Sharan Goldstein, Randi Smerud, Julie Lowenberg, and Marlene Cohen (left to right) meet with State Representative Helen Giddings (third from left) during Day on the Hill, 2013.

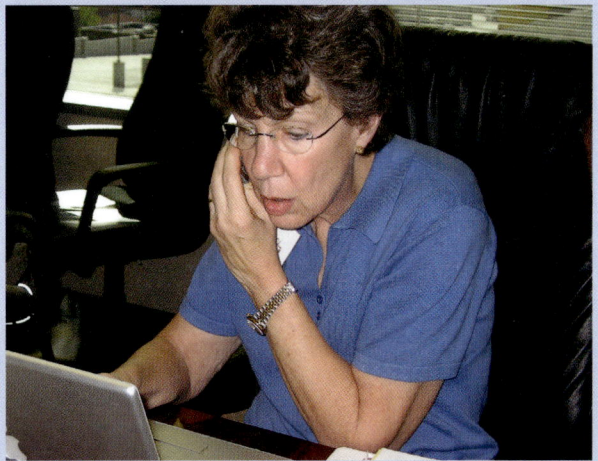

Dozens of Section volunteers responded to inquiries about the Texas voting process, as part of the "Get Out the Vote" project. (Left to right) Debra Levy-Fritts and Carol Weinstein, 2008. Photo by Laura Diamond.

Lupe Valdez, Dallas County's first woman and first Latina sheriff, was the guest speaker at the Section's opening meeting, 2005.

The Section's *Council News* heralds the panel of Judge Sarah T. Hughes and Congressman Bruce Alger as part of the effort to learn about current issues and to encourage voting, 1960. (*Council News*, November 1960.)

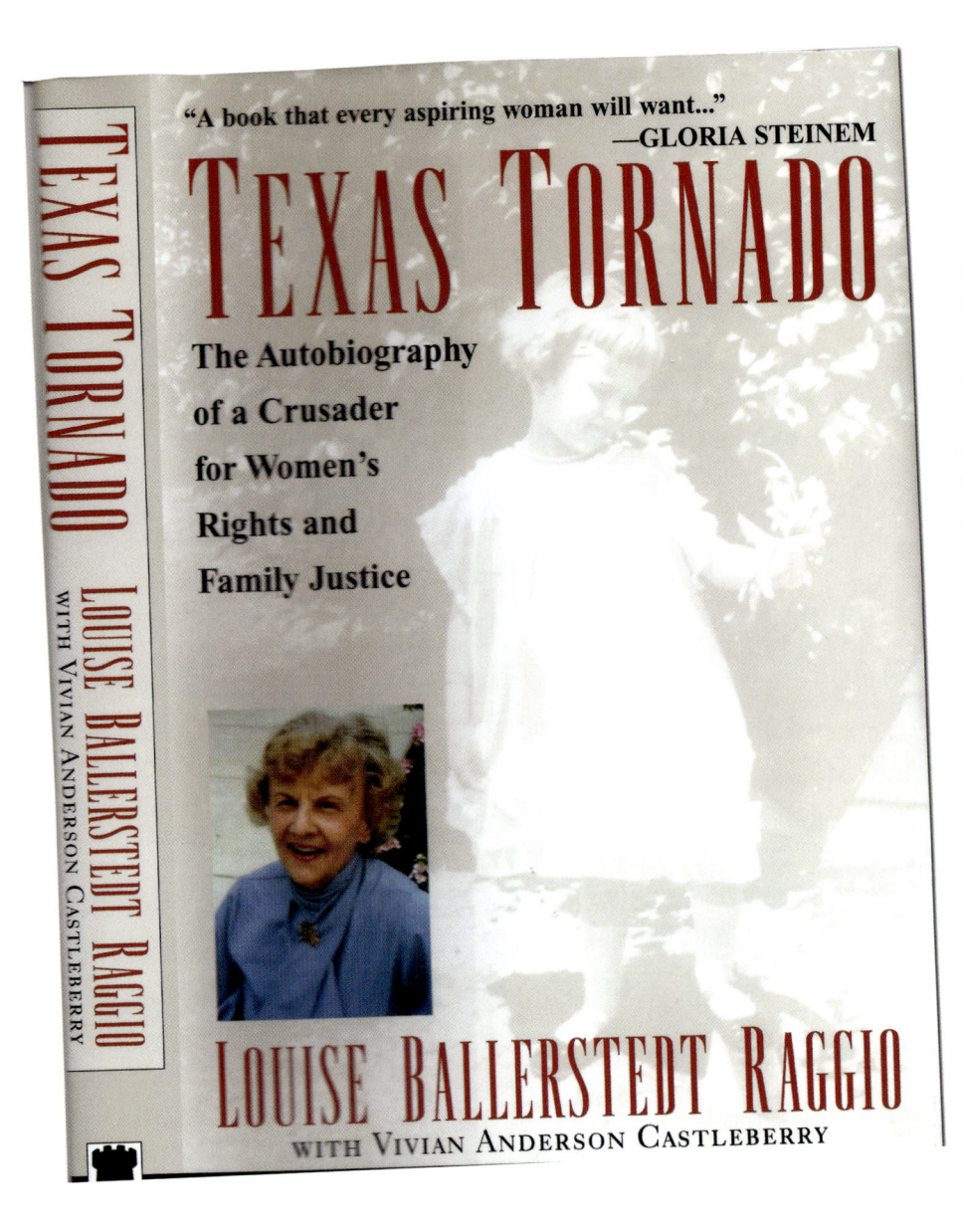

Louise Raggio's 2003 book, *Texas Tornado: The Autobiography of a Crusader for Women's Rights and Family Justice*, featured effective work of the Dallas Section. (Raggio, *Texas Tornado*.)

From Louise Ballerstedt Raggio's autobiography, *Texas Tornado* (2003, Citadel Press Books, pp. 186–187), writing about the passage of the 1967 Texas Marital Property Act, Louise says it took the support of a large group of individuals and organizations.

But it was the Jewish women who cinched a victory for us. At one time when it looked as if the bill were stuck and would die in the legislative session, Jewish women turned up en masse from all over the state to testify. Anita Marcus and Jeanne Fagadau of the Dallas Section, National Council of Jewish Women, sent out the alarm, and at their own expense, from Amarillo to Beaumont, from El Paso to Tyler, from Dallas to Brownsville, from San Antonio to Clarksville, Jewish women turned up in Austin on the appointed day. When these well-turned-out, intelligent, prepared, persistent, and articulate mothers descended on the Texas legislature, nobody would have dared tell them no. They buttonholed legislators in offices, hallways, on their way to lunch and back. It was said that on that day the only safe place for a legislator to escape was the men's room, and it was standing room only there.

The day after the group stormed Austin, I called my contact and asked if the legislators would like to have another group come and lobby. He said, "God, no, Louise! Keep those women away! We'll pass your bill!"

174

Section member Jody Platt, civil rights leader Reverend Peter Johnson, Abdur-Rahim Hasan, and Section member Maddy Unterberg (left to right) at an anti-violence press conference at Martin Luther King Center Jr. Community Center in Dallas, held on Martin Luther King Jr. Day, c. mid-1990s.

Section members Carol Rosen, Claudette Wolfe, Elaine Stillman, and Judy Hoffman, chair of the Kids in Court program, meet at the Frank Crowley Courts Building before venturing in to help children prepare to be trial witnesses, 2010.

The Texas State NCJW Day on the Hill in Austin attracted multiple generations of Dallas members. (Left to right) Debbie B. Greene and daughter Samantha, Lynne Siegel and daughter Sarah, and Ariella with her mother Beth Brand Stromberg and grandmother Brenda Brand, 2009.

Section past presidents Pat Peiser and Joni Cohan (left to right) listen intently during a briefing session at Washington Institute, 2013. Photo by Laura Diamond.

The Section joined many civic organizations to celebrate Woman's Equality Day at Dallas City Hall's Flag Room. (Left to right): Syl Benenson, Beth Konig, Sharlene Block, Beverly Tobian, Julie Lowenberg, Kathi Baum, Councilwoman Lois Finkelman, Marlene Cohen, Sharan Goldstein, Celia Schoenbrun, Mayor Laura Miller, Deborah McKnight, Saralynn Busch, Kyra Effren, Lauren Busch, Chana Robinowitz, and Robin Zweig, 2002.

Three women attorneys, Associate Justices Sonia Sotomayor, Ruth Bader Ginsberg, and Elena Kagan (left to right), members of the US Supreme Court since 2010, are part of significant Court decisions. Photo by Steve Petteway. Collection of the Supreme Court of the United States.

"Justice, justice shall you pursue."
Deuteronomy 16:20

15 : 2014 and Beyond

The world celebrated the 2014 Winter Olympics in Sochi, Russia, and Americans enjoyed average gas prices under $2 per gallon, the lowest they had been since 2005. After traveling for more than ten years, a spaceship from Earth landed on the surface of a comet for the first time.

In 2015, the Supreme Court ruled in *Obergefell v. Hodges* that states must issue marriage licenses to same-sex couples. The Supreme Court also upheld, once again, the constitutionality of the Affordable Care Act. The *Citizens United v. FEC* case allowed unlimited dollar contributions to political causes, and in the *Shelby County v. Holder* case, key provisions of the Voting Rights Act of 1965 were struck down.

The Ebola disease came to Dallas in 2014. The deaths of African American men during police encounters reminded Americans that race relations are a continuing and complex challenge. Likewise, domestic violence by professional football

Roper, the comfort dog, has an important volunteer role cheering up young victims who participate in the Section's Kids in Court project. Section member Kathy Freeman looks on, 2014. Photo by Laura Diamond.

players, campus assaults, and allegations against political, business, entertainment/media, and clerical leaders show that there is still work to be done to protect women and children.

Anticipating the Next One Hundred Years
Caren Edelstein
President, Greater Dallas Section 2014-2016

The Greater Dallas Section's work is defined and underscored by NCJW, Inc.'s current mission statement: We are "a grassroots organization of volunteers and advocates who turn progressive ideas into action. Inspired by Jewish values, we strive for social justice by improving the quality of life for women, children, and families, and by safeguarding individual rights and freedoms."

Justice for Children and Families

The Section responded to the needs of the many children from Central America who arrived at the Texas border in 2014 and then were placed in Dallas. Their parents, who had sent them alone to the United States, had hopes for a better future for their children, plus faith that this was their only recourse to keep the youngsters safe from the unrest in their countries.

These undocumented children were faced with the daunting task of appearing in federal immigration courts, with the prospect of deportation from the United States. The Section, in coordination with Catholic Charities of Dallas, took on the task of observing local Federal Immigration Court cases to assure that these children were able to receive due process under the law. Section members were trained to monitor the court proceedings as well as to assist families with the paperwork to request asylum. Data collected during the court appearances was used in a federal lawsuit to assure that unaccompanied minors were legally protected.

Kids in Court, a program designed to help children who may have been victims of felony abuse, commemorated its twentieth anniversary with a fun day of activities including lunch for the parents and children. The festivities were a positive distraction that gave families support for the task at hand: upcoming testimony in court.

Food + Fit = Fun (FFF) expanded its program to attack childhood obesity by creating a curriculum for the HIPPY program in the DISD. Home instructors and coordinators, after receiving training provided by Section volunteers, now share the lessons with HIPPY parents. This development expands the FFF program to hundreds more families. The project grew once again when the Irving ISD's HIPPY program adopted the new curriculum. FFF also has been adapted for older adults.

Justice for Women

Speakers at the Section's 2014 opening meeting, "Lurking in the Shadows," described the horrors of human trafficking. Author Alisa Jordheim shared stories about young women who had been sold or abused by predator groups. Sgt. Alfred Nunez from the Dallas Police Vice Unit and Bill Bernstein, deputy director of Mosaic Family Services, talked about what Dallas is doing to address this issue. A later "Hot Topic" study group with Ms. Jordheim continued education about human trafficking.

Other meetings highlighted the Affordable Care Act, its implementation and its effect on individuals, families, and the community. The Section collaborated with the Jewish Federation of Greater Dallas's Jewish Community Relations Council's (JCRC) Public Education Initiative on a project that works to have Jewish and Israeli content in public school textbooks presented in an appropriate manner. Further, the Section engaged a speaker on Internet safety and how to keep families—from children to grandparents—safe from electronic predators.

(Left) Section volunteers Debby Stein, Caren Edelstein, Marlene Cohen, Robin Zweig, Judy Hoffman, Pam Rieter, and Elaine Stillman (left to right) prepare to serve pizza and cake to the children and their families in celebration of the twentieth year of Kids in Court, 2014. Photo by Laura Diamond.

(Right) Judy Hoffman, Section chair of Kids in Court, presents an NCJW tote bag to Michael Loehr, district manager of Domino's Pizza, in honor of Domino's long-time support of the program, 2014. Photo by Laura Diamond.

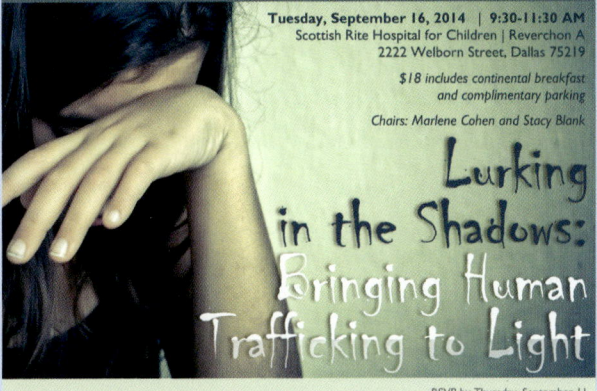

(Left) The Section's Opening Meeting, "Lurking in the Shadows," featured author Alisa Jordheim, (photo on the right), who spoke about predators in human trafficking, 2014. Photo by Laura Diamond.

(Left) Section member Kyra Effren (right) teaches Food + Fit = Fun curriculum to the DISD HIPPY coordinators, while Debbie Stein and Sharan Goldstein (back row, left to right) confer on the next lesson, 2013. Photo by Laura Diamond.

(Right) The first Section Lifetime Achievement Award was presented to Pat Peiser (right) at the 102nd Birthday Luncheon. Celebrating the honor is Pat's granddaughter Rabbi Allison Peiser, 2015. Photo by Laura Diamond.

(Left) Paint is the answer as Section member Debby Stein honors Martin Luther King Jr.'s memory with a Day of Service at Our Friends Place, 2014. Photo by Laura Diamond.

(Right) Pioneering Partner Awardee North Texas Food Bank, represented by CEO Jan Pruitt (left), celebrates with Section president Caren Edelstein (center) and past president Robin Zweig (right) at the Installation Luncheon, 2014. Photo by Laura Diamond.

Advocating for Justice

As they have done each biennium, Section members descend on Austin to visit state representatives as advocates on topics important to the Section. Topics included reproductive justice, gun violence prevention, and immigration reform. Members may have been disappointed by the some of the official responses, but they were never dissuaded from speaking up.

Honoring Ourselves and Others

The Section celebrated its 102nd birthday luncheon in January 2015, presenting its traditional awards: Hannah G. Solomon, Janis Levine Music Make-A-Difference, Emerging Leader, and Pioneering Partner. The Section also initiated a new award to recognize the longtime commitment of Section members; past president and past Hannah G. Solomon awardee Pat Peiser received the first Lifetime Achievement Award.

Like many other organizations and businesses around the country, the Section honors Martin Luther King Jr.'s birthday each January with a "Day of Service," giving members, their children, and their grandchildren the opportunity to help nonprofit agencies throughout the Dallas area. A diverse range of Dallas agencies has benefited from the Section's service, including Our Friends Place, North Texas Food Bank, Jewish Family Service, Martin Luther King Jr. Learning Center, Letot Center, and the High Risk Victim's Task Force.

The Section's Installation Luncheon, held each May, is a time to honor past leaders of the Section and to introduce the incoming leadership. I became the new president of the Section in 2014, a position I held until June 2016. North Texas Food Bank President and CEO Jan Pruitt was presented with the 2014 Pioneering Partner Award. In 2015, Vanna Slaughter, division director of Catholic Charities Immigration and Legal Services, was the recipient of the same honor.

Two longtime Section programs celebrated milestone twenty-five-year birthdays. The HIPPY program sponsored a birthday party at the Dallas Zoo. Families, home instructors, school administrators, and volunteers joined the fun. The Morton H. Meyerson Symphony Center turned twenty-five, as did the Section's Meyerson Docent Program. Since its beginning, over 176,000 people have toured the Meyerson—that's 4,000 tours and 63,000 volunteer hours!

During my presidency, the Section hired its first executive director, Catherine Horsey, who served for one year. We welcomed our second executive director, Suzi Greenman, in 2015. The new Section president, whose term began in May 2016, was Joyce Rosenfield.

Looking Ahead

Now, as the Section moves its mission into our second century, we are secure in the knowledge that there will be another hundred years after that and more to come. What does the future hold? Members will continue to make a difference because they have a faith in the future and a belief in action.

We will be working, as always, under the Principles of NCJW, Inc. that are listed below. These principles are fundamental beliefs of the National Council of Jewish Women. They are basic to and inherent in all specific resolutions.

Recent principles are:

- Individual liberties and rights guaranteed by the Constitution are keystones of a free and pluralistic society and must be protected and preserved.

- Religious liberty and the separation of religion and state are constitutional principles that must be protected and preserved in order to maintain our democratic society.

IMMIGRATION CRISIS | DEPORTATIONS
Under rocket docket, kids race time, few with a lawyer

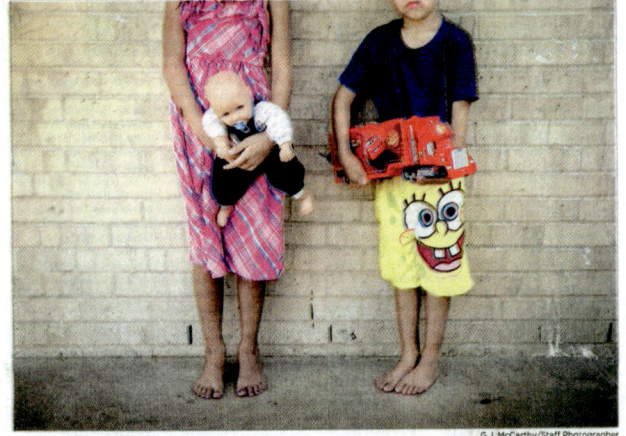

Evelyn, 8, and her 5-year-old brother, Brian, clutch their favorite toys they have received since arriving in the Dallas area in December from Honduras. Their mother received a continuance to find an attorney.

Justice jettisoned?

Section past president Cheryl Pollman was interviewed for the article above regarding the rapid immigration court hearings for unaccompanied minors facing deportation. The Section had created a court-watch program to ensure "full and fair hearings for the kids," 2014. Photo by G. J. McCarthy. (Solís, "Under Rocket Docket.")

(Left) Many cheerful hands join in at the Section's 2015 Day of Service as members took part in the Ronald McDonald House's food service and community collection program. (Left to right) Amy Schachter, Eden Schachter, Roz Katz, Judy Hoffman, Kristi Hinkamp, and Linda Skibell, 2015. Photo by Laura Diamond.

(Right) An employee of Hope's Door in Plano receives from Phyllis Stoup (right) vital supplies donated by Section members, 2014. Photo by Laura Diamond.

(Left) Section member Yolanda Clark displays the award she received as the recipient of the Janis Levine Music Make-A-Difference Award, 2014. Photo by Laura Diamond.

(Right) Member Lauren Busch promotes the Section's opening meeting that featured LEAP (Lending, Education, and Project Mentoring) for survivors of domestic violence, 2015. Photo by Laura Diamond.

Suzi Greenman, who began as the Section's executive director in 2015, is seen here signing up volunteers for the LEAP program, 2015. Photo by Laura Diamond.

Section members Carol Pinker and Phyllis Stoup (left to right) display brochures for the Section's new program, LEAP, 2015. Photo by Laura Diamond.

- Human rights and dignity are fundamental and must be guaranteed to all individuals.
- All individuals have the right to live in a world at peace.
- A democratic society and its people must value diversity and promote mutual understanding and respect for all.
- Discrimination on the basis of race, gender, national origin, ethnicity, religion, age, disability, marital status, sexual orientation, gender identity and expression, or economic status must be eliminated.
- Equal rights and equal opportunities for women must be guaranteed.
- The continuity of the Jewish people and its heritage, and respect among all streams of Judaism, must be assured from generation to generation.
- The survival and security of the State of Israel and the establishment of a just and permanent peace are central to the Jewish people and vital to the interests of the United States.
- A democratic society must provide for the needs of those unable to provide for themselves.
- Health, education, and human services must be coordinated, comprehensive, accessible, and sufficiently funded.
- An educated and informed public is fundamental to a democratic society.
- The protection and preservation of the environment are vital to a sustainable future.
- A democratic society depends on the collective efforts of the public, private, and not-for-profit sectors and is strengthened by the commitment and contribution of volunteers.

Our hopes are for a just society where every woman will be paid equally as her male counterpart, and she will be safe from domestic violence, sexism, and ageism. Every child will be free from hunger, have access to the best education possible, and grow up in a loving world. There will be sufficient safeguards in place to guarantee our civil and religious freedoms. Every family will be viewed as having value, no matter its composition, and will be treated with respect.

Newly installed Section president Caren Edelstein is proudly flanked by her granddaughter Mya (left) and daughter Allyson Raskin (right), 2014. Photo by Laura Diamond.

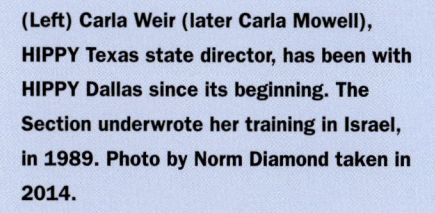

(Left) Carla Weir (later Carla Mowell), HIPPY Texas state director, has been with HIPPY Dallas since its beginning. The Section underwrote her training in Israel, in 1989. Photo by Norm Diamond taken in 2014.

(Right) Section President Robin Zweig and member Nita Mae Tannebaum (left to right) plan their route at the zoo, 2014. Photo by Laura Diamond.

(Left) Section member Debby Stein (left) leads a group of HIPPY families as they enjoy the zoo, 2014. Photo by Laura Diamond.

(Right) Section volunteer and photographer Norm Diamond (right) helps a student try out his camera, 2014. Photo by Laura Diamond.

(Left) Section members Julie Lowenberg and Caren Edelstein (left to right) cheer for HIPPY, 2014. Photo by Laura Diamond.

(Right) Syl Benenson, known as Mother HIPPY of the Dallas program, calls the celebrants together, 2004. Photo by Laura Diamond.

(Left) It's a HIPPY cheer for twenty-five years of educating families, 2014. Photo by Laura Diamond.

"One woman makes a difference, 100,000 make an impact."

This graphic tree hints that a solid base of women is needed to form the foundation of a mighty, living organization. Image courtesy of NCJW, Inc.

"Never doubt that a small group of thoughtful, committed citizens can change the world; indeed, it's the only thing that ever has."

Margaret Mead (1901-1978), American cultural anthropologist

16 : Historic Leadership

Beginning with the earliest charter members at the turn of the twentieth century, followed by subsequent dedicated officers, researchers, project volunteer chairs, and board members, many decades of Dallas Jewish women have stepped into leader shoes and moved mountains. There are not enough pages in which to identify and highlight all the outstanding leadership that the Section has enjoyed.

Following are pictures of past presidents and lists of charter groups, Section's National board members, awardees, and community awards and partners. Read on and find an amazing array of people and organizations. Positive history has been created for this area by the combined efforts of these many change agents.

100 NCJW Greater Dallas Section Presidents

1913–1915
Grace A. Goldstein (Neuman)★

1915–1919
Minnie Hexter★

1919–1921
Jennie Rosenfield★

1921–1923
Gussie Utay★

1933–1934
Sarah Strauss★

1934–1936
Amelia Mintz★

1936–1937
Estelle Shaw★

1937–1940
Ruth Koch★

1940–1941
Felice Bromberg★

1948–1950
Rosine Olff★

1950–1952
Lorraine Sulkin (Schein)★

1952–1954
Sara Waldman★

1954–1956
Edna Cohen★

1956–1958
Marie Bitterman★

1968–1970
Jeanne Fagadau★

1970–1972
Katherine Bauer

1972–1974
Janet Newberger★

1974–1976
Bette Miller

1976–1978
Betty Dreyfus

1988–1990
Darrel Strelitz

1990–1992
Joni Cohan

1992–1994
Phyllis Bernstein

1994–1996
Jody Platt

1996–1998
Madeline Unterberg

2008–2010
Cheryl Pollman

2010–2012
Barbara Lee

1923–1925
Grace Goldstein Neuman★

1925–1927
Stella Andress★

1927–1929
Rae Mittenthal★

1929–1931
Grace Florence★

1931–1933
Thekla Brin★

1941–1943
Marguerite Marks★

1943
Ann Berwald★

1943–1944
Mayme Janow★

1944–1946
Fannie Kahn★

1946–1948
Mildred Sack★

1958–1960
Bette Wedeles (Schuttler)★

1960–1962
Pat Peiser

1962–1964
Anita Marcus★

1964–1966
Selma Ross★

1966–1968
Edna Flaxman★

1978–1980
Sylvia Lynn Benenson

1980–1982
Marsha Fischman★

1982–1984
Janice Sweet (Weinberg)

1984–1986
Joy Mankoff

1986–1988
Brenda Brand

1998–2000
Kathy Freeman

2000–2002
Julie Lowenberg

2002–2004
Kyra Effren

2004–2006
Marlene Cohen

2006–2008
Sue Tilis

2012–2014
Robin Zweig

2014–2016
Caren Edelstein

★ Deceased

Greater Dallas Section Presidents

1913–1915	Grace A. Goldstein (later Grace Neuman)★
1915–1919	Minnie Hexter★
1919–1921	Jennie Rosenfield★
1921–1923	Gussie Utay★
1923–1924	Grace A. Goldstein (later Grace Neuman)★
1924–1925	Grace Goldstein Neuman★
1925–1927	Stella Andress★
1927–1929	Rae Mittenthal★
1929–1931	Grace Florence★
1931–1933	Thekla Brin★
1933–1934	Sarah Strauss★
1934–1936	Amelia Mintz★
1936–1937	Estelle Shaw★
1937–1940	Ruth Koch★
1940–1941	Felice Bromberg★
1941–1943	Marguerite Marks★
1943	Ann Berwald★
1943–1944	Mayme Janow★
1944–1946	Fannie Kahn★
1946–1948	Mildred Sack★
1948–1950	Rosine Olff★
1950–1952	Lorraine Sulkin (later Lorraine Schein) ★
1952–1954	Sara Waldman★
1954–1956	Edna Cohen★
1956–1958	Marie Bitterman★
1958–1960	Bette Wedeles (later Bette Schuttler) ★
1960–1962	Pat Peiser
1962–1964	Anita Marcus★
1964–1966	Selma Ross★
1966–1968	Edna Flaxman★
1968–1970	Jeanne Fagadau★
1970–1972	Katherine Bauer
1972–1974	Janet Newberger★
1974–1976	Bette W. Miller
1976–1978	Betty Dreyfus
1978–1980	Sylvia Lynn Benenson
1980–1982	Marsha Fischman★
1982–1984	Janice Sweet (later Janice Weinberg)
1984–1986	Joy Mankoff
1986–1988	Brenda Brand
1988–1990	Darrel Strelitz
1990–1992	Joni Cohan
1992–1994	Phyllis Bernstein
1994–1996	Jody Platt
1996–1998	Madeline "Maddy" Unterberg
1998–2000	Kathy Freeman
2000–2002	Julie Lowenberg
2002–2004	Kyra Effren
2004–2006	Marlene A. Cohen
2006–2008	Sue Tilis
2008–2010	Cheryl Pollman
2010–2012	Barbara Lee
2012–2014	Robin Zweig
2014–2016	Caren Edelstein

★ Deceased

Charter Members of the Section in 1913

Record keeping in the early years was neither thorough nor accurate. All documentation says seventy-five women came together in 1913 to organize the Dallas Section. The first printed directory in 1914–1915 records 219 names. At the October 5, 1943, opening meeting, the Section honored Charter members, past presidents, and new members. A partial list of Charter Members (year unknown) appears below with their husbands' names as was the custom of the time. It is believed that those names with a bullet (•) attended this 1943 meeting.

- Mrs. Emil Aronson (Hattie)
- Mrs. W.T. Andress (Stella)
  Mrs. Ben Ash (Mollie)
- Lillian Beekman
  Mrs. H. (Herman) Benno (Annie)
- Frances Rosenthal Bloom
- Mrs. Alfred Boas (Frances)
  Mrs. Ellis Brin (Celia)
- Mrs. Henri L. Bromberg (Felice)
- Mrs. I.G. Bromberg (Belle)
- Miss Mina Bromberg
  Mrs. A.E. (Abe E.) Bullman (Edna)
  Mrs. H.J. (Henry J.) Cohn (Florence)

Pauline Cohn
Emma Dietz
Miss Amelia Dysterbach
Mrs. S. Fleig (Clara)
Mrs. M.E. Florence (Grace)
• Mrs. Gussie Fox
Mrs. Morris Freedman (Adele)
• Mrs. S.M. Freedman (Theresa)
Mrs. Phil Garonzik (Bertha)
Mrs. Louis Getz (Edith)
Mrs. Ben Goldbaum (Sadie)
• Miss Berthe Goslin
Mrs. J.L. Goldman (Bea)
Mrs. Ben Haas (Henrietta)
• Mrs. Isaac Harris (Ella)
• Mrs. Victor H. Hexter (Minnie)
Mrs. Edgar Hurst (Esther)
Miss Sara Hyman
Mrs. Sam Hymes (Leah)
Mrs. Ben Irelson
Mrs. I. Israel (Elsie)
Miss Betsy Kahn
• Mrs. J. (Jacob) Kahn (Cora)
Mrs. Jake Kahn
• Mrs. Mayer Kahn (Sally)
Mrs. E. (Eli) Karchmer (Rose)
Mrs. Albert Kramer (Sophie)
Mrs. Arthur L. Kramer (Camille)
Mrs. I.L. (Irvin L.) Kramer (Mae)
• Mrs. Leo S. Levi
Mrs. M.C. Levi (Delano)
• Mrs. Frank J. Levin (Helen)
Mrs. Emanuel Levy (Ray)
Mrs. Henry Levy (Amanda)
• Mrs. M. Lichenstein (Marjorie)
Mrs. Albert Linz (Bertie)
• Mrs. Simon Linz (Rebecca)
Mrs. Philip Lipsitz (Annie)
Mrs. A. Lorch (Elora)
Mrs. Ed Lucas
• Mrs. Herbert Marcus (Minnie)
Mrs. Theo Marcus (Ophelia)
Mrs. J. Metzler
Mrs. W. Metzler

Mrs. Henry Miller (Carmen)
Mrs. A.H. Mittenthal (Rae)
Mrs. N.E. Mittenthal (Emma)
Mrs. Julian Morris
• Mrs. J.B. Moses (Mina Ray)
Mrs. W.S. Myers (Blossom)
• Mrs. J. Oppenheimer (Sadie)
Mrs. L. Oppenheimer (Gertrude)
Mrs. Morris Orleans
Miss Pandres (Lilye)
• Mrs. Max Philipson (Anne)
Mrs. R.C. (Reuben C.) Pollock (Jeanne)
Mrs. Gus Roos (Seline)
Mrs. I.E. Rose (Pauline)
• Mrs. I. Rosenbaum (Ida A.)
Mrs. Max Rosenfield (Hortie)
Mrs. L.B. Rosenberg
Mrs. Louis Rosenberg (Katie)
Mrs. D. (David) Rosenblatt (Grace)
Mrs. A. (A.R.) Rosenthal (Lena)
Mrs. Gus Sachs
• Mrs. Louis B. Sachs (Rebecca)
Mrs. Eli Sanger
Mrs. Elihu Sanger (Evelyn)
• Mrs. Ike (I.L.) Sanger (Mabel)
Miss Anna Shayne
Mrs. J. Schepps (Phyllis)
Miss Lilly Simon
• Mrs. Jack Smith (Pearl)
• Mrs. Arthur Star (Helen)
Mrs. Lee Swope
• Mrs. Reuben Tobolowsky (Etta)
Mrs. W. (William) Waldstein (Josephine)
• Mrs. Nathan F. Wertheimer (Minnie)
Mrs. J. (Jacob) Winterman (Rose)
Mrs. I. (Isadore) Zesmer (Jennie)

Charter Life Members

These Dallas Section Women became Life Members of National as of February 1, 1968.

Dora Aronson ★
Katherine Bauer
Margery Bernstein ★
Marie Bitterman ★

Rita Black ★
Anita Bloch
Frieda Bloom ★
Kay Blumberg ★
Carol Brin
Felice Bromberg ★
Naomi Brooks ★
Joy Burk ★
Ruth Byer ★
Cecile Cook ★
Pauline Crossman ★
Lyra Daniels
Gertrude Davis ★
Betty Dreyfus
Jeanne Fagadau★
Edna Flaxman ★
Marjorie Folgeman ★
Ann Folz
Emme Sue Frank★
Adele Freedman ★
Ernestine Freeman★
Byrna Funk★
Sadye Gartner ★
Judy Glazer
Jacquelyn Goldman ★
Josephine Goldman★
Belle Greene ★
Rose Greenspun ★
Esther Gurentz ★
Jane Guzman (later Jane Pawgan)
Iva Hochstim★
Ruth Jacobson ★
Dorothy Jacobus ★
Gloria Jacobus ★
Dovie Jaffe ★
Essie Joseph ★
Fannie Kahn ★
Louise Kahn ★
Marjorie Kahn ★
Renate Kahn★
Rita Kahn
Ruth Kahn ★
Bobbette Kamholz ★
Elaine Lansburgh★

Delano Levi ★
Marjorie Levy
Meryl Levy ★
Minnie Goldsmith Levy★
Myrtle Levy ★
Ruth Levy ★
Mollie Lipshy ★
Udys Lipshy ★
Sally Malkoff ★
Sylvia Mandell ★
Anita Marcus ★
Betty Marcus ★
Frances Marcus ★
Marguerite Marks ★
Dora Mayer ★
Carmen Miller Michael PhD ★
Bette W. Miller
Amelia Mintz ★
Patsy Nasher ★
Janet Newberger★
Rosine Olff ★
Frances Olsan ★
Elsie Pearle ★
Jeneane Pearlman
Eva Pearlstone ★
Pat Peiser
Sonia Philipson
Hortense Pollock ★
Shirley Pollock ★
Rose Rolnick ★
Annette Rosenstein ★
Leona Rosenthal ★
Rita Rubenstein
Josephine Rudman ★
Ann Salfield ★
Edythe Salzberger ★
Joan Salzberger
Carol Sandfield★
Hortense Sanger★
Fannie Schaenen ★
Lorraine Sulkin Schein★
Fonda Schwartz (now Fonda Glazer)
Shirley Shwiff ★
Ann Sikora ★

Phyllis Somer
Miriam Sternberg ★
Helen Strauss ★
Minnie Susman★
Isabelle Tobian ★
Cecile Victor ★
Carol Wadel★
Irene Wadel ★
Marie Weisberg ★
Fan Wiener ★
Marie Wolens ★
Sarah Yarrin
Barbara Zale
Edna Zale ★
Ethyle Zale ★
★ Deceased

Greater Dallas Section Members Who Served as National Board Members

Section leadership in Dallas did not stop at city boundaries. The women listed below served NCJW, Inc., either in state, district, regional, or national leadership roles.

As elected president of the NCJW State, Regional, or District organization, that member automatically served on the NCJW, Inc. National Board. Other women listed below were elected at National conventions or were appointed by National presidents to serve on the National Board. The offices of vice president, recording secretary, or assistant treasurer are elected positions.

Grace A. Goldstein (later Grace Neuman)
1918–1921 National Recording Secretary

Gussie Utay
1927–1930 President, Texas State Conference of NCJW

Fannie Kahn
1946–1955 National Board

Marguerite Marks
1949–1951 President, Southwestern Interstate Regional of NCJW

Mildred Sack
1952–1953 President, Southwestern Interstate Regional of NCJW

Lorraine Sulkin (later Lorraine Schein):
1954–1958 President, Southwestern Interstate Regional of NCJW

Marie Bitterman
1957–1961 National Board

Bette Wedeles (later Bette Schuttler)
1963–1967 National Board

Pat Peiser
1965–1977 National Board
1969–1973 National Recording Secretary
1981– Honorary National Board Member

Anita Marcus
1967–1969 First President, NCJW Southern District
1969–1975 National Board

Bette W. Miller
1972–1974 President, NCJW Southern District
1977–1981 National Board
1981–1983 National Recording Secretary
1981–2001 Board Member, NCJW Research Institute for Innovation in Education, Hebrew University, Jerusalem, Israel
1985–1993 NCJW Center for the Child Advisory Board Member
1993– Honorary National Board Member

Wanda Burger
1979–1983 National Board

Janet Newberger
1979–1983 National Board

Sylvia Lynn "Syl" Benenson
1983–1985 President, NCJW Southern District
1986–1990 National Board

Joy Mankoff
1987–1993; 1996–1999 National Board

Brenda Brand
   1989–1996 National Board

Phyllis Bernstein
   1996–2002 National Board

Jody Platt
   1996–1999 National Board

Joni Cohan
   2004–2010 National Board
   2011–2017 National Vice President

Debra "Debbie" B. Greene EdD
   2005–2008 National Board

Julie Lowenberg
   2011–2014 National Board

Sue Tilis
   2011–2015 National Board
   2015–2017 Assistant Treasurer

Greater Dallas Section Awardees through 2015

Hannah G. Solomon

The Hannah G. Solomon Award is presented to an individual:
- who has a strong NCJW identity and has changed the lives of others through personal leadership efforts and service,
- who has helped change and expand the role of women in vital areas of community life, and
- whose leadership in areas of NCJW concern—improving the quality of life for people of all ages and backgrounds—has motivated others to work for change, and has resulted in progress and enlightenment in the community.

1976 Fannie Kahn★
1978 Elsa Hirsh★
   Dorothy Jacobus★
   Marguerite Marks★
   Rosine Olff★
1979 Anita Marcus★
1980 Edna Cohen★
1982 Bette W. Miller
   Janet Newberger★
1983 Lorraine Sulkin Schein★
1984 Sylvia Lynn "Syl" Benenson
1985 Pat Peiser
1986 Jeanne Fagadau★
   Emme Sue Frank★
1987 Sara Waldman★
1989 Gerry Beer★
1990 Hortense Sanger★
1991 Annette Strauss★
1992 Shirley Tobolowsky
1993 Katherine Bauer
1994 Joy Mankoff
1995 Brenda Brand
1997 Janice Sweet (now Janice Weinberg)
1998 Ann Sikora★
1999 Marsha Fischman★
2000 Phyllis Bernstein
2001 Beverly Tobian
2002 Madeline Unterberg
2004 Edna Flaxman★
2005 Julie Lowenberg
2006 Darrel Strelitz
2007 Joni Cohan
2008 Lynn Goldstein
   Sharan Goldstein
2009 Myra Fischel
   Suzi Greenman
2010 Kathy Freeman
2011 Adlene Harrison
2012 Pauline Kress★
   Carmen Miller Michael PhD★
2014 Jody Platt
2015 Marlene A. Cohen

Janis Levine Music Make–A–Difference

The Janis Levine Music Make–A–Difference Award is presented to an individual:
- who has had a long-term commitment to NCJW,
- who has made a unique contribution to NCJW, Greater Dallas Section,

- who personifies voluntarism at its best, with characteristics such as enthusiasm and energy, willingness to work without personal recognition and making a difference wherever he or she serves, and
- who honors the memory of Janis Levine Music, a person who gave of herself with dignity and kindness of spirit.

1993 Felice Horwits★ ★★
1994 Murray Benenson★ ★★
1995 Barbara Rabin
1996 Barbara Rose
1997 Carol Wadel★
1998 Claire Lee Epstein★
1999 Dorothy Roder
2000 Tom Timmons
2001 Helen Stern
2002 Celia Schoenbrun
2003 Sue Tilis
2004 Jill Stone★
2005 Sharlene Block★
2006 Rita Doyne
2007 Cheryl Pollman
2008 Rhona Streit
2009 Phyllis Somer
2010 Linnie Katz
2011 Saralynn Busch
2012 Randi Smerud
2014 Yolanda Clark★
2015 Stacy Barnett
★ Deceased
★★ Awarded before the award was named in memory of Janis Levine Music.

Emerging Leader

The Emerging Section Leader Award is presented to an individual:
- who has the potential for assuming future Section leadership,
- who understands and supports the NCJW purpose and programs,
- who demonstrates a commitment to the Section, and
- who, if currently serving on the Section Board or is chairing a committee, has served fewer than five years.

1985 Ellen Silverman
1987 Elise Gold★
1989 Sally Regenbogen
1991 Sherry Goldberg
     Marcy Grossman
1995 Julie Bleicher
     Paula Jacobs
1996 Randi Smerud
1997 Linnie Katz
1998 Becky Bruder
     Mimi Johnson
1999 Saralynn Busch
2000 Staci Mankoff
2001 Cathy Sweet Brook
     Cynthia Feldman
2002 Sondra Perkins
     Beth Brand Stromberg
2003 Sheryl Fields Bogen
2004 Lauren Busch
     Melanie Rubin
2005 Karen Mellow Stock
2006 Stacy Barnett
2007 Karen Naseck
2008 Marla Bane
2009 Terry Greenberg
2010 Felise Leidner
2011 Joyce Goldberg
     Debra Levy-Fritts
2012 Caren Edelstein
2014 Jayme Cohen
2015 Stacy Blank

Pioneering Partner

The Pioneering Partner Award is presented to an individual (not a Greater Dallas Section member) or an organization in recognition of:
- major contributions to the Dallas community consistent with NCJW's mission and initiatives,
- strong leadership in bringing together and working with diverse groups and indivduals, and
- motivating others in the community to

strive for social justice.

2011 CitySquare (Central Dallas Ministries) and its president and CEO Larry James

2012 Cecilia Guthrie Boone, chair, Planned Parenthood Federation of America

2013 VMLC (Vickery Meadow Learning Center)

2014 North Texas Food Bank

2015 Vanna Slaughter, director of Immigration and Legal Services, Catholic Charities

Lifetime Achievement

Established in 2015, the Lifetime Achievement Award is presented to an individual in recognition of sustained, outstanding contributions to NCJW and the Dallas community. These contributions have been above and beyond the everyday and have had a long-lasting impact on the Greater Dallas Section. Also, the individual has:
- made a positive impact on NCJW,
- served NCJW for twenty-five years or more,
- earned the respect of professional and other nonprofit peers, and
- exhibited leadership and provided inspiration to others.

2015 Pat Peiser

Awards Received by the Greater Dallas Section (partial listing)

1939 Dallas Federation of Women's Clubs—Most Outstanding Club Work in the Community

1943 Community Chest—Special Commendation for day nursery work

1946 Women's Auxiliary of Dallas City-County Hospital System—Volunteer Service Award

1945–1951 Dallas City-County Hospital System—Volunteer Service Awards

1956 Terrell State Hospital—Certificate of Appreciation

1956 United Service Organizations (USO)—Certificates of Distinction (multiple years)

1958 Dallas Council of Social Agencies—Award for outstanding achievement in the field of social work

1960 NCJW, Inc.—Membership Award for largest regional gain in membership

1961 *Dallas Times Herald*—First Club of the Year Award for Operation LIFT

1964 Child Welfare League of America—Edith L. Lauer Award for "Direction for Tomorrow" program

1964 Goodwill Industries of Dallas—Community Service Award for the formation of Operation LIFT

1965 *Dallas Times Herald*—Club of the Year Award for Service to Neighborhoods for the West Dallas Study Center project

1967 Dallas Services for Blind Children—Award

1967 NCJW, Inc.—Public Relations Award for "Women on the Move" Forum

1967 *Dallas Times Herald*—Club of the Year Award (tie for first place) for services to Dallas County and its "Women on the Move" Forum

1969 *Dallas Times Herald*—Club of the Year Award for the People to People Panel

1970 NCJW, Inc. Southern District Convention—Awards for increased membership, largest percentage of enrolled national life members, and best membership retention

1973 *Dallas Times Herald*—Club of the Year Special Award for "Juvenile Justice Seminar"

1973 NCJW, Inc.—Public Relations Award for "Juvenile Justice Seminar"

1973 Dallas Home for Jewish Aged—20th Anniversary Award for Dedicated Service to Golden Acres in the "LIFE" (Love, Interest, Fulfillment, Enrichment) program

1974 NCJW, Inc. Southern District Convention—Outstanding Program Award for the "Juvenile Justice Seminar"

1974 Dallas Independent School District—Resolution for recognition and commendation for leadership in the School Volunteer program

1975 Dallas Federation of Women's Clubs—Outstanding Club Award, first place in recognition of the Section's Day Care Teacher Training Project

1976 Texas Department of Public Welfare—Highest Commendation for Family Outreach Center, "Working Parents" Forum, the seminar "Trouble in Texas—Children and the Justice System," and Aids in Medical Screening (AIMS)

1976 Eastfield College—Award for Day Care Staff Training Program

1977 *Dallas Times Herald*—Service to Senior Citizens Award for the Elder Artisan project

1978 Terrell State Hospital—Appreciation plaque for contributions made to teenage patients

1978 Dallas Volunteer Action Committee (D-VAC)—Volunteer Organization of the Year Award for Family Outreach Northwest

1979 NCJW, Inc.—Highest Increase in Membership Award

1983 Children's Medical Center—Special Recognition Award for volunteer service

1984 State of Texas—Certificate of Appreciation for exceptional and distinguished volunteer service

1984 Volunteer Center of Dallas—ARCO (Atlantic Richfield Corporation) Award for Excellence for over seventy years of service in the DISD

1985 Volunteer Center of Dallas—ARCO (Atlantic Richfield Corporation) Award for outstanding group volunteer program for the Khmer Community Development Project

1987 Women's Council of Dallas County—First Distinguished Service Award (member organization)

1988 Dallas Independent School District—Superintendent's Award for outstanding volunteer service to public education for the initiation of the DISD volunteers program and six current, active projects

1991 State of Texas House of Representatives—Special Recognition for the HIPPY program

1993 Family Outreach—Recognition on the twentieth anniversary of the first office in Richardson/Plano

1993 National Society of Fund Raising Executives, Dallas Chapter—Outstanding Philanthropic Organization of the Year

1994 Housing Crisis Center—Jeanette Early Award for outstanding organization of the year

1994 ChildCareGroup—Family Care Award presented to Dallas/Ft. Worth Marriott Interdivisional Business Council for work related to the Greater Dallas Section's "Day of the Working Parent"

1995 The *Dallas Post Tribune*—Volunteerism Award for service to Dallas Community

1997 Dallas County Adult Literacy Council—Celebrate Literacy Award for HIPPY's family literacy efforts

1997 LIFT—Key Award for Community Outreach for the conference "Literacy: Can Dallas Read the Future?"

1998 Women's Center of Dallas—Women Helping Women Special Recognition Award (Maura Women Helping Women Award)

1998 Community Council of Greater Dallas—Excellence in Human Services Programming Award for HIPPY

2000 The Dallas Southwest Osteopathic Physicians, Inc.—Humanitarian of the Year Award

2000 Dallas County District Attorney—Exemplary Service Award for Kids in Court

2001 Our Friends Place—Special Recognition and Appreciation Award

2003 Volunteer Center of Dallas—Outstanding Volunteer of the Year Award for the Parkland Hospital Infant Hearing Screening program

2004 Richardson Independent School District Board of Trustees—Recognition Award for HIPPY

2004 Dallas Community Television—Chairman's Award for Nonprofit Notes program

2005 NCJW, Inc.—Large Section Life Membership Award

2005 Jewish Family Service—Rookie of the Year Award for Safeguards for Seniors volunteers

2006 Dallas Historical Society—Award for Excellence in Community Service

2007 Texas Woman's University—Founders Day Award for scholarships for graduate studies in early childhood development

2007 Center for Nonprofit Management—Excellence in Mission Award for Kids in Court

2009 House of Representatives of the Eighty-First Texas Legislature—H.R. No. 1629 passed to honor the Greater Dallas Section of the NCJW for their distinguished community service

2011 NCJW, Inc.—Vision for America Award for Food + Fit = Fun

2011 Literacy Instruction for Texas (LIFT)—Certificate of Recognition as Champion of Literacy

2013 Women's Council of Dallas County—Distinguished Service Award (member organization)

2013 City of Dallas—Mayor Mike Rawlings's Proclamation in honor of Section's one hundredth birthday

2013 Parkland Hospital—Volunteer Award for thirty years of service at Parkland Hospital

Community Partners

Since its beginning in 1913, the Greater Dallas Section has partnered with, volunteered at, and/or cooperated with many local, state, and federal agencies, organizations, and coalitions. While an attempt has been made to acknowledge all, we apologize if we have inadvertently left any group off the list.

Adult Protective Services
Air Quality Coalition of North Texas
Alzheimer's Association (Alzheimer Disease and
    Related Disorders Association)
American Association of Retired Persons (AARP)
American Association of University Women
    (AAUW)
American Federation for the Blind
American GI Forum
American Indian Center of Dallas
American Jewish Committee (American Jewish
    Conference)
American Jewish Congress
American Red Cross
Anti-Defamation League
Anti-Poverty Coalition of Greater Dallas
Area Educational Television Foundation
Associated Women Students
Association for Retarded Citizens
Association for the Salvation of Cambodian
    Refugees
Attitudes & Attire
AVANCE Dallas
Baylor Colored Clinic (Baylor Hospital)
Bethlehem Center
Better Business Bureau
Bishop College
Boys and Girls Clubs of Dallas (Girls Club of Dallas)
Bradford Memorial Home
British War Relief Society
Bryan's House

Business & Professional Women's Club of Dallas, Inc.
Careers, Inc.
Carrollton/Farmers Branch Independent School District
Catholic Charities Dallas
Catholic Diocese of Dallas
Cause and Cure of War
Census 2000
Child Care '76 of Greater Dallas
Child Guidance Clinic
ChildCareGroup (Day Care Association of Metropolitan Dallas)
Children Health Insurance Program (CHIP)
Children's Medical Center Dallas (Dallas Baby Camp)
Children's Medical Foundation of Texas
Children's Store
Church Women United
Citizens for Community Health
City of Dallas
City of Dallas Zoo
City Park
City-County Hospital System
CitySquare (Central Dallas Ministries)
Civil Defense
CNM Connect (Center for Non-Profit Management)
Coalition for North Texas Children
Coalition for Public Schools
Coalition for Responsible Parenthood and Adolescent Sexuality
Collin County Children's Advocacy Center
Collin County Committee on Aging
Collin County Women's Shelter
Colonial School Parent-Teachers' Association
Columbia University
Communities Foundation of Texas
Communities in Schools
Community Chest of Dallas County
Community Coordinated Child Care Committee
Community Council of Greater Dallas (Council of Social Agencies)
Community Homes for Adults, Inc. (CHAI)
Community Partners of Dallas/Rainbow Room
Congregation Shearith Israel
Consumer Alliance
Council of Catholic Women, Dallas Deanery
Council on Alcohol and Drug Abuse
Dallas Alliance for Shaping Safer Cities
Dallas Aquarium
Dallas Arboretum
Dallas Area Agency on Aging (Area Agency on Aging)
Dallas Area Coalition to Prevent Childhood Obesity
Dallas Area Interfaith
Dallas Association for Education of Young Children
Dallas Association for Mental Health
Dallas Bar Association
Dallas Bar Wives Club
Dallas Big Sisters, Inc.
Dallas Birth Control Clinic
Dallas Black Chamber of Commerce (Negro Chamber of Commerce)
Dallas CASA (Court Appointed Special Advocates) (Foster Child Advocate Services/ FOCAS)
Dallas Chamber of Commerce, Criminal Corrections Resource Forum
Dallas Child Guidance Clinic
Dallas Children's Bureau
Dallas Children's Advocacy Center
Dallas City Council of PTAs
Dallas City Health Department
Dallas Coalition on Character and Values
Dallas Coalition for Hunger Solutions
Dallas Community Guidance Clinic
Dallas Concilio
Dallas Council of Catholic Women
Dallas Council of Social Agencies
Dallas Council on World Affairs
Dallas County Child Protective Services
Dallas County Child Welfare

197

Dallas County Commissioners Court

Dallas County Community Action Committee (War on Poverty)

Dallas County Community College District (Brookhaven, Eastfield, and El Centro Colleges)

Dallas County Department of Public Welfare

Dallas County District Attorney's Office

Dallas County Elder Abuse Coalition

Dallas County Elections Department

Dallas County Juvenile Department Letot Center

Dallas County Juvenile Services Advisory Committee

Dallas County KinCare Network

Dallas County Medical Society, Women's Auxiliary

Dallas County Park and Open Space Program

Dallas Federation of Women's Clubs (DFWC)

Dallas Foundation

Dallas Free Kindergarten Association (Free Kindergarten and Day Nurseries Association)

Dallas Furniture Bank

Dallas Geriatric Research Institute

Dallas Health Museum

Dallas Healthy Start

Dallas Holocaust Museum

Dallas Housing Authority

Dallas Independent School District

Dallas Jewish Coalition for the Homeless (Vogel Alcove)

Dallas Jewish Historical Society

Dallas Junior Bar Association

Dallas Legal Services Foundation, Inc.

Dallas Legislative Council

Dallas Lighthouse for the Blind

Dallas Morning News

Dallas Museum of Art

Dallas Patriotic Association

Dallas Pediatric Society

Dallas Pilot Home

Dallas Police Department

Dallas Post Tribune

Dallas Public Evening School

Dallas Public Library

Dallas Regional Chamber (Dallas Chamber of Commerce)

Dallas School for Blind Children, Inc.

Dallas Services for Visually Impaired (Dallas Services for Blind Children)

Dallas Southwest Osteopathic Physicians, Inc.

Dallas State Mental Health Clinic

Dallas Times Herald

Dallas Tuberculosis Hospital

Dallas United Nations Association

Dallas Women's Club

Dallas Women's Coalition

Dallas Women's Foundation

Day Care Action Committee

Day Care and Child Development Association of America

DFW International Community Alliance

DFWC Girls Foundation Home

Domestic Violence Intervention Alliance (DVIA)

Down Town Auditorium Committee

East Dallas Cooperative

East Dallas Health Coalition

Echad Apartments

Eckerd Drug Co.

Educational First Steps

Elder Abuse Coalition

Equal Employment Opportunity Commission

Family Life Education Association

Family Place

Farmers Foundation

Federation of Women's Clubs (City & Civic)

Free Legal Aid Bureau

Friends of the Dallas Public Library

Galerstein Women's Center at the University of Texas at Dallas

German-Jewish Children's Aid, Inc.

Gilda's Club of North Texas

Girl Scouts Troop (Section sponsored)

Girls' Adventure Trails

Girls Inc.

Girls' Protective League

Goals for Dallas

Goodwill Industries

Grand Prairie Independent School District

Greater Dallas Coalition for Reproductive Freedom

Greater Dallas Community of Churches

Greater Dallas Community Relations Commission

Greater Dallas Council of Churches

Greater Dallas Hispanic Chamber of Commerce (Dallas Mexican Chamber of Commerce)

Hadassah

Healthy Women, Healthy Families Coalition

Head Start

High Risk Victims Task Force

HIPPY (Home Instruction for Parents of Preschool Youngsters)

Hope Cottage

Hope's Door

Housing Crisis Center (Dallas Tenants' Association)

Human Relations Commission

Human Rights Initiative of North Texas

Immunize Kids! Dallas Area Partnership (Dallas Area Infant Immunization Coalition)

Infants Welfare Milk Association

Injury Prevention Center of Greater Dallas

International Rescue Committee

Irving Independent School District

Jacob's Ladder

Jewish Community Center of Dallas

Jewish Community Relations Council (JCRC)

Jewish Family Service (Jewish Federation's Social Service Bureau)

Jewish Federation of Greater Dallas (Federated Jewish Charities, Federation of Jewish Social Services, Jewish Welfare Federation)

Jewish Vocational Counseling Services (Jewish Vocational Guidance Service)

Jonathan's Place (KidNet Foundation)

Juanita Craft Summer Leadership Academy

Juliette Fowler Home for Orphans and Aged

Junior League of Dallas

Juvenile Detention Home

Juvenile Protective Association

Juvenile Welfare Association

KERA–Channel 13, FM 90

Kennedy Center Imagination Celebration

La Vida News

Ladies of Charity

Leadership Dallas

League of Women Voters of Dallas

Legal Services of North Texas

Legacy Senior Communities (Dallas Home and Hospital for the Jewish Aged-Golden Acres)

Legislative Council

Leslie K. Bedford Memorial Foundation

LIFT (Literacy Instruction for Texas) (Operation LIFT of Dallas)

Literacy Coalition of Greater Dallas

Manning House

March of Dimes

Martin Luther King Jr. Child Development Center

Martin Luther King Jr. Family Clinic

Martin Luther King Jr. Recreation Center (Crossroads Community Center)

McKinney Veterans Administration Hospital (Ashburn General Hospital)

Mental Health America of Greater Dallas (Dallas County Society for Mental Hygiene/Dallas County Mental Health Society/Mental Health Association)

Metrocare Services

Metroplex Consumer Council

Metroplex Senior Centers

Meyerson Symphony Center

Million Mom March Foundation

Mosaic Family Services

Municipal Market Committee

NAACP

Nasher Sculpture Garden

National Association of Social Workers, North Texas District

National Conference of Christians and Jews

National Council of Catholic Women

National Council of Negro Women

National Council on Crime and Delinquency in Texas

National Jewish Health-Denver (National Jewish Hospital for Consumptives)
National Jewish Welfare Board
National Retired Teachers Association
National Tay-Sachs and Allied Diseases Association, Dallas Chapter
National Youth Administration
Neighborhood Improvement Program (NIP)
Neiman Marcus
New Beginning Center
New Careers, Inc.
New Orleans Home for Jewish Children
North Texas Alliance to Reduce Unintended Pregnancy in Teens (Ntarupt) (S.A.Y. What? Coalition)
North Texas Association of Social Workers
North Texas DREAM Team
North Texas Food Bank
North Texas Planning Council for Hospitals and Related Health Facilities
North Texas United Nations Conference on Women
Oak Cliff Planning Council
Office of Civil and Defense Mobilization
Older American Legal Action Center
Older Women's League (OWL)
Open Arms, Inc. (Bryan's House)
Our Friends Place
Park Cities Baptist Church
Parkland Foundation
Parkland Health and Hospital System (Parkland Memorial Hospital)
Patriotic Association
Pepsi Kid-Around
Perot Museum of Nature and Science (The Science Place/Dallas Museum of Natural History)
Planned Parenthood Center
Planned Parenthood of Greater Texas (Planned Parenthood of North Texas)
Pollock Foundation

President's Council of Jewish Women's Organizations
Reading and Radio Resource (North Texas Taping for the Blind)
Reading is Fundamental
Reform Immigration of Texas Alliance (RITA)
Refugee Services of Texas, Inc. (Dallas Fort Worth Refugee Interagency)
Retired Senior Volunteer Program (RSVP)
Rhoads Terrace Pre-School
Richardson Child Guidance Clinic
Richardson Independent School District
Richardson Theatre Center
Ronald McDonald House of Dallas/Trains at NorthPark
Rural Life Committee
Salesmanship Club of Dallas
Salvation Army
Samaritan Inn
Senior Source (Senior Citizens of Greater Dallas)
Shalom Bayit
Social Venture Partners Dallas (SVP Dallas)
Southern Methodist University
Southwest Educational Development Laboratory
Southwest Jewish Congress
St. Vincent DePaul
State Fair of Texas
TeenAge Communication Theater (TACT)
Tejas Girl Scout Council
Temple Emanu-El
Temple Shalom
Terrell State Hospital
Texans Care for Children
Texas A&M University Agricultural Extension School
Texas Association of Services to Children, North Texas Chapter
Texas Campaign to Prevent Teen Pregnancy
Texas Coalition for Juvenile Justice
Texas Commission on Children and Youth
Texas Consumer Association

Texas Council on Crime and Delinquency

Texas Credit Union League

Texas Department of Health & Human Services (State Department of Human Resources/State Department of Public Welfare)

Texas DREAM Act Coalition

Texas Employment Commission

Texas Freedom Network

Texas Hunger Initiative

Texas Impact

Texas Instruments Foundation

Texas Jewish Post-Dallas

Texas Organizing Project

Texas Scottish Rite Hospital for Children (Shrine Hospital for Crippled Children)

Texas Society for Mental Hygiene

Texas Society on Aging

Texas United Community Services

Thanks-Giving Square

Transition Resource Action Center (TRAC)

Trinity River Mission

Tuberculosis Committee

US Department of Health and Human Services (US Department of Health, Education, and Welfare)

US Department of Labor, Women's Bureau

US Food & Drug Administration

US War Department, Women's Interest Section

United China Relief

United Way of Metro Dallas (Community Chest of Dallas)

United Ways of Texas

United We Dream

University Leadership Initiative

University of Colorado

University of North Texas (North Texas State University)

University of North Texas Health Science Center

University of Texas at Arlington, School of Social Work

University of Texas at Austin, School of Social Work

University of Texas at Dallas

University of Texas Southwestern Medical Center

Urban League

United Service Organizations (USO)

US Department of Justice/Law Enforcement Assistance Agency (LEAA)

Veterans Administration

Vickery Community Action Team (VCAT)

Vickery Meadow Neighborhood Alliance

Vickery Meadow Youth Development Foundation

Vietnamese Mutual Assistance Association

VMLC (Vickery Meadow Learning Center)

VNA Meals on Wheels

VNA Texas (Visiting Nurse Association)

Volunteer Now! (Volunteer Center of Dallas, Dallas Voluntary Action Center)

Wadley Blood Center

Wesley Inn

West Dallas Community Center

WiNGS (YWCA of Dallas)

With One Voice Coalition

Women in Community Service (WICS)

Women of Rotary (Rotary Club of Dallas)

Women's Council of Dallas County

Women's Issues Network, Inc.

Women's Museum: An Institute for the Future

YMCA, Inc.

Young Men's Hebrew Association (YMHA) (eventually became the Jewish Community Center)

Young Women's Hebrew Association (YWHA)

Zeta Phi Beta Sorority, Kappa Zeta Chapter

This 2004 version of a May 1926 group picture from National's eleventh Triennial Convention in Washington, DC, proves that NCJW is still here to advocate for women, children, and families. (See Chapter Fourteen and check out the change of fashion.) Courtesy of NCJW, Inc.

> "It literally takes a village of dedicated, tireless, type A-personality people to make a single book live up to its potential and find an audience."
>
> *Kristin Hannah (1960–), author of* The Nightingale

17 : Acknowledgments

This book is the culmination of over six years of professional and volunteer effort. The publication was created to celebrate the achievements of the National Council of Jewish Women, Greater Dallas Section's (the Section) century-old past, and to give an optimistic look into the future. It is a tribute and a hope.

Under the presidency of Barbara Lee and president-elect Robin Zweig, a Centennial Committee, chaired by Rhona Streit (also known as Rhona Frankfurt) and Jody Platt, was established to commemorate one hundred years of the Section. A history book subcommittee, chaired by Marlene Cohen, was formed to create a chronological record of outstanding accomplishments of the Section. A journalist, Harriet P. Gross, was commissioned to write the history. Work began on what was hoped to be a finished document in time for the Centennial Birthday celebration in February 2013.

As the project grew, Bette Miller joined Marlene as cochair. Later, Rose Marie Stromberg worked with Bette and Marlene as they reviewed, enlarged, and edited the manuscript, selected images, and arranged for publication of the book. What you have now in this publication is the result of thousands of hours of uncovering Section materials in the Section's office, members' homes, online, and at the Dallas Jewish Historical Society's archives, where most of the older documents are stored.

This is where the realities of life stepped in. The many skills and efforts that went into the creation of a work such as this all had to fit under the umbrella of "time." Here is how the journey was described by Bette:

> Along the way, things happened, and the book took on a life of its own. Research was followed by writing, editing, fact-checking, and culling and scanning images, plus endless hours of proofreading, all done by many devoted volunteers. As "life" got in our way, we referred to it as our dark cloud. Over the past several years, between key players, there were deaths of immediate family members, personal and family illnesses, accidents, and surgeries. And there were also simchas: family travels, weddings, births, bar/bat mitzvahs, and other life cycle events that were celebrated.

Overall, this was a labor of love by all involved. The many stories, lists, essays, and other content in this book cover just the highlights of a century of caring and service. Our thanks go out to all who have been involved and to the greater Dallas area that provided a fertile environment in which to experience our lives as American Jews through participation in the Section. We are grateful for all the blessings that go with this gift to the organization and our community.

A special "thank you" goes to the leadership of the *Dallas Morning News*, whose generous granting of permission for the use of photos, headlines, and articles from the *Dallas Morning News* and the former *Dallas Times Herald* helped authenticate the Section's actions and impact.

The many volunteers, contributors, researchers, paid professionals, and organizations that have helped put this publication together have made a good faith effort to identify and to give credit for all information, graphics, photographs, and content that is presented in the collection in this book.

The time span covered within these pages is well over one hundred years. Many of the persons represented are no longer available to verify accuracy. In fact, some of the actual contributors to this publication have passed away since their essays were submitted. Therefore, there is the possibility that someone, something, or some event may be identified or characterized in error. Any mistakes are purely unintentional. We ask flexibility and forgiveness of those who find an error.

"Section Archives" refers to the NCJW Greater Dallas Section's stored documents held at the Dallas Jewish Historical Society, housed at the Aaron Family Jewish Community Center in Dallas, Texas, or at the Section's office, also located in Dallas, Texas.

The materials that are derived from other sources and organizations are acknowledged and deemed released to the Section for use in this printed publication and any digital/electronic versions.

The collection encompasses all print and electronic publications and media that are derived from this publication. All rights for the content of this book and the collection are reserved and are the property of the Section. A copyright notice in the name of the National Council of Jewish Women, Greater Dallas Section, Inc. will protect the copyright of other intellectual property owners in the collection even if the owner is not known or cannot be found.

We acknowledge with gratitude the following:

Centennial Committee

Rhona Streit (also known as Rhona Frankfurt), cochair

Jody Platt, cochair

Barbara Lee, Section president 2010–2012

Robin Zweig, Section president 2012–2014

Donors

Special thanks for all the financial support that helped bring this book to publication.

Foundations

Tom and Jennifer Miller Hillman

Fannie and Stephen Kahn Foundation

NCJW, Greater Dallas Section

NCJW, Greater Dallas Section Centennial Benefit 2013

NCJW, Greater Dallas Section SHARE Endowment Fund

Summerlee Foundation

Kalman and Ida Wolens Foundation

National Council of Jewish Women, Greater Dallas Section Past Presidents

Katherine Bauer

Brenda Brand

Syl Benenson

Phyllis Bernstein

Joni Cohan

Marlene A. Cohen

Betty Dreyfus

Caren Edelstein

Kyra Effren

Jeanne Fagadau★

Marsha Fischman★

Edna Flaxman★ by her family

Kathy Freeman

Barbara Lee

Julie Lowenberg

Joy Mankoff

Anita Marcus★ by her husband

Bette W. Miller

Janet Newberger★ Fund of Jewish Federation Foundation

Patricia Peiser

Jody Platt

Cheryl Pollman

Selma Ross★ by her daughter

Darrel Strelitz

Sue Tilis

Maddy Unterberg

Janice Sweet Weinberg

Robin Zweig

Section Publication Team

Marlene A. Cohen

Bette W. Miller

Rose Marie Stromberg

Commissioned Staff

Maura Wright Conley, photojournalist

Tyra Damm, consolidating editor

Harriet P. Gross, journalist and voice of the book

Helene Levitan, portrait artist

Alan Lidji, Lidji Design Office

TCU Press
    Daniel Williams, director
    Kathy Walton, editor
    Molly Spain, assistant editor
    Melinda Esco, production manager
    Rebecca Allen, marketing coordinator

Suzie Tibor, photo researcher

Jay Knarr, indexer

Greater Dallas Section Staff

Suzi Greenman, executive director, 2015–2018

Nicole Gray, administrative manager

Dallas Jewish Historical Society

Debra Polsky, executive director

Jenny Claeys, administrative assistant

Alexis Joanna Ferguson, former archivist

Jessica Schneider, archivist

★ *Deceased*

Dallas Heritage Village

Evelyn Montgomery PhD, director of collections, exhibits, and preservation

Susan Finlay, collection manager

The Dallas Morning News, Inc.

Robert "Bob" Mong, former editor and current president of University of North Texas at Dallas

James M. Moroney III, publisher emeritus

Michael Wilson, editor

Mark M. Konradi, director of newsroom operations

Essay Writers/Contributors

Katherine Bauer
Syl Benenson
Phyllis Bernstein
Sheryl Fields Bogen
Denise Bookatz
Joni Cohan
Marlene A. Cohen
Rita Doyne
Betty Dreyfus
Caren Edelstein
Kyra Effren
Claire Lee Epstein★
Jeanne Fagadau★
Ann Folz
Kathy Freeman
Myra Fischel
Marsha Fischman★
Suzi Greenman
Sharon Goldstein
Judy Hoffman
Sondra Hollander
Renate Kahn★
Katherine Krause
Barbara Lee
Julie Lowenberg
Joy Mankoff
Bette W. Miller
Pat Peiser
Jody Platt
Cheryl Pollman
Janine Pulman
Myrna Ries
Joyce Rosenfield
Cynthia Schneidler, MD
Phyllis Somer
Frances "Sister" Steinberg
Darrel Strelitz
Rose Marie Stromberg
Nita Mae Tannebaum
Sue Tilis
Carol Rieter Tobias
Shirley Tobolowsky
Maddy Unterberg
Judy Utay
Janice Sweet Weinberg
Robin Zweig

Research and Assistance

All of the Section's past presidents, plus:
Carolyn Abrams
Carol Alkek
Frances Blatt
Karen Blumenthal
Anne Bromberg
Spencer Bromberg
Elinore Brown
Sharon Cohany
Annette Corman
Gerry Cristol
Laura Diamond
Janet Eickmeyer
Ann Folz
Joyce Goldberg
Sharan Goldstein
Marlene Gorin
Debbie B. Greene, EdD
Barbara Gutow
Janet Hershman
Arnold B. Kaber, PhD
Sandra Kaman
Katherine Krause
Helen Lansburgh
Zelene Lovitt
Charles Marcus★
Victor Marshall, Dallas Symphony Orchestra
Bennett Miller★
Nancy Pennington
Barbara Rose
Joyce Rosenfield
Hermine Sallinger★
Ellen Samuels
Norma Schlinger
Harriet Silverman
Phyllis Somer
Helen Stern
Norma Stone
Phyllis Stoup
Rose Marie Stromberg
T. Thomas Timmons, Legal Advisor
Nita Mae Tannebaum
Beverly Tobian
Judy Utay
William Weiss
Mark Wilson, Dallas Symphony Orchestra
Riki Rothschild Zide

75th Anniversary History Book

Written by:
Miriam Jaffe

Edited by:
Barbara Silberberg★
Rose Marie Stromberg

Research by:
Katherine Bauer
Syl Benenson
Janet Eichmeyer
Dorace Fichtenbaum★
Edna Flaxman★
Ann Folz
Helene Greenwald★
Miriam Jaffe
Fannie Kahn★
Bette W. Miller
Janet Newberger★
Norma Schlinger
Barbara Silberberg★
Helen Stern
Judy Utay

★ Deceased

Image Credits

Unless otherwise noted, images are from the archives of the National Council of Jewish Women, Greater Dallas Section, located at the Dallas Jewish Historical Society or the Greater Dallas Section's office.

Title page
p. iv: Richardson, Barbara, *Dallas Times Herald*, October 15, 1967, sec. D, 9. © 1967 The Dallas Morning News, Inc.

Foreword
p. x: "Six Staffers Salute Six Clubs." *Dallas Times Herald*, September 7, 1961. © 1961 The Dallas Morning News, Inc.

Introduction
p. 2: "A Dallas Lady Honored." The *Dallas Morning News*, January 23, 1894, 8. © 1894 The Dallas Morning News, Inc.

Decade One
p. 10: "Council of Jewish Women." The *Dallas Morning News,* March 23, 1913, 7. © 1913 The Dallas Morning News, Inc.

p. 11: "To Organize Jewish Women." The *Dallas Morning News*, February 23, 1913, 4. © 1913 The Dallas Morning News, Inc.

p. 12: "Dallas Pupils Get Lunches at Cost." The *Dallas Morning News*, December 21, 1913, part 3, 8. © 1913 The Dallas Morning News, Inc.

Decade Two
p. 16: "Lip-Reading Will Be Taught In Schools; Teacher Elected." The *Dallas Morning News*, June 7, 1934, sec. II, 1. © 1934 The Dallas Morning News, Inc.

p. 17: "Little Americans Give Russian Folk Dances." The *Dallas Morning News*, January 8, 1930, 8. © 1930 The Dallas Morning News, Inc.

p. 18: "Newly Elected Officers of Council of Jewish Women." The *Dallas Morning News,* May 5, 1932, 6. © 1932 The Dallas Morning News, Inc.

Decade Four
p. 35 (top): McKee, Ruby Clayton. "Golden Years Open Doors to Needs of the Community." The *Dallas Morning News,* September 30, 1962, sec. 6, 1. © 1962 The Dallas Morning News, Inc.

p. 35 (bottom): Castleberry, Vivian. "Where the Need is They are There." *Dallas Times Herald,* October 11, 1964, Living Section, 1. © 1964 The Dallas Morning News, Inc.

Decade Five
p. 38: McKee, Ruby Clayton. "Golden Years Open Doors to Needs of the Community." The *Dallas Morning News*, September 30, 1962, sec. 6, 1. © 1962 The Dallas Morning News, Inc.

p. 42: *Dallas Times Herald*, September 26, 1971, sec. C, 9. © 1971 The Dallas Morning News, Inc.

p. 43: Brinkerhoff, Mary. "A Community's Call to Action." The *Dallas Morning News,* June 9, 1963, sec. 6, 1. © 1963 The Dallas Morning News, Inc.

p. 45 (left): "Group to Aid Problem of 2,335 Illiterates." *Denton Record-Chronicle* (TX), April 30, 1961, sec. 3, 13.

p. 45 (right): "Workshop Planned for LIFT Teachers." The *Dallas Morning News,* May 28, 1961, sec. 1, 14. © 1961 The Dallas Morning News, Inc.

Decade Six

p. 48: McKee, Ruby Clayton. "Golden Years Open Doors to Needs of the Community." The *Dallas Morning News*, September 30, 1962, sec. 6, 1. © 1962 The Dallas Morning News, Inc.

p. 49: McKee, Ruby Clayton. "Jewish Women Do Homework Before Forum." The *Dallas Morning News,* October 2, 1966, sec. E, 1. © 1966 The Dallas Morning News, Inc.

p. 50: McKee, Ruby Clayton. "Jewish Women Plan Year of Helping Disadvantaged." The *Dallas Morning News,* October 6, 1968, sec E, 1. © 1968 The Dallas Morning News, Inc.

p. 51 (top): Young, Mildred. "New Dimension in Education." *Dallas Times Herald,* March 15, 1964, sec. D, 6. © 1964 The Dallas Morning News, Inc.

p. 51 (bottom): McKee, Rudy Clayton. "LIFE Is Concern of Jewish Women." The *Dallas Morning News*, September 26, 1971, sec. F, 1. © 1971 The Dallas Morning News, Inc.

p. 54 (left): Richardson, Barbara. "Now, Encore." *Dallas Times Herald,* October 8, 1968, sec. B, 2. © 1968 The Dallas Morning News, Inc.

p. 54 (bottom): McKee, Ruby Clayton. "Education, Not Devastation Aided." The *Dallas Morning News,* May 26, 1970, sec. C, 5. © 1970 The Dallas Morning News, Inc.

p. 56 (top right): Castleberry, Vivian. "Where the Need is They are There." *Dallas Times Herald,* October 11, 1964, Living Section, 1. © 1964 The Dallas Morning News, Inc.

p. 56 (top right): Richardson, Barbara. *Dallas Times Herald*. September 26, 1971, sec. C, 9. © 1971 The Dallas Morning News, Inc.

p. 56 (bottom left): McKee, Rudy Clayton. "LIFE Is Concern of Jewish Women," The *Dallas Morning News,* September 26, 1971, sec. F, 1. © 1971 The Dallas Morning News, Inc.

p. 56 (center right): Richardson, Barbara. "Where There's a Woman, … There's a Way." *Dallas Times Herald,* October 15, 1967, sec. D, 9. © 1967 The Dallas Morning News, Inc.

p. 56 (bottom right): "Revolving Door-Type Offender Helped." *Dallas Times Herald,* October 4, 1970, Dallas Police Department section, 6. © 1970 The Dallas Morning News, Inc.

Decade Seven

p. 60: Kennedy, Maggie. "Harrison Salutes Council for Humanitarian Work." *Dallas Times Herald,* 1976. © 1976 The Dallas Morning News, Inc.

p. 62 (center): Cobler, Sharon. "Parents Can Work It Out." The *Dallas Morning News.* January 13, 1976, sec. C, 1. © 1976 The Dallas Morning News, Inc.

p. 62 (bottom): Kennedy, Maggie. "Working Parents Need Someone on Their Side." *Dallas Times Herald*. February 5, 1976, Living section. © 1976 The Dallas Morning News, Inc.

p. 64: "Stitching Loose Ends." The *Dallas Morning News*. October 12, 1975, sec. E, 1. © 1975 The Dallas Morning News, Inc.

p. 66 (top): Richardson, Barbara. "Phil Lewis: Jail Social Worker." *Dallas Times Herald,* October 17, 1973, sec. G, 1. © 1973 The Dallas Morning News, Inc.

p. 66 (bottom) Richardson, Barbara. "$10,000 to the Rescue." *Dallas Times Herald,* September 10, 1975, sec. F, 1. © 1975 The Dallas Morning News, Inc.

p. 70:   Cobler, Sharon. "Consumer Alliance Guards Right To Get What's Paid For." The *Dallas Morning News.* October 6, 1974, sec. F, 1. © 1974 The Dallas Morning News, Inc.

p. 73:   Tucker, Jennifer. "FOCAS Executive Director is a Tough Cookie Who's Learned Not to Crumble: Marjorie MacAdams." *Dallas Downtown News*, September 8-14, 1984, 20.

Decade Eight

p. 78:   Sanchez, Erika. "Woman is Honored for NCJW Work." The *Dallas Morning News,* March 8, 1980, sec. C, 3. © 1980 The Dallas Morning News, Inc.

p. 79:   Miller, Lauraine. "A Tradition of Caring." The *Dallas Morning News*, July 20, 1987, sec. C, 1. © 1987 The Dallas Morning News, Inc.

p. 80:   Goad, Kimberly. "Fete Set." The *Dallas Morning News,* April 3, 1988, sec. E, 4. © 1988 The Dallas Morning News, Inc.

p. 82:   "E. Dallas Community Garden Grows Up." *Dallas Times Herald,* September 9, 1988. © 1988 The Dallas Morning News, Inc.

p. 83:   Marshall, Thom. "Refugee Family Faces New Fears in a New World." *Dallas Times Herald,* September 20, 1984, sec. D, 1. © 1984 The Dallas Morning News, Inc.

p. 91:   "National Council of Jewish Women Honored." The *Turtle Creek News*, September 15, 2004, sec. B, 7.

Decade Nine

p. 99:   Zethraus, Lee. "An Advocate for Children–Paula Jacobs Teaches Kids to Testify in Court." The *Dallas Morning News*, January 29, 1995, sec. E, 4. © 1995 The Dallas Morning News, Inc.

p. 102:   Silverthorn, Deborah. "NCJW Begins Its 90th Year." *Dallas Jewish Week*, September 12, 2002, 20.

Decade Ten

p. 106:   Miller, Robert. "Volunteers Still Helping Others After 90 Years." The *Dallas Morning News,* November 9, 2003, sec. D, 4. © 2003 The Dallas Morning News, Inc.

Chapter 11

p. 123:   Weinstein, Rachel Gross. "Happy Hundred: NCJW Dallas Fetes Century of Service." *Texas Jewish Post*, February 14, 2013, 1.

Chapter 12

p. 126 (top left):   McKee, Ruby Clayton. "Jewish Women Do Homework Before Forum." The *Dallas Morning News*, October 2, 1966, sec. E, 1. © 1966 The Dallas Morning News, Inc.

p. 127 (top right):   "Junior Buds to Stage Play at Temple Emanu-El." The *Dallas Morning News,* September 17, 1929, 6. © 1929 The Dallas Morning News, Inc.

p. 128:   McKee, Ruby Clayton. "NCJW Serves Fellowman." The *Dallas Morning News*, October 5, 1969, sec. E, 1. © 1969 The Dallas Morning News, Inc.

p. 129:   Cobler, Sharon. "Players following Yellow Brick Road." The *Dallas Morning News,* November 13, 1973, sec. C, 3. © 1973 The Dallas Morning News, Inc.

Chapter 13

p. 140:   The *Dallas Morning News.* "Hostesses." November 30, 1941, 12. © 1941 The Dallas Morning News, Inc.

p. 143:   Richardson, Barbara. "Encore Time." *Dallas Times Herald,* April 14, 1974. © 1974 The Dallas Morning News, Inc.

p. 146 (left):   Donaldson, Ann. "Invitations Announce Encore Sale by the Council of Jewish Women." The *Dallas Morning News.* August 09, 1964: 3. © 1964 The Dallas Morning News, Inc.

p. 146 (top right): McKee, Ruby Clayton. "NCJW Serves Fellowman." The *Dallas Morning News,* October 5, 1969, sec. E, 1. © 1969 The Dallas Morning News, Inc.

p. 147: Richardson, Barbara. "It's Second Time Around." *Dallas Times Herald*, March 14, 1973. © 1973 The Dallas Morning News, Inc.

p. 147 (top left): Castleberry, Vivian. *Dallas Times Herald,* October 11, 1964, Living Section. © 1968 The Dallas Morning News, Inc.

p. 147 (bottom right): Young, Mildred. "Encore." *Dallas Times Herald,* October 10, 1965, sec. D. © 1965 The Dallas Morning News, Inc.

p. 150 (top): McKee, Ruby Clayton. "Golden Years Open Doors to Needs of the Community." The *Dallas Morning News,* September 30, 1962, sec. 6, 1. © 1962 The Dallas Morning News, Inc.

p. 150 (bottom) McKee, Ruby Clayton. "Awareness Inspires NCJW." The *Dallas Morning News,* October 4, 1970, sec. E, 1. © 1970 The Dallas Morning News, Inc.

Chapter 14
p. 165: McKee, Rudy Clayton. "NCJW Serves Fellowman." The *Dallas Morning News*, October 5, 1969, sec. E, 1. © 1969 The Dallas Morning News, Inc.

p. 169: McKee, Rudy Clayton. "Jewish Women Plan Year of Helping Disadvantaged." The *Dallas Morning News,* October 6, 1968, sec. E, 1. © 1968 The Dallas Morning News, Inc.

p. 172: Lee, Barbara and Cohen, Marlene. "Perry Should Rethink Prayer Meet." The *Dallas Morning News,* August 3, 2011, sec. A, 14. © 2011 The Dallas Morning News, Inc.

p. 174: Raggio, Louise Ballerstedt. *Texas Tornado: The Autobiography of a Crusader for Women's Rights and Family Justice.* New York: Citadel, 2003.

Chapter 15
p. 180: Solís, Dianne. "Under Rocket Docket, Kids Race Time, Few with Lawyer: Justice Jettisoned?" The *Dallas Morning News,* September 28, 2014, sec. A, 1-2. ©The Dallas Morning News, Inc.

Selected Bibliography

This bibliography is not a complete record of all printed sources. These sources, plus many conversations with Greater Dallas Section members, helped shape this book.

Archival Collections

Dallas Jewish Historical Society Archives

National Council of Jewish Women, Greater Dallas Section Archives at the Dallas Jewish Historical Society Archives

National Council of Jewish Women, Greater Dallas Section Archives at the Section office

Books

Castleberry, Vivian Anderson. *Daughters of Dallas.* Dallas: Oldenwald Press, 1994.

Cristol, Gerry. *A Light in the Prairie, Temple Emanu–El of Dallas 1872–1997.* Fort Worth: TCU Press, 1998.

Graziani, Bernice. *Where There's A Woman: 75 Years of History as Lived by the National Council of Jewish Women.* New York: McCall Corp., 1967.

Jaffe, Miriam. *National Council of Jewish Women, Greater Dallas Section, Celebrating 75 Years of Service to the Community.* Dallas: National Council of Jewish Women, Greater Dallas Section, 1988.

Keyserling, Mary Dublin. *Windows on Day Care.*

New York: National Council of Jewish Women, 1972.

Raggio, Louise Ballerstedt. *Texas Tornado: The Autobiography of a Crusader for Women's Rights and Family Justice.* New York: Citadel, 2003.

Rogow, Faith. *Gone to Another Meeting, The National Council of Jewish Women, 1893–1993.* Tuscaloosa: University Alabama Press, 1993.

Solomon, Hannah G. *Fabric of My Life, The Story of a Social Pioneer.* New York: Bloch Pub. Co., 1946.

Weiner, Hollace Ava. *Jewish "Junior League."* College Station: Texas A&M University Press, 2008.

Newspapers, Magazines, Periodicals, Annuals, Articles, and Pamphlets

50 Years of Service. Dallas: National Council of Jewish Women, Dallas Section, 1963.

Cambodian Dallas Monthly. Dallas: East Dallas Cooperative; National Council of Jewish Women, Greater Dallas Section; and Refugee Services of Texas, Inc.

Constant Comment. National Council of Jewish Women, Greater Dallas Section, Evening Branch.

Council News/The Bulletin. National Council of Jewish Women, Greater Dallas Section.

Dallas Downtown News

Dallas Jewish Week

Dallas Morning News

Dallas Post Tribune

Dallas Times Herald

Helping Hands. National Council of Jewish Women, Greater Dallas Section, Richardson-Plano Branch.

Miller, Carmen, PhD. "For Emotionally Disturbed Children … Residential Facilities Needed in Texas," *Texas Hospitals, The Journal of the Texas Hospital Association,* March 1953: 6.

National Council of Jewish Women. *Symposium on Status Offenders Proceedings.* New York: National Council of Jewish Women, Inc. 1976.

Newsletter. National Council of Jewish Women, Professional Branch.

Texas Jewish Post

They Made a Difference. Dallas: National Council of Jewish Women, Greater Dallas Section, 2003.

Voice of Khmer Dallas. Dallas: Association for the Salvation of Cambodian Refugees; National Council of Jewish Women, Greater Dallas Section; and Refugee Services of Texas, Inc.

Yearbook. Dallas: National Council of Jewish Women, Greater Dallas Section, 1913-2016.

Index

Aaron Family Jewish Community Center (Dallas, Texas): as Section partner, 118, 119, 204

Abrams, Carolyn Marcus: pictured, 172. See also Marcus, Carolyn

Adler, Chaim: pictured, 160

Adopt-a-Grandparent program: as Section partner, 130

advocacy: of Section, 157–58, 160–75. See also specific issues

Affordable Care Act (2010): as Section issue focus, 177, 178

affordable housing: as Section issue focus, 87

Afray, Eve: pictured, 41

African Americans: relationship with, as Section issue focus, 98–99

after-school care: as Section issue focus, 11, 34, 35, 42, 49, 52, 96, 100, 118. See also childcare

After-School Recreation Program (Section), 34, 35; Councilettes and, 42

aging. See senior citizens

Aids in Medical Screening project (Section), 75

Aircraft Warning Center: as Section partner, 33

Alamo Elementary School (Dallas, Texas): as Section partner, 162

Albert, Marianne: pictured, 42

Alger, Bruce, 174; pictured, 172

Allenberg, Lauren: pictured, 112

American Cancer Society: as Section partner, 129

American GI Forum: as Section partner, 49

American Jewish Committee: as Section partner, 50, 110

Americanization. See immigration; Service to the Foreign Born project (Section)

Americanization Committee (Section), 17

Amster, Susan: pictured, 159

Anchia, Rafael: pictured, 168

Anderson, Pearlie: pictured, 83

Anderson, Ron, 68, 118; pictured, 121

Andress, Stella: pictured, 187

Anka, Paul: pictured, 101; as Section gala fundraiser performer, 101

anti-Semitism: as National issue focus, 23; as Section issue focus, 10, 23, 33, 64

ARCO Volunteer Center Award: won by Section, 78

Armstrong, Melanie, 91

Army and Navy Service: as Section partner, 33

Aronoff, JoAnn: pictured, 84

Aronoff, Valerie: pictured, 51

Asch, Gladys: pictured, 41

Attitudes & Attire (Dallas, Texas): pictured, 107; as Section partner, 94, 106

Austin Committee, 158

Austria: Section's support for Jewish shelters in, 33

awards: given by Section, listed, 192–94; received by Section, listed, 194–96. See also specific awards

Bacharach, Burt: pictured, 152, 153

Backburn, Audley: pictured, 150

Balaban, Zlona: pictured, 43

Bank, Julie: pictured, 132

Banks, Barbara, 52

Barshop, Sara Lee: pictured, 127

Barton, Joe: pictured, 173

Barzune, Dolores Gomez, 107

Bauer, Katherine: essay by, 65–66; pictured, 49, 51, 56, 122, 123, 128, 159, 172, 186

Baum, Kathi: pictured, 175

Baylor Hospital (Dallas, Texas): as Section partner, 22

Beattle, Rilla: pictured, 23

Becker, Philip, 108

Beer, Gerry, 62

Ben Milam Elementary School (Dallas, Texas): as Section partner, 162

Bendorf, Robert, 26

Benenson, Murray: pictured, 91

Benenson, Sylvia Lynn ("Syl"), 67, 72, 79, 107; essay by, 68, 70, 89–90; pictured, 56, 68, 70, 78, 85, 89, 91, 111, 113, 114, 123, 128, 143, 147, 159, 168, 172, 175, 183, 187

Benjamin, Gwen: pictured, 128

Benson, Sybil, 12

Bentsen, Lloyd: pictured, 167

Beren, Jan: pictured, 147

Berg, Rose Marion, 72; pictured, 150

Berman, Adelaide: pictured, 145

Bernice, Rose: pictured, 26

Bernstein, Bill, 178

Bernstein, Margery: pictured, 169

Bernstein, Phyllis: essay by, 83, 86; pictured, 83, 84, 98, 99, 114, 123, 128, 159, 161, 163, 166, 168, 186; on Tikkun Olam, 98

Berwald, Ann: pictured, 187

Bethlehem Center: as Section partner, 70

Biggs, Harold: pictured, 136

birth control: as National issue focus, 8; as Section issue focus, 22, 86. See also reproductive rights

Bishop College: as Section partner, 142

Bitterbaum, Evelyn: pictured, 87, 88

Bitterman, Marie: pictured, 48, 159, 172, 186

Black, Rosalind: pictured, 87

Blank, Stacy: pictured, 166

Bleicher, Julie: pictured, 153

blindness: as National issue focus, 2; as Section issue focus, 16, 17, 22, 40, 41. See also Mildred R. Sack Tribute Fund; visually challenged

Block, Sharlene, 70; pictured, 56, 85, 167, 175

Bloom, Staci: pictured, 112

Blum, Joanne: pictured, 85

Bock, Certie, 9

Bock, Jenny: pictured, 41

212

Bock, Robin Benjamin: pictured, 132

Bogen, Sheryl Fields, 72; pictured, 168

Bonnheim, Ana, 108

Bookatz, Denise: essay by, 87, 89; pictured, 88

Borley, Doris: pictured, 24

Bortz, Walter M., II, 75

Boyd, Marilyn: pictured, 86

Bradford Baby Clinic (Dallas, Texas): pictured, 127. See also Children's Medical Center (Dallas, Texas)

Bradford Memorial Home (Dallas, Texas): as Section partner, 18

Brand, Brenda, 73; essay by, 72–73; pictured, 34, 84, 106, 114, 123, 147, 159, 172, 175, 187

breast cancer: as Section issue focus, 95, 97

Breinin, Ellene: pictured, 85, 86

Brin, Fanny, 24, 25; telegram from, pictured, 158

Brin, Thekla, 18, 27; pictured, 18, 56, 159, 187

Brinker, Nancy: as CBI featured speaker, 71

Brinkman, Jim: pictured, 152, 153

British War Relief: as Section partner, 23

Brodsky, Lotty: pictured, 101

Bromberg, Felice: pictured, 186

Bromberg, H. L.: Cocktails to Coffee and, 27, 28

Bromberg Adolescent Center Tribute Fund: timeline of, 150

Brookhaven College: Theatre Department, as Section partner, 144

Brophy, Jean, 64

Brounoff, Zelman, 17; pictured, 17

Brown, Joe B., 48

Brown, Elinore: pictured, 135, 159

Brown, Michael S., 108; pictured, 108

Brown, Ruth: pictured, 41

Bruce-Starling, Joyce: pictured, 120

Bubis, Barbara: pictured, 91

Buckner Children's Home (Dallas, Texas): Councilettes and, 42

Busch, Lauren: pictured, 175, 181

Busch, Saralynn: pictured, 85, 114, 175

Bush, Laura, 95; pictured, 95

Bush, George W., 94, 105; pictured, 104, 170

Byers, Hazel: pictured, 100

Byrne, Joanna: pictured, 132

"Call Police" program (Section), 82; pictured, 81, 143

Cambodia: refugees from, Section and resettlement of, 78, 82–83, 112

Cambodian-Dallas Monthly: pictured, 82

Campos, Gloria, 71, 122

Carlson, Maurice, 44

Carpenter, Liz, 62; pictured, 62

Carrollton-Farmers Branch Independent School District: as Section partner, 88. See also specific schools

Caruth Center (Garland, Texas): as Section partner, 69

Castleberry, Vivian, 41, 147; foreword by, x-xi; pictured, x, xi, 163

Catholic Charities: Cambodian refugees and, 82; as Section partner, 112, 115, 178, 180; in Vickery Meadow neighborhood, 96, 115

Catholic Women's Guild: as Section partner, 26

Center for Nonprofit Management: as Section partner, 71

Central Dallas Ministries (CitySquare): as Section partner, 111

Cerf, Marjorie: pictured, 84, 145

Chapman, E. M.: newspaper article about pictured, 4

Chaput, Rachel: pictured, 118

charter life members: of Section, listed, 189–91

charter members: of Section, listed, 188–89

Chavenson, Jeanie: pictured, 88

Chicago World's Fair (1893), 1: pictured, xiv

child abuse: as Section issue focus, 50, 60–61, 134

Child Guidance Clinic (Dallas, Texas): as Section partner, 23

child labor: as National issue focus, 3

Child Protection Center: as Section partner, 134

Child Protective Services: as Section partner, 133

Child Welfare League of America: award presented to Section by, 41, 43

Child Welfare Study of Dallas County, 42–43, 49

childcare: as Section issue focus, 24, 51, 61, 62, 86, 134. See also after-school care

Children as Witnesses in Child Sexual Abuse Cases program (National), 79

Children's Emergency Shelter (Dallas, Texas): Councilettes and, 42

Children's Medical Center (Dallas, Texas): Councilettes and, 42, 114; Family Resource Center at, 107; Section financial support to, 82; as Section partner, 40, 66, 95, 107, 129. See also Bradford Baby Clinic (Dallas, Texas); Dallas Baby Camp

Children's Sunshine Fund: timeline of, 150

Chrisman, George: pictured, 136

Christensen, Shirley: pictured, 91

Christenson, Patricia: pictured, 143

Church Women United: as Section partner, 49, 50

Civic and Communal Affairs Committee (Section), 22

civil rights: as Section issue focus, 39-40

City of Dallas: proclamation from, 118, 123; as Section partner, 10–11, 50, 61–62, 65–66. See also specific city government departments

City of Dallas Department of Consumer Affairs: as Section partner, 64, 68, 70

City Park Elementary School (Dallas, Texas): Councilettes and, 42; as Section partner, 34, 35

Cizon, Deidre: pictured, 114

Clark, Yolanda: pictured, 166, 181

Clinton, Bill, 93; pictured 104, 170

Clinton, Hillary Rodham, 98

213

Cocktails to Coffee, 27–28, 80, 142; cover pictured, 27
Cohan, Joni: essay by, 98; pictured, 83, 84, 98, 99, 114, 123, 159, 161, 163, 168, 173, 175, 186
Cohany, Sharon, 134: pictured, 128, 138
Cohen, Edna: pictured, 78, 159, 186
Cohen, Jayme: pictured, 163
Cohen, Marlene A., 133, 172; essay by, 109–10; pictured, 99, 108, 113, 114, 123, 135, 153, 159, 166, 168, 173, 175, 179, 187
Cohen, Sandy: pictured, 168
Coker, Glynn: pictured, 56
Collin County Committee on Aging: as Section partner, 133
Collins, Jim: pictured, 167
Colonial Hill School Park (Dallas, Texas), 17
Columbian Club: founding of, 10; program from pictured, 12
Combs, Susan: pictured, 128, 138
Commer, Mamie: pictured, 41
Committee of One Thousand (National), 23
Committee on Home Defense: as Section partner, 33
Communities Foundation of Texas: as Section partner, 71
Communities in Schools project (Section), 78
Community Board Institute (CBI), 71–72; invitations pictured, 71
Community Chest: as Section partner, 17
Community Council of Greater Dallas (CCGD): as Section partner, 49, 50, 66, 67, 71. See also Dallas Council of Social Agencies
Community Homes for Adults Inc. (CHAI): as Section partner, 106, 130, 131, 133
Community Partners of Dallas: Rainbow Room of, as Section partner, 133, 137
Comroe, Jacque: pictured, 84
Congregation Shearith Isreal: as Council Sabbath venue, 17, 72; relocation of (1956), 39; as Section partner, 24; as Section Sabbath venue, 10
Connally, John, 48; telegram from pictured, 171
Consumer Alliance (Section), 64, 68, 70; Operation READY as origins of, 49, 52; pamphlet pictured, 71
Corporate and Community Groups: Section financial support to, 82
Council Comment: debut of, 18; World War II hiatus of, 24
Council News: pictured, 48, 57, 174
Council Jelly Closet, 17
Council Players, The (Evening Branch), 130; members pictured, 129. See also Travelling Troubadours (Evening Branch)
Council Sabbath, 17, 64, 72
Council Singers, The (Evening Branch), 130. See also Travelling Troubadours (Evening Branch)
Councilettes (Section), 41, 42, 126
crime and urban decay: as Section issue focus, 50
Crockett Elementary School (Dallas, Texas): as Section partner, 162

Cumberland Hill School (Dallas, Texas): as Section partner, 9, 11, 16, 162
Dallas, Texas: city government (see City of Dallas); city park in, pictured, 13; Jewish diffusion in, after World War II, 39; NCJW section (1898–1905) in, 3-4; NCJW section (1913–present) in (see Section)
Dallas Area Agency on Aging: as Section partner, 95, 102
Dallas Arboretum: pictured, 85; as Section partner, 90
Dallas Association of Young Lawyers: as Section partner, 78
Dallas Baby Camp: as Section partner, 18. See also Children's Medical Center (Dallas, Texas)
Dallas Board of Realtors: as Section partner, 81
Dallas City Jail: as Section partner, 65
Dallas City-County Hospital System: volunteer armband pictured, 34
Dallas Council of Social Agencies: award presented to Section by, 41; as Section partner, 23, 24, 42. See also Community Council of Greater Dallas
Dallas County Child Welfare Department: as Section partner, 134
Dallas County Child Welfare Unit: as Section partner, 61, 72
Dallas County Community Action Committee (DCCAC): as Section partner, 49
Dallas County Community College District, 62; as Section partner, 70. See also specific campuses
Dallas County Department of Public Welfare: as Section partner, 49, 56
Dallas County District Attorney's Office: as Section partner, 94, 99–100
Dallas County Juvenile Department: as Section partner, 78, 86, 150
Dallas County Medical Society: as Section partner, 26
Dallas County Mental Health Association: as Section partner, 61
Dallas County Mental Health Society, 34
Dallas County Society for Mental Hygiene: as Section partner, 34
Dallas County Welfare Department: as Section partner, 49
Dallas Court Appointed Child Advocates (CASA), 61, 72–73. See also Foster Child Advocate Services (FOCAS)
Dallas Cowboys: as Section partner, 81
Dallas Free Kindergarten Association: as Section partner, 11
Dallas Geriatric Research Institute: as Section partner, 64
Dallas Healthy Start: as Section partner, 94
Dallas Holocaust Museum: pictured, 95; as Section partner, 94, 106
Dallas Housing Authority: Section financial support to, 82; as Section partner, 63. See also Edgar Ward Place
Dallas Independent School District (DISD): Section financial support to, 82; as Section partner, 51, 52, 54, 64, 70, 79, 86, 87, 89, 97, 110, 111, 178. See also Dallas Public Schools; and specific schools

Dallas Jewish Coalition for the Homeless: as Section partner, 79

Dallas Jewish Federation: as Section partner, 129

Dallas Jewish Historical Society: Section archives at, 84; Section financial support to, 82; as Section partner, 107

Dallas Juvenile Detention Home: as Section partner, 34

Dallas Legal Services: as Section partner, 64, 68, 70

Dallas Memorial Auditorium Theatre, 43

Dallas Morning News, 79, 95, 172; Operation LIFT profile in, pictured, 45; Section founding noted in, 10, 11; Section's ninetieth birthday noted in, 106; as Section partner, 41, 44

Dallas Museum of Art, 56, 78, 97; pictured, 85, 86; as Section partner, 90

Dallas Police Department: pictured, 56, 66; as Section partner, 50, 55, 56, 65, 66, 83, 165

Dallas Public Evening School: as Section partner, 23

Dallas Public Library: as Section partner, 16, 65, 74, 129

Dallas Public Schools: desegregation of, Section and, 40; as Section partner, 4, 11, 22, 162. See also Dallas Independent School District (DISD); and specific schools

Dallas Services for Visually Impaired Children, Inc.: Section financial support to, 82; as Section partner, 81

Dallas School for Blind Tribute Fund, 40. See also Mildred R. Sack Tribute Fund

Dallas Society for Crippled Children: Councilettes and, 42

Dallas Southwest Osteopathic Physicians: as Section partner, 35, 97, 153

Dallas Symphony Orchestra, 17

Dallas Tenants' Association: as Section partner, 87

Dallas Times Herald: article about Section published in, 11, 34; Section named "Club of the Year" by (1961), 41; as Section partner, 11; West Dallas After-School Center awarded by, 52, 57

Dallas Tuberculosis Association: as Section partner, 162

Dallas Urban League: as Section partner, 51

Dallas Women's Issues Network, 63

Dallas/Fort Worth Marriott Interdivisional Business Council: as Section partner, 94

Danhi, Bernice E., 129

Daniel, Price, 40

Daniels, Donna: pictured, 42

Darrow, Arnold ("Scotty"): pictured, 95

Darver, Al: pictured, 145

Darver, Laura: pictured, 145; Your Thrift Store and, 142

Davis, Babette, 130

Davis, Lois: pictured, 127

Day of the Working Parent, 94

deafness: as Section issue focus, 16, 22, 75, 90, 130

Denenberg, Lys: pictured, 154

Denton Record-Chronicle: Operation LIFT profile in, pictured, 45

Denton State School: as Section partner, 130

Depression: Section during, 22–25

desegregation: as Section issue focus, 39, 40; pamphlet on, pictured, 164

Diamond, Laura: pictured, 163, 173

Diamond, Norm: pictured, 183

Diamond Shamrock: as Section partner, 81

Dickey, Kathy, 83

Direction for Tomorrow, 41, 43

divorce laws: as National issue focus, 3

Dobie Elementary School (Richardson, Texas): as Section partner, 106, 108, 111, 113

domestic violence: as Section issue focus, 66, 95, 108, 130, 182

Domestic Violence Intervention Alliance: as Section partner, 62

Donosky, Charlotte: pictured, 127

Dorfman, Judy: pictured, 51

Doyne, Rita: essay by, 101; pictured, 97, 101

Dreyfus, Betty: essay by, 71–72; pictured, 50, 61, 114, 123, 150, 159, 167, 186

drugs: as National issue focus, 3. See also substance abuse

DuBois, Barbara: pictured, 79, 90

Dulak, Roy: pictured, 49; on Section's work, 49–50

Dunlap, Margaret, 54

Eastfield College (Dallas, Texas): as Section partner, 62

Eckerd Pharmacy: as Section partner, 67, 69

Edelstein, Caren: essay by, 178, 180, 182; pictured, 99, 173, 179, 182, 183, 187

Edgar Ward Place: as Section partner, 52

Edgar Ward West Dallas Study Center program (Section): award won for, pictured, 57

EDS: as Section partner, 81

education: as National issue focus, 2; pamphlet on, pictured, 164; as Section issue focus, 8, 10, 12, 89–90, 160–61

Effren, Kyra, 97; essay by, 110–11; pictured, 96, 99, 106, 109, 113, 114, 123, 154, 159, 168, 175, 179, 187

Eickmeyer, Janet: pictured, 114

Eilbott, Paula, 99; pictured, 79, 172

Eiseman, Louise: pictured, 147, 169

Elder Artisans project (Section), 63

Eldridge, Jacqueline, 100

Ellis Island: Immigration Aid station established at, 2; as Section partner, 17, 18

Emerging Leader award: awardees listed, 193

Emmet, Rachel: pictured, 90

"Encore Fete," 144

ENCORE resale shop, 16, 130

Encore sale, 82, 130, 144; discontinuance of, 97–98; permanent space for, 51; pictured, 54, 103, 143, 145, 146, 147; start of, 41

Endow NCJW Dallas tribute fund, 109; timeline of, 151

Endowment Fund: timeline of, 149

Engle, Rae: pictured, 127

environmental activism: as Section issue focus, 13, 98

Equal Rights Amendment (ERA), 51, 62–63

Epstein, Claire Lee, 86; essay by, 87

Epstein, Sylvia: pictured, 74

Esquenaze, David., Mrs.: pictured, 38

Estes, Nolan, 51, 54; pictured, 54

Evans, Jack: as CBI featured speaker, 71

Eve, Nomi, 97

Evening Branch (Section), 126; dissolution of, 107; Encore Sale and, 144; essays about, 126, 129–30, 133, 133–34; "From Dreidels to Knaidels" booklet of, 130, 133; at Golden Acres, 64, 129, 130, 133; Hungarian refugees and, 39; launching of, 34; Morning Branch merged with, 137; pamphlet pictured, 126; presidents listed, 139; Professional Branch establishment by members of, 62; Tay-Sachs disease and, 66, 67, 91, 129, 130; various events of, pictured, 127, 128, 131, 132, 133, 135, 136, 137

Fadal, Donna: pictured, 120

Fagadau, Jeanne, 52, 65, 174; essay by, 54; pictured, 35, 54, 114, 163, 165, 186; on Section's work, 51–52

fair consumerism: as Section issue focus, 64. See also Operation READY

Fairchild, Annie: pictured, 143

Falvo, James, 83

Families on the Rise event, 106

family: as Section issue focus, 50, 56, 57, 60–61, 72–73, 78–79, 86–87, 89–90, 161–62, 178

Family Compass: as Section partner, 61

Family Outreach, 118, 134. See also Northwest Dallas County Family Outreach Center

Family Place, The, 62, 63; Section financial support to, 82; as Section partner, 134, 137

Fannin Elementary School (Dallas, Texas): as Section partner, 16

Federated Charities: as Section partner, 18

Feldman, Lenore: pictured, 83

Ferber, Edna, 17

Fine, Dorothy, 34

Finkelman, Lois: pictured, 96, 175

Fischel, Myra, 68; essay by, 111–12; pictured, 91, 111, 114, 128, 143, 145, 172

Fischman, Marsha, 112; pictured, 114, 120, 123, 159, 187

Flack, Roberta: pictured, 152, 153

Flaxman, Edna, 65; pictured, iv, 49, 114, 128, 147, 159, 187

Fleschman, Jackie: pictured, 114

Florence, Annette, 27; pictured, 127

Florence, Grace, 27, 171; pictured, 159, 187

Folz, Ann, 65; essay by, 52; pictured, 51, 128

food: as National issue focus, 3; as Section issue focus, 4 See also North Texas Food Bank; nutrition

Food + Fit = Fun (FFF) program (Section), 108, 109, 115, 178; essay about, 110–11; various activities pictured, 110, 111, 113, 179

Forest Avenue High School (Dallas, Texas): as Section partner, 22

Foster Child Advocate Services (FOCAS): as Section partner, 61, 72–73

Fowler, Claudia: pictured, 108

Frank, Emme Sue, 65; pictured, 85

Frank, Helen: pictured, 154

Frederick Douglass Elementary School (Dallas, Texas): pictured, 54; as Section partner, 51, 54

Freeman, Kathy, 101; essays by, 42, 86–87; pictured, 99, 109, 111, 114, 123, 128, 159, 163, 172, 178, 187; on Tikkun Olam, 98

Freling, Doris: pictured, 97

Fried, Barbara, 134

Friendship Fone project (Evening Branch), 129; pictured, 128

"From Dreidels to Knaidels" booklet (Evening Branch), 133; pictured, 130

Frost, Martin: pictured, 172

fundraising: of Evening Branch, 133; of Section, 141–55. See also specific funds and galas

Furneaux Elementary School (Carrollton, Texas): as Section partner, 88

galas, 144; listed, 148; programs and various events of, pictured, 152–54

Galleria Shopping Center (Dallas, Texas), 130

Garber, Diane: pictured, 133

Gartenlaub, Rochelle: pictured, 127

Geary, Wes: pictured, 136

General Mills: as Section partner, 110

German-Jewish Children's Aid (New York, New York): as Section partner, 25, 26

Germany: refugees from, Section and resettlement of, 23, 25–26, 28

Giddings, Helen: pictured, 173

Gilat, Karen Webber, 96

Gilbert, Gail: pictured, 69, 95

Girl Scouts: Section sponsorship of, 17

Glazer, Fonda: pictured, 146

Glazer, Mollie: pictured, 145

Goals for Dallas: as Section partner, 50

Gold, Rita Sue: pictured, 85, 161

Golden, Betty ("Bootsie"): pictured, 85, 168

Golden Age Recreation Club (Section), 34, 40; pictured, 34

Golden Acres retirement home (Dallas, Texas): as Council Sabbath venue, 72; Councilettes and, 42; pictured, 69;

Section branches at, 64, 129, 130, 133, 134, 137; as Section partner, 63, 67, 106
Goldman, Jackie: pictured, 128
Goldman, Josephine: pictured, 49
Goldman, Robyn: pictured, 128
Goldman, Wendy: pictured, 62
Goldstein, Amy: pictured, 84. See also Roseman, Amy
Goldstein, Ariella, 95
Goldstein, Grace A.: pictured, 8, 159, 186, 187
Goldstein, Lynn: pictured, 114
Goldstein, Marilyn: pictured, 85
Goldstein, Sharan, 65, 80, 110; essay by, 74, 91; pictured, 51, 74, 84, 91, 95, 110, 113, 163, 173, 175, 179
Golman, Grey: pictured, 118
Golman, Macy: pictured, 118
Goodman, Gertrude, 12
Goodman, Noreen: pictured, 67
Goodman, Sarah: pictured, 41
Gore, Tipper, 78
Gore, Tracy: pictured, 99
Goslin, Bertha: pictured, 23
Goyer, Emily, 43
Grace L. Florence Fund, 64; timeline of, 150
Gramm, Phil: pictured, 172
Grand Prairie Independent School District: as Section Partner, 85
Gravier, Pauline, 35
Greater Dallas Coalition for Reproductive Freedom: as Section partner, 79–80, 118
Greenberg, Terry: pictured, 108
Greenburg, William Henry, 10
Greene, Debbie B.: pictured, 94, 159, 168, 170, 173, 175
Greene, Samantha: pictured, 170, 173, 175
Greenman, Suzi: pictured, 80, 111, 182; as Section executive director, 180
Greif, Lizzy: pictured, 153
Gross, Harriet P.: Preface by, xii; pictured, 99
Gross, Marty: pictured, 136
Grossfeld, Bonnie, 112
Grossman, Marcy: pictured, 84, 95, 153
Guardians Ad Litem: as Section partner, 72
guardianship: as Section issue focus, 94, 98
Guerra, Yolanda: pictured, 70
Guggenheim, L. M., Mrs.: NCJW section (1898–1905) cofounded by, 3
gun violence: as Section issue focus, 180

Hadassah: as Section partner, 18, 24, 95, 96, 108
Hamlisch, Marvin, 82, 144; pictured, 81
Hannah G. Solomon Award, 64–65, 84; awardees listed, 192; awarding pictured, 78
Harrison, Adlene, 107; pictured, xi, 109; praise of Section's humanitarian work pictured, 60; on Section's domestic violence program, 66

Hart, Sara: pictured, 127
Harvey, Ruth, 49, 57
Hasan, Abdur-Rahim: pictured, 175
Head Start of Greater Dallas: promotion of, by Section, 49; as Section partner, 144
health care: as National issue focus, 2; as Section issue focus, 11, 16, 17, 33, 106–7, 107–8, 129, 162, 165–66. See also specific maladies and types
Health Committee (Section), 16, 17, 33
Health Special High School (Dallas, Texas): as Section partner, 79, 83, 86, 130
hearing impaired. See deafness
Hebrew Immigrant Aid Society (HIAS): as Section partner, 134
Hebrew Union College: as Section philanthropic beneficiary, 11
Hebrew University of Jerusalem, 35. See also Research Institution for Innovation in Education (RIFIE)
Heilbron, Rusti: pictured, 143
Hein, Sally: pictured, 138
Hella Temple Crippled Children Home: as Section partner, 16. See also Scottish Rite Crippled Children's Hospital
Heller, Dot: pictured, 91
Heller, Karen, 108
Hello Israel program (Section), 35, 80, 87–89, 106, 130
Hendricks, Pat: article about Section written by, 34–35
Heritage Park nursing home (Plano, Texas): pictured, 131
Hershman, Janet: pictured, 40, 56
Herskowitz, Greta: pictured, 88
Herz, Josephine (Jo): pictured, 91
Herz, Susan: pictured, 62
Herzfeld, Susan: pictured, 128
Heschel, Susannah, 80
Hesseltine, Sue: pictured, 120
Hexter, Minnie, 11, 13; pictured, 8, 159, 186
Hicks, Don: pictured, 153
Higier, Kathy: pictured, 133, 135, 159
Hillel, 12, 35
Hillyear, Louise: pictured, 16
Hinkamp, Kristi: pictured, 181
HIPPY program (Section), 35, 79, 80, 106, 118; essay about, 89–90; events pictured, 85, 86, 89, 106, 113, 161, 183; Food + Fit = Fun (FFF) program and, 108, 110, 111, 178; twenty-fifth anniversary of, 180
HIPPY/Haetgar program (National), 35
Hirsh, Margaret, 44
Hirshfelder, Blanche: pictured, 22
Hoffman, Gloria: pictured, 43
Hoffman, Judy: essay by, 99–100; pictured, 175, 179, 181
Hogue, Ilyse: pictured, 96
Hogue, Ynette: pictured, 96
Hollander, Sondra, 91; pictured, 91, 107

Holocaust, 28; survivors, aided by Section, 33. See also Dallas Holocaust Museum
Home Instruction for Parents of Preschool Youngsters (HIPPY) Fund: timeline of, 151
Home Instruction for Parents of Preschool Youngsters (HIPPY) program. See HIPPY program (Section)
Hope Cottage (Dallas, Texas): as Section partner, 34, 129, 130
Hope's Door (Plano, Texas): as Section partner, 181
Horsey, Catherine: as Section executive director, 180
Horwits, Felice: pictured, 95
hospitalized children: as Section issue focus, 16–17. See also Parkland Hospital (Dallas, Texas)
Housing Crisis Center (HCC), 87
Howard, Jorge: pictured, 67
Hughes, Sarah T., 24, 174
human trafficking: as Section issue focus, 168, 178
Hungary: refugees from, Section and resettlement of, 39; Section's support for Jewish shelters in, 33
Hunter, Victoria: pictured, 26
Hurst, Barbara, 40; pictured, 51

Immigrant, The (play), 80, 144; program pictured, 81
Immigrant Aid Committee (Section): Americanization classes offered by, 11
immigration: immigrants pictured, 3; as National issue focus, 2; rally (2010) pictured, 158; as Section issue focus, 4, 11, 17, 18, 33, 39, 78, 100–101, 107, 112, 128, 129, 130, 166–67, 168, 178, 180. See also refugee resettlement; and specific countries of origin
incarceration: as National issue focus, 2; as Section issue focus, 65
Infant Hearing Screening project (Parkland Hospital), 79, 90
infant mortality: as Section issue focus, 95
InfoVoter Technologies: as Section partner, 108
Injury Prevention Center of Greater Dallas: as Section partner, 68
Interfirst Bank: as Section partner, 81
International Council of Jewish Women, 2-3
International Council of Women, 2
Internet safety: as Section issue focus, 178
Irving, David, 96
Irving Independent School District: as Section partner, 79, 89, 108, 111, 178
Israel, 31, 39, 91, 97; as Section issue focus, 34, 35, 51, 60, 64, 78, 80, 107, 108, 160, 178, 182. See also Hello Israel program (Section); Ship-A-Box program (National)
Israel Granting Fund: timeline of, 151
Israel Granting Program (National), 35, 108

Jackofsky, Ellen: pictured, 114
Jacobs, Esther: pictured, 172
Jacobs, Paula, 99; pictured, 99, 153
Jacob's Ladder: as Section partner, 95, 106

Jacobus, Gloria: pictured, 147
Jaffe, Sam, 78
Jaffe, Miriam, xii, 91
James Madison High School (Dallas, Texas). See Forest Avenue High School (Dallas, Texas)
Janis Levine Music Make-A-Difference Award: awardees listed, 180-181, 192
Janow, Mayme: pictured, 180, 187
JCPenney Co.: as Section partner, 71
Jeanetta Foundation Day Care Center: as Section partner, 51
Jewish Children's Home (New Orleans, Louisiana): as Section partner, 17, 18
Jewish Family Service (JFS): as Section partner, 27, 68, 80, 94, 95, 98, 115, 128, 129, 130, 134, 149, 180
Jewish Federation of Greater Dallas: as Section partner, 95, 178
Jewish Welfare Relief Fund: as Section partner, 11
Jill Stone Elementary School (Dallas, Texas): as Section partner, 108
Johansen, Gayle: pictured, 80, 163
Johnson, Lyndon B., 24, 31, 48; pictured, 48. See also War on Poverty
Johnson, Mimi: pictured, 163
Johnson, Peter: pictured, 175
Johnson, Susan: pictured, 128
Jolly, Karlene: pictured, 88
Jonathan's Place: as Section partner, 94
Jones, Debbie: pictured, 136
Jonsson, Erik, 51
Jordheim, Alisa, 178; pictured, 179
Joyner, Oscar, 108; as CBI featured speaker, 72
Joyner, Thomas, Jr.: as CBI featured speaker, 72
Junior Auxiliary (Section), 42, 126
Junior Buds (Section), 15, 42, 126; pictured, 127
Junior Council (Section), 15, 42, 126; annual meeting agenda pictured, 9; founded, 11
Junior League of Dallas: as Section partner, 41, 43, 54, 65, 71, 81, 95, 102
Juniors (Section), 126
Juvenile Court Mediation Project, 78, 86–87, 170
Juvenile Detention Home (Dallas, Texas): as Section partner, 34, 129
Juvenile Welfare Federation: as Section partner, 41

K. B. Polk Elementary School (Dallas, Texas): as Section partner, 88
Kaber, Arnold: pictured, 153
Kahn, Fannie, 126; as Hannah G. Solomon Award winner, 65; pictured, 48, 65, 159, 187; Your Thrift Store and, 142
Kahn, Louise: pictured, 140
Kahn, Renate Fulda: essay by, 28; letter from pictured, 29
Kaman, Sandy: pictured, 128, 135
Kantor, Eddie: telegraph from pictured, 23

Kaplan, Bess: pictured, 145

Kaplan, Rowena: pictured, 127

Kaprow, Maurice S.: letter from pictured, 130

Karp, Renee: pictured, 118, 173

Karp, Shira: pictured, 118

Kassanoff, D. J.: pictured, 114

Kasten, Nancy, 96–97, 108; pictured, 97, 110, 161, 163

Katz, Linnie: pictured, 107, 149

Katz, Roz: pictured, 181

Kaufman, Nancy K., 115

Kay, Maxine: pictured, 127

Kennedy, John F., 36, 37, 133; assassination of, 24, 47, 48, 118

Kent, Carol: pictured, 173

KERA: as Section partner, 44, 45

Khmer refugee project (Section), 78, 82, 82–83, 112; holiday party pictured, 84

Kids in Court program (Section), 79, 92, 94, 99–100, 170, 178; comfort dog pictured, 178; pamphlet pictured, 102; pictured, 175, 179

Kimmelman, Elaine: pictured, 50, 124, 159

King, Coretta Scott: pictured, 109; as Section birthday luncheon speaker, 104, 106, 109

King, Glen D.: pictured, 165

Kirk, Ron: as CBI featured speaker, 71

Knight, Asher: pictured, 114

Knight, Gladys: pictured, 152; as Section gala fundraiser performer, 101, 148

Koch, Ruth, 26; pictured, 159, 186

Kohut, George Alexander: NCJW section (1898–1905) cofounded by, 3

Konig, Beth: pictured, 175

Kornblatt, Bridgett: pictured, 42

Kramer, Robert: pictured, 67

Krause, Katherine: essay by, 26–27

Kress, Pauline, 67

Kronick, Joan, 54; pictured, 54

Kurtz, Cindie: pictured, 131

Kurzman, Karen: pictured, 90

Ladies of Charity: as Section partner, 115

LaManna, J. L.: pictured, 97

Laos: refugees from, Section and resettlement of, 78

Lasher, Beth: pictured, 84

Lasser, Ellen: pictured, 62

L'Chaim program (Section), 76, 79

League of Women Voters of Dallas: as Section partner, 79

LEAP project (Section): pictured, 181, 182

Lee, Adrienne: pictured, 94

Lee, Barbara, 172; essay by, 115; pictured, 94, 115, 123, 163, 168, 171, 186

Lee, Jonathan: pictured, 94

Lee, Marilyn: pictured, 146

Lee, Theodore R., 99

Lefkowitz, David, 10, 23, 158

Lefkowitz, Sadie, 26, 27

Lerman, Raeann: pictured, 62

Letot Center: as Section partner, 180

Leventhal, Leah: pictured, 127

Levi, Ruth: pictured, 85

Levick, Susan: pictured, 132

Levin, Hannah: pictured, 84

Levine, Linda: pictured, 173

Levitan, Norma: pictured, 145

Leviton, Sharon, 68; pictured, 70

Levy, Beverly, 99

Levy, Helen S.: pictured, xiii

Levy-Angel, Frances: pictured, xiii

Levy, Myrtle, 27

Levy-Fritts, Debra: pictured, 111, 113, 173

Lewis, Phil, 50, 65; pictured, 56, 66

Library Volunteer Corps program (Section), 74, 80

Lichenstein, Marjorie: pictured, 127

LIFE program (Section): launched, 63

Lifetime Achievement Award, 180; awardee listed, 194; presentation pictured, 179

Lifshen, Diane: pictured, 134

Lighthouse for the Blind (Dallas, Texas), 16, 22

Ling, Laura, 118, 122; pictured, 120, 122

Lipman, Margie: pictured, 145

Lipstadt, Deborah, 96

literacy: as Section issue focus, 17, 41, 44–45, 92, 95, 100, 102, 133, 161. See also Operation LIFT

Loeb, Helen: pictured, 140

Loehr, Michael: pictured, 179

Loera, Maria: pictured, 113

Lofton, Jane: pictured, 132

Lorch, Betty: pictured, 85

Lovitt, Zelene: pictured, 42, 159

Lowenberg, Julie, 79, 106; essay by, 112; pictured, 114, 123, 158, 159, 163, 168, 173, 175, 183, 187

Lowenthal, Vivian: pictured, 35

Lurie, Ruth: pictured, 128

Lynch, Joseph Patrick, 16

MacAdams, Marjorie, 72; pictured, 73

mail campaigns. See stay-at-home fundraisers

Making the Connection (booklet), 104, 106

Maley, Allan: pictured, 49

Manaster, Jane: pictured, 114

Mandell, Madeline: pictured, 62

Mankoff, Joy, 67, 74, 79; essay by, 73; pictured, 66, 70, 80, 114, 123, 128, 143, 159, 172, 187

Mankoff, Ron, 74; pictured, 67

Mankoff, Staci: pictured, 153

Manning House: as Section partner, 129

MANOF program (National), 35

219

Marcus, Anita, 48, 61, 174; pictured, 45, 49, 61, 62, 69, 114, 123, 128, 150, 159, 172, 187
Marcus, Carolyn: pictured, 136, 138. See Abrams, Carolyn
Marcuse, Lotte, 26
Marks, Aleyne: pictured, 35
Marks, Elaine: pictured, 75
Marks, Ellen: pictured, 119
Marks, Flo: pictured, 127
Marks, Marguerite: pictured, 159, 187; telegram to, pictured, 158
Marks, Rae, 26
marriage laws: as National issue focus, 3, 162, 177
Marriott, Inc.: as Section partner, 94
Martin Luther King Jr. Learning Center: as Section partner, 180
Martinez, Maria: pictured, 97
Mary Kay Cosmetics: as Section partner, 81
Massarano, Debbie: pictured, 97
Massman, Bobbi: pictured, 90
Masterson, Dorothy, 87
Matthew, Marilyn: pictured, 42
Mawson, Sir Douglas, 17
Mayer, Dora: pictured, 24
Mayoff, Denise: pictured, 128
McCarty, Hanoch, 168
McClellen, Lu: pictured, 62
McKinney Job Corps Center: as Section partner, 134
McKinney Veterans Administration Hospital: as Section partner, 36, 41
McKnight, Deborah: pictured, 175
McLemore, Annette Florence, 27
Meadows Foundation, 44; as Section partner, 87
Meals on Wheels, 26–27, 36, 41, 106, 130, 133; delivery pictured, 84
Meissner, Doris, 107; pictured, 107, 168
Mellow, Harriet: pictured, 111, 113
Memorial and Happy Day Fund: timeline of, 148
men: in Section, 146, 149
Menorah Society, 12, 148. See also Hillel
mental health: as Section issue focus, 17, 33–34, 39, 129
Mental Health America of Greater Dallas, 34
Mental Health Association of Dallas: as Section partner, 61, 129
Meredith, James, 48
Messinger, Ruth, 109
Metropolitan High School: (Dallas, Texas): as Section partner, 70
Michael, Carmen Miller, 98. See also Miller, Carmen
Mildred R. Sack Tribute Fund: desert event invitation pictured, 40; timeline of, 150
Milk Fund. See Minnie Hexter Milk Fund
Miller, Bette, 89; Council Sabbath and, 72; essay by, 142, 144; pictured, 34, 49, 51, 56, 61, 65, 66, 80, 84, 94, 96, 98, 114, 123, 128, 159, 167, 172, 186; women's nomenclature and, 61
Miller, Carmen, 129. See also Michael, Carmen Miller
Miller, Elka: pictured, 56
Miller, Geraldine ("Tincy"), 164
Miller, Kathy, 109; pictured, 164
Miller, Laura: pictured, 102, 175
Miller, Robert: column about Section by pictured, 106
Minnie Hexter Milk Fund, 16, 33, 78, 79, 94, 165; pictured, 149; timeline of, 149–50
Mintz, Amelia, 25; Cocktails to Coffee and, 27, 28; pictured, 159, 186
Mittenthal, Rae, 17, 34; pictured, 187
Modi: pictured, 148, 153
Mondell, Allen, 78
Mondell, Cynthia Salzman, 78
Montoya, Regina: pictured, 114
Moorhead, Norman: pictured, 68
Morchower, Bette: pictured, 90, 101
Morning Branch (Section), 126; essay about, 134, 137; presidents listed, 139. See also Richardson-Plano Section
Morris, Rich: pictured, 136
Morton H. Meyerson Symphony Center: pictured, 81, 152; as Section partner, 80, 91, 180
Moses, Mike: pictured, 109
Moshenberg, Sammie: pictured, 173
Mosman, Jerry, 44
Mowell, Carla: pictured, 89. See also Weir, Carla
Music, Janis Levine: 180, pictured, 172

Nachman, Sandy: pictured, 84
Nancy Moseley Elementary School (Dallas, Texas): as Section partner, 115
Nasher, Raymond: pictured, 160
Nasher Sculpture Center (Dallas, Texas), 108; as Section partner, 90
Nathanson, Paul, 67
National: 2000 leadership conference of, 97, 102; board members from Section listed, 191–92; Eleventh Triennial Convention (1926) pictured, 156; forty-fifth national convention of, 109; founding and early history of, 1–2; logos pictured, 2; mission of, 178; one hundredth anniversary celebrations, 91; principles of, 180, 182; Resolutions pamphlets pictured, 160; Schools for CommunityAction of, 49; Section, relationship with, 4; social programs of, 2; Southern District Convention (1970) hosted by Section, 51; World War II posters of, pictured, 32
National Association for the Advancement of Colored People (NAACP): as Section partner, 108
National Audubon Society: as Section partner, 24–25, 26
National Council of Catholic Women: as Section partner,

49, 50

National Council of Jewish Women (NCJW): Atlanta Section, 71; Austin Section, 158; Dallas Section (1898–1905), 3; Dallas Section (1913-present) (see Section); Minneapolis Section, 64; national office (see National); Ohio Section, 87; Richardson-Plano Section (see Richardson-Plano Section)

National Council of Juvenile and Family Court Judges: as Section partner, 73

National Council of Negro Women: as Section partner, 49, 50

National Jewish Health Hospital (Denver, Colorado): as Section partner, 23; as Section philanthropic beneficiary, 11

National Women's Conference (1977), 62

Navarrette, Ruben, Jr., 112

Nebenzahl, Margaret: pictured, 41

Neighborhood House: health care provided at, 11; sewing class at, pictured, 10; vocational skill classes provided at, 11

Neill, Barbara: pictured, 100

New Beginning Center: as Section partner, 130

Newberger, Janet: pictured, 56, 61, 66, 69, 80, 114, 128, 159, 186; plaque honoring, pictured, 112

Nixon, Richard M., 37, 48, 59, 133

Noble, Mark: pictured, 151

nonprofit sector: training for, as Section issue focus, 71–72

Norman, Floyd: pictured, 43

North Central Expressway (Dallas, Texas): effect on Jewish population of, 39

North Texas Alliance to Reduce Unintended Pregnancy in Teens (Ntrarupt), 108

North Texas Association of Social Workers: as Section partner, 41

North Texas Food Bank: as Section award recipient, 179, 180; as Section partner, 95, 96, 114; 118, 130, 180

NorthPark Mall: trains at, 130, 133, 134

Northwest Dallas County Family Outreach Center: as Section partner, 61. See also Family Outreach

Novich, Felice: pictured, 127

Nunez, Alfred, 178

Nussbaum, Bernice: pictured, 24

nutrition: as Section issue focus, 64, 70, 95–96, 110–11, 115. See also food

Obama, Michelle, 115; pictured, 115

O'Brien, Bob: pictured, 94

Office of Civil Defense: as Section partner, 33

Olan, Levi A., 51

Olff, Rosine: pictured, 159, 186; Your Thrift Store and, 142

Operation Desert Storm: Section activities during, 130

Operation Frontline, 95–96

Operation LIFT, 44, 158, 161; advertisements and news coverage of pictured, 45; establishment of, 41; Section financial support to, 82

Operation READY, 49, 52, 64, 68; pamphlets pictured, 52

Ornish, Jeanette: pictured, 127

Oswald, Lee Harvey, 48

Our Friends Place: as Section partner, 95, 118, 119, 120, 179, 180

Owen, Kris: pictured, 90

PACE Committee (Section): establishment of, 51

Palestine: Section's support for Jewish shelters in, 33

Park Cities Baptist Church (Dallas, Texas): as Section partner, 115

Parkland Foundation: Section awarded by, 118, 121; Section financial support to, 82

Parkland Hospital (Dallas, Texas): Councilettes and, 42; Day Care Committee, as Section partner, 51; "Pink Ladies" volunteers pictured, 41; as Section partner, 23, 24, 41, 79, 83, 86, 90, 94, 106, 118, 129, 130

Passover Seder (1995), 24, 96; program pictured, 102

Patinkin, Mandy: as Section gala fundraiser performer, 101; pictured, 101, 152, 154

patriotism: as Section issue focus, 12

Patterson, Florence: pictured, 26

Patton, Evelyn, 44

peace: as Section issue focus, 24, 158

Peace in the Middle East essay contest, 97

Pearlman, Jeneane: pictured, 54

Pei, I. M., 91

Peiser, Allison: pictured, 179

Peiser, Pat: essays by, 42–43, 44, 67–68; Lifetime Achievement Award given to, 180; pictured, iv, xi, 49, 68, 80, 91, 114, 123, 128, 158, 159, 168, 172, 173, 175, 179, 187

Pelosi, Alexandra, 109

Pelosi, Nancy, 105, 109; pictured, 171

Penny Lunches program, 9, 11, 95, 157

Perot, Ross, 91

Perot Museum of Nature and Science (Dallas, Texas): pictured, 86, 89; as Section partner, 90

Perry, Rick: prayer event of, opposed by Section, 172

Peters, Bernadette: pictured, 153

Philanthropic Committee (Section), 11

Philipson, Louise: pictured, 127

Pidgeon, Sheryl Lilly: pictured, 153

Pierce, Lee, 35

Pinker, Carol: pictured, 182

Pioneering Partner Award, 179, 180; awardees listed, 193–94

Planned Parenthood: as Section partner, 168

Plaskoff, Melissa: pictured, 115

Platt, Jody, 99, 122; essays by, 98–99, 109; pictured, 97, 98, 109, 114, 119, 120, 121, 123, 145, 153, 159, 163, 168, 175, 186; on Tikkun Olam, 98

Platt, Mel, 122

Pollman, Cheryl, 106, 180; essay by, 112, 115; pictured,

221

108, 114, 123, 158, 168, 186
Pollman, Harold A.: pictured, 109
Pollock, Gwynne: pictured, 146
poverty: of women, as Section issue focus, 49, 50, 51, 52, 94
Powys, John Cowper, 17
Presbyterian Hospital (Dallas, Texas): as Section partner, 81
presidents: of branches, pictured, 159; of Section, listed, 188; of Section, pictured, 159, 186–87
Preston Hollow Elementary School (Dallas, Texas): as Section partner, 88
Prince, Kit: pictured, 106, 113
Professional Branch (Section), 62, 64, 97, 126, 137, 144; dinner announcement of, pictured, 128; discontinuation of, 97; Encore Sale and, 144; essay about, 134, 137; establishment of, 41; at Golden Acres, 64, 76, 137; presidents listed, 139; various activities pictured, 136, 138, 143, 146
Protz, Edward L.: pictured, 150
Pruitt, Jan: pictured, 179; Pioneering Partner Award presented to, 180
public policies: as Section issue focus, 167, 170–71
Public Health Nurses of Dallas: as Section partner, 26
Pulman, Janine: essay by, 137
Putter, Phyllis: pictured, 124

Rabin, Barbara, 91; pictured, 69, 91
Rabin Peace Fund: as Section partner, 35
Radford, Nina: 106–7
Radman, Bunny, 98
Raggio, Louise Ballerstedt, 174
Rainbow Room (Community Partners of Dallas): as Section partner, 133, 137
Ramirez, Maribel: pictured, 97
Ransom, Harry, 48
Raskin, Adam J., 108; pictured, 108
Raskin, Allyson: pictured, 182
Raskin, Jerry, 97; pictured, 136, 138
Raskin, Mya: pictured, 182
Rawlings, Mike, 118; pictured, 123
Ray, Eileen: pictured, 42
Razovsky, Cecilia, 25, 26
Razovsky, Fannie, 26
Reagan, Maureen, 62–63
Reba M. Wadel Scholarship Fund, 41, 51; recipients pictured, 150; timeline of, 149
Red Cross: as Section partner, 17, 18, 23, 33; telegram to Sewing Circle (Section) pictured, 18
refugee resettlement: as Section issue focus, 23, 25–26, 28, 33, 39, 78, 82–83, 112. See also specific countries of origin
Reid, Dori, 99
Reingold, Jo: pictured, 88
Reno, Janet, 98

reproductive rights: of women, as Section issue focus, 79–80, 97, 168, 180. See also birth control
Research Institute for Innovation in Education (RIFIE), 34, 35, 80, 89, 160
Rich, Nan: pictured, 98, 99
Richards, Ann: pictured, 163
Richards, Cecile, 97; pictured, 96
Richardson, Barbara: on Section's work, 49–50
Richardson Child Guidance Center: as Section partner, 130
Richardson Family Outreach Center, 60–61
Richardson Independent School District: as Section partner, 79, 89, 108, 110, 164
Richardson/Plano Branch (Section), 126; pamphlet pictured, 127; presidents listed, 139
Richardson-Plano Section, 126, 127, 130; children and youth program of, 60–61; essay about, 134; presidents listed, 39. See also Morning Branch (Section)
Ries, Myrna: essay by, 100–101
Rita O. Black Tribute Fund: timeline of, 151
Rieter, Carol: pictured, 128, 136, 138. See also Tobias, Carol
Rieter, Pam: pictured, 179
Rippy, Edwin L., 40
Robberson, Carol: pictured, 131, 159
Robbins, Debra, 96, 97
Roberts, Gwen Fine: pictured, 137
Robinowitz, Chana: pictured, 175
Roder, Dorothy, 87; pictured, 88
Ronald McDonald House: as Section partner, 130, 137, 181
Rose, Barbara, 73; pictured, 72
Rose, Jeanette: pictured, 146
Roseman, Amy: pictured, 106. See also Goldstein, Amy
Roseman, Michael: pictured, 106
Rosen, Adrienne: pictured, 120
Rosen, Carol: pictured, 175
Rosenberg, Evelyn: pictured, 127
Rosenburg, Charlot: pictured, 129
Rosenbaum, Madlyn: pictured, 114
Rosenbloom, Susan: pictured, 137
Rosenfield, Jennie: pictured, 186
Rosenfield, Joyce, 180; essay by, 126, 129–30, 133; pictured, 120, 135, 159
Rosenthal, Hannah, 109
Ross, Selma: pictured, 38, 57, 147, 159, 187
Ross, Sharon: pictured, 35
Roth, Regina: pictured, 95
Rothschild, Riki, 68; pictured, 70
Rowlett, Tracy: as CBI featured speaker, 71
Rubenstein, Rita: pictured, 45
Rubin, Felicia: pictured, 132, 135, 145, 159
Rubin, Rachel: pictured, 145
Ruby, Jack, 48
Rudberg, Marie: as Section's Junior Council president, 9
Rudberg, Peachy: pictured, 143

Rudick, Connie: pictured, 85
Russia: massacres in, as National issue focus, 2; refugees from, Section resettlement of and assistance to, 112, 130, 134. See also Soviet Union
Rydman, Edward, 57

S.A.Y. (South Advice for Youth) What? Coalition, 108, 112
Saba, Cathy: pictured, 143
Sachson, Gail, 97
Sack, Mildred, 126, 142; pictured, 159, 187
Safeguards for Seniors program (Section), 67–68, 80, 82, 95; booklet pictured, 75; brochure pictured, 68; various activities pictured, 69
Salvation Army, 87
Samaritan Inn: as Section partner, 130, 136
Samuels, Ellen: pictured, 135, 159
Samuels, Jerry: pictured, 135
San Francisco, California: earthquake in (1906), as National issue focus, 2
Sanders, Barefoot: letter to Section pictured, 39
Sandfield, Carol: pictured, 84
Sanger, Hortense, 65
Sanger, Margaret, 8, 22
Schachter, Amy: pictured, 181
Schachter, Eden: pictured, 181
Schaffer, Marilyn: pictured, 147
Scharf, Eliane, 137; pictured, 128
Schecter, Judy: pictured, 153
Schein, Lorraine: pictured, 128. See also Sulkin, Lorraine
Schepps, Emilie: pictured, 146
Schlinger, Norma, 65; pictured, 69
Schneidler, Cynthia: essay by, 122; pictured, 122, 165
Schoenbrun, Celia: pictured, 72, 175
Schoenbrun, David, 48
scholarships: offered by Section, 11, 12, 17, 35, 40, 79, 82, 90. See also Reba M. Wadel Scholarship Fund
school lunches: as National issue focus, 2; as Section issue focus, 4, 9, 11, 95
Schoolchild Welfare Committee (Section), 22
Schultz, Jaynie, 107
Schwartz, Marilyn, 95
Schwartz, Nonie: pictured, 129, 133, 159
Scottish Rite Crippled Children's Hospital (Dallas, Texas): pictured, 16; as Section partner, 16, 23, 24, 33, 134
Scrinopskie, Linda: pictured, 138
Section: advocacy of, 158; annual dues of, 8, 16, 22, 41; articles of incorporation pictured, 55; awardees of, listed, 192–94 (see also specific awards); awards given to, listed, 194–96; branches, 125–39 (see also specific branches); centennial celebrations of, 116, 118–23; charter life members of, listed, 189–91; charter members of, listed, 188–89; event programs pictured, 19; founding of, 3; funding of, 141–55 (see also specific funds and galas); future of, 180, 182; Jewish values of, 4; logos pictured, 9, 118; members who served as National Board members from, listed, 191–92; membership numbers of, 8, 11, 22, 39, 41, 42, 97; membership profile of, 142; mission of, 8; model process of, 10; name of, 50; National, relationship with, 4; ninetieth birthday celebration (2003), 106, 109, 114, 159; office fire (2005) of, 109–10; one-hundred-second birthday luncheon (2015), 180; partners listed, 196–201; permanent office of, 39, 109–10; presidents of, listed, 188; presidents of, pictured, 159, 186–87; Schools for Communication Action of, 49–50; seventy-fifth anniversary celebration of, 80, 81; social change, as goal of, 169; study groups of, 3–4, 10, 33, 53, 96–97, 163; tools employed by, 158; website of, 97
Section Sabbaths, 4, 10, 96
Segal, Marilyn: pictured, 79
Segal, Phillip: shoe store of, 35
Selby, Shayna, 42
senior citizens: as Section issue focus, 11, 17, 34, 40, 63–64, 67–68, 80, 95, 102. See also Golden Acres retirement home (Dallas, Texas); Safeguards for Seniors program (Section)
Senior Citizens of Greater Dallas (The Senior Source): as Section partner, 63, 67
Senior Safety Committee (Section), 67
Senior Safety Task Force (Section), 67
Sequoyah Junior High School (Dallas, Texas): as Section partner, 52
Service to the Foreign Born project (Section), 23
Sesame Street, 51
settlement houses: as National issue focus, 2
Sewing Circle (Section), 17–18, 18; telegram from Red Cross to, pictured, 18; in World War II, 23–24
SHARE Endowment Fund, 65, 73; founding and sustaining contributors listed, 74; timeline of, 151
Shaw, Estelle: pictured, 186
Sheinberg, Betty Sue: pictured, 90
Sherbet, Bruce, 108
Sherman, Sharon: pictured, 172
Sherwood, Roy: pictured, 136
Shidlofsky, Sherri: pictured, 133, 159
Ship-A-Box program (National), 33, 34, 35, 80; Councilettes and, 42; Evening Branch and, 129; pictured, 84
Shipp, Thomas, 57
Shrine Hospital for Crippled Children (Dallas, Texas): as Section partner, 18
Shivers, Allan: letter to Section pictured, 39
Siegel, Lynne: pictured, 175
Siegel, Sarah: pictured, 175
Sikora, Ann: pictured, 54, 65
Silberberg, Barbara, 27; pictured, 91, 94, 143, 172
Silberstein Day Nursery (Dallas, Texas): as Section partner,

23, 24
Silverman, Ellen: pictured, 145
Silverman, Pearl: pictured, 147
Skibell, Linda: pictured, 181
Skyline High School: (Dallas, Texas): as Section partner, 70
Slaughter, Vanna: Pioneering Partner Award presented to, 180
sleep: as Section issue focus, 108
Smart Shoppers program, 95
Smith, Robert: pictured, 90
Smerud, Randi: pictured, 173
Sobel, Freda: pictured, 95
Social Welfare Committee (Section), 22
social workers: professionalization of, as Section issue focus, 40–41
Society of St. Vincent de Paul Diocesan Council: as Section partner, 115
Solomon, Hannah G.: NCJW founded by, 1; pictured, xiii, 1
Somer, Karen: pictured, 54
Somer, Phyllis, 54; essay by, 35; pictured, 35, 50
Sommerfield, Elissa: pictured, 56, 127
Sommerfield, Frankie: pictured, 56
South Oak Cliff High School (Dallas, Texas): as Section partner, 70
Southern Methodist University (SMU), 8, 28, 80, 96, 118; as Section partner, 23, 34, 49
Southwest Airlines: as Section partner, 81
Soviet Union, 77; refugees from, Section resettlement of and assistance to, 134. See also Russia
Special Olympics: as Section partner, 130
Special Supplemental Nutrition Program for Women, Infants, and Children (WIC), 95
Staffin, Dolores: pictured, 137
Stahl, Judy: pictured, iv
Stahl, Sidney: on Section's work, 78
Stanley, Renee: pictured, 159
Stanley, Wendy: pictured, 101, 153
"Stay At Home" Ball (Evening Branch), 133
stay-at-home fundraisers: listed, 148; logos of, pictured, 154–55
Stein, Barbara: pictured, 153
Stein, Bobbie: pictured, 136
Stein, Debby: pictured, 114, 179, 183
Steinberg, Frances ("Sister"): essay by, 90; pictured, 90
Steinhart, Phyllis, 90; pictured, 90
stem cell research: as Section issue focus, 108
Stern, Arthur: pictured, 145
Stern, David, 95
Stern, Elizabeth (Liza), 80, 96
Stern, Freda Gail: pictured, 111
Stern, Helen, 27; pictured, 84, 145
Stern, Ruth: pictured, 88
Stillman, Elaine: pictured, 100, 175, 179
Stitch, Marjorie, 65

Stock, Karen: pictured, 85, 118
Stone, Jennifer: pictured, 136
Stone, Jill, 100; pictured, 69
Stone, Renee: pictured, 136
Stoner, Bill, 68; pictured, 70
Stonewall Jackson Elementary School (Dallas, Texas): as Section partner, 130
Stoup, Phyllis: pictured, 181, 182
Strauss, Annette, 78, 81; pictured, 84, 146, 147, 160
Strauss, Sarah: pictured, 159, 186; telegraph to pictured, 23
Streit, Rhona, 203; pictured, 120, 123, 145, 172
Strelitz, Darrel, 87, 110; essay by, 82–83; pictured, 80, 84, 114, 159, 172, 186
Stromberg, Ariella: pictured, 175
Stromberg, Benjamin: pictured, 114
Stromberg, Beth Brand: pictured, 114, 118, 132, 154, 175
Stromberg, Karen, 134
Stromberg, Rose Marie, 204; essay by, 52
Student Education Fund: timeline of, 148–49
Stuhl, Helen, 65
substance abuse: as Section issue focus, 79. See also drugs
Sulkin, Lorraine, 34, 134, 137; as National staff member, 40; pictured, 159, 186. See also Schein, Lorraine
Summer of Decision (film), 41
suffrage. See women's suffrage
Svidlow, Libby: pictured, 129
Swartz, Susan: pictured, 119
Sweet, Janice, 50, 65, 73, 87; pictured, 51, 114, 120, 123, 128, 153, 159, 161, 187. See also Weinberg, Janice Sweet
Switner, Betty, 91

Tamid: An Everlasting Legacy giving campaign, 109
Tannebaum, Nita Mae: essay by, 133–34; pictured, 38, 69, 127, 159, 183
Tate, Willis, 49; pictured, 51
Tay-Sachs disease: as Section issue focus, 66, 67, 91, 129, 130
teen pregnancy: as Section issue focus, 79, 82, 83, 86, 107–8
teens and youths: Section branches for, 126
Temple Emanu-El (Dallas, Texas): as Council Sabbath venue, 17; Girl Scout troop at, 17; as immigration conference venue, 168; pictured, 9, 127; relocation of (1957), 39; as Section history exhibit venue, 122; as Section partner, 3, 18, 23, 24, 27, 96, 108, 115; as Section Sabbath venue, 10; as Section storage location, 39; as twenty-fifth anniversary tea venue, program for pictured, 28
Temple Shalom (Dallas, Texas): as Council Sabbath venue, 72; pictured, 97; as Section partner, 96
Terrell Hospital Adolescent Center Tribute Fund. See Bromberg Adolescent Center Tribute Fund
Terrell State Hospital: as Section partner, 36, 41, 130
Texas A&M AgriLife Extension Program: as Section

partner, 83
Texas Department of Public Welfare: as Section partner, 62, 63, 75, 134
Texas Capitol Building: Section advocacy at, pictured, 163, 173; Section quilt displayed at, 91
Texas Coalition for Juvenile Justice (TCJJ): as Section partner, 61
Texas Jewish Post: Section highlighted in, 118, 123
Texas Marital Property Act (1967): as Section issue focus, 174
Texas Society for Mental Hygiene (TSMH): as Section partner, 33–34
Texas State Fair, 17, 22, 27, 51, 78
Thanks-Giving Square (Dallas, Texas): pictured, 60
Thielman, Mark: pictured, 84
Thelma Boston Home: as Section partner, 129
Thomas, Casey: pictured, 108
Thomas, Marlo: pictured, 152
Thompson, Sydney, 17
Thornton, Heidi: pictured, 96
Tikkun Olam, 98, 160
Tilis, Sue: essay by, 35; pictured, 85, 123, 153, 163, 168, 187
Timmons, Tom, 97; pictured, 98, 138
Tobian, Beverly: pictured, 168, 175
Tobian, Carolyn, 65; pictured, 165
Tobias, Carol: essay by, 134, 137; pictured, 120, 135. See also Rieter, Carol
Tobolowsky, Hermine Dalkowitz, 51; pictured, 48
Tobolowsky, Shirley: essay by, 67–68
Tower, John: pictured, 172
Transition Resource Action Center (TRAC): pictured, 112; as Section partner, 111
Traub, Patty: pictured, 120
Travelling Troubadours (Evening Branch), 129, 130
tribute funds: listed, 148–51. See also specific funds
Trubitt, Peggy: pictured, 69
tuberculosis: as Section issue focus, 16, 17, 23, 33, 162
Tuberculosis Committee (Section), 16
Tuberculosis Hospital (Dallas, Texas): as Section partner, 18
tutoring: as Section issue focus, 35, 51, 54, 78, 79, 83, 96, 115
Tycher, Laurie: pictured, 42

Unell, Phyllis: pictured, 136
United China Relief: as Section partner, 23
United Service Organizations (USO): as Section partner, 24, 129
United Way: as Section partner, 71
University of Texas at Arlington, 151; social work program at, 41, 50–51
University of Texas at Austin: social work program at, 41
University of Texas at Dallas: as Section partner, 95
University of Texas Southwestern Medical School, 90; as Section partner, 66

Unterberg, Madeline ("Maddy"), 112; essay by, 100; pictured, 98, 114, 120, 128, 153, 159, 175, 186
US Department of Agriculture: as Section partner, 95
Utay, Gussie: pictured, 159, 186
Utay, Judy: essay by, 66, 91; pictured, 91, 127, 135, 143, 159
Utay, Robert: pictured, 135

Vaca, Nina: as CBI featured speaker, 71
Valdez, Lupe: pictured, 174
Veeder, Sandra: pictured, 136
Veeder, Stacy: pictured, 136
Vickery Meadow (Dallas neighborhood): as Section issue focus, 96, 100, 112, 115
Vickery Meadow After-School Care Program, 100
Vickery Meadow Elementary School (Dallas, Texas): as Section partner: 96, 100, 115
Vickery Meadow Food Pantry: pictured, 114, 149; as Section partner, 106, 115
Vickery Meadow Learning Center (VMLC): pictured, 107, 110, 112, 114; as Section partner, 100–101, 106, 115
Vickery Meadow Neighborhood Alliance, 115
Victim's Task Force: as Section partner, 180
Vietnam: refugees from, Section resettlement of and assistance to, 78, 89, 130
Villalba, Jason: pictured, 173
Visiting Nurse Association (VNA), 26–27; as Section partner, 64, 67
visually challenged: as Section issue focus, 16, 75, 81, 169. See also blindness
Vogel, Thelma: pictured, 50
Vogel Alcove, 79; as Section partner 130, 132
Voice of Khmer: pictured, 82
Volunteer Center of Dallas: Section awarded by, 90; as Section partner, 65, 67, 71
Volunteer Management Education Coalition, 65
voter participation: as Section issue focus, 108
V'Shalom (Evening Branch pamphlet), 130; pictured, 128

W. T. White High School: (Dallas, Texas): as Section partner, 70
W. W. Samuel High School: (Dallas, Texas): as Section partner, 70
Wadel, Carol, 73; pictured, 38, 143, 150, 169
Wadley Blood Center: as Section partner, 129
Waldman, Jackie: pictured, 95, 115
Waldman, Sara: pictured, 75, 159, 186
Wallace, Kevin: pictured, 97
war bonds, 11, 24, 33, 142
War on Poverty: effect on Section's planning of, 49–50
Warwick, Dionne: pictured, 152, 153
Washburne, Evy Kay: pictured, 111
Wasserman Schultz, Debbie, 109

Watel, Rose: pictured, 114
Watkins, Craig: as CBI featured speaker, 71; pictured, 99
Ways and Means Committee (Section), 16
Ways and Means Department (Evening Branch), 133
Weathers, Beck, 97
Weber, Louis J., Jr.: as CBI featured speaker, 71
Wedeles, Bette: pictured, 45, 48, 172, 187
Weenick, Raye Ann: pictured, 146
Weinberg, Evelyne: pictured, 88
Weinberg, Janice Sweet: essay by, 72. See also Sweet, Janice
Weiner, Hollace Ava, 2
Weinstein, Carol: pictured, 114, 173
Weinstein, Max: pictured, 119
Weinthal, Joel, 108
Weir, Carla, 89; pictured, 183. See also Mowell, Carla
Weiss, Susan: pictured, 169
West Dallas After-School Study Center, 52
West of Hester Street (film), 78, 144
Wetherington, Ron, 164
Wettreich, Zara: pictured, 79, 90
WFAA-TV, 8; as Section partner, 41, 44, 45
White, W. T.: pictured, 51
White House, 77, 115
White House Conference on Aging, 40
White House Conference on Child Welfare (1909): National's participation in, 3
Wigder, Carol: essay by, 134
Wilder, Thornton, 17
Wills, Debbie: pictured, 136
Wilonsky, Margaret: pictured, 90, 91
Wilson, J. E., Mrs.: pictured, 35
Wiman, Rosalie: pictured, 145
Wise, Wes, 60, 66; pictured, 56
With One Voice coalition, 112; flier pictured, 112
Wohlner, Barbie: pictured, 138
Wolens, Jackie: pictured, 146
Wolfe, Claudette: pictured, 100, 175
Wolff, Gretel, 28
Wolff, Paul, 28
Wolfram, Rhea: pictured, 146
Wonderland Express, 130
World War I: preparedness parade pictured, 9; Section activities during, 11, 18
World War II: National posters during, pictured, 32; refugee resettlement during, 23, 25–26, 28; Section during, 33; Sewing Circle (Section) in, 18, 23–24, 33
Wormser, Gloria: NCJW Section (1898–1905) cofounded by, 3
Wormser, L. Nora: NCJW Section (1898–1905) cofounded by, 3
women: employment of, as National issue focus, 2; generally, as Section issue focus, 61–63, 79–80, 178; health of, as Section issue focus, 106–7, 107–8, 111–12; poverty of, as Section issue focus, 49, 51, 52, 94
Women in Community Service (WICS): as National partner, 49; as Section partner, 134
Women of Rotary: as Section partner, 23
Women on the Move conference (1966), 49, 52; planning meeting pictured, 127; telegram about pictured, 171
Women's Access to Comprehensive Health Services (WACHS) program (Section), 107, 111–12; class pictured, 112
Women's Council of Dallas County: as Section partner, 26–27, 65
Women's Seder (1995). See Passover Seder (1995)
Women's Seder (2008), 108
women's suffrage: as National issue focus, 8; program cover supporting, pictured, 5; suffragists pictured, 2
Wood, Susan: pictured, 165
Woodrow Wilson High School (Dallas, Texas), 28
Wright, Beth, 129
Wright, Linus: pictured, 163

YACHAD program (National), 35
Yad b'Yad (Hand in Hand) Fund, 108; establishment of, 35; timeline of, 151
Yarrin, Sarah: pictured, 115, 127
Yollick, Liny: pictured, 88
Young, Mildred: pictured, 57
Young Professional Branch (Section), 126; establishment of, 62; pictured, 62; presidents listed, 139
young women: in Section (see Councilettes (Section))
Your Thrift Shop, 16, 41, 142, 144; Councilettes and, 42; donation advertisement for pictured, 41, 147; Evening Branch and, 129; opening of, 34; pictured, 143
YWCA: as Section partner, 23

Zale Corporation: as Section partner, 81
Zesmer, Miriam: pictured, 127
Zimmerman, Abe, Mrs.: pictured, 23
Zimmerman, Mimi Platt: pictured, 114
Zimmerman, Molly: pictured, 114, 119
Zimmerman, Saul: pictured, 119
Zionist Organization of America: as Section philanthropic beneficiary, 11
Zweig, David: pictured, 114
Zweig, Lauren: pictured, 114
Zweig, Louis: pictured, 123
Zweig, Robin, 133; essay by, 122; on Evening Branch, 126; pictured, 72, 89, 99, 114, 120, 123, 135, 137, 153, 159, 175, 179, 183, 187

Remembrances

Remembrances

10

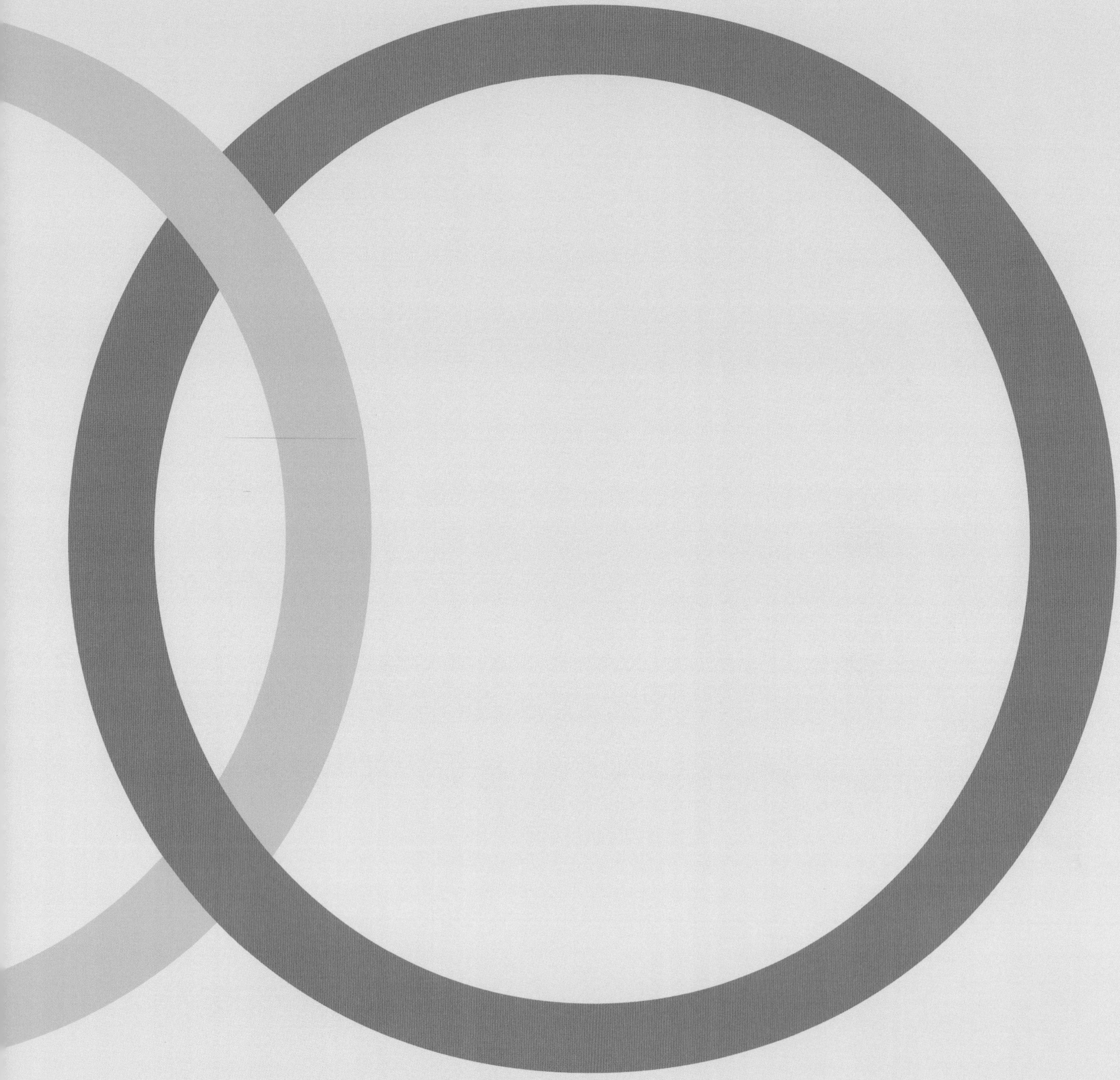